Theodore Roosevelt
and the Progressive Movement

Also by George E. Mowry

The Urban Nation: 1920–1960

Theodore Roosevelt

AND THE

PROGRESSIVE MOVEMENT

By

GEORGE E. MOWRY

HILL AND WANG — NEW YORK
A division of Farrar, Straus and Giroux

FIRST AMERICAN CENTURY SERIES EDITION SEPTEMBER 1960

*Theodore Roosevelt and the Progressive
Movement* is reprinted by special arrangement with The Regents of the University
of Wisconsin of University of Wisconsin,
Madison, Wisconsin.

PRINTED IN THE UNITED STATES OF AMERICA

FOR MY FATHER
A Progressive Then and Now

Preface

THIS VOLUME is not a history of the progressive movement, a book which the author hopes to write some day. Nor is it a biography of Theodore Roosevelt. Rather it is an attempt to study the influence of the man upon the movement and the movement upon the man. For this reason little is said of Roosevelt's early career and much has been made of the months in 1909 and 1910 when the ex-president was out of the country. Foreign affairs are discussed only as they affected the course of internal politics.

The book is based in large part on the voluminous Roosevelt manuscripts in the Library of Congress. Other collections of manuscripts used are indicated in the bibliography. The unfortunate gaps in the papers of Jonathan Dolliver and Albert B. Cummins explain the infrequent references to these collections at various periods. The other principal sources are the newspapers of the period, the spoken and printed words of many scholars, including some of my teachers, and, of course, a host of printed monographs and general works. The books listed in the bibliography include only the works cited in the footnotes, and in no way represent my total debt to others. During the three-year period between the completion of the manuscript and its publication some additional pertinent material has been published. A few references have therefore been subsequently inserted, but these additions have made little, if any, change in the interpretation of the more important elements of the study.

To the many persons and institutions that have aided me in the preparation of this book I am deeply grateful. The photographs are from the collection of the Library of Congress. In particular I wish to thank Dean John D. Hicks of the University of California for his constant help and encouragement; Professor William B. Hesseltine of the University of Wisconsin, who read part of the manuscript and offered valuable criticism; Professor Howard K. Beale of the University of North Carolina, who, in the course of his extensive research on Theodore Roosevelt, has generously shared with me some of his findings; Miss Livia Appel of the University of Wisconsin Press for her able editing; and my wife, who enjoyed none of the fun and gladly suffered most of the drudgery in the making of the book.

G.E.M.

Contents

Illustrations

Theodore Roosevelt
and the Progressive Movement

CHAPTER ONE

Genesis

WHEN THE youthful and energetic Theodore Roosevelt accidentally became president in September of 1901, the United States came to the end of an era. As William McKinley lay dying in Buffalo from an assassin's bullet it was not apparent that a new order was being born upon the death of the old. The new president belonged at least in name to the party of his predecessor. From his first few cautious moves it appeared in Washington as if nothing had changed from the days of McKinley, or for that matter of Harrison, Arthur, Garfield, or Hayes. "I wish to say that it shall be my aim to continue, absolutely unbroken, the policy of President McKinley," Roosevelt had said as he quietly took the oath of office.[1]

If Roosevelt had clung to that resolution, the first four years of the new century would have been politically uneventful indeed. For at least McKinley's domestic policies had been, with some minor variations, monotonously similar to those of preceding Republican administrations. Since Lincoln's day the party had gathered every four years to nominate and usually to elect estimable and unessential gentlemen. Altogether their policy, if one stretches the point, had been one of masterful inactivity.

In fact, in the thirty years from the Civil War until 1896 American politics had been a never-never land without much rhyme and with less reason. Except in the years presided over by Grover Cleveland the party of Lincoln had controlled the presidency. Yet Republican dominance was more apparent than real. During most of the stretch the Democrats held a majority in the lower house of Congress. Throughout the same

[1] *New York Times*, September 15, 1901.

3

years Republican unity in the Senate was torn to shreds by rowdy and belligerent gangs of Mugwumps, Stalwarts, and Liberal Republicans fighting over precious little save pap and place.

Even the noisy fights between the traditional parties had an air of unreality about them. Scarcely more than sentiment and issues irrevocably settled years before on the battlefield differentiated them. For a time it appeared, until Cleveland broached the question, that the tariff might serve as a delineating line. But even that issue disappeared in the impotent struggles centering around the Wilson bill of 1894. The tariff was what a long since forgotten Democratic presidential nominee said it was, a local question.

In retrospect the entire game of politics seemed to be a local and unimportant question as compared with other developments in the country. For the national directing force in the years following the Civil War lay not in the realm of politics but in industry and finance. There a group of remarkable men enjoyed the privilege of being born to the trade at exactly the right time in history. John D. Rockefeller, Andrew Carnegie, J. Pierpont Morgan, William H. Vanderbilt, Jay Gould, and Philip D. Armour, to mention only a few, made ample use of their opportunity. While the politicos were furiously fighting their inconsequential battles these men from their kingdoms of steel, oil, and finance were blueprinting the future of America.

Before the Civil War both the Federalists and the Whigs had appreciated the immense industrial opportunities afforded by the nation's abounding natural resources. But the followers of Hamilton and Webster had never obtained the indulgent government necessary to the full realization of their dreams. An agrarian majority marshalled together with the artisans of the youthful cities had always stood in the way. The Jefferson–Aaron Burr pattern of planters and proletariat had been too strong for them at the ballot box. Up to the eve of the great conflict ending at Appomattox the Democratic soft-money, low-tariff, anti-corporation principles had prevailed in the law of the land.

Before the cannons thundered at Sumter, however, the Democratic party was torn asunder. And with their foes divided the ex-Whig element of the new Republican party seized their chance of a century. By skillful alchemy they quickly transformed the reform republicanism of Lincoln into the more materialistic concepts of Roscoe Conkling, Marcus Alonzo Hanna, and Nelson W. Aldrich. Before sweet peace returned the pattern had been set. The Morrill tariff provided adequate protection, a national banking system promised stable finance, and the immigration act of 1864, authorizing the importation of contract labor, insured low wages. With alacrity the Homestead Bill was passed, opening up the national domain to settlement—and to corporate exploitation. Finally, with remarkable prescience, the foundations of federal judicial protection for corporate wealth were stealthily constructed. A decade and a half later the federal courts were effectively safeguarding vested property from reform-minded state legislatures.

From that point the Rockefellers, the Morgans, and the Carnegies took up, and the next three decades were theirs. Their accomplishments were little short of incredible. With a genius for business organization that has seldom been equaled they created an industrial America almost overnight. By ruthlessly crushing their competitors they, together with a few others, came close to controlling the nation. In a few years they had dotted the country with their workshops, criss-crossed it with iron rails to carry their goods to every hamlet, and had even reached out to the ends of the earth for new materials and new markets.

As a result of their efforts America became a world power. A never-ending stream of capital flowed from abroad to feed the hungry maw of industrial America. European bourses sagged when the news from New York and Pittsburgh was bad. In the sixties the proud ancient market centers of civilization still considered this land as a half-barbarous place filled with savages. A few years later in European stores and Asiatic stalls little tags began to appear bearing their fateful messages "made in Philadelphia," Chicago, Boston.

The future implications of this new industrial system were tremendous. Properly greated to social needs, it was capable of producing for all an abundance such as the world had never dreamed of. At that time, however, only a small minority was reaping its full benefits. At the top, a few thousands of the new business classes were amassing stupendous fortunes. Below them a hundred thousand or so smaller operators and entrepreneurs were sharing the rewards of the age in more modest fashion. But on the other side of the ledger the masses of people created much and earned little. For thirty years American agriculture suffered starvation. Homesteads were given up; mortgages were foreclosed and free farmers either became renters on the land of their fathers or drifted to the cities. There they joined a growing mass of underpaid, underfed, politically impotent workers. The sharp economic dualism of America was strikingly reflected in Henry George's *Progress and Poverty*, published in 1875. In thirty years over two million copies of the book were sold.

But the business element controlling American society between 1865 and 1900 rarely heard the underprivileged. Its eyes were focused on the heights above. There the dazzling progress of telegraph boys to steel kings and of produce merchants to multimillionaire oil barons was at once soothing and provocative. Success was measured in dollars, and what one man accumulated could be acquired by another provided he were able. This spirit of materialism not only controlled its own domain of workshop and counting house but pervaded the very fabric of American society. Colleges produced their apologists for the system, churches approved it, and both institutions shared its wealth. The Alger book had become the urban counterpart of agrarian folklore.

Government was not least affected by this emphasis upon the acquisition of wealth. In fact, politics, which in good part had made big business possible, now became its handmaiden and sometimes its courtesan, selling favors where and when offers were made. Collectively the business classes asked little from government. An amenable president who would continue the lavish land subsidies, pursue sound financial policies, and correctly control foreign affairs was their chief desire. Such a man could also be depended upon to select safe men for the nation's courts. Vested privilege was to look increasingly to the courts for protection not only against the irresponsible acts of reforming legislatures but also against the rising labor unions. Beyond that the group demands of business were modest. They had achieved what they wanted during the Civil War. To be let alone now to direct the nation they were fast possessing—their definition of laissez faire—was all they asked.

Individual wants of the industrial tycoons were sometimes less easily satisfied. More often than not the politicians were privately sympathetic to their desires. Many a statesman of the period was a man of affairs himself, far too many more were paid retainers. But there were always public pressure and troublesome elections. Often the wants of one financial giant conflicted with the wants of another to embarrass an aspiring congressman or state senator. At other times, as Messrs. Gould and Vanderbilt uncomfortably learned in their struggle for the Erie, some politicians and judges were using the business methods of the age a shade too expertly even for these masters of acquisitiveness.

But all in all these were happy years. Business indexes, production figures, and census statistics all testify to that. Grover Cleveland caused a few tremors with his tariff ideas, but they were stilled by Congress. The Interstate Commerce Act, the Sherman Anti-Trust Act, the income tax, and the Granger activities were birds of evil omen. But the courts had been staffed with sympathetic men, and what they did not do by decision the executives did by inaction.

Thus surrounded with a favorable political environment, economic America progressed with giant strides. On the other hand, the political development of the nation seemed to stop almost totally for thirty years. Since the day of the Mayflower Compact, American political evolution had been pointed in the direction of more democracy and a broadening of civil rights. But now the march toward universal suffrage begun under Jackson and extended beyond the color line in Lincoln's day came to an abrupt halt and possibly even retreated. Armed protection of Southern ballot boxes and other types of extra-political persuasion in the North soon wiped out the gains of the fifteenth amendment. It was not until the very end of the period that women's suffrage won its first few feeble victories in the West.

Innovations in the machinery of government were few from 1868 to 1897, and old mechanisms were slanted in an undemocratic direction. Jacksonian democrats had once fashioned the convention to "let the people rule." Now in the hands of a new species of local political bosses it was used more to obstruct than to further the popular will. The indirect election of United States senators apparently worked well enough before the Civil War. In the age of materialism economic pressure and corruption produced different results. The Senate of the United States was often spoken of as the millionaires' club, and senators were almost as widely known by the particular interest they represented as by the states from which they came. Economic representation in practice antedated by a good many years the theories of some modern political scientists.

The popularly elected House of Representatives responded to the tides of the times. Speaker Thomas B. Reed's ironclad rules may have made that body more efficient. They also dangerously centralized the power of the House in the hands of the Speaker, who might or might not reflect majority sentiment. The arrogation by the federal judiciary of the power to review state laws under the fourteenth amendment again circumscribed the democratic process. In some measure the power to determine the legality of socio-economic legislation was now transferred from the hands of popularly elected bodies into the hands of men appointed for life.

Simultaneously the increasing judicial predilection to use the injunction in labor disputes was threatening some of the basic principles of the Bill of Rights. A study of labor decisions handed down by the courts from 1880 to 1900 is a study of the restrictions placed upon the freedom of speech, the freedom of assembly, and the ancient right of trial by jury.[2] The use of the injunction and attending contempt proceedings in the two decades was not without some similarity to the issuance of *lettres de cachet* by the pre-revolutionary French monarchy.

Corruption ran from the bottom of the American political structure upward into state and national government. The mass moral sense which had in part made possible the antebellum reform crusade ending in the antislavery cause had long since almost vanished from American politics. In its place was a general willingness either to play or accept the game of "multiplication, division and silence." E. H. Harriman was much too inclusive in his alleged remark that he could "buy" state legislatures, Congress, and, if necessary, the judiciary,[3] but he had certain grounds for the observation. The story of the Credit Mobilier, the career of Charles Tyson Yerkes, the Chicago traction magnate, and the devious course of Judge Barnard of the New York State Supreme Court are all historical cases in point.

This was the political world of which Theodore Roosevelt accidentally found himself master in 1901. This was the nineteenth-century order of American life which in the first moments of his presidency he had promised to preserve. It had existed since the conscientious but inept Grant had sat in the White House, and except during the Cleveland interim and the rebellion of 1896 it had appeared to be growing stronger with the years. And yet before the seven Roosevelt years were over this system conceived and nourished by conservative Republicanism was tottering to its very founda-

[2] Selig Perlman, *History of Trade Unionism in the United States* (New York, 1923), 156–160.
[3] Henry F. Pringle, *Theodore Roosevelt* (New York, 1931), 452.

tions. Everywhere in local, state, and national government it had been put on the defensive by the progressive movement.

In its essence the progressive movement was a great social reaction against the preceding age. Compounded of moral, political, economic, and intellectual revolt, it was not restricted to one party but ran through the entire gamut of political organizations. Nor was it a product of a single economic class. Farmers and laborers were at its core, but they were soon joined by multitudes from the white collar and small business classes and even by some of the very rich. In fact, few reform movements in American history have had the support of more wealthy men. Charles R. Crane, Rudolph Spreckels, Tom Johnson, F. A. Filene, Joseph Fels, George W. Perkins, and Frank Munsey were merely a few of the financial angels who contributed to one or another of its phases. Politically the movement had a Middle Western tinge at the start. But by 1910, with the election of Woodrow Wilson in New Jersey and Hiram Johnson in California, it was nationwide. Finally the progressive movement was a way of thought that separated an old and a new America. The perspicacious Henry Adams sensed that when he spoke of his generation of Americans becoming "instantly old."[4]

It was this movement that in the course of fifteen years attempted, with a certain amount of success, to change the whole moral, economic, and political face of the country. Undoubtedly it altered the standards of political honesty and public morals. It inquired into the national structure of production and tried to redistribute wealth more equitably among all the nation's people. It made drastic changes in some of the old concepts of property which the race had held for centuries. It modified the organization of the American government as that government had not been changed since the Civil War. And, in not the least of its actions, it demonstrated that the federal government in the plenitude of its powers was the master of even the largest industrial combinations. One of the great accomplishments of the progressive

[4] *The Education of Henry Adams* (New York, 1918), 147.

movement was to fasten Jeffersonian idealism on a Hamiltonian structure in a partial realization of social democracy. Twenty years later another great reform movement was built upon that foundation.

Theodore Roosevelt did not beget the progressive movement. In spirit it was as old as America itself. For the same flame had burned in the men gathered around Samuel Adams, Tom Paine, Daniel Shays, Thomas Jefferson, in fact, wherever the many have fought the privileged few for economic, political, and intellectual liberty. The more material beginnings of the movement likewise antedated Roosevelt by years. For its origins were dispersed in the 1870's between the Greenbackers, the Granger groups, the anti-monopolites, the youthful labor parties, and what remained of the old Charles Sumner–Wendell Phillips faction of the Republican party. These small beginnings were stoutly nourished by the economic and political tracts of Henry George, Edward Bellamy, and Henry Demarest Lloyd. They were at least acknowledged by the pale realism of Hamlin Garland, William Dean Howells, and Mark Twain. Howells succeeded in mentioning a labor strike objectively for the first time in polite American literature. And Twain's Senator Dilworthy in *The Gilded Age* was not one to inspire confidence in the American politico.

But the real seedbed of progressivism was of course Populism. The progressive movement was cradled in the home of the Populists, the Middle West. The progressive program was grounded upon the Populist platform. As the historian of the Populist movement has pointed out, almost every plank in that platform was written into law during the progressive years.[5] Moreover, there was a direct political bloodline from Bryan to Wilson and on to a young assistant secretary of the navy, Franklin Delano Roosevelt.

Likewise in the Republican party it was true that Roosevelt "cursed Bryan and then aped his ways." But Vachel Lindsay's line of poetry told only a part of the truth. Republican progressivism began where Populism left off. Before it was

[5] John D. Hicks, *The Populist Revolt* (Minneapolis, 1931), 421.

through, however, it had grafted many new things on the original stock, not the least of which was a national scope for the movement. The Populist center of gravity was, and remained, among the farmers. Roosevelt in 1912 polled a larger percentage of votes in the big cities than he did elsewhere in the country. Against that background it is not surprising that the Progressive platform in 1912 had more in common with a New Deal document than it had with Bryan's program of 1896.

One fundamental weakness of the Populists was their inability to capture any sizeable fraction of national Republican strength. They acknowledged their weakness when they joined the Democrats in 1896, only to find that even that combination was not strong enough to win. Bryan was beaten worse in 1896 than any presidential candidate had been in forty years. In fact, it was by opposing Bryan and Populism that the Republican party had become a real majority party for the first time in its history.

The period following that election was the high summer of corporate influence. Never had industrial leadership seemed more expansive, more powerful. The census of 1900 reported the existence of seventy-three industrial combinations whose capital exceeded ten million dollars. Only twenty of these had their origins before 1898, whereas fifty-three had been organized in the two closing years of the century. Following hard on the century mark, the United States Steel Corporation was formed, the first industrial concern in the world with a capitalization of more than a billion dollars. A short time thereafter the creation of the Northern Securities Company, the American Tobacco Company, the Bethlehem Steel Company, and the American Portland Cement Corporation, to mention only a few of the better known consolidations, were announced. Indeed, scarcely a month went by without the formation of another business giant from erstwhile competitors. From 1895 to 1905 traditional industrial competition was committing suicide.[6]

[6] Consolidation did not stop at national boundaries. In 1901 American

Meanwhile organized conservatism dominated politics. Bryan had been defeated; Hanna and McKinley ruled. The nation under Republican guidance had fought a glorious little war with Spain which had neither cost too much in blood and treasure nor returned too little in empire and public satisfaction. The highest tariff bill in American history and the Gold Standard Act were passed with little opposition. At the peak of their power Hanna and conservatism re-elected McKinley over Bryan by a larger majority than in 1896.

The history of American politics is a study of the laws of the pendulum. Action has followed reaction as regularly as night the day. By 1901 conservatism had dominated the political scene for four decades. It was high time for a change. Prior to 1900, with the exception of the Republican Populists, there had scarcely been a successful reforming Republican politician. Here and there a man like Governor Hazen S. Pingree of Michigan disturbed his complacent colleagues. But Pingree was exceptional. And then in the same year that marked McKinley's second triumph Robert M. La Follette was elected as an anti-corporation, anti-machine governor of Wisconsin. To the north Minnesota had elected the radical-talking Samuel R. Van Sant to the same position. A year later the trust-baiting Albert B. Cummins was made governor of Iowa, and a single-taxer, Tom L. Johnson, mayor of Cleveland. In September of 1901 Theodore Roosevelt became president of the United States. The progressive movement had begun.

For years before 1900 the presidents of the United States had been relatively old men and perhaps they had been tired. Many of them had been selected as a compromise between warring congressional leaders whose names and deeds were often more familiar to their countrymen than those of the man thus elected. The fortunate nominees were soon made aware, if they had not previously appreciated the fact, that

producers of sewing thread joined a world thread cartel dominated by the J. and P. Coats Company of England. See John A. Hobson, *The Evolution of Modern Capitalism: A Study of Machine Production* (London, 1907), 208–212.

the political center of gravity lay in Congress and not in the White House. Roosevelt was a political accident. So he was relatively free. He was also the youngest man who ever sat in the White House and undoubtedly the most energetic. Soldier, scholar, and practising politician besides a half dozen other things, Roosevelt was boyishly eager to make the world feel the weight of his hand. One thing was certain: the days of White House placidity and dignified inaction were over. Whether the new administration was steered left or right or straight down the center, with T.R. at the helm it would be steered with vigor and a whoop.

Politicians and businessmen were both edgy after McKinley's death, wondering what direction the concentrated presidential energy would take. Rumors flew about Washington that Roosevelt had broken with Hanna and the Old Guard. The stock market wavered in New York. But when nothing happened to disturb the calm along the Potomac, both groups breathed easier. Wall Street recovered from its case of nerves, and the Old Guard went confidently on its way again, assuring itself that kings had changed but not dynastic policies.

At the time only a few people in Washington understood the significance of what was happening in the Middle West. Among these few was Theodore Roosevelt. From the beginning of his administration the new president held a weather eye on the West and was ready to trim his sail and shift his course whenever the reform winds freshened. But this much can be said for Roosevelt. Opportunist though he was (which of course is another way of saying that he was a good politician), he was an opportunist with strong reform leanings, who had little in common with the Conkling, McKinley, Aldrich concept of politics and less with the social pretensions of the reigning industrialists of his day.

Roosevelt was born of a family that had acquired its money and position early in American history. By the time Theodore was born the Roosevelts wore what wealth they had with ease and grace. It had been with them too long to demand display or to elicit reverence. Neither were they likely to be impressed by staggering dividends or excited by huge personal accumulations. There were other ends in life besides material ones for young Theodore. There were the arts, literature, and a duty to the nation. Moreover, there was the Calvinist obligation to take care of the unfortunates around one. But Roosevelt needed no Calvinist doctrine of stewardship to evoke that feeling. He was born with a warm impulsive heart, which he carried with him into the presidency.

In Roosevelt's many-sided character perhaps the dominant urge was his desire for power, a desire always tempered by his strong conviction that he could that power in the interest of the public. Just a little less demanding in the determination of his actions was the brightly burning flame of nationalism within him. Quick to resent national insult and with a certain fondness for the trappings of war, he was likely in times of international stress to forget his domestic aims, buckle on his armor, and go jousting. Still another clue to his character was his love for the Republican party and his monumental disdain for all things labeled Democrat. Born in an era when to be a gentleman in the North was to be a Republican, Roosevelt throughout his life viewed the Democrats with a feeling akin to contempt.

All these things tempered his reforming spirit, causing many people to view his liberal professions with suspicion. But at heart Roosevelt did have a certain fundamental sympathy for the plight of the underprivileged. In the pulling and hauling of the many emotional and moral forces of his character, this sympathy was always more or less apparent.

This basic liberal strain in Roosevelt's personality did much for the success of the progressive movement. His very coming to the White House imparted to the whole government a vitality and a will to action which it had not known for years. His attacks on big business and its attendant evils made the American people ever more conscious of the problems presented by a new industrial era. His continued sermonizing from the White House stirred many a hitherto placid citizen into a state of righteous indignation. Speaking from the most prominent tribune in the nation, he found the ear not alone of the West but also of many in the East who would not have listened to the more radical doctrines coming from the statesmen across the Alleghenies. In short, he aroused the entire nation to the need for action. And while he did little himself to solve the numerous questions he broached, he did create a national demand that these questions be met and answered. Roosevelt was the best publicity man progressivism ever had.

When Roosevelt entered the White House in 1901, he found Congress dominated by a small group of elder Republican statesmen in the Senate. This small cabal composed of Nelson W. Aldrich of Rhode Island, J. C. Spooner of Wisconsin, W. B. Allison of Iowa, and O. H. Platt of Connecticut, aided by a few more independent lights such as M. A. Hanna of Ohio, practically controlled the Senate and a subservient House. These were men satisfied with affairs as they had been and they wished to run the government as it had been run for the past forty years. Their leader was Aldrich, the acknowledged representative of big business in the nation's legislative halls. Ever since his determined fight on the Interstate Commerce Act of 1887 he had been an automatic political reflex of organized industrial and financial conservatism.

What few Republican progressives there were in the House and Senate in 1901 can scarcely be called an opposition. Here and there sat a man like old Senator G. F. Hoar, who had been protesting for years against the trend of national affairs. But their numbers were few and for the most part their names unknown. Clearly if Roosevelt was to work with Congress in any degree of harmony he would have to do it through the small conservative directorate. Otherwise his first term would achieve nothing in legislation accomplishments and there might be no second term. "Before I write my message," Roosevelt wrote Nelson W. Aldrich a few weeks after he had taken office, "I should like to have a chance to go over certain subjects with you."[7]

From the time of that letter until he was elected on his own

[7] September 30, 1901, in Pringle, *Roosevelt*, 244.

in 1904 Roosevelt's personal legislative achievements consisted chiefly of obtaining an amendment to the Elkins Act and setting up a bureau of corporations to investigate corporate practices. He secured the amendment against the opposition of the conservatives by simply letting out for publication the slightly untruthful information that John D. Rockefeller had been deluging the Senate with telegrams insisting that the amendment be defeated.[8] But beyond that for three years Roosevelt did little. In fact, so slight was his interference with the legislative process that the alleged agreement at Oyster Bay, September 16, 1902, seems plausible. Here, according to Aldrich's biographer, Roosevelt sealed a bargain with Aldrich which gave him a free hand in foreign affairs in return for Aldrich's noninterference in legislative matters.[9]

Whether from agreement or pure expediency it must have been difficult for Roosevelt to keep his fingers out of the legislative hopper. However, there were other things a president might do without congressional sanction to show the people that his heart was right. One of them was to enforce the Sherman Anti-Trust Act. For a decade the law had rusted on the statute books. When it had been used effectively by Roosevelt's predecessors it had been pointed against labor unions, not corporations.

In 1901 two great railroad men backed by the most powerful financial concerns in America were locked in a titanic struggle for control of the railroad network stretching from Chicago to Seattle. In the end James J. Hill, E. H. Harriman, the House of J. P. Morgan, and Kuhn, Loeb, and Company with Rockefeller connections fought to a draw. And then, like the sensible men they were, they compromised by chartering the jointly controlled Northern Securities Company with a capitalization of four hundred million dollars.

Here was the perfect situation. The crescendo of public clamor against the business leviathans was rising day by day. The men implicated represented the very inner council of

[8] *Ibid.*, 341.
[9] N. W. Stephenson, *Nelson W. Aldrich: A Leader in American Politics* (New York, 1930), 198–199.

American big business; some of them were also the chief public villains of the day. To the agricultural West they were Wall Street, the monstrous thing that prevented an honest poor man from making a decent living.

Without warning on February 19, 1902, Attorney General Philander C. Knox announced that the government at the president's request would soon start suit to dissolve the Northern Securities Company. For the first time since its passage the Sherman Anti-Trust Law was to be sincerely and energetically enforced. Prosecutions of other business combines were to follow. As the ticker tape jerked out the sad story in descending quotations, the reform element in the country took heart for the first time since 1896.

The year 1902 was, in fact, the *annus mirabilis* for progressive political action. A month after the announcement of the Northern Securities suit the anthracite coal miners of Pennsylvania went out on strike to enforce their demands for a living wage. Leading the miners was John Mitchell, a labor statesman of the first order and a man whom Roosevelt grew to respect. On the other side of the quarrel were a group of hard-headed coal operators who believed in the inviolability of the right of an owner to conduct his business as he pleased regardless of public consequences. They were determined not to add a cent to their meager wage scale, and the strike went on through the spring and summer and into the early autumn of 1902.

Meanwhile the country faced a coal shortage. Homes, offices, and schools were cold. Public resentment flared up at the operators who steadfastly refused to arbitrate their differences. Their refusal had been given not only to non-official groups but also to the president, who had personally interceded in the struggle. With the congressional elections and winter approaching, Roosevelt waited no longer. He let it be known that if arbitration was not soon accepted the United States Army would temporarily dispossess the owners and mine the coal. Faced with the horrible specter of state socialism, the operators finally backed down. Some ten years earlier

Grover Cleveland had used federal troops to quell Eugene V. Debs and his striking railway workers. Now the use of federal troops had been at least threatened to force the arbitration of a labor dispute. For the first time in American history the federal government had officially acknowledged that at times justice might lie with labor in its disputes with capital. From the anthracite coal strike to the National Labor Relations Board was a long journey but the steps were connected if not continuous.

Two other actions of Roosevelt in the year 1902 brought heart to progressives everywhere. The first was his constant and effective support of the Newlands Act while it was passing through Congress. The Newlands Reclamation Act was significant because it permitted the government to engage in the construction of great irrigation dams throughout the West. The second was his appointment of Oliver Wendell Holmes to the Supreme Court. Holmes was appointed, in part, because of his labor views. He had been successful, Roosevelt wrote to Lodge, in sustaining "his sympathy for the class from which he has *not* drawn his clients."[10] Roosevelt probably did not know that he was appointing one of the great English-speaking jurists of all times. For Holmes was a fellow of Coke, Blackstone, and Marshall.

Roosevelt's chief aid to the reform cause during his presidency lay perhaps more in the response he invoked than in his own positive acts. Throughout the year 1902 the president incorporated in his public addresses suggestions for national control of corporations and revision of the tariff, two things which he would continue to talk about for the rest of his incumbency without doing anything about either. A few members of Congress took Roosevelt at his word and introduced specific measures. In the 1902 session a bill was introduced by the chairman of the Senate Judiciary Committee contemplating federal control of all interstate corporations. A more

---

[10] *Selections from the Correspondence of Theodore Roosevelt and Henry Cabot Lodge, 1884–1918*, edited by Henry Cabot Lodge (New York, 1925), 2: 228.

radical measure to put all iron and steel goods made by a trust on the free list was proposed in the House. The chairman of the House Judiciary Committee even sounded out his committee on the advisability of nationalizing all coal mines and coal deposits in the country.[11] When once these measures were seriously proposed Roosevelt remained silent, and none saw the light of legislative day. But they did serve at least to feed the public interest in and stimulate discussion of the problems.

The reform spirit was in the air in America and for that matter throughout the whole Western world. The progressive movement in America, the struggle for representative government and a Duma in Russia, the "new deal" of Asquith and Lloyd George in England, social reforms in France, the rise of the Social Democrats in Germany, and the attainment of manhood suffrage in Italy and Austria were merely various local manifestations of an intellectual environment that spread across continents and oceans.

In October of 1902, according to the historian of the muckrake clan, the first truly muckraking magazine article was published in the United States. Perhaps no other single force was more responsible for the success of the progressive movement than the group of popular writers that emerged to write for the fast-flourishing muckrake magazines. Nothing was too holy for their prying eyes, no institution too sacred for their debunking pens. If at times they bordered on the sensational they at least exposed a picture of American politics and social conditions that had never before been revealed. The American public gasped with consternation and anger at what they saw.[12]

Very little less influential in creating a climate of reform were the great liberal daily newspapers. Sired by the Spanish

[11] *Congressional Record*, 57 Congress, 2 Session, vol. 36, pt. 1, p. 393.

[12] C. C. Regier, *The Era of the Muckrakers* (Chapel Hill, 1932), 55. The muckrake magazines, so called by Roosevelt, were a group of low-priced periodicals whose investigations into political, economic, and social problems were the sensation of the day. They reached a vast audience and their influence was great.

War, the sheets of Hearst and Pulitzer were already by 1902 turning to "liberal" journalism. And in the universities doughty champions of the new day had risen up to contest the philosophy of William Graham Sumner. It is significant of the *Zeitgeist* of the period that an unknown from the far Northwest antedated by nine years a revolutionary thesis of a leading American historian dealing with the making of the federal constitution. The federal constitution, he wrote in a letter to the *Outlook*, "was written primarily for the defense of property, and hence of necessity, the powers of government were placed in the hands of private property owners by those who made the constitution."[13] The writer then intimated that little could be done with the crusade for a social democracy until that power was placed squarely in the hands of the people. Perhaps he had sat in the classes of James Allen Smith at the University of Washington. Smith was to publish in 1907 one of the first truly critical works on the evolution of the American government.[14]

One of the last institutions to feel the impress of the movement, and in turn the last to contribute to it, was the church. But already by 1902 a sizeable wing was arguing for socialized Christianity. The social program of the Methodist Episcopal church in 1908 was nothing if not advanced. In the counterattack thousands of pages were written against this attempt to substitute social service for Christian worship. But by the end of the decade it was not uncommon for the Baptist World Alliance to adopt at its yearly meeting a comprehensive program of social and economic reform.[15] Indicative of the march of religion was the conservative warning that the nation's clergymen were inclined to "take up the cause of the users of dynamite and fighters of militia too easily in times like these."[16]

With the reform spirit fermenting in all parts of the nation Roosevelt, having voiced its aspirations clearly for the first

[13] *Outlook*, 73: 181–182 (January 17, 1903).
[14] *The Spirit of American Government* (New York, 1907).
[15] *Outlook*, 98: 473 (July 1, 1911).
[16] *New York Times*, January 26, 1912.

time in national government, did a characteristic thing. Apprehensive that irate Republican conservatives might obstruct his renomination in 1904, he beat a strategic retreat. The demand for corporate control was absent from his speeches. He began to doubt "whether it would be wise" to make a tariff reduction in the year preceding a presidential election.[17] He acquired a new "respect and regard" for Aldrich and his conservative following, who had often differed with him but who in the last analysis always sought "to do what is best for the government."[18]

Dominating the Republican convention in 1904, Roosevelt selected Elihu Root and Joseph G. Cannon as its presiding officers and his friend Henry Cabot Lodge as chairman of the Committee on Resolutions. It would have been difficult to find three more reverent archbishops of high conservatism in the entire Republican apostolic succession. They did what was expected of them. The notorious "Addicks Republicans" from Delaware were seated in place of a reform faction from that state. The La Follette delegates selected by the legally constituted Wisconsin Republican convention were denied their seats in favor of a bolting conservative faction led by Senator Spooner. The platform was completely innocent of anything savoring of progressive action. Conservatives everywhere rejoiced—they had misjudged Roosevelt.

In the following election Roosevelt, supported by the usual Hannaesque campaign contributions, met the feeble efforts of Alton B. Parker, the Democratic candidate, with much noise and little else. Roosevelt was elected by a popular majority of two and a half million votes. Elected along with the president in the East were the usual Republican machine candidates. Out in the Middle West, however, there was trouble. La Follette and Cummins had once more carried their states on progressive platforms. The red-haired radical, William R. Stubbs of Kansas, had elected his man governor over the opposition of Regular Republicans, and Coe Crawford had come perilously

[17] Roosevelt to J. B. Bishop, April 27, 1903, in Pringle, *Roosevelt*, 353.
[18] Roosevelt to W. H. Taft, March 13, 1903, in Stephenson, *Aldrich*, 218.

close to defeating the standpat machine of Senator Alfred B. Kittredge of South Dakota. Elected on the Democratic ticket were Joseph W. Folk and John A. Johnson as reform governors of Missouri and Minnesota.

On scanning the election results Roosevelt must have been elated and apprehensive at the same time. He had won a handsome victory, but the party instead of gaining had lost cohesiveness. Aldrich and his lieutenants had gained support for the president in the East on the strength of a conservative platform. To the West, Cummins, La Follette, and Stubbs had campaigned not for the friend of Aldrich but for the Roosevelt of the Northern Securities case and the coal strike of 1902. There was danger of a split in the party if something was not done to appease the growing radicalism of the West. Governors La Follette and Cummins soon received invitations to a White House conference.[19]

Not long after the conference with the Middle Western governors Roosevelt began to talk about tariff revision. Conservative congressional leaders were "surprised" at the president's feelings. Hurrying to Washington, they persuaded him to drop the matter only after a long discussion.[20] But Roosevelt had not forgotten the ominous clouds rolling up in the West. Just a few days before the end of 1904 James A. Garfield, commissioner of corporations, issued a report recommending that Congress pass legislation to bring all corporations engaged in interstate trade under federal supervision. A shiver ran through the nation's business circles. Garfield's report was just the shower before the storm.[21]

A month later the president spoke to the Union League Club of Philadelphia, which included the very cream of Pennsylvania's industrial and financial leadership. Only a few months before many of these men had made sizeable contributions to Roosevelt's campaign fund. They had been satisfied with the president's moderate yearly address to Congress

[19] *Ibid.*, 252.   [20] *Ibid.*, 253.
[21] *Report of the Commissioner of Corporations* (House Document 165, 58 Congress, 3 Session), 45.

and they had gathered together expecting at the very worst to hear a pleasant moralistic lecture phrased in generalities. But for once Roosevelt was in no mood for generalities. He grew specific that night, painfully specific. Business, the president said, had grown so powerful that a wide extension of governmental supervision was necessary. No free people on earth could tolerate the private use of the "power conferred by vast wealth," Roosevelt continued, without endowing government with "the still higher power" of directing its employment in the interest of the people as a whole. Business had become interstate in scope, and state control was no longer desirable nor adequate. If the Supreme Court ruled against national regulation of corporations an amendment to the Constitution would be necessary.

What was true of business in general was also true of the railroads, the president continued: "there must be lodged in some tribunal the power over rates" to protect both the railroad and the shipper. Roosevelt did not intend, he remarked, to allow this country to fall because of a class government under which the poor plundered the rich or the rich exploited the poor.[22] As his listeners left that night they must have asked themselves whether William Jennings Bryan or Theodore Roosevelt was president.

The effect on the country was electric. Trust regulation and railroad rates became a topic of general discussion. And while the country talked, the Esch-Townsend bill was introduced into the lower House, embodying the presidential demands for railroad rate-making.[23] The bill passed the House with a rush, but in the Senate, meeting with the determined opposition of the conservative phalanx, it was smothered in the dark recesses of the Committee on Interstate Commerce. The resourceful man in the White House, however, was not of a mind to watch the cabal utterly disregard the growing dissent in the country. All the year in speech after speech he pounded away in the interest of railway regulation. Having built up

[22] Theodore Roosevelt, *Works* (New York, 1925), 15: 215–226.
[23] *Congressional Record*, 58 Congress, 3 Session, vol. 39, p. 952.

public sentiment to the point where the Senate could no longer refuse to act, he repeated his demands in the annual message to Congress in December of 1905 in language that fairly joined the issue.[24]

The conservative coterie in the Senate once more prepared for the coming struggle. But in doing so it found that its battle lines lacked the solidarity of the old days. The final roll call had taken some of its ablest leaders. In May, 1904, Matthew Quay, the perennial senator from Pennsylvania, had died. Just a year later Senator O. H. Platt turned his face away from the strife of congressional battles forever. This was a serious loss, for Platt, along with Aldrich, Spooner, and Allison, had captained the conservative forces. A tower of strength on the floor and an able parliamentarian, Platt was all but irreplaceable.

Desertion further depleted the Stalwart ranks. Soon Spooner of Wisconsin, irritated at the direction the political winds were blowing in his state, was to refuse to stand for reelection. And W. B. Allison had shown signs of disaffection.[25] Watching the situation in the West, Allison had long been uneasy. In 1901 he had broken temporarily with Aldrich over the matter of reciprocity. The next year found him again in opposition to the leader of the Senate when he voted against a bill for the subsidizing of steamship lines.[26] Now fearful of Cummins' attacks at home, he was preparing to veer for shelter. Aldrich himself refused to do other than march stoutly along the conservative path which he had first mapped out in 1886.[27]

Simultaneously with the decline of conservative leadership, there began to develop in the Senate a small group of senators devoted to progressive action. Jonathan Dolliver of Iowa and Moses E. Clapp of Minnesota had always been more sympathetic with Western radicalism than with the

[24] *New York Times*, December 6, 1905.
[25] Stephenson, *Aldrich*, 266.
[26] *Outlook*, 70: 695 (March 22, 1902).
[27] William B. Allison MSS., Historical Memorial and Art Department of Iowa, Des Moines, Iowa.

narrow conservatism of Aldrich. Spurred on by Roosevelt's eloquence, they voted with the minority in 1905 in favor of the Esch-Townsend rate proposal.[28] Repeatedly in the next few years they indicated that they were departing from the old conservative domination. In the van of this liberal group forming in the Senate was also to be found Indiana's impeccably dressed Beveridge. Becoming more progressive with each passing year of the decade, he broke entirely with conservative doctrines in 1906 by advocating the direct primary system and the inheritance tax. Beveridge soon followed up with a sweeping demand for revision of the tariff, a demand which did not cease even after the president had written him that he did not see how it was to be accomplished "just at this time."[29] Then there was La Follette. Upon the death of Senator Quarles the Wisconsin legislature, in January, 1905, had elected him to a seat in the upper house. The old guard must have had strange musings indeed as they watched "Battle Bob" walk down the Senate aisle on the arm of his archenemy Spooner to take the oath of office. Surely some of the more realistic in the chamber must have perceived that this was the beginning of the dusk of the gods.

But the conservative force had little thought of twilight as it prepared to defeat Roosevelt's proposed railroad legislation in January of 1906. Assailed though it was by a temporary coalition between the president and the radical West and torn by dissension in its own ranks, it still stood firm in the mid-afternoon of its power, confident in its leaders and complacent in its strength. The result of the next three months' battle was a draw between the two forces. The Hepburn rate bill was neither the stringent measure that the West had hoped for, nor was it the innocuous one that Aldrich and his forces would have passed. It was a compromise after Roosevelt's own heart. The president had advanced the bill to pacify the West and so to heal the widening breach in the party. He had no thought of utterly crushing the conservative majority and

---

[28] *Independent*, 58: 918 (April 27, 1905).
[29] Roosevelt to Beveridge, August 23, 1906, in Claude G. Bowers, *Beveridge and the Progressive Era* (Boston, 1932), 239.

alienating it from the party. Even in the heat of the conflict when tempers were short he and Aldrich continued their cordial personal relations. The two had even dined together in the White House, and Roosevelt had accepted the advice of the other to drop the tariff question when the restless chief executive again expressed a desire to tinker with the custom rates.[30]

In the railroad legislation Roosevelt had secured what he wanted, but he failed to appease the West for long. The rate-bill had only whetted its appetite. Soon the prairie stumps were ringing with demands for physical evaluation of railroads, income and inheritance taxes, more rigid regulation of trusts, a downward revision of the tariff, and direct election of senators. Consonant with the swell of this chorus, the widening split of the party in Congress became more and more evident. In the skirmishes over Roosevelt's pure food legislation of 1906 angry words were bandied on the Republican side of the Chamber which would not be forgotten. Progressive legislators, as they watched their cherished measures consigned to the legislative scrap heap, began to wonder if the forces aligned behind Aldrich and Speaker Cannon were not more inimical than friendly. After the defeat of his child labor bill Beveridge speculated on the problem to a friend: "Sometimes I feel that public life is not worth the effort when a man gives his best efforts for the passage of righteous laws, and then, by the 'ethics' of party regularity is compelled to go out and work for the very men who were the enemies of these measures."[31]

The day had not yet come when progressives were ready to indict their fellow Republicans in public. But an ominous open break had already appeared in Congress. In the voting on the Aldrich-Vreeland bill sixteen Western Republican representatives and six senators joined the Democratic minority in an unsuccessful attempt to defeat the measure.[32]

[30] Roosevelt to Aldrich, August 31, 1905, in Stephenson, *Aldrich*, 279; Roosevelt to Allison, November 9, 1905, Allison MSS.

[31] Beveridge to C. W. Miller, August 15, 1908, in Bowers, *Beveridge*, 291.

[32] *Congressional Record*, 60 Congress, 1 Session, vol. 44, pt. 1, pp. 3861–3864.

As the Middle West became more radical Roosevelt became more active in his attacks on the "malefactors of great wealth." Through the two years of 1907 and 1908 the Bureau of Corporations and the attorney general's office were busy starting suits against corporate combinations. In the space of eighteen months the government entered suit against three of the country's largest industrial combines, the Standard Oil Company, the American Tobacco Company, and the Sugar Trust. And then in January, 1908, the president sent to Congress the most radical of all his messages. In burning paragraphs he scourged the nation's courts for their promptness in using the injunction against labor unions. He proposed a whole series of reforms for the federal government to enact. Workingmen's compensation, physical evaluation of railroads, more power over rates for the Interstate Commerce Commission, and a measure designed to control speculation and to prevent gambling in the stock markets were all vitally needed. In a string of caustic explosives Roosevelt concluded the message with a tirade against the dishonest and corrupt businesses that had made the "name 'high finance' a term of scandal" and reproach.[33]

The conservative hierarchy of the party fumed at the speech. Senator Foraker irritably suggested the obvious, that "there does not seem to be any substantial difference between what is represented by Mr. Bryan and Mr. Roosevelt."[34] Important Republicans wrote to the president that they could no longer follow where he led.[35] There were even suggestions that a new organization be formed "which shall comprise the conservative men of both great political parties."[36] The conservative leaders, however, did not take this last suggestion very seriously. The proper course of action, according to Al-

[33] *New York Times,* January 31, 1908.
[34] Joseph B. Foraker to J. F. Babcock, February 19, 1908, Foraker MSS., Ohio Philosophical and Historical Society, Cincinnati, Ohio.
[35] Nicholas Murray Butler to Roosevelt, February 4, 1908, in Pringle, *Roosevelt,* 480.
[36] James R. Day to Foraker, February 15, 1908, Foraker MSS., Cincinnati, Ohio.

drich, was to keep the party intact but eliminate from it those men whose election in the West promised "nothing but mischief and destruction."[37] If Beveridge and his progressives were not quite ready for open warfare the conservatives were. And apparently only the necessity for unity in the coming presidential campaign prevented the outbreak of the inter-party war then and there.

One of the president's chief concerns in 1907 and 1908 was the selection of a successor. That was to be a difficult choice. The right man had to be sympathetic enough with the Roosevelt philosophy to carry out "my policies" and to keep the Middle West in line. On the other hand, he had to be acceptable to the majority conservative faction of the party. The ideal man, of course, was Roosevelt himself. But the president in an unwise moment of jubilation after the 1904 elections had counted himself out. So in 1908, however regretfully, it had to be another.

On the basis of ability alone Elihu Root apparently was Roosevelt's first choice. But Root was too closely affiliated with corporations to be acceptable to the West and perhaps even to Roosevelt personally. A movement was under way for Charles Evans Hughes, who had acquired some status as a liberal by his investigation of the New York life insurance concerns. But the frosty and independent governor of New York did not suit the presidential fancy. Finally after much soul-searching Roosevelt settled on William Howard Taft, his secretary of war, as the solution to the problem.

Taft had been the loyal errand boy of the administration. He had capably carried out every task assigned to him, and at times with his direct and frank manner he had seemed more liberal than the hard-hitting but compromising president. The very soul of geniality, Taft had few personal enemies. Moreover, because of his faithful service to a progressive administration he was more acceptable to the Middle West than any other presidential aspirant.[38]

[37] Aldrich to Foraker, August 21, 1908, Foraker MSS., Cincinnati, Ohio.
[38] Oscar K. Davis, *Released for Publication* (New York, 1925), 47–54;

To the extent that Taft's candidacy was favored by Roosevelt and other Republican progressives, it was opposed, strangely enough in the light of future events, by the party's conservatives. Taft had been too much a Roosevelt man to suit their tastes. His tariff views were painfully in conflict with Republican orthodox doctrines. Either Joseph G. Cannon of Illinois, C. W. Fairbanks of Indiana, or Joseph B. Foraker of Ohio, who had all announced their candidacies, would have been far more acceptable. A list sent to Foraker in January, 1908, after Roosevelt had announced his preference, indicates that the Ohio senator was being given steady financial support by Senators Murray Crane and Henry Cabot Lodge of Massachusetts. Aldrich promised a sizeable contribution later. And Senator Jacob H. Gallinger of New Hampshire wrote that he was busy lining up other support for the "stop Taft" movement.[39]

Roosevelt did little at first to advocate Taft's candidacy openly, but he soon became convinced that unless he did so his own renomination would result. From that time on the president pulled every string within reach to secure Taft's nomination. Southern state conventions were martialed and run in the usual way, federal patronage was dispensed with judicious care, and Republican officeholders were carefully instructed in the nature of their duties.[40] To complete the rout of the opposition a whisper was circulating that if Taft were not accepted, Roosevelt for another four years would be the only al-

Henry R. Stoddard, *As I Knew Them* (New York, 1927), 443; Mark Sullivan, *Our Times* (New York, 1932), 4:18; Pringle, *Roosevelt*, 497–502; George H. Haynes, *The Life of Charles G. Washburn* (Boston, 1931), 120.

[39] Gallinger to Foraker, November 27, 1907, January 11, 1908, and Joseph W. Henderson to Aldrich (copy), January 14, 1908, Foraker MSS., Cincinnati, Ohio; Julia B. Foraker, *I Would Live It Again* (New York, 1932), 330.

[40] Governor W. O. Bradley to Foraker, February 10, 1908, and N. C. Murphy to Foraker, January 25, 1908, Foraker MSS., Cincinnati, Ohio; James S. Clarkson to Grenville M. Dodge, June 8, 1908, Grenville M. Dodge MSS., Historical Memorial and Art Department of Iowa, Des Moines, Iowa; Roosevelt to William D. Foulke, February 3, 1908, in Pringle, *Roosevelt*, 501.

ternative. At that Aldrich and most of his companions gave up.[41]

In the ensuing convention Roosevelt, as in 1904, compromised with the conservative faction. He agreed to the choice of the conservative Senator Burrows of Michigan as temporary chairman of the body after he had indicated Beveridge as his preference.[42] He wrote to his close friend Lodge, chairman of the committee on resolutions, referring to the efforts of Crane and Aldrich to write the platform: "I hope that in the platform you will refuse to allow them to shape it in any way, and that you will put in a straight thorogoing platform as free from the Hale type of reactionary policy as from the La Follette type of fool radicalism."[43]

That to Lodge, a reactionary in his own right, meant anything but a reform platform. A minority report given by a delegate from Wisconsin obtained scant hearing in the committee. A labor delegation was accorded even less courtesy.[44] One of the very few progressive spots in the whole platform was a promise to revise the tariff. And although the document did not indicate which way the revision should be made, Taft had already promised revision downward. In fact, the progressive faction of the party accepted the platform in silence mainly because the party's nominee had been guaranteed to them by Roosevelt as a progressive, as one who would carry on where he had stopped.

The subsequent election was less significant for its immediate results than for its adumbrations of the future. Once more the unhappy Bryan was defeated and the Republican party victorious on a wave of votes. But as a portent the Republican lead in terms of popular votes was just half of what it had been in 1904. More to the point, the revolt in the West had

[41] W. F. Draper to Foraker, February 10, 1908, Foraker MSS., Cincinnati, Ohio; Stephenson, *Aldrich*, 474.

[42] William D. Orcutt, *Burrows of Michigan and the Republican Party* (New York, 1917), 2: 293.

[43] Roosevelt to Lodge, June 8, 1908, in Lodge, *Correspondence*, 2: 293.

[44] Samuel Gompers, *Seventy Years of Life and Labor* (New York, 1925), 2: 293.

gathered strength. Taft had lost Colorado, Oklahoma, Nevada, and Nebraska. At the same time Democratic governors carried Ohio, Indiana, Minnesota, North Dakota, and Montana, states which had all sent in their electoral vote for the national Republican ticket.[45] The Middle West had been partially willing to vote for a Republican candidate for president certified by Roosevelt, but it had refused to vote for Stalwart Republican governors.

The spirit of revolt manifest in the elections of 1908 soon infected the House of Representatives. For five years that body had been largely dominated by Speaker Joseph G. Cannon. A reactionary extraordinary, Cannon had used the ironclad rules of the House to stifle progressive legislation and to frustrate the opposition. With some justice Cannon was called a "Tsar" and his handpicked judiciary committee "the legislative crematory." Many progressive measures were sent to the committee; few ever came out.

In December, 1907, one lone Republican from Wisconsin voted against re-electing the Speaker. But as Cannon continued to obstruct progressive measures opposition to him grew. By December, 1908, thirty progressive Republican congressmen were meeting weekly to consider ways and means of preventing his re-election. Entering into a coalition with the Democratic minority, they were just barely beaten on a roll call vote 168 to 163.[46] The next day the same group of Western Republicans again joined the minority to defeat a ship subsidy bill sponsored by the Regular Republican organization.[47] Thus a party within a party was being born and the first faint foreshadowings of 1912 were etched across the capital.

Developments in the Senate were likewise portents of troublesome days ahead for the Republican party. There as in the House the split between progressive and conservative was widening daily. And as the days passed even Roosevelt, the

[45] Frederick Logan Paxson, *Recent History of the United States* (Boston, 1929), 375.
[46] *Congressional Record*, 60 Congress, 2 Session, vol. 43, pt. 4, p. 3572.
[47] *Ibid.*, 3694.

astute politician, was unable to obtain any unity of action from Congress. In fact, in the last three months of his presidency the conservative majority in both Houses, anticipating their day of liberation from "Roosevelt Rex," played fast and loose with the president. They refused to accept Roosevelt's messages, wrecked his legislative program, and slapped him in the face with frankly critical resolutions. Long afterward Roosevelt himself admitted that he was unable to get anything done in the face of this conservative revolt.[48] In the House and in the Senate even before Roosevelt left office the Republican party was being torn asunder.

The progressive movement owed much to Theodore Roosevelt as he left office. He was not the first honest president of the United States. But he was a president who hated corruption enough to look for it and dig it out. He was not the first president who sympathized with the more unfortunate of his countrymen. But he was the first president since the Civil War who, when he saw mass poverty, became agitated and insisted that government do something about it. Moreover, Roosevelt was the only president to his day who had the inclination and the courage to challenge big business. He did sincerely attempt to enforce the Sherman Anti-Trust Law. As much cannot be said for his three predecessors. Finally, Theodore Roosevelt was the first president since 1868 who, while in office, acted on the assumption that the public and organized labor as well as capital had rights that ought to be protected by the public law.

Detractors of Roosevelt have claimed that he had little part in the origins of the progressive movement, that he simply reaped where other men had sown, and that he then usually proceeded to vilify his benefactors. Both charges are unquestionably true in part. Roosevelt owed more to William Jennings Bryan than he ever cared to admit. Perhaps this, with the fact that Bryan was a Democrat, was the reason that he was so savage toward the Great Commoner at times. But among other national political leaders and particularly

[48] Theodore Roosevelt, *An Autobiography* (New York, 1921), 352.

among those of his own party Roosevelt was a true pioneer in the reform movement. The year 1902 marked the rebirth of progressive political action in the United States. During that year, sharply punctuated by the Northern Securities case, the anthracite coal strike, the Newlands Reclamation Act, and the appointment of Holmes to the Supreme Court, Roosevelt stood virtually alone as a nationally known progressive Republican. At that time Robert M. La Follette was still in his first term as a state governor, Cummins had just been elected, Beveridge was more an imperialist than a progressive, and William E. Borah and George W. Norris were unknowns. Five years later a future progressive, Woodrow Wilson, voiced the hope of all conservative Democrats that William Jennings Bryan be knocked "into a cocked hat."[49]

Roosevelt has been assailed by critics for his willingness to compromise on virtually every legislative issue. He has also been charged with talking reform loudly and accomplishing little or nothing at all. But it should be remembered that Roosevelt had very little if any progressive strength to work with in Congress except at the very end of his second term. Confronted by hostile majorities, he secured what he could. To Roosevelt democratic statesmanship was the art of achieving the possible.

The president was also serving the progressive movement by his continual preaching. For although he never personally achieved half of the many things he told his countrymen ought to be done, he did awaken in the masses of the people an acute desire for progressive action. Roosevelt was the advance agent of progressivism. And therein lay grief for his successor.

For seven years Roosevelt had held before the American people a vision of a Nirvana. In enthusiastic and compelling words he had painted such glowing pictures that many Americans had come to believe in them as a part of their national heritage. But he himself had just started the country

[49] Ray S. Baker, *Woodrow Wilson, Life and Letters* (New York, 1931), 3: 23.

along the rocky legislative path to this land of green meadows. Most of that difficult task was left to his successor under personal contract to achieve the deed. The few halting steps Roosevelt had taken had already opened an ugly seam in the party's ranks. The widening of that seam in the next administration was the inevitable result of the Roosevelt years. For the outgoing president left to his successor a progressive country demanding that much be done. He had also bestowed on him a Congress dominated by conservatives who had stoutly set their faces in the opposite direction. The Republican party that William Howard Taft inherited was already a house divided against itself.

CHAPTER TWO

Taft, Tariff, Trouble

ON INAUGURAL DAY, March 4, 1909, William Howard Taft awoke to one of the bitterest storms the capital city had witnessed in many years. During the night a screaming blizzard had swept in, bringing with it marrow-freezing cold. Ice and snow cut the city off from all outside communication. Only a thin crowd of the stalwart lined the edges of Pennsylvania Avenue that morning to cheer the new president as he rode with the old, and for the first time in sixty-three years the president took the oath of office inside the Senate chamber.[1]

Were these bitter north winds a portent of the tempest of sentiment that was to sweep his administration into a four-year record of controversy and party wreckage? Few in the nation on inaugural day would have thought so. For when Theodore Roosevelt left the White House for his home at Oyster Bay a temporary truce was declared in the ranks of the Republican party. As both progressive and conservative factions of the party turned from the old occupant of the White House to the new they saw what they thought was good and claimed the new man as one of their own.

Glad to be freed from the rule of the "mad messiah," the business world contemplated the new president with assurance. "It will be such a comforting thing to have old times restored again," noted John Wanamaker as he speculated on Taft's future policy. For the most part the industrial and financial fraternity agreed with Wanamaker that in Taft lay the answer to their seven-year prayer of "Let us have peace."[2]

---

[1] *New York Times*, March 5, 1909; M. A. DeWolfe Howe, *George von Lengerke Meyer* (New York, 1920), 424.

[2] Herbert A. Gibbons, *John Wanamaker* (New York, 1926), 2: 273; E. H.

If the conservatives of the party were pleased by the ascendancy of Taft, no less delighted were the progressives. Was he not Roosevelt's personally chosen man to carry on his policies? Had not Taft himself in speeches throughout the country fully endorsed the unenacted program of his predecessor and promised that before another inaugural day the program would be written into national statutes? What more could anyone ask of an incoming president? These same progressives were somewhat taken back when they heard that the president had appointed an official family made up largely of conservative corporation lawyers. A few were fearful that he had "overloaded his cabinet with calm." But this slight temporary shadow was dispelled when his inaugural address was read. Here was a progressive confession of faith and a straightforward promise to translate the Roosevelt preachings into legislative enactment. "Roosevelt has cut enough hay; Taft is the man to put it into the barn," was the progressive chorus.[3]

Thus both Republican camps viewed their new leader with complacency, but only because they saw in him two different persons. Both sides were confident that the president would align himself with their own philosophy of government. Only a few realized that Taft, large as he was, could not hope to cover two horses, especially when the horses were going in opposite directions. Moorfield Storey was one of the few. He wondered what would happen when the president had to choose: "As to Roosevelt's policies, Taft is either for them or against them. Publicly he is for them, privately he allows it to be understood that he will not carry them out." That to Storey spelled trouble in the future.[4]

William Howard Taft, the object of all this speculation,

Harriman to James Stillman, January 24, 1909, in Anna R. Burr, *The Portrait of a Banker: James Stillman* (New York, 1927), 261; S. M. Dack Brothers and Company to Joseph B. Foraker, February 27, 1909, Foraker MSS., Cincinnati, Ohio; *Bankers' Magazine*, 78: 179 (February, 1909).

[3] George von L. Meyer to Roosevelt, March 8, 1909, Roosevelt MSS., Library of Congress; *Kansas City Star*, March 5, 1909.

[4] Moorfield Storey to Charles Francis Adams, August 9, 1908, in M. A. DeWolfe Howe, *Portrait of an Independent: Moorfield Storey* (New York, 1932), 281.

was fifty-two years old when he entered the presidency. At an early age he had begun public service and had held no less than nine public offices, of which only one was elective. He had served ably under Roosevelt as governor general of the Philippines and later as secretary of war. Always in these years he had been a firm supporter of Roosevelt's policies and at times in his frank manner had seemed to out-Roosevelt Roosevelt. For this reason, among others, he had been selected as the heir apparent, and by his acceptance had contracted to carry on the Roosevelt doctrines.

Taft brought with him to his office many of the qualities that make a successful president. Agreeable in manner and with an extraordinary good nature, he was one of the most likeable persons who ever filled the presidential chair. So infectious was his humor that to see and hear him laugh was to feel that everything in the universe was as it should be. Combined with this personal charm was a mind which, once stirred to action, was as good as, if not better than, most of those around him. In his political and personal activities the man possessed unquestionable integrity. One might question the advisability of Taft's actions but never the sincerity of purpose behind them.

This is what made it so strange that Taft should have been wearing, quite unconsciously, false clothing when he became president. Roosevelt at first believed—and led the country to believe—that Taft was a progressive cut out of the Roosevelt cloth. Even Taft believed it when he took office. But he was as wrong in his self-estimation as were Roosevelt and the country. Under the immediate spell of his dynamic predecessor he continued to act and talk in the spirit of progressivism. Once that influence was removed he returned to his basic conservative self. For Taft, slow to action, tolerant and suspicious of all excesses, was of the same pattern as John Morley's classic conservative, "with his inexhaustible patience with abuses that only torment others, his apologetic words for beliefs that may not be so precisely true, and institutions that are not altogether so useful as some might think possible; his

ON THE JOB

Cartoon by Bushnell in the *Cincinnati Times-Star*, reproduced in the *Literary Digest*, March 20, 1909, with the following comment: "This cartoon, representing President Taft obliterating Mr. Roosevelt's footprints, derives special interest from the fact that it appears in Mr. Charles P. Taft's paper."

cordiality toward progress and improvement in a general way and his coldness or antipathy to each progressive proposal in particular." Taft began his term under the banner of progressivism, a philosophy alien to his nature. At the end of it he was defending the conservative cause, all his overt political actions mirroring the more profound strains in his basic self. This inward struggle of the man to align himself with his true nature at the same time that he sought to fulfill the promises he had given his predecessor was one of the more fundamental reasons why his term was a political nightmare. The progressives in Congress regarded Taft as a captain who had deserted the cause. And for such a man there is always more hatred than for the acknowledged enemy.

Many other things in Taft's nature marked him as a poor chief executive. He was far too heavy and he ate far too much. As a consequence he was willing to let other people make his decisions and do his work. This personal laziness was to be disastrous many times in his administration. Whereas Roosevelt prepared a speech weeks in advance, emending it again and again, Taft would often write a speech on a train just before delivery and would sometimes make an address without any formal preparation.

In fact, the new president was poorly prepared for his high post. Before he had been in office a year friend and foe alike were saying that he was worse than a novice at the high art of politics. Even Taft in his candid manner admitted that in this sinuous game he was a failure. It would have been difficult enough for a master politician to steer a course that would leave him relatively unscathed in the four turbulent years between 1909 and 1913. For Taft, political tyro that he was, the four years inevitably to be filled by factional warfare in the party promised nothing but misfortune.[5]

Discord was not slow to appear. Taft's immediate action in March was to call for a special session of Congress to consider the question of tariff revision. But before this delicate subject could even be broached an insurgent revolt against Speaker Cannon threatened the solidarity of the Republican organization. This opposition was nothing new, but merely the continuation of the struggle that had started in Roosevelt's administration and had just missed being successful in December of 1908. Now with only a majority of forty-seven in the House of Representatives the rebellion of thirty progressive Republicans or insurgents threatened the Republican control of that body.

Joseph G. Cannon had come to Congress in 1873 as a representative from Illinois. Re-elected regularly, he had worked

[5] Letters to Roosevelt from Elihu Root, February 11, 1910, Henry C. Lodge, April 22, 1910, and Joseph B. Bishop, January 2, 1911, Roosevelt MSS.; *Review of Reviews*, 42: 387 (October, 1910); *New York Times*, September 23, 1911.

his way to the top of the Republican House machine. In the thirty-six years he had so thoroughly schooled himself in parliamentary practices that by 1909 he was the master of every dodge that ever profited a politician. Slim and erect, weighing slightly over 140 pounds, Cannon was a curious mixture of the country bumpkin and the city sophisticate. His speech, clothing, and manners savored of the crossroads country store, but his ways were the ways of a fox.[6]

If Nelson W. Aldrich was the uncrowned king of the Senate, Cannon was equally royal in the House. Backed by the powers of the speakership and consummately skilled in the art of parliamentary fencing, he almost controlled that body as he wished. He appointed all its committees, bestowing the loaves and fishes upon whom he pleased. Among these was the powerful rules committee, which to a large degree determined the fate of legislation. In addition the Speaker could alter the course of debate in the House by granting or refusing recognition.

In part the insurgent revolt was a democratic protest against these dictatorial powers, in part against the way the powers had been used.[7] For Cannon was a thoroughgoing reactionary who had obstructed progressive measures with devastating regularity. He remarked once that three-fourths of the proposals for change were conceived in an atmosphere of corruption and the other fourth in ignorance. So long as Cannon dominated the legislative procedure in the House there was little hope for the passage of any comprehensive progressive program. With that in mind, Congressmen George W. Norris of Nebraska, Victor Murdock of Kansas, and Au-

---

[6] Charles W. Thompson, *Party Leaders of the Time* (New York, 1906), 182.

[7] George W. Norris, "The Fight on Rules," *La Follette's Magazine*, January 8, 1910. Some historians have seen fit to distinguish between the insurgents in the House and the progressive Republican movement, claiming that the majority of the insurgents were interested only in limiting Cannon's power. As this study will show, insurgency in the House of Representatives was simply one manifestation of the broader movement, and it will be treated as such.

gustus P. Gardner of Massachusetts began to enlist votes for a reform and, with the pledged support of the Democrats, soon obtained a favorable majority.

Joseph Cannon, tough old warrior, was not one to take defeat without fighting. On the morning of March 9 the Speaker, Nelson W. Aldrich, and Chairman Payne of the Ways and Means Committee of the House, called on the president to warn him that unless the plans of the rebels were quashed the tariff bill would be endangered. They then asked Taft for support in the fight over the powers of the Speaker. The president was in a quandary. If he backed the conservative leadership he might be pictured as an ally of the reactionary forces in Congress. On the other hand, could he afford the hostility of the powerful Speaker? Taft disliked Cannon personally and sympathized with the insurgent demands. In fact, shortly after his election he had suggested to Roosevelt the possibility of removing the Speaker, but the outgoing president, though he believed the step desirable, advised against it on the grounds of expediency.[8]

Because of Roosevelt's advice and the warnings of Aldrich and Cannon as to the future of the tariff, Taft agreed to support the Regular organization, apparently overlooking the possibility of taking no stand on the matter. In return for presidential help Cannon promised that he would loyally carry out the pledges of the Chicago platform.[9] Accordingly the broad hint came from the White House to the insurgents that unless they fell in line their patronage suggestions might be overlooked. Principle won over pap, however, when thirty-two progressive Republicans, despite presidential displeasure, absented themselves from the Republican organizational caucus. When the House met, thirty-one of them voted with the

[8] Henry F. Pringle, *The Life and Times of William Howard Taft* (New York, 1939), 1:404–409; Archie Butt, *Taft and Roosevelt* (New York, 1930), 1: 10, 201; Roosevelt to Taft, October 12, November 10, 1908, Roosevelt MSS.

[9] Taft to Horace Taft, May, 1909 (copy), Roosevelt MSS.; Herbert S. Duffy, *William Howard Taft* (New York, 1930), 237; George von L. Meyer diary, March 12, 1909, in Howe, *Meyer*, 427.

NEW WINE IN OLD BOTTLES
Cartoon by Darling in the *Des Moines Register and Leader*, reproduced in the *Literary Digest*, December 25, 1909.

minority on the motion to accept the old rules of the House. And only the desertion of a group of Tammany and Southern Democrats kept the Speaker and President Taft from being totally defeated. Breaking away from Champ Clark, the minority leader, the Democrats supported a compromise that made only slight changes in the House rules.[10]

Emphasizing their dissatisfaction with the outcome of the skirmish, twelve Middle Western Republicans refused to vote with their fellows in the re-election of Cannon as Speaker and publicly reiterated their determination to attack him at the first opportunity. Moreover, this struggle over the rules at

[10] *New York Sun*, March 14, 1909; *Congressional Record*, 61 Congress, 1 Session, vol. 44, pt. 1, pp. 21, 22, 33–34. Cannon obtained the support of the Democrats by promising the Southerners tariff concessions and giving assurances of Republican support in New York for a Tammany election proposal. Henry C. Lodge to Roosevelt, July 20, 1910, Roosevelt MSS.; *Philadelphia North American*, March 17, 1909.

the outset of the Taft administration had more significance than was indicated in the rising hostility toward Cannon. The incident marked the opening wedge of the estrangement between the president and the progressive forces in the Republican party, an estrangement that was to grow until outright civil war within the party brought it to defeat.

At his inauguration the progressive Republicans had regarded Taft as a friend. When he used his position to support Cannon they were surprised and irritated. For all the president's reasoning about the future safety of his legislative program, this coalition with the Speaker seemed like the friendship of the lion and the lamb. How, they asked, could the president expect to enact a program of advanced legislation by first destroying the power of the progressive bloc in Congress? When Cannon removed some of the insurgent leaders from important committee posts, they mistakenly assumed that Taft had given "tacit sanction," for he made no public objection. And when the president continued to maintain cordial relations with Cannon after the Speaker had violated his promise to support the Chicago platform, a suspicion of Taft's sincerity entered the progressive mind. Thus the administration moved toward the delicate business of tariff-making with a group in the party which, if not actually hostile to it, was at least suspicious of White House promises; and which was likely to be increasingly critical of the president if his words again proved fairer than his deeds.[11]

The demand for tariff revision within the Republican party first came from the Middle West. Mainly a producer of exportable commodities, the section had been since the Civil War a thorn in the side of Republican tariff orthodoxy. Historically anti-trust, it began early in the century to connect the rise of industrial combinations with the high protective tariff. Soon the phrases "the mother of trusts" and the "Iowa Idea" became common political idioms throughout the Mid-

[11] William D. Foulke to Roosevelt, May 17, 1910, Roosevelt MSS.; *Philadelphia North American*, March 17, 1909; *La Follette's Magazine*, March 27, 1909.

dle West. The latter referred to Governor Albert B. Cummins' plan to destroy the trust by removing all duties on competing products coming into this country. So popular did this "trust" remedy grow that it was a plank in numerous Republican state platforms as early as 1902.

Thereafter the movement for a lower tariff became national. Small business men suffering from the sharper competition of an advancing industrial system blamed this "pinch of privilege" on the trusts operating under the protection of unfair tariff schedules. Fully forty per cent of the membership of the National Association of Manufacturers, its secretary wrote in 1907, were heartily in favor of tariff reduction. Then too, the period after the passage of the Dingley bill in 1897 was one of currency inflation partially attributable to the increased gold supply. During these years commodity prices rose steadily, and complaints about the high cost of living were heard in both East and West. To a public that knew little about the intricacies of economics the high tariff was a convenient explanation for the shrinking of its real income.[12]

While president, Roosevelt was aware of the the discontent with the Dingley law and occasionally talked about the necessity of tariff revision. But every time he moved in that direction Aldrich and Cannon advised against it as politically inexpedient. And toward the end of his administration Roosevelt admitted to Cannon that the advice had been eminently sound.[13] However, since he was no longer to be in office after 1909 he came to the conclusion that the party could not risk another campaign without promising revision downward, a conclusion with which William Howard Taft readily agreed. After studying under William Graham Sumner in his college days, Taft had been consistently against the principle of an extremely high tariff. "Mr. Taft is a very excellent man," an Ohio politician wrote in 1909, "but there never was a minute

[12] H. E. Miles to Joseph B. Foraker, August 28, September 9, 1907, Foraker MSS., Cincinnati, Ohio.
[13] Roosevelt to Jacob Reis, April 18, 1906, and to Joseph Cannon, February 28, 1907, Roosevelt MSS.

since I first knew him when the tariff was not too high to suit him."[14] In a speech at Bath, Maine, in 1906 Taft had maintained that business conditions in the nation had changed so radically "as to make it wise and just to revise certain schedules of the tariff." Two years later the Republican nominee clarified this rather ambiguous statement by calling for "a revision which shall reduce excessive rates."[15]

To most conservative and protectionist Republicans in Congress the Dingley schedules would best be left alone. But the White House pressure at the 1908 Chicago convention forced a consideration of tariff revision. Much against its desires the convention included in the platform a plank stating with masterful ambiguity that "the Republican Party declares unequivocally for a revision of the tariff." The document did not explicitly promise a revision downward, but the people interpreting the platform in the light of the candidates' statements considered the party bound to reduce the custom rates.

It was to discharge this obligation that Taft upon taking office convened Congress in special session on March 15, 1909, and shortly thereafter sent it his tariff message. That message was a great disappointment to the progressives. Leading the country to expect a ringing demand for downward revision, the president merely stated, in a very brief note, that the Congress had been called for the business of revising the tariff. Busy with some inconsequential politics in Ohio, Taft in his usual manner had failed to write the trenchant message he had originally planned. It was a poor beginning indeed, to treat so explosive a matter as tariff reduction in thus casual a fashion.[16]

The Payne bill reported to the House on the third day of the session was an attempt at a real downward revision. In

---

[14] Joseph B. Foraker to R. A. Benedict, January 20, 1909, Foraker MSS., Cincinnati, Ohio.

[15] Sullivan, *Our Times*, 4: 365.

[16] W. A. Day to Philander C. Knox, December 17, 1908, Knox MSS., Library of Congress; Albert Shaw to Roosevelt, May 29, 1912, Roosevelt MSS.

harmony with the president's campaign speeches it contained important decreases from the Dingley rates on pig iron, machine tools, agricultural implements, lumber, print paper, and sugar, to name just a few. Middle Western representatives and progressives in general acknowledged it as "thoroughly satisfactory," and even the father of the "Iowa Idea" admitted that there were a good many more reductions in it than he had expected.[17]

The bill's progress in the lower chamber was even more pleasing to the progressives, for whereas more than two hundred amendments were made, most of these were in the direction of greater reduction. At Taft's request coal, hides, and iron were put on the free list despite strenuous objections from Speaker Cannon. One of the few untouched high rates was in the glove and stocking schedule which Cannon, paying a debt to a friend, protected from amendment. The only other direct presidential intervention in the tariff-making resulted in an agreement between Taft and Representative Joseph W. Fordney of Michigan, congressional spokesman for the beet sugar growers. The president guaranteed Fordney that there would be no further reduction in the sugar schedule provided that 300,000 tons of Philippine sugar be permitted entry duty free annually.[18]

The Payne bill ran into difficulties in the House only in its last moments. At that time a group of forty representatives from raw material producing states, angered at the president's success in placing lumber, coal, and hides on the free list, threatened to defeat the bill on the final vote. Organized and led by Senator Stephen Elkins of West Virginia, they were finally won over to supporting the measure when they were assured "on highest authority" that these rates would be taken care of in the Senate. With the raw material bloc appeased, the bill came to a vote on April 9 and passed by a party alignment 217 to 161.[19]

[17] *Des Moines Register and Leader*, March 18, 1909.
[18] *New York Sun*, April 5, 1909; *Congressional Record*, 61 Congress, 1 Session, vol. 44, pt. 1, p. 333.
[19] *New York Sun*, April 1, 4, 5, 1909.

Not too surprised nor disturbed at the easy passage of the revision bill in the House, the high tariff forces complacently awaited its consideration by the Senate, where, assured the *New York Sun*, "things really happen to a tariff bill."[20] Doubtless with this in mind one of the outnumbered Democrats in the House remarked in debate that it was useless to spend more time on the measure, for the bill that would finally be enacted was not yet written. "It is being prepared," Henry D. Clayton of Alabama continued, "by the master of your party, the distinguished Senator from Rhode Island, across which a tobacco chewer can spit into the blue waters beyond and not violate any town ordinance on the subject."[21]

The senator referred to was Nelson W. Aldrich, and the implication that he had power to frame the tariff bill to his liking was little short of the truth. Aldrich, in March, 1909, stood a giant among his fellows, boss of the United States Senate and, some people believe, boss of the Republican party. Many times a millionaire, in a chamber containing twenty other millionaires, he had won his place by virtue of a dominating personality, a mentality far above the average, a record of long service to the party, and a pervading faithfulness to the industrial interests of the nation. He was six feet tall, erect and confident, with luminous and penetrating eyes that sparkled with wit and candid appreciation in a gathering of friends and flashed across the Senate floor to seize upon an enemy in debate. Charming to his friends, Aldrich could be arrogant and even cruel to those who dared oppose him. But there were few in his own party who cared to cross him; for as the congressional representative of the "fat cats" Aldrich could be relied upon to supply ample financial support whenever the fate of the faithful was in doubt on election night. And though he could give benevolently, he could also coolly refuse. Interlocutor extraordinary between government and the great business interests, there was no question which side Aldrich would take in the coming tariff struggle. As chairman

[20] *Ibid.*, April 5, 1909.
[21] *Congressional Record*, 61 Congress, 1 Session, vol. 44, pt. 1., p. 850.

of the Committee on Finance he would report the bill to the Senate.

Powerful as Aldrich had been in the Senate for more than a decade, in March of 1909 his old strength was already waning. Just the year before one of his most able lieutenants had died, and another, irritated at the rising tide of radicalism in his home state, had declined to stand for re-election. When William B. Allison and John C. Spooner followed Orville H. Platt from the Senate, Aldrich, their captain, was the only one left of the four who had dominated that body in the name of high conservatism for so many years. As the Senate convened on March 15, 1909, Aldrich's three most trusted lieutenants were the two senators from Massachusetts, Henry Cabot Lodge and Murray Crane, and Eugene Hale of Maine. The distinguished looking Lodge, his narrow eyes cold as Arctic ice floes, was scarcely the equal of the eloquent Platt. Nor did Crane and Hale entirely take the place of Allison and Spooner. Gargantuan Boies Penrose of Pennsylvania was not to be discounted; but neither could he be bossed, and at times he exhibited a distressing sense of political whimsy. The rest, Reed Smoot of Utah, John Kean of New Jersey, Jacob Gallinger of New Hampshire, and a dozen others, were more pliable and certainly less capable.

Opposing Aldrich in the coming epical tariff struggle was a group of Middle Western senators led by Robert M. La Follette of Wisconsin and Jonathan P. Dolliver of Iowa, foemen worthy of any steel in the clash of parliamentary swords. La Follette was elected to the Senate in 1905, leaving behind him a record as a progressive governor that few men have equalled in the history of state government. In five years of tireless effort La Follette had transformed a state ruled for and by the corporations into an object lesson in social and economic democracy. The ever-ready champion of the underdog, he came to the Senate an uncompromising foe of almost everything Aldrich believed in. His short rugged frame, topped with a mop of unruly hair, his powerful voice intense in its earnestness, and his flair for self-dramatization were all familiar qualities in Washington. Since his first days in the Senate "Battle Bob" had been an *enfant terrible* to complacent conservatives.

At La Follette's side throughout the tariff struggle stood Jonathan P. Dolliver of Iowa. Dolliver had become a rebel against the conservative wing of the Republican party after many years spent in faithful support of it. His friendship for Allison, whose protégé he was, had kept him regular many times when his natural idealism would have led him to oppose his party. Finally upon the death of his friend he made peace with his deeper convictions by arriving at an understanding with Albert B. Cummins, who had taken Allison's place in the Senate and against whom Dolliver had so many times fought under the hot Iowa sun.

Before Congress met, Dolliver wrote to Aldrich resigning from his place on the Interstate Commerce Committee in favor of Cummins and asking that he be transferred to the Committee on Finance. When Aldrich announced the committee lists Cummins had been placed on the Commerce Committee, but Dolliver's name was missing from Finance, although three senators who were all his juniors in seniority had been put in that favored spot. Aldrich felt that he had got rid of a troublemaker; instead he had made an inveterate progressive and a dangerous foe.[22]

The addition of Dolliver to the progressive ranks was not a mean one. A giant of a man, tolerant and genial, Dolliver could be an aggressive opponent. He was a finished orator. When angry only the Puckish appearance of his kindly round face with its shaggy mustache softened the impact of the most caustic congressional wit of the decade.

Besides these two powerful leaders the progressive forces in the Senate included the eloquent Albert J. Beveridge, sartorially perfect, Albert B. Cummins of Iowa, slender and

---

[22] Champ Clark, *My Quarter Century of American Politics* (New York, 1920), 2: 314; Cyrenus Cole, *I Remember, I Remember* (Iowa City, 1930), 324–325; James E. Watson, *As I Knew Them* (Indianapolis, 1936), 138; Stephenson, *Aldrich*, 345.

graceful, the tall and ungainly Joseph L. Bristow of Kansas, and Moses E. Clapp of Minnesota, considerate of opponents and harmonizer of the progressive group. Supporting this small coterie from time to time were Norris Brown and Elmer J. Burkett of Nebraska, Coe Crawford of South Dakota, Knute Nelson of Minnesota, and William E. Borah of Idaho.

Such was the personnel of the bloc that lined up in opposition to the tariff plans of the Senate's conservative leadership. As time went on the amorphous character of the group was to be altered by continuing concerted action into a more formal organization which eventually became the basis of a party within a party. But in March, 1909, these men were only progressive Republicans representing the Middle West. They had been staunch supporters of Taft and were intent upon carrying out his platform promise of revision downward.

At the same time, however, Henry Cabot Lodge, a member of the Senate Finance Committee, revealed that the Senate leaders had no intention of making any sweeping reductions in the Dingley rates. The House tariff bill was "pretty good," Lodge wrote to the absent Roosevelt, but it did contain some "strange incoherences and contradictions." The articles put upon the free list would reappear with substantially the old rates. And in the main, the Senator concluded, "I think that we shall bring out the Dingley bill with some improvements in detail and classification."[23]

Lodge's prediction proved remarkably accurate. For in a very short time Aldrich introduced the Senate bill with the remark that his committee had made more reductions in the tariff than had the House. A close examination of the bill, though, proved the Rhode Island man a bit wrong in his mathematics. For the Senate bill as introduced on April 12 offered 847 amendments to the Payne bill, the majority of which contained increases in the custom rates. Increases were made on sugar, iron and steel goods, cottons, hosiery, lumber,

[23] March, 1909, Roosevelt MSS.

lead, and a host of fabricated articles. The Senate bill struck out the inheritance tax passed by the House and added a provision for maximum and minimum rates.[24]

As the true nature of the Aldrich bill was gradually revealed, public sentiment rose, but in no section of the country was the criticism so general as in the Middle West. Almost to a sheet the newspapers of the area urged their senators to revolt against the "New England Tyrant" who had broken faith with the president and the country. In Washington the silence was ominous. And then on April 22 oratorical lightning played across the Senate chamber as La Follette and Dolliver in smashing speeches declared they would have no part of the Aldrich bill. Several times its author got up to defend his legislative child, but each time he sat down worsted by the vehemence of the criticism. Thereafter as the Democratic section cheered the division of their ancient enemy, the rest of the progressive group attacked the bill with a fiery barrage of condemnation.[25]

Supporting their remarks with Taft's campaign speeches, La Follette, Dolliver, Cummins, Bristow, and Clapp all maintained that in opposing the bill they were fighting the president's fight. The question came up repeatedly whether the bill reduced or increased the Dingley rates. Aldrich and Lodge at first stoutly maintained that the bill measurably decreased the Dingley rates. Disputing these assertions was a long statistical table which the Bureau of Statistics of the Department of Commerce and Labor had prepared at the request of La Follette. Reading the tables into the *Congressional Record*, the Wisconsin senator produced reliable evidence that the Aldrich bill levied an ad valorem tax of 41.77 per cent on incoming goods, whereas the equivalent ad valorem of the Dingley bill was only 40.21.[26]

[24] *Congressional Record*, 61 Congress, 1 Session, vol. 44, pt. 2, p. 1332; F. W. Taussig, *Tariff History of the United States* (New York, 1914), 373–374.

[25] *Kansas City Star*, April 17, 1909; *Des Moines Register and Leader*, April 18, 1909; *Congressional Record*, 61 Congress, 1 Session, vol. 44, pt. 2, p. 1447.

[26] *Ibid.*, pt. 3, pp. 2752–2832.

After discrediting the bill generally the Middle Western senators set to work on its many divisions. Aware that no individual could study the entire bill, they divided the burden among them. Dolliver took the cotton schedule, La Follette the wool, Cummins metal and glass, and Bristow the lead and sugar rates. After toiling on the floor of the Senate all day long each of them went home to study the intricate sets of figures far into the night. Perhaps no other group of men ever labored so hard on a congressional project. Several of them worked themselves into a state of physical breakdown. Often they met in conference, usually at the home of La Follette or Beveridge, to discuss some knotty problem or to plan the next day's attack. There the strain of their work clearly showed in irritable tempers which occasionally clashed only to be soothed by the fellowship of Clapp and Dolliver.[27]

The results of their labor were soon evident on the floor of the Senate. Even Aldrich, the author of the tariff bill, was at times virtually helpless before an attack based upon such profound familiarity with the most veiled of its clauses. When the progressive Republican senators began to tear the bill apart schedule by schedule, the result was some of the greatest tariff debates in the history of the United States Congress. As point followed point the shade of Calhoun must have echoed a fervent amen at an equally shadowy Webster.

Jonathan Dolliver led off the great series of speeches on May 4, with a tremendous arrangement of the wool and cotton schedules. In a three-hour speech which the conservative *Boston Transcript* called "the most damaging criticism of Republican tariff making . . . in recent years," the senator from Iowa attacked both the bill and its originators. "Never before," noted one Washington correspondent, "has Aldrich been talked to as he was today by Dolliver." His face getting redder and redder as each of Dolliver's shots went home, the chairman of the Finance Committee lost his composure completely when it was charged that the cotton schedule was in reality written by a group of New England cotton manufac-

[27] Bowers, *Beveridge,* 347.

turers. And Aldrich's discomfiture increased daily as Cummins, Bristow, Beveridge, and La Follette followed Dolliver in speeches that fairly burned their way through the Senate air.[28]

"Aldrich and the old crowd are gone," Beveridge exulted to his wife after a particularly savage speech. "He has lost his cunning. Thrice in two days has he gone all to pieces." But that was slightly inaccurate. Worsted in the crossfire of debate, Aldrich, announcing that the Republican party had not promised to lower the tariff rates any more than to raise them, quietly set about to pass the schedules as they had been written by the committee. As early as April 22 Aldrich asked the Senate where and when the Republican party had made a promise to revise the tariff downward. Ignoring the president's forthright statements, Lodge added that "nobody ever pledged me to revision downward any more than to revision upward." But the most consistent explanation was made by Senator William B. Heyburn of Idaho. Even if the pledge had been made, Heyburn said, the people surely did not believe it. "The people know the Republican party well enough to know," Heyburn continued, "that even though inadvertently it might make expressions that sounded badly, it could be trusted in the hour of its responsibility."[29]

Conservative Republicans generally gloried in this cavalier treatment of Taft's solemn statements. The suggestion was made to the Senate that the presidential promises of 1908 were out of date and that the best thing to do was to pass the Dingley bill again. The bulk of Middle Western and progressive opinion, however, viewed these remarks as a betrayal of the president. Prominent Republicans urged Taft to fight Aldrich and his party-wrecking schemes. Frank B. Kellogg observed that he had been a member of the 1908 conven-

[28] *Boston Transcript*, May 5, 1909; *Philadelphia North American*, May 5, 1909; *Congressional Record*, 61 Congress, 1 Session, vol. 44, pt. 2, p. 1707.
[29] Albert J. Beveridge to Mrs. Beveridge, June 1, 1909, in Bowers, *Beveridge*, 345; *Congressional Record*, 61 Congress, 1 Session, vol. 44, pt. 1, pp. 1450, 1858; pt. 2, p. 3316.

tion's resolutions committee and that "no protective apostle thought of such a thing as a declaration that the tariff should be revised upwards; in fact the entire discussion was reduction of certain schedules that had proven to be too high."[30]

The progressive press took up the cry against this betrayal of the people by the "princes of privilege." In particular they sharpened their attack against Aldrich, the man whom the country held responsible for the deception. "The history of American government furnishes no parallel to the insults which are now being heaped on the doctrine of popular government by the Senatorial boss from Rhode Island," lamented one Middle Western sheet; another wondered whether there was one senator who really believed Aldrich patriotic or honest. All of them concurred in the warning that if Aldrich was not dealt with speedily the people would hold a day of reckoning at the polls.[31]

This criticism, at first confined to Aldrich, soon began to envelop the president. As the tariff rates mounted closer to the heavens after each roll call, the public began to wonder why Taft did not move to stop this violation of his pledges. The course of the president during the time was a strange one indeed. Neither consistent nor effective, its lack of political sense was all but incredible.[32]

Taft was sincerely desirous of a lower tariff—of that there can be no doubt. The main trouble lay in his complacency. He had been advised by Lodge not to use his influence to secure lower rates while the bill was in the House or the Sen-

[30] Frank B. Kellogg to Taft (copy), May 5, 1909, Roosevelt MSS.

[31] *Kansas City Star*, May 13, 1909; *Des Moines Register and Leader*, April 26, 1909; *Outlook*, 57:145 (May 22, 1909); *Philadelphia North American*, May 11, 1909.

[32] Henry F. Pringle, Taft's recent friendly biographer, cites Taft's constitutional scruples as a reason for his lack of leadership. The president hesitated to coerce with patronage because of his concept of a limited executive, Pringle explains. See Pringle, *Taft*, 425. Taft, it is true, held to this position in theory and he never used the patronage against a conservative. But, as this study will show, the president in cooperation with Aldrich did use the appointing power to its limits in an attempt to defeat progressivism in the spring of 1910.

ate but to wait and make his fight in the conference committee. The slippery Lodge well knew, and the president should
have known, how ineffectual the plan would be. But then had
not Cannon and Aldrich promised him that they would cooperate? Taft was shocked when the sky-high Aldrich bill
was reported to the Senate. Shortly thereafter he remarked
to one of his cabinet that he was afraid that Aldrich was
"ready to sacrifice the party." Soon he was urging the progressives to rebel and fight for lower rates. If the final bill was
not to his liking, he assured La Follette, he would veto it.[33]

But then something happened. The president had been
holding many conferences with Aldrich and Cannon. In the
latter part of May, Dolliver, white of face, whispered to
Beveridge on the Senate floor that Taft had deserted them.
The next day when Beveridge went to the White House he
was met with the "coldest atmosphere" he had ever encoun-
tered. But the president so changed the tune again that by
June 12 Beveridge could write his wife, "Saw Taft—he is
with us." Only four days later, however, the president once
again incurred the wrath of the progressives. Beveridge wrote
that the president was impossible and that "the administration is doomed."[34]

These bewildering vacillations in the president can only be
explained in the paradox of Taft the conservative trying to
enact a progressive program. Fundamentally he distrusted
reformers and preferred the company of solid conservatives,
who were far less disturbing. He admired Aldrich as much as
any other man in the Senate. Before his election Taft had
written to the Rhode Islander that he was anxious to see and
talk "with the levelest headed man in the country." Now in
the middle of the tariff battle, as the progressive attack on
Aldrich grew violent, Taft's own conservatism and his increasing fondness for Aldrich personally led him to associate

[33] Henry C. Lodge to Roosevelt, July 31, 1909, in Lodge, *Correspondence*,
2: 343; Butt, *Taft and Roosevelt*, 1: 41; Robert M. La Follette, *Autiobiogra-
phy* (Madison, Wisconsin, 1911), 440.
[34] Bowers, *Beveridge*, 337–349.

the criticism with himself. When he was urged to veto the bill he made the surprising statement that he thought "too highly of Aldrich" to do that, and he did not care "to be popular on those terms."[35]

Seemingly Taft, if not pushed, would interfere in no way with the Senate. Even some of his well-wishers began to have "misgivings" about his policy of inactivity. Unless the president intervened, ex-Attorney General Bonaparte opined, "it would have been far better politics not to have had the special session at all."[36] And as Aldrich and Taft seemed to be getting more friendly, there appeared in the Middle Western press the first outright criticism of the president. According to these reforming journals, the country would no longer tolerate presidential inaction. They urged Taft to take the opportunity to aid his true friends who were seeking real tariff reform. "For if all this brave talk in recent years is to come to nothing but an Aldrich revision, but little attention will be paid to further brave talk during his *four* or eight years."[37]

It was at this critical stage in his administration that Taft took a step which to the progressive mind committed him totally to reaction. In the midst of the tariff debate Senators William E. Borah and Joseph W. Bailey introduced an income tax measure as a substitute for the inheritance tax deleted from the Payne bill. Since the Supreme Court had declared the income tax act of 1894 unconstitutional a belief had grown that a new law could be drawn in such terms that the court would approve. Roosevelt had so spoken in a message to Congress in 1907. Taft, in his acceptance speech, had echoed his predecessor by declaring that a measure "can and should be devised which under the decisions of the Supreme Court, will conform to the Constitution." The president was so sure of his legal ground that he had a measure drawn up and presented to the House Ways and Means Committee

[35] Stephenson, *Aldrich*, 331; F. L. Dingley to Roosevelt, June 3, 1910, Roosevelt MSS.

[36] Charles J. Bonaparte to H. C. Gauss, June 23, 1909, Bonaparte MSS., Library of Congress.

[37] *Des Moines Register and Leader*, April 24, 1909. Italics mine.

which was withdrawn only when that body declared for the inheritance tax.[38]

As the income tax bill supported by a progressive-Democratic coalition came up for consideration, Aldrich and his supporters were inalterably opposed. They heartily disliked the dangerous principle of taxing the rich in proportion to their wealth. There was also the added danger that "the scheme would produce so much money . . . that it would involve in a short time another revision of the tariff and a large destruction of protection."[39] But the devil's broth was brewing, for the progressive-Democratic opposition had a temporary majority and was threatening to filibuster the tariff to death unless the income tax measure was brought to a vote.[40]

Throughout the next few days Aldrich worked feverishly to trade tariff advantages for pledges against the income tax, but a week before the vote was to be taken the measure still had a majority of five in its favor. Hurrying to the White House, the Republican leader explained the situation to Taft. After many conferences the president agreed to use his influence to stop the income tax if Aldrich would supply the votes to pass a tax on corporations which was to be recommended to the Senate by the president. Against his will Aldrich agreed. But so many Republican senators feared an irate public opinion that before the necessary votes could be gathered assurances had to be given that an income tax amendment would be submitted to the states.[41]

Two days before the vote on the income measure, Taft sent a special message to the Senate advocating the adoption of his corporation tax and indirectly condemning the income proposal. His measure would be a great step forward in the regulation of interstate business, he declared, because it per-

[38] *New York Times,* July 29, 1908; *New York Sun,* July 1, 1909.
[39] Henry C. Lodge to Roosevelt, June 21, 1909, Roosevelt MSS.
[40] Elihu Root to Charles F. Mathewson, June 26, 1909, in Philip C. Jessup, *Elihu Root* (New York, 1938), 2: 230.
[41] Henry C. Lodge to Roosevelt, June 21, 1909, Roosevelt MSS.; George von L. Meyer diary, June 15, 1909, in Howe, *Meyer,* 434; *New York Sun,* June 15, 1909.

mitted the government to examine the books of corporations.[42] Privately he told his brother that he was opposed
to the income tax because he was "afraid of the discussion"
and the "criticism" that would ensue if there were to be
another close division in the high court on the subject. Two
years later the president revealed in a public interview what
was probably his more fundamental attitude. On that occasion he declared he did not favor the laying of an income
tax "except in an emergency like war." Under Roosevelt's
influence in 1908 Taft was for an income tax; a year later he
was wavering; by 1911 he was against it. Slowly but surely
at 1700 Pennsylvania Avenue the sands of progress were
running out.[43]

On the floor of the Senate the genial Clapp, incited by the
presidential deal with the conservative forces, bitterly ar-
raigned Taft's actions as the first step away from the Roosevelt policies. That was unfair. But out in the country a progressive Republican paper wondered what next could be
expected of a president who declared he had no right to interfere with the course of legislation and then "allowed Senator
Aldrich to persuade him to sit up all night to write a message
against the men who had been fighting for what he had recommended." This air of suspicion, widespread throughout
the progressive wing of the party, boded ill for Taft in the
trying days to come. Any legislation that he might now obtain by working with Aldrich would be viewed with a critical
if not a disparaging eye.[44]

[42] This despite Aldrich's admission that the corporation tax was proposed solely to defeat the income tax and that the measure would be
dropped at the end of two years. *Congressional Record*, 61 Congress, 1
Session, vol. 44, pt. 4, p. 3931.

[43] Butt, *Taft and Roosevelt*, 1: 134; Taft to Frances E. Leupp, in "President Taft's Own View," *Outlook*, 99:316 (December 2, 1911). For a
different interpretation see Pringle, who depicts the affair as a presidential
victory over Aldrich, which in part it was. But Pringle says nothing of
Taft's own retreat on the income tax. Instead, quoting a presidential letter
of explanation *after* the passage of the corporation tax, he suggests that
Taft had been opposed to congressional enactment of the tax from the
first. Pringle, *Taft*, 1: 433–436.

[44] *Congressional Record*, 61 Congress, 1 Session, vol. 44, pt. 4, p. 4009;
Des Moines Register and Leader, June 20, 1909.

After his victory over the income tax Aldrich was never in serious trouble again while the tariff bill was in the Senate. One could always hold most of the Republican senators in line by threatening to reduce the tariff on products of their own states. And Democratic senators were occasionally willing to trade a few votes for protection of Southern lumber, sugar, and fruit. It was only when Aldrich left Washington for a few days' rest that the Senate became refractory. The grip the Rhode Island senator had over most of his colleagues was amply illustrated by the lamentations of Stephen Elkins as he tried to explain a year later why he had not voted for the income tax. "I was then in slavery," said the West Virginian, remarking that every time he wanted to get off the conservative reservation he was warned by Aldrich "to keep right where you are if you know what is good for you."[45]

The Middle Western senators, however, free from the necessity of obtaining tariff advantages for their section, could afford to oppose Aldrich. And in answer to the popular cry to reduce the cost of living they voted almost as a bloc on schedule after schedule against the Republican majority. The numerous roll calls on the tariff reveal that La Follette, Clapp, Beveridge, Bristow, Cummins, Dolliver, and Nelson voted oftener against the Aldrich rates than for them. This group was joined many times by a small number of progressive Republicans from the range states of the Northwest. But William E. Borah, Jonathan Bourne, and George S. Nixon represented grazing and mining empires that were demanding protection for themselves. To obtain substantial tariffs on hides, lumber, and mineral products, they frequently voted against their inclinations. Specific protection has a way of preceding general principle in tariff legislation.

The vote on the Aldrich bill provided a perfect picture of economic representation. Sectionally the Middle West and the South were in opposition to the Far West and the East;

thus manufacturing, cattle, and extractive industry were lined up against the farm. Significantly, industrialized Illinois and Ohio and sugar-conscious Louisiana departed from the sectional vote. The Aldrich bill as finally passed on July 8 without the votes of progressive Republicans completely revamped the House rates. It restored the duty on hides, iron ore, and lumber, greatly increased the rates on cottons and wools, and contained an exaggerated amount of protection for silks, cutlery, sewing machines, typewriters, and machine tools. The bill substituted the corporation tax for the income tax, provided for a tariff commission, and eliminated the maximum and minimum provision.

The bill's passage provoked a storm of protest throughout the country. Newspapers joined the muckrake magazines in denouncing the measure as a wanton repudiation of a party pledge. Some of the Eastern news sheets, such as the *Philadelphia North American*, were undoubtedly against the bill on principle. Others may have been actuated by the bill's high duty on Canadian wood pulp. But in no part of the country was the opposition so united as in the Middle West. The Nebraska Republican state convention, meeting in July, called on the president to veto the bill and commended the stand of the state's two senators in voting against the Republican majority. From Minnesota, North and South Dakota, Wisconsin, and Iowa came hearty concurrence.[46]

Seeking to still the wave of criticism, Taft hurriedly let it be known that he was going to work directly with the conference committee to secure lower rates. He also intimated that he was ready to confer with progressive leaders in an effort to write their demands into the final legislation. But the Middle West was dubious. "Too late," it rejoined with conviction. "Does a man show his teeth to those with whom he is working in harmony?" The question was entirely pertinent, for just at that time Taft was writing his brother that Aldrich was quite with him and that the two were working together

[46] *New York Sun*, July 29, 1909; *Philadelphia North American*, July 10, 1909.

to secure lower rates. Moreover, as the summer of 1909 progressed, Washington seldom saw Taft in company with a progressive Republican. Instead he was dining with Aldrich, motoring with John Kean, playing golf with Reed Smoot, or in the congenial fellowship of a stout conservative, going out to see the Wright brothers pilot their flying machine.[47]

The conference committee that met in the middle of July had a long and stormy life. With the possible exception of Sereno E. Payne, chairman of the House Ways and Means Committee, its membership was completely devoted to the principle of sky-high protection. Speaker Cannon and Aldrich had made sure of that in their selections by skipping over several capable moderates, much to Payne's disgust. The latter several times walked out of the committee when his House colleagues voted unanimously to set aside the House bill and accept the Aldrich rates. The last time the irritated chairman took his leave, he threatened to discharge his committee and make an adverse minority report. To bring him back took all the president's persuasive powers.[48]

Meanwhile Taft had moderated his demands for lower rates to the point of asking only for free raw materials and reductions in the woolen, glove, and hosiery schedules. Representing Eastern manufacturing interests that would not be adverse to less expensive raw materials, Aldrich was reasonable. But the speaker of the House was a man apart. Cannon was soon threatening to adjourn the House with the bill still in conference unless his high tariff demands were met. Moreover, Western senators who had supported the bill only because of the promised duties on hides, metal, and lumber now became troublesome. Soon they served a written ultimatum on Aldrich that they would oppose the entire bill unless the duties were retained on Western products. With the low tariff Middle Westerners meeting in one end of the capitol and the Western high-tariff bloc in the other, and each group issuing

[47] *Chicago Tribune,* July 10, 1909; *Des Moines Register and Leader,* July 3, 18, 1909; Taft to Charles P. Taft, July 13, 1909, in Stephenson, *Aldrich,* 358; Thomas H. Carter to Mrs. Carter, July 16, 1909, Carter MSS.

[48] *New York Sun,* July 22, 1909.

daily ultimatums to mingle with Speaker Cannon's growling, the fate of the tariff bill was dark. "The tariff bill may not pass at all this session," Senator Carter of Montana gloomily wrote his wife.[49]

For a while the harassed president thought seriously of encouraging the progressives to revolt and defeat the conference report. At the last moment, however, Cannon and the Western senators yielded to the threat of a presidential veto, and Taft believed he had won a total victory. He obtained free hides and reductions on glass, lumber, coal, and iron ore. In the final conference report the House had acquiesced completely in 522 of the Senate amendments to the original Payne bill, the Senate had yielded on 124, and the remaining 201 amendments had been compromised. The victory rested with Aldrich and high protection.

With the two houses of Congress at last in agreement, the president tried to persuade the Senate progressives to support the bill. La Follette and Cummins he recognized as hopeless, but the cheer of the White House table was spread before Beveridge, Borah, Brown, Clapp, and Dolliver. For a long time these moderates were on the fence. They heartily disliked the idea of voting against a Republican measure and against the president. Still the reductions secured by Taft were negligible and plainly in the interests of the manufacturers. On the last day of the July meeting in Beveridge's committee room they decided to vote in the negative. Following them twenty Republicans voted against the Republican measure in the House of Representatives. Even Speaker Cannon was dissatisfied. As the vote was announced a half-hearted cheer echoed from the floor. The bill, like Cinderella, was an unwanted stepchild.[50]

The Payne-Aldrich bill, which the president signed just as a terrific thunderstorm broke outside the White House, was in general a re-enactment of the old Dingley bill with slight

[49] Thomas H. Carter to Mrs. Carter, July 17, 21, 26, 1909, Carter MSS.

[50] *Des Moines Register and Leader*, August 3, 1909; *Congressional Record*, 61 Congress, 1 Session, vol. 44, pt. 5, p. 4755; *New York Sun*, August 1, 1909.

changes. In addition to reductions obtained by Taft, oil was put on the free list, and decreases were made in the steel and iron goods rates, but the duties on silk and cotton goods were slightly advanced. The remainder of the bill, including the notorious woolen schedule K, against which so much criticism had been centered, was left largely as it had been in the Dingley tariff. Only in some administrative features did the bill differ from preceding Republican tariffs. It provided for a tariff board to recommend "scientific" schedules, the corporation tax, and the European principle of maximum and minimum rates. The last provision gave the president the authority to raise the rates twenty-five per cent against the goods of any country he believed to be discriminating against the United States.[51]

That the tariff bill had been framed by and for the interests of the east coast and New England was evident to a political realist. Henry Cabot Lodge admitted as much when he petulantly wrote that Massachusetts, which had fared better than any state in the Union from the tariff, had ungratefully reduced the Republican vote for governor.[52] Massachusetts, remarked a Maine member of Congress, had never gone away from the halls of Congress with "more in her craw" than she obtained in the Payne-Aldrich bill.[53] What was clear to Eastern statesmen was equally manifest to Westerners. Even Middle Western regulars complained bitterly of this sectional discrimination: "It was New England and Pennsylvania that made the new tariff law," wrote James S. Clarkson of Iowa, "and it is largely for New England and Pennsylvania interest. The people and the states who constitute a real majority in the nation were largely ignored."[54]

This mild criticism of Eastern Republicanism was no clue to the real feeling of the trans-Allegheny country. In daily

[51] See F. W. Taussig, *Free Trade, the Tariff and Reciprocity* (New York, 1920), 150–165, for a history of the tariff board.

[52] Henry C. Lodge to Roosevelt, November 30, 1909, Roosevelt MSS.

[53] Quoted in Sullivan, *Our Times*, 4: 369.

[54] James S. Clarkson to Grenville M. Dodge, September 17, 1909, Dodge MSS.

jeremiads the section newspapers inveighed against the East and Eastern party leadership. Taft, the easy-going soul, they admitted might have been duped and could be forgiven if his future actions warranted it; but for Aldrich and the rest of his "trust serving Senators" they had nothing but implacable hatred. Aldrich must go even if the removal meant civil war within the party. And as for the Aldrich senators, they were frankly told by some of their constituents that their continued stay in Washington depended on how soon they "cut loose from the Aldrich leash." When Governor John A. Johnson of Minnesota in a speech at Seattle urged the progressive West and the Democratic South to unite in rebellion against the East, there was applause from not a few Western Republican journals.[55]

Thus the West was re-examining and redefining its Republicanism. Was the specter of 1896 again stalking over the prairies? Only the future would tell. But already Westerners in both houses of Congress had fused themselves into informal voting entities against the regular organization of the Republican party.

[55] *Des Moines Register and Leader*, August 3, 1909; *La Follette's Weekly*, August 14, 1909; Samuel Gordon to Thomas H. Carter, January 29, 1910, Carter MSS.; *Kansas City Star*, August 4, 1909.

CHAPTER THREE

The *Cause Célèbre:* Pinchot-Ballinger

THE FUTURE OF THE Taft administration hung in a delicate balance during the hot August and September days of 1909. Through the heartland of Republicanism, the Middle West, rebellion seethed against the tariff and the party leadership. Coming home from Congress, Republican senators and representatives continued to add fuel to the flames. Within a week Beveridge of Indiana was at work on an article for the *Saturday Evening Post* attacking both Aldrich and his tariff. In Iowa, Cummins, speaking to a convention of "progressive"[1] Republicans, demanded the election of men who would carry out platform promises. Elsewhere La Follette, Clapp, Dolliver, and Bristow were campaigning against "Aldrichism." Division and defeat were the prospects for the party unless the president through some political magic were able to reunite it.

But before Taft could possibly induce harmony he had to restore lost confidence. For the president's course in the tariff struggle had changed the temper of the Mississippi Valley from enthusiastic support to watchful if not suspicious waiting. By agreement the congressional dissenters refrained from open criticism of Taft. Their public utterances expressed the hope that the president would abjure the Aldrich-Cannon leadership and use the newly created tariff board to make substantial reductions in the immediate future. But among themselves they wondered if Taft had not been "permanently

[1] Apparently this was the first time "progressive" Republicans as distinguished from Republicans held an open meeting. *Outlook*, 92:907 (August, 1909).

hypnotized" by Aldrich, Lodge, and Smoot. Cummins believed that his proposed trust control measures would be rejected by the "friends" of the president who were advising him how not to regulate corporations "in all the dialects of equivocation and uncertainty." And this distrust of the administration was soon amplified by rumors from Washington.[2]

At a meeting of the National Food Conference early in August, Secretary of Agriculture Wilson surprised the nation by roundly condemning his assistant, Dr. Harvey W. Wiley, patron saint of the country's pure food crusade. Shortly thereafter the news came from Washington that Wilson was seeking the dismissal of his chief chemist and that the president was not at all opposed.[3] Dr. Wiley, one of the most prominent of Roosevelt's "little crusaders," had endeared himself to the public by his struggle against the great commissary concerns. Almost simultaneously the nation got its first intimation of the struggle developing between Gifford Pinchot and the secretary of the interior, Richard A. Ballinger, over the conservation of national resources. In each instance the press reported that the Roosevelt men were in danger of losing their jobs because of their zeal in carrying out what had been Roosevelt's policies.[4]

On August 5, 1909, Speaker Cannon added to the uncertainty of the public mind by announcing his selections for the permanent committees of the new House of Representatives. An examination of the lists showed that Charles N. Fowler of New Jersey, Augustus P. Gardner of Massachusetts, and Henry A. Cooper of Wisconsin, insurgents all, had lost their chairmanships. The reaction against the speaker's arbitrary

[2] A. B. Cummins to Roosevelt, July 7, 1910, Roosevelt MSS.; Cummins to Beveridge, September 13, 1909, Cummins MSS., Historical Memorial and Art Department of Iowa, Des Moines, Iowa; *La Follette's Weekly*, August 14, 1909; H. D. Ticknor to Jonathan Dolliver, August 1, 1909, Dolliver MSS., Iowa City, Iowa; Cummins to Beveridge, September 13, 1909, in Bowers, *Beveridge*, 370.

[3] The press was wrong. Taft supported Wiley and considered discharging Secretary Wilson. Pringle, *Taft*, 2: 729.

[4] *Des Moines Register and Leader*, September 9, 1909.

action was instant and sharp. Throughout the Middle West progressive sentiment began to mobilize for a decisive battle with the conservative autocrat of the House. So-called "progressive" Republican candidates began to announce themselves against Republican incumbents who had supported Cannon and the tariff. In answer the tough old speaker demanded that all insurgents in both the Senate and the House be considered party traitors. "I know of only one way to treat them," Cannon declared, "and that is to fight them just as we fight Mr. Bryan and his following." Soon thereafter it was announced in Washington that Cannon would have the aid of the Republican Congressional Campaign Committee in removing these noxious weeds from the garden of Republicanism. The president said nothing about the pronouncement, and there were those who considered that silence lent consent.[5]

To the progressive Republican mind the Wiley, Pinchot, and Cannon episodes added together looked suspiciously like a concerted wave of reaction officially endorsed if not inspired by the White House. With outspoken skepticism the Middle West prepared to meet the president, who had started a thirteen-thousand mile speaking tour which was to take him from coast to coast. Urged to make a countrywide defense of his administration against the rising tide of criticism, Taft left Beverly, his summer home, early in September. But even before he had started on his pacification mission the Mississippi Valley warned him that it was to be a delicate business. The president would be cheerfully welcomed, proclaimed the *Kansas City Star* editorially, but his speeches would be watched with "great interest" because of the somewhat "ambiguous" position he had recently adopted.[6]

With progressive Republicanism holding its judgment in abeyance, Taft in the next thirty days, through a series of most injudicious speeches, succeeded in squarely arraying the

[5] *La Follette's Weekly*, September 4, 1909; *Kansas City Star*, October 16, 20, 1909; *Des Moines Register and Leader*, October 22, 1909.
[6] *Kansas City Star*, September 11, 1909.

reform forces in his party against him. At the very outset of his trip he made public his growing friendship for Nelson W. Aldrich. Speaking in Boston, he characterized the Rhode Islander as "one of the ablest statesmen in financial matters in either House" and as "the real leader of the Senate," who had "an earnest desire to aid the people."[7] He then went on to praise the Aldrich plan for a central bank, a plan as cordially hated in the Middle West as was its author. From the viewpoint of the Middle West that was a bad beginning. For was not Rooseveltism dead and buried when Aldrich ruled in the Senate? And now it seemed as if the president had not only confirmed the burial but had shaken hands with the gravedigger as well. The sick Dolliver, chagrined at the Taft statements, turned for comfort to the future: "It is an incredible thing," he wrote to Beveridge, "that as sensible a man as Taft should start out by tying the Aldrich millstone around his neck and travelling like a peddlar of damaged goods. 'Leader of the Senate'—we will jar that myth in the next three years. Wait for results my boy. . . . With Pinchot knocked out and Aldrich put in command I think you can hear a lion roar in East Africa."[8]

But Taft either knew not or cared not; for three days later he journeyed to Winona, Minnesota, to make a speech in defense of the standpat Congressman Tawney and the Payne-Aldrich bill, a speech still cited as a masterly example of political ineptitude. To an already irritated Middle West he offered not the hand of conciliation but the rod of rebuke. "Was it the duty of the members of Congress who believed that the bill did not accomplish everything that it ought to accomplish, to vote against it?" the president asked. "I am here to justify those who answer the question in the negative. I am not here to defend those who voted for the Payne bill[9] but to support them."

[7] *Des Moines Register and Leader,* September 15, 1909.
[8] Dolliver to Beveridge, September 14, 1909, Dolliver MSS.
[9] Taft was at least being political in calling it the Payne and not the Aldrich bill.

After slapping the Middle Western progressives squarely in the face, the president went on to identify himself thoroughly with this political pariah by describing it as "the best tariff bill that the Republican party has ever passed and therefore the best tariff bill that has been passed at all."[10] Meanwhile administration acolytes were glossing Taft's statement. A few days before the Winona address Vice-President Sherman remarked with evident satisfaction that the party had fulfilled every campaign pledge in passing the Aldrich bill. A few days after the Winona effort Aldrich announced that he would make no further speeches on the tariff, since that question "had been settled for a number of years." Taft, Sunny Jim Sherman, and Aldrich. The harmony was obvious; the timing evident.[11]

The Winona address was unquestionably a major milestone in the alienation of progressive Republican sentiment from the Taft administration. Up until that time the progressives had been hopeful that the president would eventually give them at least backhanded support. After Winona they were sure that their victories would have to be won over the opposition of the president as well as the leaders of the House and Senate. The sentiment that the speech could only be construed as a "definite alignment on the part of the president with the reactionary forces" resounded from Ohio to Colorado. But its effects were not confined to a section. Beveridge noted that "it raised a storm of dissent in the East. Little else was talked about in New York and Philadelphia." Later on he wrote to Amos Pinchot that Horace Lorimer, editor of the *Saturday Evening Post*, after reading the address announced that "from that moment his magazine would become insurgent."[12]

The Winona speech had one other important result; it started the "back from Elba" movement for the re-election

---

[10] *Des Moines Register and Leader*, September 17, 1909.

[11] *Kansas City Star*, September 14, October 20, 1909.

[12] *Ibid.*, September 18, 1909; Beveridge to Dolliver, September 25, 1909, Dolliver MSS.; Beveridge to Amos Pinchot, March 24, 1910, Roosevelt MSS.

of Theodore Roosevelt in 1912. Taft had scarcely left Minnesota when Henry Allen of Kansas announced that he was from now on looking to Africa for the 1912 Republican nominee. Republican papers joined in the declaration of the *Des Moines Register and Leader* that Roosevelt could now have the honor for the asking. Even the bitterly anti-Roosevelt *New York Times* suggested that Taft's efforts had opened the path to the White House for the Colonel.[13] Quite understandably the good-natured president deeply resented these references to Roosevelt. Like a prominent son of a more famous father Taft grew touchy about the inevitable comparison. And when progressive circles kept reiterating the Roosevelt suggestion, Taft naturally moved closer to the conservative wing of the party, where he was better appreciated.

The rest of the president's trip through the Middle West was described as a "polar dash through a world of ice." Everywhere the president was greeted courteously, but nowhere enthusiastically. Wrongly or rightly, the section now felt that he was more foe than friend.[14] Taft himself did little to change this attitude; the sharp-eyed Butt noted that everywhere the president went he consorted with the people whom Roosevelt had been wont to call "the enemy." It was on this trip that the president and Speaker Cannon were photographed with their arms about each other, a picture of perfect accord.[15] The president's proposals, made in speeches throughout the country west of the Mississippi, to reform the powers of the Interstate Commerce Commission and to redraw the Sherman Anti-Trust Law did little to re-establish his lost popularity. The plan he enunciated at Des Moines to establish a commerce court to try cases arising from the

[13] *Des Moines Register and Leader*, September 23, 24, 1909.

[14] *Chicago Tribune*, September 21, 1909; *World's Work*, 19: 121 (November, 1909).

[15] Butt, *Taft and Roosevelt*, 1: 202. It is interesting to note that invariably Taft put the arrangements for his receptions in various states into the hands of tried and true conservatives. Taft to Thomas A. Carter, July 30, 1909, Carter MSS.

activities of the Interstate Commerce Commission and to transfer the power to defend such cases from the Commission to the attorney general's office, his scheme to narrow the anti-trust law so that the government to be successful at suit would have to prove intent to establish a monopoly, and his remarks on the income tax at Denver were all viewed by the Western press as retrogressive.[16]

By the time Taft returned to Washington the Republican party was in a critical state. The revolt of the West was assuming ominous proportions. Lodge in a letter to Roosevelt spoke of the rampant radicalism of La Follette and Cummins across the Appalachians and was sure it spelled trouble for the future. Apparently on his trip the president shared none of Lodge's anxiety. Surrounded by standpat local leaders who told him only what he wanted to hear, he was quite unaware of the real temper of the country. Almost at the end of his journey Taft wrote to Secretary Knox that the trip had accomplished everything he had wished for. The insurgents, he indicated, were so noisy simply because they were at the end of their rope: "They have become desperate and their cry is heard above the quiet chant of contentment that exists every where in this country."[17] But back in Washington there were different tidings. One member of the Cabinet warned Taft that the Roosevelt following had a plot afoot to force an issue between the two men. Another told him that he simply must dismiss Pinchot for disloyalty, and a third informed him that the entire reform section of the party distrusted his intentions and "hell was to pay everywhere."[18]

Taft was a courageous man and perhaps his years on the bench had imparted a rigidity of judgment that would not permit an opinion once held to be changed. Whatever the reason, the president refused to shift his ground. Privately

[16] *Kansas City Star*, September 21, 22, 1909.

[17] Lodge to Roosevelt, October 20, 1909, Roosevelt MSS.; Thomas H. Carter to Fred W. Carpenter, October 2, 1909, Carter MSS.; Taft to Philander C. Knox, October 24, 1909, Knox MSS.

[18] Dolliver to Beveridge, September 14, 1909, Dolliver MSS.; *Philadelphia North American*, November 15, 1909.

he did admit that the Winona address had been prepared on the train and that he had given it only a superficial examination before he delivered it. The use of the comparative "better," he thought later, might have been more advisable than the use of "best" to describe the virtues of the Payne-Aldrich bill. But he would not change a jot of his praise of Aldrich, his general estimate of the tariff, and his criticism of the progressives. He confessed to Attorney General Wickersham that he may have made a political error in defending the Rhode Island senator, "but I have the satisfaction of knowing that I said what I believed." And to all comers, friend and foe alike, Taft's reply was the same. "I meant every word of my Winona speech," he answered a critical letter from Indiana. Butt thought that he had been won over largely by Aldrich and he feared for the future.[19]

During the autumn of 1909 most of America was heatedly lining up in two great controversies. In August the spectacular news flashed through the nation that the American explorer Dr. Frederick Cook had discovered the North Pole. Scarcely had the shouting subsided when word came on September 6 that Admiral Robert E. Peary of the United States Navy had been to the top of the world. Cook's story was declared a fraud. At once the country divided into camps of Cook and Peary devotees, and throughout the winter an acrimonious battle raged in the barber shops of the nation.

Less dramatic but certainly of more significance was the outbreak of a heated controversy between two conspicuous members of Taft's official family, Secretary of the Interior Richard A. Ballinger and Chief Forester Gifford Pinchot. Ultimately the struggle between the two men was to become a *cause célèbre* of American history about which a literary battle continues to this day.[20] Immediately it had profound effects

[19] Butt, *Taft and Roosevelt*, 1: 201–202, 222; Taft to William Dudley Foulke, November 18, 1909, Foulke MSS.

[20] When Henry F. Pringle published his study of William Howard Taft in 1939 he reversed the existing historical judgment on the Ballinger-Pinchot episode by coming to the defense of Taft's administration and of Ballinger. Subsequently Harold L. Ickes, present secretary of the interior,

upon the Taft administration and the history of the Republican progressive movement.

The prelude to the drama was written years before Taft became president. Before the turn of the century a group of public-spirited citizens, observing the wholesale exploitation of natural resources by private interests, began to fear a national exhaustion of basic materials. Accordingly the movement to preserve what resources were left in the national domain was born. Hitherto the accepted policy had been the simple one of distributing the public lands and other national riches as rapidly and as cheaply as possible to any private interest guaranteeing to exploit them. Rapid exploitation, it was thought in the nineteenth century, would benefit both the nation and private individuals.

However, with the real or fancied threat of exhaustion, a growing opinion demanded conservation. Contributing to this growth was the contemporary campaign against the "trusts." It was feared that if governmental dispensation of the natural wealth was not curtailed these great business combinations would soon own all the wealth of the country. The old reckless handout policy should be stopped, and the government should dispose of such natural resources as were left in the national domain only when it was in the national interest.

In the foreranks of the early conservation apostles stood Gifford Pinchot of Pennsylvania. Born to wealth, Pinchot,

published an undocumented article in the *Saturday Evening Post* (May 25, 1940) in which he completely exonerated Ballinger and indicted Gifford Pinchot. From all appearances neither Pringle nor Ickes used to any extent the thirteen volumes comprising the investigations and reports of the congressional investigating committee. It is also interesting to note that previous to the appearance of Secretary Ickes' article, Gifford Pinchot had opposed the plan of the present secretary of the interior to transfer the Forestry Bureau to his own department.

In answer to both the Pringle and the Ickes' interpretation, Alpheus T. Mason published *Bureaucracy Convicts Itself* in 1941. The first draft of this chapter, which agrees substantially with Mason's general interpretation, was written in 1938 and incorporated in a Ph.D. thesis at the University of Wisconsin.

after studying forestry abroad, spent most of his young life in the public service where he dedicated all the fierce energies of a true crusader against the nation's vested interests. Appointed chief forester in the Department of Agriculture, Pinchot soon became a close friend of Theodore Roosevelt. A member of the famous Tennis Cabinet, Pinchot probably inspired the president to take up conservation as his own cause. In propagandizing for conservation, Roosevelt used all his peculiar genius for public persuasion. By ballyhoo and by withdrawing from public entry millions of acres rich in resources Roosevelt in seven years had made conservation a national movement. On leaving office he considered it as one of his most valuable contributions to national life.

If Pinchot had been Roosevelt's source of inspiration in the conservation crusade, James R. Garfield, another member of the Tennis Cabinet, had really done the spade work. As secretary of the interior Garfield had charge of most of the national domain. Roosevelt was delighted, therefore, when Taft told him in an "off-hand"[21] manner that Garfield would continue as his secretary of the interior. There would be a direct continuity of "my policies" as long as Garfield held his position. Consequently when Taft later appointed Richard A. Ballinger instead, both Garfield and Roosevelt were keenly disappointed.

To Pinchot, who had been kept on as chief forester, the replacement of Garfield was more than a disappointment; it was a tragedy. Pinchot was described by a contemporary as "a combination of an enthusiast and a politician" who could be a "useful agency under firm and tactful control but a dangerous compound under other circumstances."[22] He was not a man given to meditation when events met with his disapproval. Perhaps he would have found fault with even the most zealous conservationist unlucky enough to have taken the place of his friend Garfield. And Richard Achilles

[21] John J. Leary, Jr., *Talks with T.R.* (New York, 1920), 42.
[22] Charles J. Bonaparte to H. C. Gauss, January 15, 1910, Bonaparte MSS.

Ballinger, though he had been a Roosevelt appointee, was no conservationist. Instead, reflecting the dominant sentiment of the Far West, he believed that conservation obstructed the logical development of the country. At a time when most of the country rejected it Ballinger still held to the nineteenth-century doctine of "division, disposition and dividends." Between Pinchot and Ballinger, reformer and business man, collectivist and individualist, the issue had to be joined. It was a struggle not only of personalities but of two Americas. In Ballinger from the West the economic individualism that had made possible the Vanderbilts, Rockefeller, and Jay Gould found its dying voice. Pinchot spoke for the new day of social democracy.[23]

The first intimation of trouble between the two men came when Ballinger restored certain water power sites to the public entry lists. Just at the end of Roosevelt's term Garfield, without specific congressional authority, had withdrawn from public entry about a million and a half acres of land in close proximity to possible power sites. Early in April of 1909 the new secretary, against the advice of Arthur P. Davis, chief engineer of the Reclamation Service, reversed Garfield's action on the ground that his predecessor had acted without proper authority. When attacked later, Ballinger maintained that the Reclamation Service had advised the move because it lacked funds for taking care of the land. At this point the chief forester held a conference with President Taft, who subsequently advised Ballinger to again withdraw the lands. This the secretary of the interior did, somehow managing to find the necessary maintenance funds.[24]

Further friction was generated between the two men when the Interior Department refused Pinchot's request that land be withdrawn for the establishment of ranger stations. Never had Frank H. Hitchcock or Garfield in Roosevelt's Cabinet

[23] For a contrary report of Ballinger's conservation views see Pringle, who calls him "a friend and not the enemy of conservation." *Taft*, 1: 473.

[24] *Investigation of the Department of the Interior and of the Bureau of Forestry* (Senate Document 719, 61 Congress, 3 Session), vol. 4, pp. 1172, 1181.

denied the forester's petitions.[25] By this time, irritated and suspicious, Pinchot gave a willing ear to an investigator of the Interior Department, one Louis R. Glavis, who came to him in the summer of 1909 with the charge that Ballinger was illegally aiding a group of Seattle men to deliver the richest coal lands in Alaska to the Morgan-Guggenheim Syndicate. Assuring himself that the accusation was just, the forester urged Glavis to present a written version of his charges directly to the president. The public first heard of the affair when Pinchot in a speech before the National Irrigation Conference in August charged Ballinger with being a virtual traitor to Roosevelt's conservation doctrines.[26]

Meanwhile Glavis had written his bill of particulars to the president. No charge of corruption was made, but throughout the document the implication was strong that Ballinger was a foe of conservation. Glavis cited as evidence the secretary's actions over a period of years in the case of the Alaskan coal claims, which became known the country over as the Cunningham Claims.[27] Taft read the letter and referred it to Ballinger, who in turn submitted a rebuttal which both the president and the attorney general studied at length. After a discussion with the Cabinet Taft exonerated Ballinger and authorized him to discharge Glavis for insubordination.[28]

Aware that Glavis' dismissal would anger Pinchot, the president hastened to placate the forester, whom he secretly considered a "fanatic," by writing him a long, gracious letter stating how much his valuable services had been appreciated. But the letter, which began with the salutation, "My Dear Gifford," also contained a veiled hint that the attacks on the secretary would have to stop. Taft sincerely hoped that Pinchot would not make Glavis' cause his own. A short time later the president sought to end the matter by praising Bal-

[25] Rose M. Stahl, *The Ballinger-Pinchot Controversy* (Northampton, Massachusetts, 1926), 85.

[26] *Philadelphia North American*, August 11, 1909.

[27] *Investigation of the Department of the Interior*, 2: 60–63.

[28] Diary of George von L. Meyer, September 5, 1909, in Howe, *Meyer*, 445.

linger's work and at the same time assuring the public that the administration was pledged to the Roosevelt policies—although, he added, such a pledge "does not involve me in any obligation to carry them out unless I have Congressional authority to do so." He then went on to promise that he would take every step "and exert every legitimate influence upon Congress to enact legislation which shall best subserve the purpose indicated."[29]

The presidential hint did not persuade Pinchot to let the matter rest. Throughout the autumn he secretly supplied newspapers with damaging anti-Ballinger material. November found him again writing to the president criticizing the secretary of the interior. In a few days Taft received another letter in the same vein from Pinchot's good friend James R. Garfield. The fat was really thrown into the public fire, though, when Louis Glavis published an article on the affair in a November issue of *Collier's Weekly*. Sensational in tone, it so stirred up public opinion that a showdown in a congressional investigation seemed inevitable.[30]

Meanwhile out in the country the progressive Republican press almost to a paper had come to the support of Pinchot. Even before the facts of the conservation quarrel were known they began to attack the administration on the grounds that Pinchot's record as a public servant was certified by the years, whereas Ballinger was at best an unknown quantity. When the news leaked out in August that the president was supporting his secretary of the interior, most of the newssheets cited the action as one more piece of evidence that Taft was returning to McKinleyism. In particular did the progressive journals ridicule the reliance of the president and his secretary upon strict construction of congressional authority as an excuse for their actions. The same strict con-

[29] Butt, *Taft and Roosevelt*, 1:193; *Des Moines Register and Leader*, December 2, 3, 1909; *Kansas City Star*, September 29, 1909.

[30] Louis R. Glavis, "Whitewashing of Ballinger," *Collier's Weekly*, 14: 13–17 (November 13, 1909). In the course of the article there were strong implications that Ballinger was corrupt. On the basis of evidence presented that was palpably unjust.

struction, they argued, would have made the Louisiana Purchase impossible, Tawney right and Dred Scott wrong, Lincoln unconstitutional in freeing the slaves, and Jackson a marplot in quashing the South Carolina nullification.[31]

As public disapproval increased, Taft came to the conclusion that the concerted attacks on Ballinger and the administration's conservation policy were political in their nature and not in the interest of conservation. He felt that there was a great conspiracy in the West, headed by Pinchot, of all the men who were interested in electing Roosevelt president in 1912. When his brother suggested that he let Pinchot go, he replied that this was exactly what Pinchot wanted so that he could appeal to Roosevelt against the administration.[32]

This judgment was not altogether unwarranted. Not a few of Roosevelt's friends, while sympathizing with Garfield and Pinchot, deplored their more pointed statements as calculated to start a back from Elba movement. In addition, there was no denying that the congressional progressives were delighted by the turn of events and were happy to help the quarrel along. Confident that Aldrich, Cannon, and the administration would oppose them in the next Republican primaries, the Middle Western rebels were eager to welcome any new allies. Pinchot and Garfield would be particularly useful additions, for both of them were intimate and influential with Roosevelt. And a Roosevelt loosening his sibilant thunderbolts against the standpatters in the heat of the next summer's campaign would more than balance any loss of administration support.[33]

When Congress met in December, 1909, the progressive Republicans, with Democratic blessings, forced an investigation of the Interior Department. But even then, had it not been for the dramatic actions of Gifford Pinchot, the investigation might have turned out to be a routine suppression of

[31] *Kansas City Star*, September 26, 1909.
[32] H. C. Gauss to Charles J. Bonaparte, December 24, 1909, Bonaparte SS.; Butt, *Taft and Roosevelt*, 1: 245.
[33] Bonaparte to H. C. Gauss, January 13, 1910, Bonaparte MSS.

opposition criticism scarcely noticed by an apathetic public. Pinchot, however, focused the attention of the nation upon the investigating committee by outmaneuvering the president. In effect, he forced Taft to discharge him. Early in January, 1910, the crusading forester sent a letter to Senator Dolliver, which the latter read by permission in the Senate. In the course of the document Pinchot admitted that the Forest Service had been aiding the attack on Ballinger by supplying Glavis and others with confidential information from government files. Pinchot then went on to praise Glavis as "a defender of the people's interests," thus implying that the president who had discharged him was something else.[34]

There was nothing for Taft to do but to dismiss Pinchot. Everyone agreed to that. But in haltingly relieving the forester of his duties the president let pass a golden opportunity for dismissing Ballinger. As subsequent events proved, Ballinger was innocent of corruption. He was also innocent of being a conservationist; and he was a great and continuing liability to the Taft administration. Had the president secured his immediate resignation, he would have stilled Pinchot, would possibly have allayed Roosevelt's later irritation, and certainly would have cut the ground from under the feet of the progressive Republicans. As it was, the Republican rebels in Congress rushed to Pinchot's side, giving aid and undoubtedly expecting the same in return. Uniting squarely with them for the first time was the *Outlook*, a periodical influential with the moderate and clerically tinged reform element in the East. *Collier's Weekly*, threatened by friends of the administration with a million-dollar suit for printing Glavis' article, also joined the band. Pinchot and Garfield, the *Outlook*, *Collier's*, and Dolliver, La Follette, Cummins, Beveridge, and Norris—it was becoming a formidable band no longer confined to the Middle West. Prophetically the *Outlook* stated that if the progressive element in the Republican party was further ignored, a new party or a new alignment of parties would result.[35]

[34] *Investigation of the Department of the Interior*, 4: 1284.
[35] *Outlook*, 94: 374 (February 19, 1910).

What of Roosevelt and his reaction to the dismissal of
Pinchot? The cagey Elihu Root and Taft had both spent long
moments of thought on that point before they had agreed to
discharge Pinchot. Many people believed, the progressives
undoubtedly prayed, and perhaps the president feared that
the action would immediately take the Colonel into the opposition camp. Roosevelt, however, deep in the African jungle, at first heroically remained silent. When the news of
Pinchot's dismissal first reached him he could not believe it,
and in a letter to Lodge he expressed the hope that his information had been incorrect.[36] Beyond that he offered no
clue to his feelings. But after a succession of letters from the
men close to him, his thoughts began to crystallize. Roosevelt
heard from Dolliver that the president had taken "the certificate of character" which Roosevelt had given him and had
"turned it over to the Senator from Rhode Island."[37] Nicholas Longworth, his son-in-law and a firm supporter of Taft,
wrote that the substitution of Ballinger for Garfield seemed
to him "almost a crime."[38] Sometime in January, 1910,
Roosevelt condemned the Cunningham people as violators of
the law.[39] Now with the supporting evidence of some of his
friends he must at least have thought that Taft's course was
a disastrous one. This conclusion was undoubtedly strengthened by the findings of the congressional committee as they
proceeded to investigate the whole affair.

The joint congressional committee to investigate the Interior and Forestry departments began work on January 28,
1910, and was in almost constant session until June. An attempt was made to handpick the committee from the ranks
of administration supporters.[40] That the intention to apply
whitewash liberally was not altogether carried out was
largely due to the progressives and the work of Louis D.
Brandeis, employed by *Collier's Weekly* to defend Glavis and

[36] Roosevelt to Lodge, January 17, 1910, Roosevelt MSS.
[37] Dolliver to Pinchot, March 25, 1910, Roosevelt MSS.
[38] Nicholas Longworth to Roosevelt, April 27, 1910, Roosevelt MSS.
[39] Roosevelt to W. D. Hulbert, January (?), 1910, Roosevelt MSS.
[40] *Outlook*, 95: 140–142 (May 28, 1910).

Pinchot. Acting almost as a prosecutor at times, Brandeis went behind the evidence given by the administration's witnesses to produce a quantity of damaging information. From a veritable mass of testimony Brandeis reconstructed the whole story of the history of the Cunningham claims and thus adduced a picture of Ballinger that left little doubt where the secretary of the interior stood on the conservation question.

The story of the Cunningham claims was a long and involved one. Under the land laws of 1900 and 1904 Congress extended the coal land laws of the United States to Alaska. By these acts a person could stake out a claim of not more than one hundred and sixty acres of land. The federal statutes required that he swear that he had acted in his own interests alone and not for some other person or corporation. On payment of a small sum the claimant received a certificate of entry, and the claim passed to the General Land Office, where an investigative bureau held inquiries to assure itself of the good faith of the claimant. When the General Land Office was convinced that these conditions had been met, it ordered the claims to be clear-listed and patents issued.

In 1906 Roosevelt realized that there would be no legal development of the coal fields in Alaska under the law as it stood. Certainly no individual would undertake the expensive operations necessary for the opening of coal fields with the guarantee of only one hundred and sixty acres of coal deposits. He therefore ordered the lands withdrawn from entry until some legislative solution was found by Congress. Previously, however, some thirty-three alleged private claimants had obtained certificates of entry. Consequently the General Land Office was ordered to investigate and clear-list the holdings if their findings warranted it. These thirty-three claims comprising the famous Cunningham claims covered about fifteen per cent of the Bering River coal field, then thought to be the richest deposit of its kind in Alaska.[41]

[41] *Investigation of the Department of the Interior,* 1: 7.

In 1907 Ballinger was appointed by the Roosevelt administration commissioner of the General Land Office, and as the Cunningham claims were held by several prominent Seattle business men, Ballinger was well acquainted with the men involved before he took office. Meanwhile the special investigating agents, one of whom was Glavis, charged that the claimants were in collusion to sell their claims, once clear-listed, to the Morgan-Guggenheim Syndicate, which had been organized the year before. Despite these reports Ballinger ordered the claims clear-listed, only to revoke the order when a strong telegram of protest arrived from Glavis. Commissioner Ballinger then indicated to the claimants that the delay was only temporary, and in a few days he appeared before a committee to argue for the Cale bill, which would have automatically validated the Cunningham claims.[42]

Shortly thereafter Ballinger resigned his position to practice law in Seattle. At the same time Glavis was called to Washington and put in full charge of the investigation. In the following year Glavis, journeying to Seattle, secured from Clarence Cunningham, the attorney representing the claimants, a private journal indicating that the thirty-three entry men had made an agreement to act jointly, which under the existing law automatically invalidated their claims. The investigator then obtained from Cunningham an affidavit to the effect that the claimants ever since the start of the transaction had common action in mind. This he filed along with the journal as government testimony.[43]

Cunningham soon grew worried over the affidavit he had made and consulted Ballinger in the interests of his clients. Together Ballinger and Cunningham drew up a second affidavit full of half truths which sought to explain away the first document by falsely declaring there had never been any intention among the entrymen to combine. Ballinger then took the document to Washington and presented it with argument to the General Land Office. In so doing and accepting

[42] *Ibid.*, 7: 3960.
[43] *Ibid.*, 3: 108–109.

a fee from the claimants he was breaking an administrative regulation which forbade a former officeholder from appearing before his own department in the interest of a claim pending before his resignation. It is a question, however, whether Ballinger was aware at that time of an agreement signed on July 20, 1907, between the Cunningham claimants and the Morgan-Guggenheim Syndicate.[44]

When President Taft took office in March, 1909, Ballinger became secretary of the interior. Although he subsequently refused to correspond officially with the Cunningham claimants, he did continue privately to advise the group of the status of their claims.[45] Moreover, a short time after Ballinger's assumption of office, Glavis was removed as investigator of the claims on the grounds that he was working too slowly. And despite the fact that his successor agreed that more time was needed to obtain evidence, the Interior Department announced that it would hear and decide the cases at once. Whereupon Glavis appealed to Pinchot and later to Taft, an appeal that resulted in his dismissal.[46]

In its effects on public opinion the conduct of Ballinger's counsel, John J. Vertrees, before the congressional committee was most disastrous. During his opening defense of the secretary's actions Vertrees branded the conduct of conservation policy by Roosevelt and Garfield as the lawless work of deluded visionaries. "There was the reign of men," Vertrees exclaimed. "March 4, 1909, there came the reign of law."[47] The country cared not for subtle definitions of law but wanted results. The administration was either for or against Roosevelt's policy, which had produced results. The impeachment

[44] *Ibid.*, 7: 3601. Pringle states (*Taft*, 1: 501) that "there was nothing improper about the fee." The agreement between the Cunningham group and Daniel Guggenheim is printed in full in vol. 5, pp. 2132–2133, of the committee hearings. By this agreement Daniel Guggenheim agreed to pay $250,000 for a half interest in the claims and advance other sums for their development. Thus the Guggenheim interests had a little more than the "remote connection" which Pringle admits. *Taft*, 1: 473.

[45] *Investigation of the Department of the Interior*, 2: 74.

[46] *Ibid.*, 3: 262.

[47] *Ibid.*, 5: 2393.

of that policy by Ballinger's counsel was construed as evidence of the secretary's hostility to conservation. That such a construction was not invalid became obvious in 1912, when Ballinger himself characterized the Roosevelt conservation doctrines "as too absurd to warrant serious consideration" and urged that the control of water power and mineral sites be given back to the individual states.[48] Unfortunately in 1910 the public incorrectly inferred from Vertrees' remarks that the president too was a foe of conservation.

Still another series of facts elicited by the committee brought severe public criticism of the hapless president. When the committee called for the evidence upon which Taft had exonerated Ballinger and discharged Glavis, the president sent it an impressive document of some fifty thousand words. This long report carried the date of September 11, 1909. Brandeis, however, with the testimony of a government stenographer, proved that the document had not been prepared on that date but three months after Glavis had been discharged. It was then revealed that the documentary evidence upon which the president had acted was a much shorter memorandum prepared by Assistant Attorney General Oscar W. Lawlor, who had submitted it to Ballinger for corrections before it was given to the president. This so-called Lawlor memorandum had not been produced when the committee asked for all the relevant papers, and its use by the president as the basis of his decision was denied by the administration witnesses until Brandeis forced a counter admission. The predating of public papers is common enough. But the falsehoods surrounding the document in addition to its predating further convinced the public of official skullduggery.[49]

At the conclusion of the investigation, the Republican members of the committee, with the exception of the progressive Edmond H. Madison of Kansas, voted Ballinger a complete bill of health. That was expected. For the majority

[48] *Milwaukee Sentinel*, August 25, 1912.
[49] For the best account of this whole episode see Mason, *Bureaucracy Convicts Itself*, 157–177.

committee members had been chosen from the trustworthy who agreed with Senator Carter that it was only the "cranks" who really believed in conservation.[50] But that decision was only the official one. Another was made by the people at large: that Secretary Ballinger, even if his personal integrity remained unsullied, was a sworn enemy of conservation and thus was unfit to occupy his office. And they felt that their judgment was corroborated when a year later the General Land Office declared the Cunningham claims canceled.[51] The president himself backhandedly added to the general agreement by appointing Walter L. Fisher, a friend of Pinchot and Garfield, as Ballinger's successor when he voluntarily left his post with presidential felicitations in March, 1911.

Taft's eventual curtsy to public opinion in appointing a friend of conservation as secretary of the interior did him little good. It was too late by a year. He should have dismissed Ballinger along with Pinchot. Failing that, he should have secured the resignation of the secretary in March, 1910, when Brandeis was filling the public ear with untoward information. Instead he made no effort to appease the progressive Republican element, shouting that Ballinger must go. Never admitting any grounds for that attack on Ballinger except those of "muckraking and slander,"[52] Taft defended his secretary all through the summer. Day by day he was thereby making Democratic votes for the coming elections. Perhaps Charles J. Bonaparte's assertion that the whole affair was characterized by "the most notable unbroken succession of colossal blunders known in American politics" was a little strong. But it had its point.[53]

Nor was this strengthening of the enemy the most harmful effect the president's course had on the fortunes of the Republican party. Some erudite student of politics once said that the party in power is never defeated by the opposition

[50] Thomas H. Carter to Louis W. Hill, October 2, 1909, and to C. R. Miller, April 22, 1910, Carter MSS.

[51] *New York Times*, June 27, 1911.

[52] Taft to Carter, July 28, 1911, Carter MSS.

[53] Bonaparte to H. C. Gauss, March 10, 1911, Bonaparte MSS.

but defeats itself. Taft in 1910 was preparing for such a defeat by allowing the schism in his party that had appeared in the tariff struggle to widen farther. Progressive Republicans alienated by the tariff were further estranged by the unsuccessful rebellion against Speaker Cannon. Taft's support of Ballinger led to the belief that new leadership was imperative if progressivism was to become the dominant philosophy of the party.

More significantly, Taft had incurred the hostility of two men very close to Roosevelt, who was soon to emerge from the African jungle to cast an appraising eye on the doings of the man he had left in charge at home. In Africa Roosevelt took no definite stand, but in America many of his best friends were already mobilizing. Pinchot, Garfield, and other disaffected Republicans had joined the opposition alliance of the Middle Western rebels; and even as the deed was done, shadows of the future began to envelope the White House.

"There is a growing disposition to look to Roosevelt's return as a signal for a break to progressive leadership," jubilantly shouted the men of the prairies.[54]

[54] *Des Moines Register and Leader*, September 11, 1910.

CHAPTER FOUR

Prelude to Revolution

W HEN CONGRESS ASSEMBLED for a new session in December, 1909, the leaders of the Republican party were jittery. Less than a year remained before the congressional elections of 1910, and the people were in an ugly mood. Coming back to Washington, standpat leaders reported a public aroused about the tariff, apprehensive about conservation, and ready to oust Joseph G. Cannon as speaker. A poll taken by the *Chicago Tribune* revealed that eighty per cent of the Republican editors west of the Allegheny Mountains wanted Cannon removed from office. To the east the conservative *Wall Street Journal* characterized his control of the House as "sordid and narrow" and likewise demanded his retirement.[1]

Responding to the public pressure, Republican regulars began to feel that Cannon was too heavy a burden to carry much longer. In November of 1909 Henry Cabot Lodge wrote Roosevelt that there had to be some understanding that Cannon was not to be re-elected as speaker in the next session. "It would be impossible in my judgement to elect a House if it was known that Cannon was again to be Speaker if the Republicans won." President Taft, despite his support of Cannon during the tariff fight, intimated to Secretary Knox that the speaker was causing him great concern. The president did not object to Cannon's reactionary views. Instead he urged the speaker's retirement because he felt that Cannon had lost his hold on the American people by his continual "vulgarity and blackguardism." The president asked Knox

[1] *Chicago Tribune*, February 14, 1910; *Wall Street Journal*, January 20, 1910.

to suggest in "certain Senatorial and other quarters" that it was a most propitious time for the speaker to announce his voluntary retirement.[2]

For years progressive and moderate Republicans in the House had been seeking either to limit or eliminate Cannon as a force in legislation. Twice they had failed openly to curtail the extensive powers of the speaker, and after the last insurrection some of them had felt his heavy retaliating hand. Jubilant over the turn of sentiment, they avidly set about to perfect an organization of the anti-Cannon forces, silently hoping that the president would not again change sides in the middle of the struggle. Fully aware of the situation, Cannon refused to take in sail to meet the coming storm. Instead the valiant old warrior's attacks on the progressives grew more violent as he threatened to encompass their defeat in the coming primaries. Then to the surprise of conservatives and progressives alike, he blandly announced that the administration would support him in the "snake hunt."[3] As if to emphasize the speaker's remarks the January 9 news letter of the Republican Congressional Campaign Committee announced that it would oppose the principle of insurgency in the coming elections and would advocate the nomination and election of "Regular and loyal" Republicans.[4]

It was soon being whispered in the press that Cannon and Taft had come to an understanding and were leagued against the progressives. That had not fully happened yet. But when the progressives' patronage was cut off in January, 1910, they were positive that the newspapers were right.[5] Taft's rather lame excuse that he was merely "preserving the status quo to impress them with their obligations" to his legislative program explained nothing. If the president had made a bargain

[2] Lodge to Roosevelt, November 30, 1909, Roosevelt MSS.; Harold Blake to Thomas H. Carter, March 15, 1910, Carter MSS.; Taft to Philander C. Knox, October 24, 1909, Knox MSS.

[3] *Des Moines Register and Leader*, November 26, December 1, 1909.

[4] *New York Sun*, January 10, 1910.

[5] One of the most Regular Middle Western papers, the *Chicago Record Herald*, was "disgusted" by such "peanut politics."

with the speaker, the progressives reasoned, then they could expect nothing but a Payne-Aldrich hoax all over again. Taft gave further credence to the theory that he had sold his progressive soul to the conservative devil by writing an Indianapolis publisher that in view of the unfairness toward Cannon and the good work he had done as speaker, he would do nothing to force his resignation: "I think Mr. Cannon represents a certain sort of control in the House that I do not agree with, and I am hopeful that he will announce his retirement . . . but that Cannon did a great deal of good work while he was Speaker goes without saying, and I cannot help attributing a great deal of the bitterness of this controversy to the counting rooms of the newspapers which have been affected by the failure to reduce the tariff on print paper in the tariff bill."

The president then went on to say that he would not attack the men who were sincerely working to carry out his program. Nor would he help those who were trying to defeat his efforts, namely La Follette, Cummins, Clapp, Bristow, and the House insurgents. The publisher concluded that Taft by his own admission had chosen the reactionary side and sent a copy of the letter to Roosevelt in Africa as incontestable proof that the president was already well along the road to Damascus.[6]

Sadly disappointed but no longer surprised by presidential vagaries, the House progressives were determined to continue their fight against Cannon even if it meant conflict with the president. That was manifest in the middle of January when they defeated Taft's plan for selecting a "congenial" investigating committee to inquire into the Ballinger-Pinchot affair. The president wanted Cannon and Aldrich to appoint the joint committee, but his proposal was defeated when twenty-six insurgents in the House, led by George W. Norris and Victor Murdock, joined the Democrats in a vote to elect the committee by the full House. Moreover, to persuade the insurgents to attend the Republican caucus Taft was forced

[6] Taft to Lucius B. Swift (copy), February 19, 1910, Roosevelt MSS.

to send a written promise to Representative Norris that he would not use his patronage against a subsequent attack on the speaker. As it was, six insurgents walked out of the caucus in the midst of the session.[7]

Two months later a coalition of progressive Republicans and Democrats under the leadership of Norris made a final move against the speaker. After some parliamentary jockeying in a rules debate, Norris, claiming privilege under the Constitution, rose to introduce a resolution. As the revolutionary nature of his amendments to the rules of the House became clear, there was a deep silence. Calmly the Nebraska insurgent proposed that the powerful rules committee be enlarged from five to fifteen members, that its members be elected by the House instead of being appointed by the speaker, that the speaker be prohibited from a place on the committee, and that the committee be allowed to select its own chairman. Reduced from its technicalities, the resolution proposed to change the speaker's position from that of a near dictator to that of a presiding officer.[8]

In the hubbub that followed, the Regulars opposed the motion on the ground that it was not privileged. And the resulting debate lasted without intermission all through the night and the next day. Stalling for time to gather up all possible strength, the speaker refused to rule on the motion. But when he attempted to adjourn the House at the end of the day the progressive-Democratic coalition kept the body in session. James Watson, ex-Republican whip, was hurried to the House to use his persuasive powers, and telegraphic appeals for help were sent to Senator Penrose in Pennsylvania and to President Taft speaking at Erie. The president wired back that he was sorry to be absent from the capital "at so critical a period" and then went on his way.[9] Penrose, however, hurried to Washington, where he used his influence in an attempt

[7] *Congressional Record,* 61 Congress, 2 Session, vol. 45, pt. 1, p. 404; *Philadelphia North American,* January 13, 1910.

[8] *Congressional Record,* 61 Congress, 2 Session, vol. 45, pt. 3, p. 3290.

[9] Butt, *Taft and Roosevelt,* 1: 306.

to win over enough votes to save the speaker.[10] But it was all in vain. In spite of everything the speaker could do the coalition remained firm and in the majority.

In the meantime the battle raged in the House. Cannon was virtually driven out of the chair by the thunderous yells of the Democratic minority of "Rule! rule! rule!!" Tempers grew hot as it was charged that the organization was making no attempt to bring recalcitrant members in to make up a quorum. A motion was made to elect a new sergeant at arms, and when Dalzell, spelling the tired speaker in the chair, ruled the motion out of order, he was in turn overruled from the floor. The new officials were immediately given warrants to bring in the missing Republican members, and that night many Republican congressmen, along with Nicholas Longworth, were arrested in their beds and unceremoniously hauled to the House. As the night dragged on, ragged nerves gave way, and violent imprecations were hurled across the aisles of the House, only to be drowned in the piercing scream of the rebel yell from joyous Democrats.[11]

Throughout the next day the fight continued, punctuated with numerous but abortive conferences between Republican progressives and Regulars. At four o'clock on Friday afternoon, after the House had been in session continuously for thirty-six hours, Cannon announced that he was ready to rule on the point of order. But the legislators, weary from their long vigil, saw fit then to adjourn the body until the next day. When the House reconvened the galleries were jammed with spectators anxious to view the end of one of the most remarkable legislative battles of the decade. A hush fell over the gallery and floor alike as the speaker took the chair. In a few minutes he announced that Dalzell's point of order had been well taken and therefore the Norris resolution could not be considered. An appeal overruling the speaker was quickly

[10] Watson, *As I Knew Them*, 123–124.

[11] *Ibid.*, 125; *Des Moines Register and Leader, Chicago Tribune, New York Times,* and *New York Sun,* March 19, 1910; Clark, *My Quarter Century,* 2: 274; Alice Longworth, *Crowded Hours* (New York, 1933), 174; L. White Busbey, *Uncle Joe Cannon* (New York, 1927), 251.

voted. A motion to lay the matter on the table was beaten, and the Norris resolution to change the rules of the House was adopted 191 to 156 with forty-six insurgent Republicans shouting their approval as the tally clerks indicated that the rebellion had ended with a revolution.[12] As the last episode of the struggle the speaker, slightly pale but otherwise calm, mounted the rostrum to make a statement. With an un-wavering voice Cannon told the House that only two courses were open to him and that, since he did not choose to resign, he would entertain a motion for his dismissal. Congressman Burleson of Texas made the motion. But when it was put to a vote, enough insurgents rejoined their party to save the speaker his office and what remained of his prestige.[13]

As the jubilant shouts of the victors filled the Washington air even the president must have viewed the outcome with some satisfaction. For Taft had long since been determined that the speaker should not be re-elected. But if Cannon had lost face with the country, so had the president. Cannon's loss was Taft's loss to the progressive Republicans, who were posi-tive that the president had been supporting Cannon. It was true that Taft had explained his withholding of the patronage on other grounds and that he had refrained from approving the campaign committee's open attacks on progressive sena-tors and congressmen. But it was also true that the president, in a position to command, had done nothing to stop the com-mittee's onslaught. Moreover, Taft had continued to write letters in defense of Cannon and had fraternized with him in public on what appeared to be intimate terms. With his usual lack of political sense, he had chosen this unfortunate time to revive the executive dinner in honor of the speaker —a function his predecessor had carefully avoided.[14]

Throughout January, 1910, the president fairly peppered Congress with suggestions for legislative enactments. Among these was a proposal to amend the Interstate Commerce

---

[12] *Congressional Record,* 61 Congress, 2 Session, vol. 45, pt. 4, p. 3436.
[13] *Ibid.,* 3439.
[14] *Philadelphia North American,* March 4, 1910.

Act, a statehood enabling act for New Mexico and Arizona, several conservation measures, a plan for setting up postal savings banks, and a provision for voluntary federal incorporation of business. The first and last of these suggestions Taft sent to Congress together, but because of conservative opposition to the federal incorporation plan he withdrew it from consideration. Consequently in the next few months Congress was mainly concerned with the regulation of common carriers.

Since the passage of the Hepburn rate bill in 1906 there had developed nation-wide agitation to strengthen the powers of the Interstate Commerce Commission. During the autumn of 1909 Taft himself had proposed that a new commerce court be erected to facilitate the decision of cases arising from rate regulations, that railroads be prohibited from owning stock in competing lines, and that the Interstate Commerce Commission be given full power to regulate the issuance of railroad securities.[15] Meanwhile La Follette was demanding the enactment of his plan for physical evaluation of carriers as a basis for scientific rate-making. And other radical Western leaders were proposing a more stringent long and short haul clause and an amendment to implement the commodities clause in the Hepburn Act, which had been severely weakened by a Supreme Court decision in May, 1909.

Meeting in New York City in September, 1909, by presidential request, a group of six men under the direction of Attorney General Wickersham attempted to draw up a bill for congressional consideration. With an "unusual unanimity of opinion,"[16] Wickersham wrote, the conference succeeded in translating Taft's general suggestions into specific measures, most of which substantially increased the power of the Commission. Immediate objection, however, was raised to the Commerce Court which Taft thought would expedite

[15] *Kansas City Star*, September 20, 1909.
[16] George W. Wickersham to James R. Mann, September 14, 1909, to be found in Mann's *Personal Legislative History* of the Interstate Commerce Act. The history, which is partly in manuscript, is in the Library of Congress.

the settlement of railroad cases. Wickersham's scheme gave the Commerce Court original jurisdiction in entertaining appeals on both law and fact from the decisions of the Interstate Commerce Commission. Appeals could be taken in turn from that court to the Supreme Court only when a constitutional question was involved. And though to the layman's eye the legal distinction between law and fact is almost indistinguishable, opponents of the Commerce Court idea claimed that in practice the scheme would transfer from the Commission to the Court all powers to determine rates and classifications.[17]

Especially throughout the West the Interstate Commerce Commission had won the respect and admiration of the public. That was less true of the courts, at least in railroad decisions. James R. Mann, Regular Republican and chairman of the House Committee on Interstate Commerce, reflected Western sentiment when he wrote Wickersham: "I have helped to defeat this proposition on several occasions and so far have seen no reason to change my opinion."[18] The conference must have been less unanimous than Wickersham had led Mann to believe, for soon chairman Knapp of the Interstate Commerce Commission was likewise criticizing the Commerce Court proposal.[19] When the contents of the bill became more widely known, objections were also raised to the omission of a long and short haul clause and the physical evaluation scheme.

With the proposed legislation in his hand the president invited criticisms of it from many sources. Senator Cummins was seen frequently at the White House, as were Wickersham, Aldrich, and Elkins. But not the least important people coming to the White House were the representatives of the nation's big railroads. Early in November, 1909, the executives of the country's first-class railroads had appointed

[17] Memorandum of George W. Wickersham to James R. Mann, September 14, 1909, in Mann, *Personal Legislative History*.

[18] James R. Mann to George W. Wickersham, October 25, 1909, *ibid*.

[19] *New York Sun*, February 19, 1910.

a committee to work for "safe" legislation. Soon the committee was reporting that the president was amenable to some of their suggestions. The railroad men objected mainly to the provisions in the bill allowing the shipper to choose his route and regulating railroad securities. Apparently, to judge from their correspondence, the rest of the bill was more to their liking. They had full opportunity to go over it carefully, for confidential copies of it had been sent them in advance by Attorney General Wickersham.[20]

Early in January, just before the bill was sent to Congress, the presidents of six major railroads had a final three-hour conference with the president. Afterwards the *New York Sun* told its readers that the president had made concessions and that the attorney general was at work rewriting the measure, modifying some of its more stringent provisions.[21] A few days later the public also read a statement by President Brown of the New York Central railway that the bill "should not alarm the investor nor embarrass any railroad that wants to do business in a straightforward and orderly manner."[22]

These press notices worried progressives. They had objected to some of the president's suggestions before the bill was written and were now fearful that the final draft would be even more unpalatable. Their alarm increased when it became known that Aldrich would support the president's measure. They recalled that the Senate leader had persistently opposed any real advance in railroad regulation from the introduction of the original Interstate Commerce Act of 1887 down through the Hepburn bill. On these grounds progressives were almost solidly predisposed against the measure.

[20] Frank Trumbull to Grenville M. Dodge, November 7, December 3, 1909, Grenville M. Dodge to William Howard Taft, December 22, 1909 (copy), Martin A. Knapp to Frank Trumbull, December 23, 1909, Frank Trumbull to Dodge, April 30, 1909, Wickersham to Dodge, December 30, 1909, Dodge MSS.

[21] *New York Sun*, January 3, 7, 1910. Months later the semi-official railroad journal reported that important concessions were made in the conference to the railroad interests. *Railway Age Gazette*, July 1910, p. 7.

[22] *Philadelphia North American*, January 5, 1910.

The bill introduced into the House as HR7536 was, in the multiplicity of its provisions, almost identical to the bill drawn by the conference in New York City. One important exception dealt with railroad mergers. The first draft of the bill provided that the major railroads must dispose of all their stock holdings in competing lines. As introduced into the House the bill permitted a railroad to purchase a competing line in which it controlled more than fifty per cent of the stock. It also legalized certain mergers of noncompeting companies.

With stricter government regulation, railroad efficiency could undoubtedly have been increased by cooperation and combination without sacrificing public interest. But that conclusion the progressive mind, tinged by the nineteenth-century doctrine of competition, refused to admit. A progressive-Democratic coalition in the House soon struck out all the sections of the bill contrary to the Sherman Law, added clauses providing for physical evaluation and for long and short haul regulation, and defined telephone and telegraph companies as common carriers. The Commerce Court was barely saved when a progressive amendment to strike it out resulted in a tie vote of 140 to 140.[23]

Long before the bill had passed the House a furious skirmish occurred in the Senate committee, where Cummins and Clapp had attempted to append over a hundred amendments to the Wickersham bill. In the face of so much zeal for renovation Aldrich refused to consider any changes at all. The measure was reported out exactly as written by Wickersham with the result that Clapp and Cummins joined the Democrats in a stinging minority report.[24] They argued that the grant of power to the Commerce Court would permanently cripple the Commission and that the abrogation of the Sherman Law would create "numerous vicious monopolies." They charged that the measure was a step backward in rate regulation, thus impugning the good faith of the president. Un-

[23] *Congressional Record*, 61 Congress, 2 Session, vol. 45, pt. 5, p. 5578.
[24] *New York Sun*, March 4, 1909.

doubtedly from the viewpoint of effective regulation some changes were desirable, but the hundred amendments looked suspiciously as if the progressives were judiciously mixing reform and politics.[25]

The president had come to the end of his rope with the progressives. By January he was convinced that the real purpose of the rebels was to wreck his administration and defeat him in 1912. He told Butt that if the party did not come to his point of view he would step down and allow the radicals to "Bryanize" it, but until that time came he would fight them.[26] And as the president moved away from progressive Republicanism he identified himself more completely with Aldrich reaction. In a Lincoln Day address in New York City he echoed Aldrich of the year before by remarking that the tariff bill had materially reduced the custom rates, despite the fact that it had not been "expressly said in the platform that this revision was to be a downward revision." He reiterated, this time advisedly, that the bill had been the best tariff law in the nation's history.[27] A week later, appearing with Aldrich in Rhode Island, Taft effusively praised the Senate leader. The president could have written in all sincerity to Aldrich in March of 1910 what he did a year later: "I long for your presence. I feel about as Scott said of Rhoderick Dhu—a blast upon your bugle horn were worth a thousand men."[28]

Now when the progressives were attacking his railroad bill Taft took the final step in a political evolution. He joined the conservatives in a well-planned effort to exterminate progressivism root and branch from the party, and by so doing finally made peace between his professions and his true nature. On March 1 he conferred with Aldrich and Cannon at the White House. The three decided to use the railroad bill

[25] *Chicago Tribune*, March 4, 1910.
[26] Butt, *Taft and Roosevelt*, 1: 272. To standpat Senator Carter the progressives by this time were nothing short of "crooks." Thomas H. Carter to Samuel Gordon, February 7, 1910, Carter MSS.
[27] *New York Sun*, February 13, 1910.
[28] Taft to Aldrich, January 29, 1911, in Stephenson, *Aldrich*, 385.

exactly as it had been drawn up as a final test of party regularity. It was agreed that the measure should be passed without amendment and that anyone who opposed it should be treated as an enemy of the party.[29]

A week later the president drove to Aldrich's home to discuss the strategy of the coming struggle. He told Aldrich that he had been in conference with the conservative leaders of Iowa and that they had promised to defeat Dolliver and Cummins if they were assured of financial and patronage support. Both Taft and Aldrich agreed to start the standpat fund by personal contributions. The rest could be raised, Aldrich promised, by private subscriptions from his friends. Simultaneously the plan called for an estoppage of progressive patronage and for sending out into the prairie country a battery of standpat evangelists to wrestle with all the districts "possessed of the progressive devil."[30]

When the news of the standpat campaign seeped through the country, progressive tempers grew hot. Taft was bluntly warned to keep the "Cannon-Aldrich crowd" out of the Middle West if he was interested in Republican success in the autumn elections. Prairie newspapers invited the president to come ahead with his "standpat crew." "Kansas is mighty keen for a war of that kind," Rooseveltian William Rockhill Nelson grimly wrote in his *Kansas City Star*.[31] In the Senate Cummins of Iowa opened up on the railroad bill with a four-day tirade that spared neither the bill nor the president. And for two solid weeks thereafter every oratorical fuse in the Senate chamber was set off in attack and defense, in which accusations and name-calling substituted for statesmanship.

In the end, however, it became apparent that amendments would have to be made. Many Regular Republican senators told Aldrich that they would not dare in an election year to vote for the bill as it stood. Lodge wrote to Roosevelt that the Wickersham version "did not sufficiently enlarge the

[29] *New York Sun*, March 2, 1910; *Des Moines Register and Leader*, March 5, 1910.
[30] Butt, *Taft and Roosevelt*, 1: 299–301; *Kansas City Star*, March 8, 1910.
[31] *Ibid.*, March 6, 1910.

powers of the Interstate Commerce Commission. That was admitted by all."[32] And so, to win votes, Aldrich withdrew the bill and Wickersham set to work once more. When it reappeared in the Senate the powers of the Commerce Court had been substantially reduced.

But if the administration had been forced to make concessions it was still capable of issuing ultimatums. On April 9, at the Hamilton Club in Chicago, Attorney General Wickersham gave a last warning to the progressives. "The time of running with the hare and hunting with the hounds is over, and everyone must choose whether or not he is for the President and the Republican party." The Republican members of the Congress must prove their Republicanism or read themselves out of the party "by their actions on the bills in Congress." "By their fruits," the Attorney General ended, "ye shall know them."[33]

"Wickersham's speech," wrote Beveridge, "which voices the real sentiments of the administration, has made things much worse than ever and I haven't the slightest doubt Dolliver isn't going after him horse, foot, dragoons, mounted batteries, and heavy artillery."[34] It was not Dolliver's rapier wit, however, that flashed in the Senate in answer to Wickersham, but La Follette's impassioned, truculent logic. Three days later Battle Bob slowly rose to his feet to speak for the Republicanism of the West. Characterizing the railroad bill as a "mask" behind which lurked "unknown and unnumbered villainies," La Follette went on to pay his respects to its author as the arbiter of who was and was not a Republican. The senator then outlined the growth of the New York, New Haven and Hartford Railroad monopoly, revealing a tale of almost unbelievable corruption, and ended by pointing out that Wickersham had ordered the suit against the company to be discontinued just twenty-four hours after the United

[32] Lodge to Roosevelt, April 30, 1910, Roosevelt MSS.
[33] *Milwaukee Sentinel*, April 10, 1910.
[34] Beveridge to Dr. Albert Shaw, April 11, 1910, in Bowers, *Beveridge*, 376.

States district attorney had set the day for the opening of the case.[35] The implication was clear that the president might do well to cease his attacks on the West and examine his own official family.

Immediately after La Follette's speech a progressive-Democratic coalition threatened to rewrite the railroad bill completely. On May 3, when the president was absent from Washington, the coalition cut out all the sections of the bill contrary to the Sherman Law. And as the clauses for the regulation of railroad securities and long and short haul were scheduled next for debate, the outnumbered Regulars were in a state of consternation. Hurried telephone calls were put through for the president, and a party caucus was called. But still no Regular majority could be obtained. Many Stalwarts, in a panic because no "safe legislation" could be assured, were in favor of a quick vote on appropriation bills and adjournment. But the wiser council of Aldrich to stall until the president returned prevailed. Even then the progressives managed to win a partial victory by passing a more stringent long and short haul provision.[36]

With the president back in Washington a determined effort was made to find a majority pledged to pass the legislation without severe modification. Dinners were held at the White House at which Taft tried his persuasive powers on recalcitrant Republicans. Aldrich himself held a conference with some of the more moderate progressives. But all the wheedling was in vain. Borah reported back after the president's "peace dinner" of May 14 that no promises had been made.[37] Temporarily defeated, Aldrich turned to the Democrats. There he found an ally for a price. At the opening of the session Taft had recommended a statehood act for the New

[35] *Congressional Record*, 61 Congress, 2 Session, vol. 45, pt. 5, p. 4561. The senator's charges were subsequently verified. The suit was dropped when Wickersham advised Taft that there was no ground for action. *Report of the Interstate Commerce Commission*, vol. 31 (1914), pp. 34-35; Taft to Norman H. White (copy), April 8, 1912, Roosevelt MSS.

[36] *Des Moines Register and Leader*, May 5, 1910.

[37] *Philadelphia North American*, May 14, 1910.

Mexico and Arizona territories, a measure which the Democratic party heartily supported. Republican Regulars and some progressives were opposed because it would undoubtedly add four more Democratic senators to Congress. An initial effort to compromise on Republican support for the statehood in return for Democratic help with the railroad measure was halted because of Democratic objection to the control of railroad securities. Aldrich, only too pleased at this demand, finally induced Taft to bow to the compromise, and the bargain was sealed.[38]

Against this lineup of Regulars and Democrats there was little hope for progressive amendments. One by one they were voted down, with the one exception that telegraph and telephone companies be defined as common carriers. But so materially had the progressives altered the measure that all of them approved in the final vote on June 3. The Mann-Elkins Act was a real advance in railroad regulation. Whereas under the Hepburn Act the Commission was empowered to annul an act only after a shipper had entered a complaint, it could now examine any schedule or classification on its own initiative, make modifications at its discretion, and forbid a scheduled advance until it approved. Furthermore, the burden of proof to show that the advance was reasonable was put upon the common carrier, not the Commission.[39]

Some of the credit for the legislation undoubtedly belongs to William Howard Taft, but not all, as some historians claim. By their activity the progressives had eliminated from the bill many reactionary features that Aldrich and his cohorts had slipped into its pages. In addition they had added much to its strength. Their stand on the merger clauses in the light of today seems foolish, but subsequent years bore out to some extent their fears of the Commerce Court. Reduced though its powers were by progressive amendments, the court proved all too friendly to the railroads. When its

[38] Confidential source of information; cf. George E. Mowry, "Theodore Roosevelt and the Progressive Movement," unpublished Ph.D. thesis, 1938, in the Library of the University of Wisconsin.

[39] House Document No. 967, 61 Congress, 2 Session, p. 16.

prestige was lost altogether with the impeachment of one of its judges, it was abolished.[40]

Taft had the unhappy faculty of giving good measures bad names. Early in the special session he had recommended the establishment of federal postal savings banks. This Populist-born proposal had been endorsed by the Republican platform and was popular throughout the country. When the measure was shelved early in the session by the Republican organization, public protest ran high. Six months later, when it was reintroduced into the Senate with renewed presidential blessings and promptly supported by Aldrich, the public was bewildered and quizzical. The progressives in Congress were downright suspicious. They awaited the Trojan horse.

As reported from committee, the bill was with one exception the old Populist measure. It provided for banks in every post office, where the poor and the timid could deposit their small savings in perfect security. It also forbade the banks to pay more than two per cent interest on deposits. A further clause empowered the postal banks to invest their deposits in government bonds. That, to the conservatives, was its *raison d'être*. For in January of 1910 the national banks of the United States held 730 million dollars worth of United States bonds drawing two per cent interest. Upon the basis of these bonds national bank notes were issued in accordance with the National Banking Act of 1863.

In 1910 the Aldrich monetary commission had already determined to propose a central bank of issue for the entire country to replace the old national banking system. But unless some way was found to relieve the national banks of their vast holdings of two per cent bonds, the scheme was doomed. Under the new scheme the two per cent bonds would be practically unnegotiable because of the much higher interest rates on the then current federal issues. Masterfully conceived was the proposal to purchase the bonds with postal savings deposits. The progressives would be forced to sup-

[40] *Cases Brought in the Commerce Court* (Senate Document No. 789, 62 Congress, 2 Session, 1912).

port the bill, the national banks would be happy, and the central bank of issue would no longer be imperiled.[41]

When the bill came up in the Senate for the first time, however, the Borah amendment limiting the investment of postal savings funds was adopted by a progressive-Democratic coalition. And as the amendment forbade investment without a minimum interest return of two and a quarter per cent, the postal savings measure held no further attraction for the Senate leadership. Temporarily it was dropped like a hot potato. Three months later, after some judicious vote-trading the president and Aldrich won support for a compromise measure more to their liking. As finally passed over progressive opposition the bill permitted the investment, at presidential discretion, of thirty per cent of the postal funds in two per cent bonds.[42]

And so the session ran its fiery course, the friction mounting daily between the progressives on the one hand and the president and his conservative supporters on the other. On the bill to limit the use of labor injunctions, the McCall campaign publicity measure, the conservation acts, and the plan to extend the powers of the tariff commission, Republican progressives found themselves opposed by the Regulars supported by the president. By the end of the session, days before Roosevelt came home from Africa, the progressives and Taft had come to the parting of the ways. This was manifest in the tariff commission debates. The tariff commission was one of the president's favorite projects. Throughout the first half of 1910 he was busy urging its passage. Unfortunately in his public remarks he mixed support for the commission with heavy praise for the now bedraggled Payne-Aldrich bill and equally heavy censure of the progressives. In answer, on June 13, Jonathan Dolliver arose to make what proved to be his valedictory speech in the Senate. In many ways it was to be his greatest. Stung by the president's

[41] *Circular of the National City Bank*, July 1910, reprinted in *La Follette's Weekly*, July 8, 1910.

[42] Taft to Carter, June 23, 1910, Boies Penrose to Carter, April 21, 1910, Carter to Mrs. Carter, June 19, 1910, Carter MSS.

remarks and his patronage activities in the primaries, Dolliver pulled few punches. Significant for its rolling eloquence,
the speech was a portent of just how far apart the two wings
of the once compact Republican party had drifted.

He spoke, Dolliver said, in defense of the little group of
men impeached "for the offense of taking the President's
campaign speeches seriously, and for the still higher crime of
regarding the platform of the Republican party as a binding
moral obligation." It was a very disagreeable but necessary
duty since the president had so misused the prestige of his
great position. In attempting to carry out Taft's program,
Dolliver exclaimed, the progressives had met nothing but opposition from the White House, acting together with the
"'constructive statesmen' who derided the candidates' opinions when they were uttered in the campaign and laughed out
loud when they were repeated in Senate debates."

If the progressives had made any mistake, Dolliver continued, it was in remaining silent too long "while an organized
defamation of our political characters has been set on foot,
proceeding from the highest public offices of the government . . . and from a so-called campaign committee, presided over by a multi millionaire promoter of street car fran-
chises." The progressives could never be pushed out of the
Republican party by such lying vilification, Dolliver asserted,
and "least of all" by removing from their necks the millstone
of political patronage *through which even presidents of the
United States have more than once been drowned*[43] in the
middle of the political sea.

The senator from Iowa then paid his respects to the tariff.
The bill itself he described as "brutal and sordid" and Taft's
defense of it at Winona as "grotesque." "Last year witnessed
two important hoaxes," he said, "the discovery of the North
Pole by Mr. Cook and the revision of the tariff downward by
Senator Aldrich." After the laughter had died down he went
on to observe that executive felicitations had been tendered
upon both events. With a few more remarks about the trust

[43] Italics mine.

problem Dolliver ended his manifesto of rebellion as wild cheering broke out in the galleries.[44] The speech had a profound effect upon sentiment in the country, for Dolliver reached an audience that the more radical La Follette was unable to approach. "What La Follette says doesn't seem to hurt . . . but Dolliver's attitude has poisoned a good many against the Republican party," wrote a Republican state politician.[45]

Dolliver was not the only one who was bitter. On the last day of the congressional session the president went as usual to the executive chamber just off the Senate floor to sign the bills passed in the dying minutes of Congress. In that usually happy scene, where it is customary for senators to bid the president goodbye, not one outright progressive appeared. Even Borah, who had once been close to Taft and who was in the room for a few minutes, left without even looking at the head of his party.[46] The rift was obvious.

The progressive opposition to Aldrich and his conservative followers was understandable, but their bitterness and hostility toward the president can be understood only in the light of the strange events taking place in the Republican party. For out on the local hustings the very political lives of the progressive senators and representatives were being threatened from the White House. The president, after his conference with Aldrich early in March concerning the defeat of Dolliver and Cummins, had expanded his base of operations. Word soon came from the White House that an organized campaign would be waged by the administration against all progressives.[47] Proof of this rumor came when the Republican Congressional Campaign Committee began flooding progressive constituencies with sharp attacks on their congressional representatives, advising that such men be defeated in the coming primaries.[48] Still more alarming to progressives was a

[44] *Congressional Record*, 61 Congress, 2 Session, vol. 45, pt. 8, p. 7908.
[45] J. Adam Bede to Carter, March 5, 1910, Carter MSS.
[46] Butt, *Taft and Roosevelt*, 1: 414.
[47] *Philadelphia North American*, March 9, 1910.
[48] Lucius B. Swift to Roosevelt, May 5, 1910, A. B. Cummins to Roose-

current Washington rumor that not only would progressives be militantly opposed in the primaries, but if they won there they would be given no aid against their Democratic rivals in the autumn elections.[49]

It was soon evident to the progressives that many of these rumors were valid. In Washington the campaign committee was busy signing up standpat speakers to invade the Middle West before the primaries. As early as April seven conservative senators and representatives, including Senator Burton of Ohio and Speaker Cannon, announced that they would stump Iowa for the purpose of defending the administration and attacking its progressive detractors.[50] Long before, the president had appointed referees of patronage in the progressive states in place of the senators representing them. He told Secretary MacVeagh that he would help the Republicans of Indiana, but not Beveridge.[51] Meanwhile it was also evident that the great campaign fund which Aldrich had promised to collect was beginning to pour into the Middle West to help the standpatters. Conservative organizations were quickly established in every state with local "Taft Republican" clubs in almost every town and village.[52] Great volumes of printed matter in the interest of standpatism continued to flow from Washington. And every possible means was used to secure the support of the press throughout the insurgent country. In Iowa, where no conservative paper of any consequence existed to challenge the radical *Register and Leader*, particularly great efforts were made to acquire support. James S. Clarkson, former conservative editor of the *Register* and at that time surveyor of the port of New York, was offered a half million dollars by a group of "Iowan and Eastern" men to establish a standpat newspaper in Des Moines. When that

velt, July 7, 1910, Roosevelt MSS.; *Boston Transcript*, April 18, 1910.
   [49] *Washington Times*, March 9, 1910.
   [50] *Des Moines Register and Leader*, April 16, 1910.
   [51] Butt, *Taft and Roosevelt*, 1: 356.
   [52] *Des Moines Register and Leader*, May 3, 1910; F. G. Steele to Thomas H. Carter, April 14, 1910, and Carter to Steele, April 26, 1910, Carter MSS.

offer was declined, another group offered to buy out the *Register and Leader* for him. He refused both these proposals, however, because, as he wrote a friend, he would not contemplate fighting Dolliver, whom he considered as a son.[53]

Goaded almost to fury by the actions of the administration, progressives in private communications changed their cautious criticism of the president to direct accusations of apostasy. Roosevelt soon heard from Dolliver that the policies of his administration would be lost irretrievably "unless a way could be found to overthrow the present management in Congress which is now the guardian of the President's opinions, and to all appearance the keeper of the Executive conscience."[54] A much more eloquent and terse communication from a progressive Republican Indianapolis publisher informed Roosevelt that "Taft is a damn, pig-headed blunderer."[55]

Nor were the radicals much less sharp in their public addresses. Before a progressive rally at Des Moines in early May, Dolliver struck out at the president and his standpat cohorts with equal fury. "The future of the Republican party," he shouted, "lies in the success of the movement, now nation wide, to disown and put aside a leadership which has betrayed the welfare of the party and the country."[56] As for Cummins, he had long before raised the shout to turn the standpat rascals out in the coming primaries. La Follette, Clapp, Bristow, Beveridge, Garfield, Pinchot, Poindexter, Stubbs, and a host of other progressives were saying "amen" in every speech. The liberal press answered the threat by advising their readers to forget party lines. "What inheritance have we in Taft," wrote Henry Wallace, editor of the powerful *Wallace's Farmer*, "or what portion in the President? 'To your tents O Israel.' " The Republican *Philadelphia North*

---

[53] James E. Clarkson to Grenville M. Dodge, September 17, 1909, April 11, 1910, Dodge MSS.

[54] Dolliver to Gifford Pinchot, March 25, 1910, Dolliver MSS. This letter was written to Pinchot, but it was really addressed to Roosevelt. It was written just a few days before Pinchot sailed for Europe.

[55] Lucius B. Swift to Roosevelt, March 4, 1910, Roosevelt MSS.

[56] *Des Moines Register and Leader*, May 12, 1910.

American advised its readers to vote either for liberal Republicans or for Democrats, but at all events to beat the men who had betrayed them, from Dalzell on down, in the Pennsylvania delegation. In opposition to the "Taft Republican" clubs "Progressive Republican" clubs were formed in the Middle West to support the progressive senators and representatives.[57]

With the Republican family thus split into two opposing forces, each bent on defeating the other, the barrage of abuse broke all bounds. The Democrats were quite forgotten. As early as January Joseph B. Foraker returning from Washington noted that the city was full of fight, "but all the fighting talked about was among Republicans. I did not hear of any Republican, from the President down, talking or planning about any fighting with the Democrats." James S. Clarkson, once a director of Republican fortunes in Iowa, was "astonished by the bitterness the two elements show toward each other." The feud even involved the dead. In Iowa the secretary of the Allison Memorial Committee complained loudly that although Dolliver and Cummins contributed, the rest of the progressives in the state almost to a man refused to give anything to the fund for the erection of a statue to the standpat leader of former days.[58]

Meanwhile the first skirmishes between the two forces to secure control of the state conventions were taking place. In Indiana the position of Beveridge was too secure to permit any real opposition to his renomination. So the Stalwart forces concentrated their efforts on getting control of the state Republican convention in order to censure the senator for his recent course in Congress. The business men of the state were rapidly organized by ex-whip James E. Watson and ex-Senator James A. Hemenway to demand an endorse-

[57] Henry Wallace, "What the Middle West Wants," *World's Work*, 20: 12891–12898 (May, 1910); *Philadelphia North American*, April 25, 1910; *Des Moines Register and Leader*, April 15, 1910.

[58] Joseph B. Foraker to James Boyle, January 24, 1910, Foraker MSS.; Thomas H. Carter to H. J. Burleigh, May 3, 1910, Carter MSS.; James S. Clarkson to Grenville M. Dodge, March 16, 1910, and Caroline Y. Smith to Dodge, January 30, 1910, Dodge MSS.

ment in the state convention of both the tariff and the president. By assiduous work the resulting organization managed
to swing many district delegations away from the senator
and under the Taft banner.[59] With the counting of noses,
however, the state convention was found to be safely progressive, and as a result Beveridge was elected temporary chairman. Thus from the keynote speech to the last sentence in
the platform there was not a single mention of the Payne-
Aldrich Act. On the other hand, a prompt revision of the
tariff was demanded, Beveridge's course in the Senate was
commended at length, and the president was endorsed and
was pledged support only "in any efforts to secure the enactment of genuine progressive legislation." Cummins, upon
hearing of the proceedings, jubilantly wrote to Beveridge:
"You have fired a shot that will be heard around the world,
especially on the shores of the Mediterranean."[60]

The mood of the Stalwarts about the matter was far different. "Indiana undoubtedly will go Democratic next fall,"
exclaimed Dalzell when he heard of the standpat rout. "I
hope she will, and then we will have in the Senate a real
Democrat and not a half-baked one like Beveridge."[61] The
president, despite the urgings of Senator Crane and Vice
President Sherman to read Beveridge out of the party, refused to make a statement and called off his scheduled speech
in Indianapolis, where he had intended to deliver a militant
defense of the Payne-Aldrich bill. He did, however, continue
to confer long and often with Beveridge's two most powerful
enemies in the state, Watson and Hemenway, and flew into a
rage when Beveridge himself called at the White House.[62]

But the intra-party battles in Indiana were mild as compared with the warfare that raged in other states of the
Middle West. As early as November, 1909, statements had
come indirectly from the White House that the national

---

[59] Bowers, *Beveridge*, 389–390.
[60] *Des Moines Register and Leader*, April 6, 1910; Cummins to Beveridge,
April 6, 1910, quoted in the *Des Moines Register and Leader*, April 7, 1910.
[61] *New York Sun*, April 7, 1910.
[62] Bowers, *Beveridge*, 377, 383.

leaders of the party, backed by the solid support of Eastern
business men, would endeavor to defeat La Follette in the
Wisconsin primaries.[63] This threat was repeated in the Stalwart press many times during the early spring of 1910. When
S. A. Cook early in April announced his candidacy against
La Follette, the Washington correspondent of the *New York
Tribune* interpreted this as merely the initial step in the
determined fight which would be waged against the radical
senator by a faction that would enjoy the unswerving support
of the White House. Spurred to action, the Stalwart press in
Wisconsin opened upon Senator La Follette with a Billings-
gate campaign that savored more of a tavern brawl than a
political campaign. "Factional rats," "party wreckers,"
"party carrion," and "elephadonks," used to imply the half
Republican and half Democratic qualities of the progressives, were a few examples of the terminology in this exchange
of political felicitations.[64]

The practical work in this effort at party surgery was
started when a group of twenty-five "Taft Republican" leaders, meeting at Milwaukee on May 20, agreed to call a state
Republican "conference" on June 8, 1910. County conferences were scheduled for the first week in June to select members to attend the state meeting. The purposes of the meeting
were clearly stated in the "convention" call: the conference
was to consider ways and means of redefining and purging
Republicanism in the state, an action made necessary by the
perfidy of its representatives in the national legislature, who
were "persistently voting with the Democratic minority in
that body to delay the enactment of Republican measures,
to embarrass the Republican administration, and to defeat
or make difficult the redemption of Republican pledges."[65]

Despite the fact that the meeting was called in defiance of
the regular and legal Republican organization in the state,
the convention received presidential endorsement. The meet-

[63] *Bostoi Transcript*, cited in the *Des Moines Register and Leader*, November 2, 1909.
[64] *Milwaukee Sentinel*, April 19, 1910.
[65] *Ibid.*, May 19, 20, 21, 29, 1910.

ing was opened by Vice-President Sherman, who had travelled all the way from Washington to make the keynote address. In response to a congratulatory telegram Taft himself replied that he was gratified to receive the support of the meeting and asked that his hearty thanks be expressed "to the Wisconsin Republicans assembled in convention."[66]

Never before, perhaps, in all the history of the state, did a Wisconsin political convention so identify itself with predatory reaction as did the meeting in the Milwaukee Auditorium on June 8, 1910. Under a screaming banner demanding death to those traitors who ran for office as Republicans and became Democrats after election, the hosts of Stalwartism were drawn up that afternoon to eliminate from the Republican party the virus of progressivism. This half-dead, half-forgotten spirit of ancient Bourbonism was reawakened by every speech from the platform and by every cheer from twelve hundred delegates. Vice-President Sherman's opening speech set the tone for further oratorical displays. He piously inveighed against the progressives for arraying "class against class and interest against interest," and demanded that such apostles of unrest be unceremoniously ejected from the party ranks. After the vice president the temporary chairman, Michael E. Dillon, continued the attack against these hoisters of the "black flag of politics" who preached "the gospel of pessimism and despair" and to whom "optimism and brotherhood" were strangers. But the Stygian darkness of Bourbonism was left for Levi H. Bancroft to penetrate. Denouncing La Follette and his followers in perfervid paragraphs, this high priest of Stalwartdom branded as "treasonable and revolutionary," unconstitutional and irreligious, the progressive appeals to the passions and prejudices of the masses. For, continued Bancroft, "God's patient poor have made no contribution to world progress." They belong to a class of "political junk" along with the Negro slave and the Russian serf. "Without energy or inspiration they constitute a drag on the wheels of progress." He ended his speech with a solemn warning that if the progressives succeeded in their

[66] *New York Sun*, June 9, 1910; *Milwaukee Sentinel*, June 2, 1910.

attempt to make this dependent class the rulers of society, something worse than revolution would follow.[67] In the reactionary corner of Valhalla, Metternich must have muttered a fervent "amen." To such a class of men did William Howard Taft, the "liberal" friend of Roosevelt, entrust his political fortunes in the spring of 1910.

Before the "convention" adjourned, it set up a permanent organization for the state, including a "State Central" and a "State Executive" Committee. The latter was empowered to call a convention at any time and to do anything it thought necessary to fulfill the purposes of the organization. No endorsement or selection of candidates was made by the convention, but its purpose was plainly stated by one of its officers as an attempt to carry Wisconsin "for Taft and Republicanism over La Follette and Insurgency."[68]

In Iowa, where standpatters were also warring upon the progressives, events followed much the same pattern. After many conferences with the president in Washington,[69] a group of Iowa standpat politicians, led by ex-Congressmen W. P. Hepburn and Colonel Lacey, came home to work day and night to build up an anti-Dolliver-Cummins organization. Immediately after the breakup of a state highway convention in Des Moines, two hundred Stalwart politicians held a second convention to perfect a Taft Republican organization with the four-fold purpose of capturing the state convention in June, of defeating the progressive Republican congressman in the autumn, of defeating the two liberal senators when they again came up for re-election, and of controlling the state delegation to the Republican National Convention in 1912.[70] As a result of the meeting in Des Moines, Taft clubs were established throughout the state and were soon federated into a statewide organization. Paradoxically, as in Wisconsin, the leaders of the movement were men who in 1908 had devoted all their efforts to blocking the

[67] *Ibid.*, June 9, 1910.
[68] *Ibid.*, June 14, 1910.
[69] *New York Sun*, March 6, 1910; *Des Moines Register and Leader*, March 6, 7, 8, 1910.
[70] *Sioux City Journal*, March 10, 1910.

nomination of Taft, the man they were now supporting.

The state's progressive forces began to organize clubs also, and when William Gorst, backed by Cummins and Dolliver, announced that he would run against the Stalwart gubernatorial incumbent, the name Gorst-Dolliver-Cummins Republican Clubs was adopted. The political atmosphere became even more sultry when senatorially backed progressives announced their candidacies against the four remaining standpat congressmen representing the state. On May 10, 1910, at the Des Moines Coliseum, the progressives formally inaugurated their organized effort to encompass the defeat of all standpatters in the state. Taking advantage of a lull in the fight over the railroad bill, both Senators Dolliver and Cummins came home to speak on the same platform in the interests of the progressive candidates and to lash the Payne-Aldrich tariff before a wildly cheering crowd of twelve thousand people.[71]

In answer to the progressive attacks all four standpat congressmen left Washington a month before Congress adjourned to enter the fray. They were shortly followed by Speaker Cannon, Congressman William B. McKinley, chairman of the Republican Campaign Committee, and other exponents of reaction. The president directly threw his weight behind the conservative forces by appointing Lacey and ex-Congressman Hepburn the patronage referees for the state. He even entered the gubernatorial fight by withdrawing the names of two postmasters, after he had sent them to the Senate, who had announced that they would support the progressive Gorst in preference to the standpat incumbent Carroll.[72] He wrote special letters of recommendation for the standpat congressman and sent the secretary of agriculture, Tama Jim Wilson, into his home state on a speech-making tour in defense of the conservatives.[73]

As the time for the primary neared, the whole state of

[71] *Des Moines Register and Leader*, May 11, 1910.

[72] *Ibid.*, April 16, June 17, 1910.

[73] Letters to Dodge from Taft, May 11, 1910, and Walter T. Smith, May 7, 1910, Dodge MSS.; *Sioux City Journal*, May 27, 1910.

Iowa was ablaze with the propaganda of both sides. The conservative newspapers maintained that the single issue at stake was "the endorsement of Cumminsism as opposed to Republicanism." They charged that an "Insurgent" vote was a Democratic vote, and that such a victory would mean business and financial chaos. "A vote for Cummins and Dolliver means less work for the American workingman and lower wages. It means lower prices for farm products and more mortgages on the farm. It means precisely what a vote for Bryan meant in 1908," rang out the *Sioux City Journal*. In exchange the progressive Republican papers thoroughly castigated the state's standpat Republican congressmen for serving as the tools of Aldrich and Cannon. They charged the president with being the creator of "party anarchy" and suggested that the progressives follow the president's example and refuse to support all Regular Republicans nominated in the autumn election. The *Cedar Rapids Gazette* even went further: it predicted that Taft in inviting a fight to the finish with the progressives would get both, the fight and the finish.[74]

The results of the Iowa Republican primaries held on June 8, following hard on the reversal in the Indiana convention, constituted another severe defeat for Taft and his standpat allies. Full returns revealed that all the progressive congressional incumbents had been victorious, that two of the four Stalwart incumbents, including John T. Hull, a congressional veteran of twenty years, had been retired, and that although the conservative governor had beaten the progressive candidate by a handful of votes, Dolliver and Cummins had retained their control of the state by capturing a sizeable majority of the delegates for the coming state convention.[75] Altogether progressivism had won a stirring victory and had occasioned the man in the White House still another headache.

[74] *Ibid.*, May 12, 27, 1910; *Cedar Rapids Gazette*, cited in *Des Moines Register and Leader*, March 18, 1910.
[75] *Des Moines Register and Leader*, June 10, 1910.

The two sharp reversals in Indiana and Iowa, however, gave the president little pause in his campaign, which seemed more foolhardy with each passing day of the summer. Using the power and patronage of his office and the great campaign fund that Aldrich collected, Taft and the Republican Congressional Campaign Committee continued to wage merciless war on progressivism. In Kansas the progressives, led by Governor Stubbs, Senator Bristow, William Allen White of Emporia, Henry Allen, Congressmen Victor Murdock and Edmond H. Madison, were confronted with the same forces as were Cummins and Dolliver in Iowa. At the head of this opposition were D. W. Mulvane, national committeeman, Senator Curtis, later to be vice-president, and Thomas Wagstaff, candidate for governor against Stubbs. Supplied with money from Aldrich's corporation slush fund and with federal patronage, they formed the customary "Taft Republican" organization and raised the cry over the Kansas prairies of "Death to Progressives."[76] And as the president battled in Kansas against progressivism, so he did in Ohio against James R. Garfield, in Washington against Miles Poindexter, in New Jersey, in Nebraska, and in the Dakotas.

About the middle of May, 1910, the American people were tremendously agitated by the approach of two great forces to the continent of North America. The first of these was the return of Haley's comet. As this cosmic wanderer came nearer the earth, excitement became mass hysteria. Comet pills were sold on the streets of New York to ward off the effects of the evil cosmic genius, thousands of miners in the hard-coal fields in Pennsylvania refused to go to work on what they believed to be the last day of their earthly lives, two men committed suicide in the city of Milwaukee, and an Iowa farmer took his family, livestock, and personal goods into a cave.[77]

The other event that excited popular imagination was the return of Theodore Roosevelt from his long holiday spent in

[76] *Kansas City Star*, March 21, April 24, June 19, 24, 1910.
[77] *New York Sun*, May 19, 1910; *Milwaukee Sentinel*, May 19, 1910; *Des Moines Register and Leader*, May 13, 1910.

BACK IN THE OLD PLACE
Cartoon by Harding in the *Brooklyn Eagle*, reproduced in the
Literary Digest, April 9, 1910.

cutting a tumultuous swath through the depths of the
African jungle and the royal and diplomatic society of
Europe. A feverish welcome was being prepared. The name
of Roosevelt had never left the front pages of the papers,
even after he had disappeared into the heart of the jungle.
And as the split between Taft and most of the rest of Roosevelt's friends in the country grew wider, the name of the
ex-president loomed up even larger from newspaper and
periodical type. For the question on every Republican's lips
during the spring days of 1910 was which side Roosevelt
would espouse in the civil war. Claims were made on both
sides,[78] telegrams flew around the country with predictions,

[78] Bonaparte to Count Molke Huitfeldt, February 7, 1910, Bonaparte
MSS.; Thomas H. Carter to O. M. Lanstrum, April 26, 1910, Carter MSS.;
Kansas City Star, March 9, 1910; *Milwaukee Sentinel*, May 25, 1910; *Sioux
City Journal*, May 29, 1910.

and long ex-cathedra articles appeared describing what pur-
ported to be the exact state of the Roosevelt mind. Roosevelt himself had said very little, and he had promised close
friends that he would make no public statement until he had
studied the situation thoroughly.[79] Despite his silence, however, the progressives were positive that he would champion
their side of the quarrel.

In February the *Chicago Tribune* published the results of a
poll of all Republican editors west of the Alleghenies asking
for whom they would cast their vote if a presidential election
were to be held the next day. The *Tribune* was not surprised
to find that Roosevelt led Taft by three hundred votes. This
mood to desert Taft for Roosevelt was manifest in the public
pronouncements of many leading Republicans. In April Congressman Miles Poindexter declared to an audience in New
York City that the only way to keep the country out of the
hands of thieves in 1912 was to elect Roosevelt. This point-
blank notice of opposition to President Taft was followed by
similar ones from William Allen White, Henry Allen, and
other lesser lights in the official Republican galaxy.[80]

Early in June, just before Roosevelt's return, the country
was electrified by a meeting of the Roosevelt Club of St.
Paul. At a dinner attended by both Gifford Pinchot and
James R. Garfield, the president of the club drew a round of
loud applause when he predicted the birth of a new third
party with Roosevelt, Pinchot, and Garfield as its leaders.
In their subsequent addresses neither Pinchot nor Garfield
denied or doubted the prescience of the statement. The liberal Republican press seized upon the suggestion, and many
others were enthusiastic.[81] "Back from Elba" became a progressive watchword.

[79] Roosevelt to Lodge, March 1, 1910, and to John Hays Hammond,
May 11, 1910, Roosevelt MSS.
[80] *Chicago Tribune,* February 14, 1910; *Philadelphia North American,*
April 18, 1910.
[81] *Milwaukee Sentinel, Des Moines Register and Leader,* June 12, 1910;
Kansas City Star, June 13, 1910.

These wishes, however, did not take into account the basic strains of Roosevelt's character. Most potent, perhaps, of the inner wellsprings of Roosevelt's overt actions were his vaulting ambition, his dislike and fear of defeat, and a curious pride in what he deemed his own infallibility. Certainly, political realist that he was Roosevelt in 1910 could have seen little hope of ultimate victory for a new third party that must battle against the tremendous odds of the two old parties' power, wealth, and organization. To establish a third party would also be tantamount to making a public confession that he had been wrong in his selection of Taft as successor. That in itself would be extremely distasteful. Moreover, it would probably assure Democratic success in the next presidential election, and to the normal Roosevelt way of thinking even a reactionary Republican of the deepest hue was an infinitely better citizen than the best of Democrats. All these things, together with the fact that several of his closest friends, including Lodge, Root, and Longworth, were standing solidly with Taft, would militate against his formation of a liberal third party. It would have been much more logical to suppose that after his return he would devote his efforts to bridging the chasm that existed in the party. Had he not done that in the old days? And could he not do it again?

But such an attempt to heal the widening fault in the Republican party was foredoomed even if essayed by the political genius of Roosevelt. It was an attempt to reconcile the irreconcilable, to pluck fruit from cactus, and squeeze blood from the turnip. The wounds incurred in the raging battle on the prairies were too deep to be healed by the salve of mutual conciliation, however skillful the physician who applied it. For the invisible bands that had held the Republican party together in the past were parting one by one. The old common prophecies were exciting no enthusiasm. The old common battle cries were falling on deaf ears. A new political order was seeking to establish itself upon the grave of the old.

CHAPTER FIVE

Compromise and Disaster

IF THERE IS TO BE a great crowd, do arrange so that the whole crowd has a chance to see me and that there is as little disappointment as possible," wrote Theodore Roosevelt to the friend who in the spring of 1910 was directing the plans for his welcome.[1] On the heels of this characteristic bit of self-extollment the ex-president came home on June 18, 1910, amid the thunder from the naval guns of New York harbor. From the Battery up through the city thousands of the faithful lined the streets to greet him and the inevitable Rough Riders.

While the masses were shouting, the politicians were narrowly watching the returning wanderer in the hope of resolving some of the perplexing questions that had been troubling them. The Sphinx-like silence Roosevelt had maintained since emerging at Khartum had kept them in ignorance of his political leanings, which would go far to determine the outcome of the Western rebellion. Each of his actions was therefore judiciously diagnosed for a possible suggestion of future intentions. It was carefully noted, with much accompanying speculation, that Roosevelt's first act after meeting the official welcoming committee was to single out Gifford Pinchot with a cheery "Hello Gifford."[2] This, together with the fact that he did not accept the president's invitation to visit him at the White House, convinced many that Colonel Roosevelt was thoroughly impatient with William Howard Taft.

As a matter of record, Roosevelt did come home from

[1] Roosevelt to William Loeb, April 21, 1910, Roosevelt MSS.
[2] *Milwaukee Sentinel*, June 19, 1910.

Europe personally estranged from his onetime friend. This coolness was born not of a single incident but of a series of events. One of the first differences between the two men arose over Taft's selection of his Cabinet.[3] There is every reason to believe that the Colonel was piqued when the president appointed successors to James R. Garfield, Luke Wright, and Henry White after telling him that he would retain the trio. Roosevelt wrote to Henry White that Taft had told both Lodge and him that he intended to keep White. "It was not a promise, but it was an unqualified declaration of intention."[4] Later when the dismissal came, Roosevelt wrote a letter from the depths of Africa which showed unmistakable signs of vexation. Soon he was telling his close friends that Taft had dismissed White because of a trivial incident between the two men years before in London.[5] Taft at least thought that it was because he had replaced the three men that Roosevelt did not write him while he was in Africa and did not acknowledge his farewell present. Roosevelt's Attorney General Bonaparte, while later speculating to a friend about the estrangement, also intimated that the rift started when Taft was deciding upon his Cabinet after the election.[6]

Matters of a far more personal nature fostered this initial ill feeling. Mrs. Taft, ambitious for her husband and perhaps resentful of the tag "made in Oyster Bay," was deeply suspicious of Roosevelt and constantly encouraged her husband

[3] Roosevelt's most recent biographer states that Taft's actions in choosing his own Cabinet and in refusing to continue Henry White as ambassador to France were not issues between the two men until Roosevelt seized upon them later as a rationalization of his anger. Pringle, *Roosevelt*, 525.

[4] April 9, 1909, cited in Allan Nevins, *Henry White* (New York, 1930), 299; Stoddard, *As I Knew Them*, 385.

[5] Roosevelt to Henry White, July 21, 1909, in Nevins, *White*, 298; Arthur Lee to Roosevelt, July 7, 1910, Roosevelt to George Trevelyan, October 1, 1911, Oscar S. Straus to Roosevelt, March 13, 1909, Roosevelt MSS.; Oscar S. Straus, *Under Four Administrations* (New York, 1922), 263–264; Watson, *As I Knew Them*, 131; Laurence F. Abbott, *Impressions of Theodore Roosevelt* (New York, 1919), 67; Butt, *Taft and Roosevelt*, 1:285.

[6] Charles J. Bonaparte to H. C. Gauss, March 19, 1912, Bonaparte MSS.

to take a course independent of his predecessor's. Predisposed to regard as inevitable a break between the two men, she was apparently willing to believe the wildest rumors circulating about Washington of Roosevelt's desires to regain the presidency. Feeling so, it may have been that she went out of her way in a feminine fashion to show the women of the Roosevelt family that she, at any rate, did not need to turn her face toward Sagamore Hill. It is also probable that Alice Roosevelt, with her talent for bitter speech, did little to smooth the relations between the feminine members of the two households.

In any event, Roosevelt, after he left the country, was incensed by stories from various sources that the members of his family were being treated rather cavalierly by the mis-

THE MEETING

Cartoon by Johnson in the *Philadelphia North American*, reproduced in the *Literary Digest*, July 16, 1910.

tress of the White House. None of his letters dealing with the matter have been kept, but two in reply to his complaints, written by Lodge and Nicholas Longworth, his son-in-law, give some clue to the state of his feelings. Lodge wrote that both he and Longworth had been "hurt and galled by the attitude of the White House toward Edith and Ethel, of which you speak." But he went on to state that the president was entirely unconscious of those things. They came, Lodge said, from the source that had been the cause of many mistakes.[7] Longworth, writing at greater length, said he did not believe the president's personal feelings about his onetime chief had changed a whit, that whatever appearance of change there was should be attributed to other sources. The colored gentleman in the wood-pile was not a gentleman at all, Longworth wrote, "but is Mrs. T."[8] For Roosevelt, however, it was difficult to distinguish between the actions of the president and those of Mrs. Taft, and these slights, real or fancied, undoubtedly colored considerably his thoughts about the man he had left in charge back in Washington.

Charles Taft, the president's half brother, also contributed to the growing coolness between the two men. For while Roosevelt was abroad he had received clippings from Charles Taft's papers which were anything but friendly. One of these Lodge branded as "infamous," having only the merit "of relieving us of any possible obligation."[9] Subsequently Roosevelt referred on numerous occasions to the part played by the president's wife and brother, who, he thought, had made the president jealous of him "and anxious to emphasize the contrast between our administrations."[10]

All these complexities naturally affected Roosevelt's appraisal of the Taft administration. Perhaps it was significant that his first sharp criticisms of Taft appeared at about the

[7] Lodge to Roosevelt, April 25, 1910, Roosevelt MSS.
[8] Longworth to Roosevelt, April 27, 1910, Roosevelt MSS.
[9] Lodge to Roosevelt, April 25, 1910, Roosevelt MSS.
[10] Roosevelt to Gifford Pinchot, June 28, 1910, to Lodge, July 20, 1910, to Cecil Spring Rice, August 22, 1911, and to Longworth, July 22, 1910, Roosevelt MSS.

time he was complaining about the actions of the president's wife and brother.

Kept informed of the boilings of the political pot by Lodge's adroitly written letters, Roosevelt was not at all surprised at the outcome of the 1909 tariff battle. He thought that the administration had "come out as well as we could hope on the tariff question" and even conjectured that the tax on corporations was "the best way out on the income tax business."[11] So at the end of 1909 he was apparently as satisfied as a Roosevelt could be with the shaping of political things in the United States.

Apparently, too, he continued to be satisfied for some months thereafter. Then came the first slight change. In January he wrote that he thought the actions of the Guggenheim people in Alaska indefensible "unless we are willing to condone every species of violation of law."[12] When he first heard that Gifford Pinchot had been dismissed he could not believe it, and later, after some consideration, he wrote Lodge that perhaps it had been impossible for Taft to take any other route, but he was nevertheless sorry that it had happened. On March 4 he wrote Lodge that they would probably have to renominate Taft and fight the campaign on his administration, implying that he would himself actively enlist in the battle. He added, however, that he knew nothing of the situation; but from the scant evidence at hand, his own candidacy did not seem wise.[13]

Presently, though, Roosevelt began to hear from others besides Lodge.[14] And as the progressive chorus of disapproval began to burst in upon his ears, he began to take issue with some of Lodge's statements. By April 6 he was writing that the tariff issue had not been met as it should have been, that

[11] Roosevelt to Lodge, September 10, 1909, July 26, 1909, in Lodge, *Correspondence*, 2: 342, 345.
[12] Roosevelt to W. D. Hulbert, January (?), 1910, Roosevelt MSS.
[13] Roosevelt to Lodge, March 4, 1910, in Lodge, *Correspondence*, 2: 362.
[14] Letters to Roosevelt from Lucius B. Swift, March 4, 1910, and L. E. Thompson, March 17, 1910, Roosevelt to Frank B. Kellogg, March 10, 1910, Roosevelt MSS.

things which ought to have been done had been left undone, and that the whole had been handled in a way that "caused trouble."[15] In the same letter he indicated that he was disregarding Lodge's advice not to grant Pinchot's request for an interview; he had written Pinchot that he would be "delighted" to see him.

Roosevelt met Pinchot in a woods near Porto Maurizio, where the two talked for a couple of hours. After that Roosevelt never felt the same again about the Taft administration. Exactly what the two men said will probably never be recorded, but Pinchot had not gone to Europe unarmed. With him he had taken a sheaf of letters written by some of Roosevelt's closest friends, including Albert J. Beveridge, Jonathan P. Dolliver, and William Allen White. Having been prepared for the specific purpose of acquainting the ex-president with the true state of affairs at home, the letters fairly bristled with acrid comment. They also contained a carefully prepared bill of particulars against the Taft regime. Beveridge asserted that the tariff law was "just plain dishonest," Dolliver that the president had taken "the certificate of character which Mr. Roosevelt had given him and turned it over to the Senator from Rhode Island." All agreed that because of the "recent reaction" the re-election of either President Taft or a Republican Congress was impossible.[16]

That the Porto Maurizio conference had a positive influence on Roosevelt is fairly obvious. On the same day he wrote a long letter to Lodge which revealed just how he felt about the Taft administration and the political situation in general. The senator from Massachusetts was now urging Roosevelt to save the party from defeat by supporting the Taft administration wholeheartedly or becoming a candidate himself in 1912.[17] Roosevelt testily replied that since the administration had "completely twisted around the policies I

[15] Roosevelt to Lodge, April 6, 1910, in Lodge, *Correspondence*, 2: 365.
[16] Letters to Gifford Pinchot from Dolliver, March 25, 1910, and Beveridge, March 24, 1910, W. B. Colver to Thomas R. Shipp, March 25, 1910, Roosevelt MSS.
[17] Lodge to Roosevelt, April 4, 5, 1910, Roosevelt MSS.

advocated and acted upon" such a course was impossible. He charged Taft with blindly following Aldrich and Cannon in a course that had alienated the friends of his policies, as well as most of the country. In a postscript he added that having done his part he emphatically desired that he should not be put into the position of having to run for the presidency, "staggering under a load which I cannot carry, and which has been put upon my shoulders through no fault of my own." The movement in the West, he maintained, had come about because of the "totally unfit" leadership of the "Cabinet of lawyers" surrounding the president. "I might be able to *guide* this movement, but I should be wholly unable to *stop* it, even if I were to try."[18]

From that day on every mail brought its sheaf of letters from complaining progressives. Common to all was the accusation that Taft had abandoned the ways of his predecessor and thus had caused a hopeless split in the party.[19] Roosevelt came home thoroughly convinced that Taft, though sincere, had permitted reactionary forces to lead him into a position that had inevitably occasioned the revolt of the progressive faction. Conferences with progressive leaders sustained that judgment. A fortnight after his arrival he stated categorically in a letter to Longworth that the original Taft-Wickersham railroad bill was "indefensible," that if it had been passed as originally drawn up, it would have "irretrievably" wrecked the Republican party, that the Ballinger people had tried to check his policies completely, and that the thing for the administration to do was to "completely alter its course of procedure." Roosevelt was convinced that Taft had consciously tried to be a success "by acting in as strong a contrast as possible."[20]

Meanwhile the warfare within the party continued. Throughout the Middle West, in Wisconsin, the Dakotas,

[18] Roosevelt to Lodge, April 11, 1910, in Lodge, *Correspondence*, 2: 367–374.

[19] Letters to Roosevelt from W. R. Nelson, April 7, 1910, Pearl Wight, April 30, 1910, and William D. Foulke, May 17, 1910, Roosevelt MSS.

[20] Roosevelt to Longworth, July 11, 1910, Roosevelt MSS.

Iowa, Nebraska, Kansas, Illinois, Indiana, and Ohio, on the west coast in California and Washington, and in the East in New Hampshire, Pennsylvania, and New York the two factions fought each other with increasing bitterness. Before the state primaries Regular and progressive orators harangued from every stump. In Wisconsin alone within the space of seven days Jonathan P. Dolliver, Albert B. Cummins, Moses E. Clapp, Joseph L. Bristow, William E. Borah, Gifford Pinchot, James R. Garfield, Judge Ben Lindsey, Francis J. Heney, and Congressman George W. Norris of Nebraska delivered a hundred and eighty speeches in support of Senator La Follette and progressive congressmen.[21]

As the struggle neared its culmination, name-calling was indulged in freely. Cannon, McKinley, Sherman, and Ballinger branded the progressives as traitors, socialists, populists, and anarchists.[22] In one speech John Hays Hammond, president of the National League of Republican Clubs, called them "calamity Howlers," "Simon pure socialistic demagogues," "unintelligent intellectuals," and "unctuous rectitudists."[23] Regular orators lost no opportunity to depict the progressives as something other than Republican, and in their vocabulary "Elephadonk" became synonymous with "progressive." The progressives in turn flung dead cat for dead cat. Lodge vigorously protested to Roosevelt that Senator Cummins had perverted the truth when he called him "a slave of the steel trust."[24] Aldrich was even more roughly handled by the "prophets of discord." Senator Bristow openly charged the leader of the Senate with being dishonest. "Whether or not Senator Aldrich is guilty of a technical violation of the statutes I do not know," he said in a speech at Topeka, Kansas. "But I do know that he is guilty of violation of political decency, of political honesty." Bristow

---

[21] *La Follette's Weekly*, September 17, 1910; Lincoln Steffens to James B. Dill, April 8, 1910, *Letters of Lincoln Steffens*, I: 241.

[22] *New York Sun*, July 7, 1910; Martin J. Hutchens to Thomas H. Carter, June 28, 1910, Carter MSS.

[23] *Kansas City Star*, August 21, 1910.

[24] Lodge to Roosevelt, August 4, 1910, Roosevelt MSS.

finished the speech by accusing Aldrich of boosting the tariff on rubber to increase his personal fortune invested in that industry.[25] The president himself, constantly supporting the Regulars, was not above the reproach of the progressives. As a matter of political strategy they made few public attacks upon him, but private letters furnish an accurate barometer of rising anger against him. "It is needless to tell you that the hostility to Taft in the Middle West is fierce and is becoming fiercer," wrote one standpat journalist.[26]

For Taft the summer was one long list of political reverses. As the returns of one primary followed another it became increasingly clear that the country, for the most part, rejected the Republicanism of Aldrich, Cannon, and Ballinger. In the Iowa state convention, controlled by Dolliver and Cummins, an attempt to endorse Taft for 1912 was met with a roar of boos and catcalls, and was voted down by a majority of 244 votes.[27] A short time later when a huge picture of Theodore Roosevelt was lowered over the platform a wave of applause swept over the delegates. The platform was an out-and-out declaration of progressive doctrines. It refused to recognize the Payne-Aldrich tariff "as a satisfactory fulfillment of the party promises." Time and time again, by contrast, it referred to the policies of Theodore Roosevelt. It endorsed only "such efforts as President Taft and his advisers have made to fulfill the promises of the national platform."[28]

Almost at the same time that the Republican state convention of Iowa was damning Taft with faint praise the Kansas Republican primaries again exhibited the temper of the West. Four of the six remaining standpat congressmen fell before progressive foes, and the radical Stubbs was once again renominated over an opposition candidate backed by

[25] *Des Moines Register and Leader,* July 19, 1910.

[26] *La Follette's Weekly,* August 13, 1910; Dolliver to Chester H. Rowell, July 16, 1910, Dolliver MSS.; Cummins to Roosevelt, July 7, 1910, Roosevelt MSS.; Martin J. Hutchens to Thomas H. Carter, July 26, 1910, Carter MSS.

[27] *Des Moines Register and Leader,* August 4, 1910; *Milwaukee Sentinel,* August 4, 1910.

[28] *Iowa Official Register* (Des Moines, Iowa., 1910), 345–347.

the congressional Campaign Committee, Senator Curtis, and President Taft. And as every Regular congressman had campaigned on the issue that a vote for a progressive was a vote against Taft, the president's prestige declined still further.[29]

These progressive victories in the Middle West were soon followed by a smashing administration defeat in California. Backed by the Lincoln-Roosevelt Republican League, Hiram Johnson, who had declared that he went for his Republicanism to Wisconsin and Iowa and not to Washington,[30] was nominated for governor on the Republican ticket. In the backwash of this revolution that temporarily destroyed the power of the Southern Pacific Railroad in the state, three standpat congressmen were defeated by progressives, and the nomination for the senatorial election went to John D. Works, an ardent prophet of the new day.[31]

But by far the greatest progressive victories occurred in September. On a single day the dismal returns coming into the White House indicated that Robert La Follette had again carried Wisconsin by an overwhelming majority, that in New Hampshire young Robert Bass had smashed the Regular forces supported for years by the Boston and Maine Railroad, and that standpat Senator Burrows had been unsuccessful in his fight for renomination in Michigan. As an anticlimax Congressman Miles K. Poindexter, a leader of the House insurgents, was nominated a week later for the senatorial race in Washington.[32]

This series of progressive triumphs damaged the president's prestige, for in each contest except the Townsend-Burrows race in Michigan, Taft had strongly supported the Regular clan. He had used the patronage in New Hampshire and in Washington as he had in Wisconsin.[33] He spoke of the Washington defeat as a personal "body blow," and

[29] *Kansas City Star*, August 1, 2, 3, 1910.
[30] *Nation*, 91: 49 (July 21, 1910).
[31] *Ibid.*, 91: 156 (August 25, 1910).
[32] *New York Sun*, September 14, 1910.
[33] Henry C. Lodge to Roosevelt, September 3, 1910, Roosevelt MSS.; Butt, *Taft and Roosevelt*, 2: 513.

even regarded Maine's action in returning the first Democrat in forty years to the Senate as less of an administration defeat than the results in Wisconsin and Washington.[34]

As the battle of the primaries came to an end progressive leaders had every right to be jubilant. They had carried a successful fight to their Regular opponents throughout the country west of the Mississippi. They had even made important gains in the more hostile territory to the east. When all was over, by the end of September, forty-one Republican incumbent congressmen had been defeated, of whom only one, Congressman Fowler of New Jersey, was classified as an insurgent. Most of them, including such organization leaders as Boutell and Lowden of Illinois, McKinley of California, and James A. Tawney of Minnesota, had been defeated by avowed progressives. In the senatorial nomination all the progressive incumbents had been victorious, and in Washington, California, and North Dakota new progressive names were to appear on the senatorial ballot. The only severe progressive losses throughout the entire summer were the defeat of James R. Garfield, who had announced himself as a "Progressive Republican" candidate for governor in Ohio and the unexpected death of Senator Dolliver in October.[35]

Meanwhile Theodore Roosevelt had finally decided upon a course of action. Even before his return he was indisputably at odds with Taft personally and with his policy; and since then his many conferences with party leaders of all shades of opinion had removed his last doubt that Taft had deviated from the course he had tacitly promised to follow. Conceding that Taft had "meant to act with full regard for the interest of the people," he was nevertheless convinced that the president had been captured by the skillful blandishments of Aldrich and Cannon.[36]

But what infuriated Roosevelt most was not that Taft was holding hands with Aldrich and Cannon rather than with

[34] *Ibid.*, 2: 513.
[35] *Kansas City Star*, October 16, 1910.
[36] Roosevelt to W. S. Cowles, July 28, 1910, Roosevelt to Sidney Brooks, October 17, 1910, Roosevelt MSS.

Dolliver and Beveridge, but that in so doing he had split the Republican party to a point where its success in the coming elections was gravely imperiled. Roosevelt's boundless contempt for the Democratic party unconsciously made him antagonistic to anything that might enfeeble Republicanism and thus enhance the possibility of a Democratic victory. Then too he was supremely proud of the fact that he had, seemingly through his own efforts, left the party in what had appeared to be an impregnable position. Now when he saw it in shambles, an artist's pride in his own creation was touched, and a sense of irritation grew against the man who, he reasoned, had destroyed it. In his letter to Lodge from Porto Maurizio he complained bitterly of the "hapless" condition of the party, spoke often and at length of possible disaster ahead, and castigated a leadership that had followed the desires of ten per cent of the party only to alienate the remaining ninety per cent.[37] He reverted to this theme many times in the next few months. In July he wrote Nicholas Longworth that the president had fallen far short in one most important respect, that of maintaining within the party an essential solidarity. "Whether through its fau[lts] or its misfortunes I cannot say, but the administration has certainly wholly failed in keeping the party in substantial un[ity], and what I mind most is that the revolt is not merely among political leaders, but among the masses of the people. I am n[ot] prepared to say that the masses of the people are insurgent, b[ut] very large fractions of them are; and the Insurgent leaders represent not themselves but those big aggregations of voting units behind them."[38] Roosevelt was condemning his successor not for being a conservative but rather for not being a politician.

Distraught as he was over the state of the party, Roosevelt determined to devote the summer to bringing the two wings together.[39] He was still annoyed with Taft, but he strove to

[37] Roosevelt to Lodge, April 11, 1910, in Lodge, *Correspondence*, 2: 370.

[38] Roosevelt to Nicholas Longworth, July 11, 1910, Roosevelt MSS.

[39] Two years afterward Charles J. Bonaparte believed that Roosevelt in the summer of 1910 was trying "to rehabilitate the Taft administration

soften the animosities of the past and unite the party for future action. He refused consistently, in the face of extreme pressure from both sides, to endorse publicly either the Taft administration or the progressives. For he well knew that either step would automatically vitiate any influence he might have on the other faction. He was in a position of "unconceivable difficulty," he wrote. The ultra-Taft people were bent on having him endorse the administration. Not only would such an endorsement be an "insincerity" but it would destroy his hold on the progressives and therefore deprive him "of all power of helping" the president. On the other hand, the "extremists" were wild to have him break with Taft.[40]

Roosevelt insisted that the newspapers make it known that he was seeing men of all faith, "regulars and insurgents, party men and independents." He made it clear, after repeated calls for help from both sides in the primary fights, that he intended to eschew all factional struggles.[41] When it came to his ears that the progressive Hiram Johnson, struggling in California, would be exceedingly thankful for his support, Roosevelt wrote a letter to his son, then in California, telling him to show it to Johnson and Fremont Older. "I am with the insurgents in this fight," he ended, "but not for publication."[42] Through conferences and letters he argued Gifford Pinchot out of his desire to form a new third party. Roosevelt repeatedly cautioned the volatile Pennsylvanian to speak with more moderation and to say nothing that could be "twisted into something in the nature of a factional attack." He agreed with Pinchot that Taft had disappointed them, but pointed out that it was not only "possible but probable"

by getting control of its policy." Bonaparte to Count Moltke Huitfeldt, December 3, 1912, Bonaparte MSS.

[40] Roosevelt to Lodge, July 19, 1910, in Lodge, *Correspondence*, 2: 385; Roosevelt to Arthur Lee, July 19, 1910, Roosevelt MSS.

[41] *Des Moines Register and Leader*, July 13, 1910; Roosevelt to General J. M. Ashton, July 22, 1910, and to E. F. Waggoner, July 14, 1910, Lodge to Roosevelt, July 5, 1910, Roosevelt MSS.

[42] Roosevelt to Theodore Roosevelt, Jr., August 10, 1910, Roosevelt MSS.

that circumstances would force them to renominate the president two years hence, and it would be "eminently desirable" to elect him over any possible Democratic candidate. Moreover, he declared, Taft would probably have done enough by that time to "justify" such a renomination; to deny him renomination would be a serious thing "only to be justified by really strong reasons." From his own standpoint, he ended, renomination of the president would be "eminently desirable," for he thought that he himself would not be nominated "unless everybody believed that the ship was sinking."[43]

When it was argued that his personal desires should not interfere with his "duty" to solidify the forward movement and insure its success, so as to make reactionary control of the Republican party impossible for six years at least, Roosevelt stated that to go beyond what the people wanted was "worse than useless." He was sure that if the progressives went on with their "ultra reform" plan the public would become more antagonistic toward them than toward the "ultraregulars."[44]

In the same vein Roosevelt wrote to both his progressive and Regular friends in Ohio, urging them to get together on a platform progressive enough to defeat Harmon in the autumn elections and thus save the president from a rebuke in his home state. The one aim, he told Longworth, was to try and get the people backing up the party in Indiana, where it was under "insurgent control," and the party in Ohio, where it was under "Regular control." With this in mind, he advised the Ohio Republicans to compromise on past issues, to endorse the Payne-Aldrich tariff as an improvement upon any of its predecessors but one that needed revision, to cite the railroad bill as an example of the good results attending the "cooperation" of progressive and Regular Republicans. The administration should be commended for writing into the bill certain provisions representing "great improvement in the law," but equally so the progressives for "inserting excellent

[43] Roosevelt to Gifford Pinchot, June 28, 1910, Roosevelt MSS.
[44] Roosevelt to Gifford Pinchot, August 16, 1910, Roosevelt MSS.

amendments" which rounded out the bill, making of it "a real and substantial measure of progress."[45] Although he was dissatisfied with Taft's record, he felt the president had done enough to warrant his support and this he would give with "entirely good grace" if Taft did not in the future tie himself closer to the reactionary wing.[46]

But Roosevelt was sadly disappointed in the results of the Ohio convention. The Regular Republicans, disregarding Garfield and the progressive contingent, wrote a straight conservative platform fulsome in its praise of the Aldrich principles. In perfect harmony with the platform, Warren G. Harding, a disciple of the Foraker-Cox school of politics, was nominated for governor.[47] Despondently Roosevelt wrote his friend Garfield that the platform was "extremely reactionary" and that the Republican powers in Ohio had foolishly made "the average politician's platform and put on it the average politician's candidate" in a year when very much more needed to be done to insure victory.[48]

Only this desire to reunite the party can logically account for Roosevelt's precipitate entrance into the New York primary fight after he had announced that he would abjure such factional struggles. The background for the New York fray, in which Roosevelt fared so badly, was a complex one. After Thomas C. Platt had been unhorsed as Republican boss of the state in the early part of the decade, the once airtight machine had gradually gone to pieces. By 1910 New York Republican politics consisted chiefly of an unceasing war between Governor Hughes and Timothy Woodruff, state Republican chairman, supported by allied regional bosses. Backed by the remnants of the once-famous New York "black horse brigade," the regional bosses had defeated so many of the Hughes policies that Taft and Root decided early in 1910 that to carry the state in the fall elections

[45] Roosevelt to Nicholas Longworth, July 11, 1910, Roosevelt MSS.
[46] Roosevelt to Garfield, (?), 1910, Roosevelt MSS.
[47] *Milwaukee Sentinel*, July 28, 1910; Alexander C. Sunds to Foraker, July 29, 1910, Foraker MSS., Cincinnati, Ohio.
[48] Roosevelt to Garfield, August 6, 1910, Roosevelt MSS.

Woodruff, William Barnes, Jr., and William Ward must be defeated. Accordingly they exerted themselves to the utmost to get Woodruff to resign. But by the time Roosevelt came home, such action had been productive of exactly nothing.[49]

Shortly after Roosevelt's return the Old Guard completed its demolition of the Hughes policies by voting down the Cobb-Hinman direct primary bill. Soon Roosevelt met Hughes at a Harvard class reunion, where the governor persuaded him to champion the cause of reform. That night the ex-president jarred the state by demanding by telegram that the state legislature pass the direct election measure.[50] Some Roosevelt biographers have attributed this move to his restless energy and his desire to court public attention. But despite the fact that there was in Roosevelt, as someone has said, much that made him want to be the bride at any wedding and the corpse at any funeral, it is probable that his action was born of a much more logically developed reason. The situation in New York state was exactly tailored to fit the plans for healing the schism running through the party. Here was the one place in the United States where he could strike a blow at the bitter-end reactionaries without crossing the purposes of the administration. Here was one position where the progressives and the administration could fight together.

After the telegram had been sent, the wheels of chance moved fast. The "Old Guard" in the state, resentful of this intrusion, answered the challenge by once more bringing up the bill and defeating it.[51] Roosevelt probably would have dropped out of the skirmish then and there had not Hughes and Lloyd C. Griscom, chairman of the New York County Republican Committee and an administration representative, urged him to carry the fight to the state convention. As a consequence Roosevelt soon announced his candidacy for

[49] William Loeb to Roosevelt, April 8, 1910, Roosevelt MSS.; *Des Moines Register and Leader*, March 15, 1910; *New York Sun*, April 9, May 11, 1910; Butt, *Taft and Roosevelt*, 1: 282, 309.
[50] *New York Sun*, June 30, 1910.
[51] *Milwaukee Sentinel*, June 29, 30, 1910.

the temporary chairmanship. And a few days before the state committee met, Griscom, after conferences with both Taft and Roosevelt, publicly declared that the two men were as one on the state issues.[52]

With the support of both Hughes and Taft, an easy Roosevelt victory seemed inevitable. But then things went awry. Months before the primary bill episode, Taft had offered Hughes a seat on the Supreme Court. Belatedly accepting the offer, Hughes, after urging Roosevelt into the New York fight, now told him that as a prospective justice he could no longer engage in politics. The air around Oyster Bay must have been electric after that incident, judging from Roosevelt's reflections on the character of the later chief justice.[53] But Roosevelt's troubles were not yet over. For at that point William Howard Taft, in whose interests Roosevelt believed himself fighting, deserted and possibly joined the enemy.

While Roosevelt was still disporting himself in the jungle, Taft had become uneasy about his friend. He mentioned to Major Butt that Roosevelt had not even answered his cordial letter of goodbye or thanked him for the present he had given him upon his departure. After Pinchot sailed for Europe the president was apprehensive that the discharged man would fill the ex-president's ears with "prejudicial tales." These fears were played upon and enlarged by his conservative associates, who came to him almost daily with scarehead stories of what Roosevelt would do upon his return.[54] As the time neared for Roosevelt's arrival, the press and the country focussed their attention so closely on New York harbor that Taft seemed but a sideshow to the wanderer's return. Naturally this had its effect on the president; Butt remarked that he looked bad and was under a great "nervous strain." Other men close to the president reported that he became increasingly irritable as the date of Roosevelt's arrival neared.[55]

[52] *New York Sun*, August 16, 1910.
[53] Roosevelt to Lodge, September 15, 21, 1910, Roosevelt MSS.
[54] Taft to Roosevelt, March 21, 1909, Roosevelt MSS.; Butt, *Taft and Roosevelt*, 1: 327, 364.
[55] Charles J. Bonaparte to Jerome Bonaparte, June 8, 1910, H. C.

Home at last, Roosevelt declared in his address of welcome that he was "ready and eager to be able to do my part"[56] in resolving the questions before the nation. But to Taft's long and hearty letter of welcome he replied that he would express no opinion of the administration for at least two months. To Taft such a remark, pregnant with things unsaid, could only mean outright disapprobation. "I don't care if he keeps silent forever," snapped the president. "Certainly the longer he keeps silent, the better it will please me."[57] Later in the month when a conference between the two men was being arranged by Henry Cabot Lodge, the president hoped to the last that Roosevelt would not come.[58] With this spirit manifested beforehand the conference had little chance of success.

Unfortunately for both Taft and Roosevelt and for the Republican party, neither understood the position of the other in the summer of 1910. And considering the pride of each man, the pattern of events gave neither much opportunity to make his position clear. There is no question that for numerous reasons Roosevelt was highly irritated with the president. It is also clear that he intended to work toward reuniting the party and thus toward the success of the Taft administration. On surveying the situation, however, he concluded that an outright endorsement of the Taft administration would not only be construed as insincerity but would make unification impossible. Taft, however, fully expected such an endorsement, for it is apparent that he regarded his legislative record as ample token of his intention to follow the Roosevelt road. When that endorsement was not forthcoming, he became suspicious of Roosevelt's designs and concluded that his former friend had joined his enemies. This suspicion grew daily as the press reported that one progressive after another was being received with open arms at Oyster Bay. Thereafter when movements anticipating the nomi-

---

Gauss to Charles J. Bonaparte, June 3, 1910, Bonaparte MSS.; Butt, *Taft and Roosevelt*, 1: 312–313, 331; *Outlook*, 95: 125 (May 28, 1910).

[56] *New York Times*, June 19, 1910.   [57] Butt, *Taft and Roosevelt*, 1: 416.

[58] Lodge to Roosevelt, June 26, 1910, Roosevelt MSS.; Butt, *Taft and Roosevelt*, 1: 416.

nation of Roosevelt in 1912 grew, mushroom-like, Taft was sure the Colonel had drawn on his sparring gloves. "I do not see how I am going to get out of having a fight with President Roosevelt," he remarked to Butt the first week in July,[59] and the news of the bout soon spread among the politicians. "If I mistake not we are in for a big row," wrote Senator Carter to his wife.[60]

Perhaps it was Taft's feeling that he would have to deal with Roosevelt if he were to be renominated that led to the involved administration policy in New York. Or perhaps Taft was not personally responsible for all that followed. At any rate, just before the New York state Republican executive committee announced their choice for temporary chairman of the state convention, the president sent what Roosevelt took to be an ultimatum through Lloyd C. Griscom. The message, according to Roosevelt, contained a promise and a threat. The president promised in return for an unequivocal Roosevelt endorsement of the administration to cast out Cannon and Aldrich as advisers, replace them with Senator Crane and his private secretary Norton, and give the Colonel a voice in the selection of Ballinger's successor. The threat was an implied one. The president revealed that he was losing his patience with Roosevelt and hinted that if an endorsement was not soon forthcoming he would feel obliged to fight him. In a letter to Lodge, Roosevelt related how thoroughly he was amused by Taft's "futile" actions. Both Edith and he had laughed so hard that Griscom had become embarrassed trying to explain the "silly" threat away.[61]

But evidently during the conference Roosevelt quickly shed this contemptuous amusement. Grimly he told Griscom, he later wrote, that he might have to support Taft in 1912 simply as a matter of expediency, but the hour was a little late to choose him then as a White House adviser. That

[59] *Ibid.*, 2: 434–435.

[60] July 8, 1910, Carter MSS.; Joseph B. Foraker to J. M. Swank, October 28, 1910, Foraker MSS., Cincinnati, Ohio.

[61] Roosevelt to Lodge, August 17, 1910, Roosevelt MSS.

would have been "the natural and wise thing" for the president to have done eighteen months before. But an attempt to assume the old relations now, after Taft had so "deliberately abandoned" them, was but the "wildest folly."[62]

Roosevelt was a history-conscious person. Before his death he placed all his papers in the Library of Congress, apparently willing to let his record speak for itself. Unlike so many other manuscript collections, Roosevelt's indicates that he preserved all his letters, including those that shed an unfavorable light. In the entire collection there is little evidence of deletion or selection. For that, among a great many other things, posterity should respect him. But in his correspondence with Lodge about Taft's actions in New York three pages of two letters are missing. Why is a matter for speculation. Whatever the answer, the fragmentary letters to Lodge show that his friendship of years with the large jolly man in the White House was irretrievably broken.

On August 1 the Republican executive committee met to nominate a man to preside over the New York state convention as temporary chairman. But instead of nominating Roosevelt, whose name had been suggested by administration men, the committee unexpectedly named Vice-President James S. Sherman, a leader of the New York reactionary element and a close friend of Timothy Woodruff. It is certain that the president was greatly pleased by this public humiliation of his old friend. To what extent he had encouraged and directed it is doubtful.[63] Griscom told Roosevelt that Woodruff, Barnes, and Ward had promised Taft that they would deliver the New York state delegation to him in 1912 and that Taft had urged their continuance in power on that account.[64] Both Woodruff and Sherman stated that they had been in close communication with Taft by telephone, and that their action was with the full approval of the president.[65] Butt

[62] Roosevelt to Lodge, undated and with the first page missing, and August 23, 1910, two pages missing.
[63] Despite Pringle's statement to the contrary. See his *Roosevelt*, 537.
[64] Roosevelt to Lodge, August 17, 1910, Roosevelt MSS.
[65] *New York Sun*, August 17, 1910.

afterward related that Sherman was in constant telephonic connection with the president, apprising him daily of the plans being laid to defeat Roosevelt in the convention. When the news finally came over the wire, both the president and his secretary, Norton, began to laugh. "We have got him— we've got him, we've got him as sure as peas," exclaimed Norton, and they both laughed again.[66]

The New York press interpreted the incident as an "open declaration of war."[67] But Roosevelt, although he felt he had been "double-crossed," had no intention of pressing the issue.[68] In fact, he was extremely glad to be out of the struggle, for it relieved him of the necessity "of leading what would in all probability be a losing fight," a burden he had in the first instance only "reluctantly" accepted. He wrote Lodge that the course of the administration had so angered the New York Republicans that they would vote against anything Republican, reform, anti-reform, Taft, Roosevelt, or Old Guard Republicanism.[69]

But Achilles was not allowed to retire to his tent. The older heads in the party began to fear that defeat would be the consequence and a split in the party inevitable. The most consistent administration paper in the country, Ambassador Ogden Reid's *New York Tribune*, was soon advising Sherman to decline in the interests of party harmony.[70] Taft and Norton suddenly stopped their laughter and bent every effort to make it appear that the president was utterly innocent of any connection with the scheme. Taft himself issued a public statement declaring that he had never heard Sherman's name suggested for the position until he saw it in the news-

[66] Butt, *Taft and Roosevelt*, 2: 480–481; Lodge to Roosevelt, September 3, 1910, Roosevelt MSS.; *New York Sun*, August 17, 18, 19, 1910; Watson, *As I Knew Them*, 145–146.

[67] *New York Herald*, August 17, 18, 1910; *New York Times*, August 17, 18, 1910.

[68] Roosevelt to Gifford Pinchot, August 17, 1910, Roosevelt MSS.; *Kansas City Star*, August 18, 1910; *New York Times*, September 20, 1910.

[69] Roosevelt to Lodge, August 17, 1910, Roosevelt MSS.

[70] *New York Tribune*, August 19, 20, 1910.

papers. In support of his statement he published a telegram to the vice-president dated a few days before the committee meeting, advising Sherman to consult with Roosevelt before any decisions were made. The president, however, said nothing about the Griscom conference nor about the constant telephone communications and directions delivered from Beverly thereafter.[71] In the following days Woodruff and Barnes corroborated the White House declaration, although they later retracted the corroboration.[72]

Never in his life had Roosevelt quit in the middle of a fight. Never had he better reasons for quitting than he had now. In the face of probable defeat, he nevertheless chose again to carry through. When the Stalwarts intimated that they would fight to the last ditch, the Colonel, just before departing on his Western trip, declared that he would carry the fight to the convention floor, where the bosses would get "all the fight they want."[73] But although he continued to struggle in what he thought to be the interests of the Republican party, Roosevelt had less and less respect for the man nominally at its head. In no way did he acknowledge the explanation of the White House concerning the New York affair. In letters to friends his tone became increasingly critical of the president. Where Taft had been sincere and well intentioned before, he was now only "feebly well-meaning; but with plenty of small motive"; so completely did he reflect the coloring of his immediate surroundings that he repeatedly broke his word or "betrayed" some former associate.[74] Whereas only a few months earlier Roosevelt had thought it likely that he would support Taft for the nomination, he now bluntly wrote Root that if his support was given, it would be under no illusions, "but simply as being the best thing that conditions present."[75] Roosevelt did not quickly forget the incident, for

[71] *New York Sun*, August 23, 1910; Butt, *Taft and Roosevelt*, 2: 489–490.
[72] *New York Sun*, August 24, 26, 1910; *New York Times*, September 27, 1910.
[73] *New York Sun*, August 25, 1910.
[74] Roosevelt to Arthur Lee, August 16, 1910, Roosevelt MSS.
[75] Roosevelt to Elihu Root, October 21, 1910, Roosevelt MSS.

he mentioned it repeatedly in letters during the next two years.[76]

In this state of mind Roosevelt set out, in late August, on a Western trip which was eventually to lead him through sixteen states. With him went a special car of correspondents, and from the moment of his first speech Taft's name dropped out of the daily headlines to make way for the thousands of stories written about the activities of the ex-president. The trip had been planned and most of his speeches outlined before the New York episode. That he had not given up his intention of uniting the party was obvious from his last-minute remarks to Lodge. He dreaded, he said, the effort to combine the enunciation of his own beliefs with "freedom from anything looking like criticism of the Taft administration."[77] It is probable, however, that his feeling toward Taft left its impress on his speeches. At any rate, throughout the course of his Western journey Roosevelt went further in his advocacy of radical doctrines than he had ever gone before.

In Denver he roused the crowd to a "frenzy" with his militant demands for advanced social legislation.[78] Speaking before the Colorado state legislature, he struck at the Supreme Court of the United States as a fundamental barrier to social justice, plainly stating that if the court continued to hand down decisions as in the Knight sugar case and the New York bakeshop case the whole American system of popular government would soon be overturned. He criticized the Court sharply for developing by successive interpretations a whole "neutral" area between the jurisdictional reach of the state and that of the national government where no power penetrated the anarchy.[79]

The West rose with a shout to greet the espouser of such doctrines. All through the night, as the Roosevelt train passed from Colorado into Kansas, crowds of whooping partisans

[76] *Ibid.;* Roosevelt to Lucius B. Swift, March 5, 1911, and to Lodge, February 27, 1912, Roosevelt MSS.

[77] Roosevelt to Lodge, August 18, 1910, Roosevelt MSS.

[78] *New York Sun*, August 30, 1910.

[79] *New York Times*, August 30, 1910.

stood in the rain for hours to cheer his train. But the enthusiasm of the scattered hundreds in small towns was but a prelude to the fervor that was to seize every corner of the Middle West after Osawatomie. For there in Kansas in the grove where old John Brown, fifty-four years before, had written abolitionism in blood, Roosevelt scaled the heights of radicalism in his New Nationalism.

Right at the opening of the speech he interpolated a paragraph in the written version that was considered a criticism of the administration. A broken promise, he maintained, was bad anywhere, but was worse in the field of politics. "No man in public life should be content to make a pledge on the stump that after his election he doesn't keep. If he makes a pledge and doesn't keep it, hunt him out of public life," he snapped as the great audience fairly howled.[80]

With that introduction Roosevelt turned to the subject of reform. Social justice could never be attained in the nation until the power of the federal government was greatly increased. When that day came the executive power should be regarded as the "steward of public welfare," and the national judiciary subsidiary to that power. Moreover, contrary to its historic position, the judiciary must "be interested primarily in human welfare rather than in property." Disturbing as that doctrine was to the Union League clubs of the country, much worse was to follow. In elaborating on the "square deal" Roosevelt tersely stated that he advocated having "these rules changed so as to work for a more substantial equality of opportunity, and of reward for equally good service." The nation was "face to face" with new concepts of the relation between property and human welfare. "The man who wrongly holds that every human right is secondary to his profit must now give way to the advocate of human welfare, who rightly maintains that every man holds his property subject to the general right of the community *to regulate its use to whatever degree the public welfare may require it.*"[81]

[80] *Ibid.*, September 1, 1910.
[81] Italics mine.

Labor, Roosevelt continued, always had been "the chief element of wealth," and as such the government should regulate its terms and conditions "directly in the interests of the common good." Ordinarily Roosevelt was content to make a moral generalization, but here at Osawatomie he became specific. Without quibble he endorsed the graduated income and the inheritance tax, a comprehensive workingman's compensation act, laws to regulate the conditions and terms of child and female labor, a thoroughgoing revision of the tariff, and greatly increased power for the Bureau of Corporations and the Interstate Commerce Commission for the purpose of obtaining complete publicity for and strict supervision of the capitalization of all corporations engaged in interstate business.[82]

When Roosevelt finished at Osawatomie he had probably delivered the most radical speech ever given by an ex-president. His concepts of the extent to which a powerful federal government could regulate and use private property in the interests of the whole, and his declarations about labor, when viewed by the eyes of 1910, were nothing short of revolutionary. The Eastern Brahmins of property bayed like hounds on a strong scent. Lodge wrote Roosevelt that his use of the word property had "startled" people everywhere in the East and that his enemies were holding him up as "little short of a revolutionist."[83] Lodge was particularly disconcerted by Roosevelt's attacks on the courts. "I think that to encourage criticism of and hostility to the decisions of the courts," he protested vigorously, "tends to a disregard of the law itself."[84] The conservative press became almost apoplectic in its rage. Branding the New Nationalism as a "fraud," a "lie," and a colossal exposition of "moral impudence," it charged Roosevelt with a desire to be a "Little Father" and of having even more sinister designs.[85] The *New York Sun* declared that

[82] *New York Times*, September 1, 1910.
[83] September 3, 1910, Roosevelt MSS.
[84] Lodge to Roosevelt, September 5, 1910, Roosevelt MSS.
[85] *New York Times*, *New York Evening Post*, and *Chicago Inter-Ocean*, September 2, 1910.

the third great crisis in the history of the nation had come, and warned every honest and patriotic citizen to prepare himself against this new Napoleon who deemed it his mission, along with the other "assailants of organized institutions" throughout the history of the world, "to overthrow and destroy in the name of public opinion and for the sake of personal advancement."[86]

Roosevelt would not have called his New Nationalism radical. For him its doctrines were essentially conservative. Nevertheless the New Nationalism was not only radical in a larger sense but was in some measure a break from the American reform pattern. Up until Roosevelt the progressive tradition in America after Jefferson had been on the whole a compound of physiocratic doctrines and egalitarianism modified by the American frontier. Its leaders—Jefferson, Jackson, and Bryan—had lived most of their lives close to the soil, and their doctrines appealed mostly to the workers of the soil. Their dream had been of a land of small farmers, small entrepreneurs, small business men regulated by traditional competition. They feared bigness wherever they found it, in business or in government. Jefferson was opposed to the powerful Federalist state, Jackson to Biddle's bank, and Bryan to industrial combination. Perhaps Bryan's love for the spoils system may have been partially predicated upon a dislike for a trained bureaucracy foreshadowing a master state. In Jacksonian equality there was no place for an administrative élite.

Faced by giant industry and lusty labor unions in the latter part of the nineteenth century, progressivism, reacting historically, demanded unworkable anti-trust measures. In so doing it adopted, in a sense, a reactionary position. It was the position of a Cobbett and of the Luddite rioters when the Industrial Revolution was young.[87] Combining Hamiltonian means with Jeffersonian ends, the New Nationalism was the

---

[86] *New York Sun*, September 2, 1910.

[87] Herbert Croly points up the significant difference between the reform movements. Possibly Roosevelt in talking with Croly was in-

first real break from that great but now seemingly anti-quated tradition. The more recent New Deal, if something else in spirit, was in many ways only a step away from the New Nationalism.

Roosevelt had come by his New Nationalism slowly. He had always been a nationalist in foreign affairs. But the concept of a master regulatory state was a gradual development. During his presidency he had been impressed with the power and the wrongdoings of unrestrained capital. On the other hand, he had feared the increasing strength of labor and still more the increasing votes of the Socialist party. Yet by the end of his term Roosevelt must have known that his trust-busting and other reforms had neither curbed business nor soothed the restless masses. The fateful reform legacy left to Taft was evidence of that.

In England during the spring of 1910 Roosevelt had talked with Henry Herbert Asquith, Lloyd George, and Sir Edward Grey. These leaders of the Liberal party were doing strange things to Gladstonian liberalism. Lloyd George's historic budget of 1909, providing the means for four years of reform, had brought liberals and conservatives to their sharpest division since 1830. And then, coming home, Roosevelt read Herbert Croly's *The Promise of American Life*. Perhaps no author had influenced him more since Mahan.[88] In plain English Croly said the things that Roosevelt had been groping for. Much that was said at Osawatomie came straight from the pages of *The Promise of American Life*. Indeed, the phrase "the New Nationalism" was one of Croly's.[89] But whatever the origin of the New Nationalism, its doctrines were pointed

fluenced in calling some of the Western progressives of both parties "agrarian tories." See Herbert Croly, *The Promise of American Life* (New York, 1909), 106.

[88] In many ways Herbert Croly was a remarkable person. His father had been a reformer before him and his mother was perhaps the first woman journalist in the United States. Editor of the *Architectural Record*, Croly became the chief theorist for the progressive movement. His two books, *The Promise of American Life* and *Progressive Democracy* foreshadow the New Deal under a second Roosevelt.

[89] *The Promise of American Life*, 169.

in a different direction from that of traditional American progressivism.

As the news of Osawatomie penetrated to the hamlets and the farms of the trans-Mississippi West, there was spontaneous rejoicing. On the train leaving Lawrence, Kansas, progressives William Allen White, Governor William R. Stubbs, Senator Bristow, and William Rockhill Nelson, "hysterically jubilant," gathered to celebrate. Up and down the aisles went the word, "Roosevelt for 1912."[90] The next day at the Commercial Club of Kansas City the ex-president was met with a rousing song predicting his victory at the next election.[91] Before he crossed the Mississippi River the Nebraska "Progressive Republicans" were called to a statewide conference to organize for Roosevelt and Dolliver as nominees in the next election.[92]

Roosevelt, however, had no intention of permitting the movement to gain headway. The following day at Sioux City, Iowa, he commended Taft for his efforts to secure an effective tariff commission and at the same time heartily endorsed Senator Dolliver.[93] Having gained the confidence of the progressives by the Osawatomie speech, he sought now to get that of the Regulars, and to make both see that their interests lay not in separation but in fusion. He expressed as much in a letter to Lodge, who had taxed him with having given Dolliver and the progressives too much credit for the passage of the tariff board measure. He granted that perhaps he had given Dolliver too much praise, but he had had both progressives and Regulars on the platform with him. By mentioning them all together with Taft he was trying to make them understand that their interests were identical and that if they split instead of acting together "there would be disaster."[94]

[90] *New York Times*, September 2, 1910.
[91] *Milwaukee Sentinel*, September 2, 1910.
[92] *Des Moines Register and Leader*, September 2, 3, 1910; *Kansas City Star*, September 1, 1910.
[93] *Des Moines Register and Leader*, September 4, 1910.
[94] Lodge to Roosevelt, September 12, 1910, Roosevelt MSS.

Roosevelt followed this policy for the rest of his trip. At the St. Paul Conservation Congress, though he disagreed on some minor points with President Taft, who had spoken the day before, he paid him a generous compliment and heartily endorsed the administration's policy laid down in connection with coal, ore, and phosphate lands.[95] At the same time he took occasion to smash at Congressman James A. Tawney, whom he believed to be so reactionary as to constitute a major obstacle to getting the party on "a middle of the road progressive basis." Later, while speaking in Milwaukee, Wisconsin, he carefully refrained from endorsing La Follette.[96] Shortly thereafter, at the Hamilton Club in Chicago, Roosevelt publicly censured the reactionary Senator Lorimer, who was under investigation for buying his way into the United States Senate. Taft objected strongly to this prejudicing of a man; but in general all elements of the Republican party applauded heartily.[97] Despite the criticism from Eastern conservative centers about his radical speeches, Roosevelt felt that his Western trip had done a great deal to unite the party. He wrote that Regulars, moderates, and insurgents, including "the machine mayor of Pittsburgh," had told him as much and had expressed their gratitude for his visit. "I do not think they were utterly insincere," he ended.[98]

Coming home, Roosevelt set out to do in the East what he thought he had done in the West. His plan was to support both moderate Regulars and moderate progressives for office. At Oyster Bay he announced that he would make speeches in support of Senators Lodge and Beveridge as well as for the progressive Robert Bass and the Regular Congressman Bascom Slemp. In New York, although he felt that nothing could save the party from a "tremendous drubbing," he went ahead with his efforts to unseat the reactionary elements so as to bring all shades of Republican opinion to its support.[99]

[95] *New York Times*, September 6, 1910.

[96] *Milwaukee Sentinel*, September 8, 1910.

[97] *New York Times*, September 9, 10, 1910; Butt, *Taft and Roosevelt*, 2: 509; *Literary Digest*, 41: 475 (September 24, 1910).

[98] Roosevelt to Lodge, September 12, 1910, Roosevelt MSS.

[99] Roosevelt to Lodge, September 12, 15, 21, 1910, Roosevelt MSS.

Shortly thereafter Lloyd C. Griscom, chairman of the New York County Republican Committee, asked Roosevelt to meet Taft and thus quiet the numerous rumors flying about and show the public that they were united in the New York scrap. Roosevelt agreed, and the conference took place at New Haven in the house of a friend of both. Roosevelt later described the meeting as "cordial," but Taft thought Roosevelt anything but "genial" and in fact quite "offish." No federal politics were discussed, but Taft volunteered to help Roosevelt in the fight on New York bossism and labeled Barnes and the rest as "crooks."[100] Roosevelt came away from the conference in a more charitable frame of mind toward Taft. But he was greatly agitated again when the president's secretary, Norton, gave out the story that Roosevelt had desired the meeting because he was in trouble in New York and that during the conference he had asked for aid, which Taft had magnanimously promised. So worked up was Roosevelt that he immediately made a public statement of the truth of the matter, which Lloyd C. Griscom confirmed.[101] To Lodge, however, Roosevelt described the connivance of Norton and Taft in such petty prestige politics as "outrageous." He was glad, he said, that it had happened, because now when people asked him why he did not see the president he could simply point to that incident as proof that intercourse was impossible.[102] Only a few days later Taft significantly told Major Butt that he and Roosevelt had come to the parting of the ways.[103]

Disregarding this personal friction with the president, Roosevelt continued in his effort to rehabilitate the party in New York state. In a bitterly contested pre-convention fight, he completely whipped the triumvirate of bosses and was elected temporary chairman of the convention by a substantial margin.[104] During the course of the convention not a sin-

[100] Roosevelt to Lodge, September 21, 1910, Roosevelt MSS.; Butt, *Taft and Roosevelt*, 2: 524.
[101] *New York Times*, September 21, 1910.
[102] Roosevelt to Lodge, September 21, 1910, Roosevelt MSS.
[103] Butt, *Taft and Roosevelt*, 2: 529.
[104] *New York Sun*, September 27, 1910.

gle incident occurred that could be interpreted as implying criticism of the administration except that the platform was silent on endorsements for the next presidential race. Roosevelt even went so far in his keynote address as to laud the president for his achievements in the first eighteen months of his administration. The platform enthusiastically praised the president and even endorsed the Payne-Aldrich tariff as a downward revision. Thanks to Roosevelt's support, Henry L. Stimson, a Taft man for 1912, was nominated for governor.[105] Roosevelt, though expecting inevitable defeat, believed that he had done yeoman's service in getting the party on a basis where both progressives and Regulars would support it.[106]

He was soon disabused of this idea, however, as the progressive West rose in a storm of protest against his endorsement of the president and of the Payne-Aldrich tariff.[107] He was fairly deluged with letters, some "really offensive" in their criticisms.[108] The press, representing all shades of opinion, joined in lampooning the "man on two horsebacks." "But jest to decide 'twixt stan'pat an' insurgent, He finds ain't expedient, not to say urgent," wrote one rhymester.[109] He was attacked from the East for his radical Osawatomie doctrines and from the West for his reactionary condonation of the president and the tariff. He had failed to see that the party was split on issues so fundamental that it was impossible to draw the two wings together. His characteristic approach to any political problem had led him into the impasse

[105] *New York Times,* September 29, 1910.

[106] Roosevelt to Bonaparte, October 5, 1910, and to Sidney Brooks, October 17, 1910, Roosevelt MSS.

[107] Just previous to the New York convention Roosevelt in a signed article in the *Outlook* had praised the Payne-Aldrich bill. *Outlook,* 92: 102 (September 17, 1910).

[108] Benjamin I. Wheeler to Roosevelt, October 7, 1910, W. C. White to L. F. Abbott (copy), December 5, 1910, Henry C. Wallace to Gifford Pinchot, November 5, 1910, Roosevelt to Theodore Roosevelt, Jr., October 19, 1910, Roosevelt MSS.

[109] Hosea Biglow in the *Indianapolis News,* cited in the *Nation,* 91: 351 (October 20, 1910).

THE PIED PIPER
Cartoon by Minor in the *St. Louis Post-Dispatch*, reproduced
in the *Literary Digest*, November 12, 1910.

of trying to reconcile the irreconcilable. Now he was reaping
the whirlwind.

Even before the New York convention Roosevelt was sick
of his "pointless" activity in trying to reunite the party. To
give up all privacy, he wrote, and to be forced into all "the
frowsy and fussy activity of public life, with none of its power
or reward, is simply intolerable."[110] Now with little but criticism descending upon his unhappy head, the intolerable became altogether insufferable. With supreme disgust and keen
disappointment he lashed out in his correspondence at both
"the wild irresponsible folly" of the ultra-insurgents and the
stupid course of the "Bourbon-Reactionaries." On the one
hand he wrote that he had "split definitely with the Insurgents" and on the other, in replying to a request from

[110] Roosevelt to Lady Delamere, September 22, 1910, Roosevelt MSS.

Root to help the president out in his fight in Ohio, he bluntly declared that it was "simple folly" for Taft to expect his support "when all possible care is taken to show that I am not in any real sense to be consulted . . . before the nomination or after the election."[111] But because of the promises he had made he continued with his thankless task. He injured his voice in New York in a ten-day stumping tour of the state advocating the election of Stimson. He spoke for Lodge in Massachusetts and for Bass in New Hampshire. He made two trips to the West before election day, speaking in Iowa and Indiana for progressives. Reconsidering his refusal to talk in Ohio, he even partially endorsed Harding as he pleaded for a Republican victory in the state to give proof of the people's belief in Republicanism.

"The results of the Maine election and nomination of Poindexter seems to me to have placed the Administration in a position so clearly untenable that some change of policy on its part may be reasonably expected in the near future," Charles J. Bonaparte wrote to a friend early in September.[112] A few days later Taft began to take in sail in an attempt to steer the party in a more progressive direction. Rumors came from Beverly that Aldrich, Cannon, and Ballinger would soon be dropped as administration advisers for more forward-looking men. Administration leaders announced that they would not support Cannon again for Speaker. Taft himself in speeches reversed the position he had taken at Winona by declaring that he realized the tariff was not a "complete compliance with the promises made."[113] And then the president, by a letter from his secretary to an Iowa politician, attempted to call off all intra-party hostilities. Admitting that the patronage had been used against certain Republicans in the primaries, the letter stated that this policy

[111] Roosevelt to Root, October 21, 1910, to Sidney Brooks, October 17, 1910, and to Theodore Roosevelt, Jr., October 19, 1910, Roosevelt MSS.

[112] Bonaparte to Clinton R. Woodruff, September 15, 1910, Bonaparte MSS.

[113] *Milwaukee Sentinel*, August 7, 12, 13, 15, 18, 1910; *Des Moines Register and Leader*, August 6, 1910.

had come to an end, and that the distribution of political plums would be put on the old basis. Furthermore, it urged all Republicans of whatever shade of opinion to support all Republican nominees and to forget the bitter strife of the summer months.[114]

But such a last-minute attempt at conciliation failed to bring peace to the strife-ridden party. The progressives merely viewed these professions as a deathbed repentance, which was likely to be forgotten the moment the crisis had passed.[115] They pointed out that Aldrich, in fact all the "old crowd," was regularly visiting Beverly. The invective between the two camps all through the summer months had been too caustic, the issues too sharply defined to be forgotten.[116]

Everywhere, Roosevelt wrote Lodge, the two factions "intend to cut the throats of the other at the polls." He went on to report that in Indiana the Hemenway-Watson faction was doing everything it could to elect a Democrat against Beveridge, that in Illinois and Ohio there was "sullen discontent," that the Regulars in Iowa were planning and hoping for a Democratic triumph, and that even the Cannon people were hostile to Taft and "would a thousand fold" rather see a Democratic victory than a Congress that wouldn't elect Cannon Speaker. The split looked "as deep as it could be." And though Taft had not the power to heal it, the president's position made it "an absolute impossibility" for Roosevelt or anyone else to do the work, the Colonel gloomily concluded.[117]

Other men were convinced that the party was beyond repair. Bonaparte was looking ahead to a "great disaster." In

[114] *Philadelphia North American*, September 17, 1910.
[115] Bonaparte to Elliot H. Goodwin, September 21, 1910, Bonaparte MSS.; *Kansas City Star*, August 18, 1910; *Philadelphia North American*, September 17, 1910.
[116] *Milwaukee Sentinel*, August 13, 16, 1910.
[117] Roosevelt to Lodge, August 17, 1910, Roosevelt MSS.; Joseph B. Foraker to Albert Clarke, October 29, 1910, Foraker MSS., Cincinnati, Ohio.

despair Senator Carter predicted that the whole country would "go to pot." And Foraker even surpassed Carter in his dismal prophecies.[118] In New York, where Roosevelt had tried his hand, conditions were even worse. For many of the progressives in New York, angry with Roosevelt for his endorsement of Taft and the tariff, bolted the party. On the other hand, conservatives, charging that Roosevelt was using the New York gubernatorial election as a stepping stone to the presidency in 1912, advocated the election of a Democrat. The *New York Sun* repeated for a month before the election: "The time to beat Roosevelt in 1912 is on November 8, 1910."[119] As a result, the party found it almost impossible to collect money for campaign purposes.[120] Wealthy men throughout the state, calling themselves "Taft-Hughes" Republicans, formed Republican leagues for the election of the Democrat John A. Dix.[121] In such an atmosphere a Republican victory in the state was a forlorn hope.

The secession of the men of "property and principle" from the Republican party was not peculiar to New York. Fearing that progressivism and Rooseveltism would capture the Republican party everywhere, they began to look at its Democratic rival, apparently freed from the Bryan incubus, as a haven. Mr. Dooley with his customary insight warned his friend Hennessey not to step on the feet of a well-dressed man reading a statistical report but to speak to him as a fellow "Demmycrat."

There was a time, continued Mr. Dooley, that "gin'rally speakin' a Demmycrat was an ondesirable immygrant that had got past Ellis Island. But it's different this year, Hennessey. The Demmycrat party is no longer low an' vulgar. Its the hite iv fashion an' th' home iv wealth. I blush to read

[118] Bonaparte to John B. Hanna, September (?), 1910, Bonaparte MSS.; Thomas H. Carter to Mrs. Carter, August 12, 1910, Carter MSS.
[119] *New York Sun*, October, November, 1910.
[120] Roosevelt to J. B. Bishop, October 20, 1910, Roosevelt MSS.; Butt, *Taft and Roosevelt*, 2: 550, 554.
[121] *New York Sun*, October 7, 1910; Lidell Tilghman to Grenville M. Dodge, October 31, 1910, Dodge MSS.; Roosevelt to Isaac Russell, September 12, 1911, Roosevelt MSS.; *New York Sun*, October 3, 1910.

whats said about me in the paper. I'm a boolwork iv th' constitution. I'm th' savior iv property; the supreme coort can
sleep a dhramless sleep knowin' that I'm on guard."[122]

But if the richer elements in the country were disaffected
from the party in power, no less was the farmer and the laboring man. Taft's ostensible conservative leanings, his attitude
toward the use of the labor injunction, and the constantly increasing "cost of Payne Aldrich living" along with the rebellion to the west all militated against success. The Republican leaders, although they admitted that a reverse was coming, were not prepared for the magnitude of the defeat.

The day after election reports came in of one fallen Republican stronghold after another throughout the country. In
New England and the Atlantic coast states alone, Republican
aspirants for the governorships lost to their Democratic rivals
in Maine, Massachusetts, Connecticut, New York, and New
Jersey. And while the loss in New York was celebrated as a
smashing defeat for Roosevelt, the president also had his
cross to bear: Ohio, his home state, had been carried by a
wave of Democratic votes.[123] With Ohio went Indiana, and
the border states of Maryland, Kentucky, and Missouri. Thus
in the East, where the party was dominated by conservative
interests, the minority progressive faction had drifted into
the Democratic ranks to elect Woodrow Wilson and Eugene
N. Foss. Most of the progressives had probably stayed with
the party only in New York. The strength of the progressive
Republican revolt in the East was manifest in Pennsylvania,
where the candidate for governor of the new Keystone party
fell short of victory over the Penrose Republican machine by
only thirty thousand votes.[124]

Only in the West, where progressivism had captured the
party, did its ranks remain relatively undepleted. In the
nine most progressive states of the West[125] the Republican

[122] *Kansas City Star*, November 6, 1910.
[123] *New York Sun*, November 3, 1910.
[124] *Philadelphia North American*, November 10, 1910.
[125] Wisconsin, Iowa, Kansas, Nebraska, North Dakota, South Dakota,
Minnesota, California, and Washington.

losses in congressional elections amounted to only three, whereas in the four Eastern states of New York, New Jersey, Pennsylvania, and Ohio the number totalled twenty-six. In the senatorial election likewise such Eastern Republican Regulars as Eugene Hale of Maine, Kean of New Jersey, Dick of Ohio, Chauncy M. Depew of New York, and Scott of West Virginia had been retired. The only loss in the nine progressive Republican states enumerated was Burkett of Nebraska, who had seldom aligned himself with the reforming faction. Moreover, three new out-and-out progressives, Miles Poindexter of Washington, Works of California, and Gronna of North Dakota had been sent to the Senate by the returns of 1910.

All in all, the results of the election had important effects upon the future pattern of events. In the first place, the Democratic party in November of 1910 stood rehabilitated in the eyes of the country. With the election of Wilson, Foss, Baldwin, and Harmon, the party had acquired able leaders of national stature who could take the place of the quadrennial loser Bryan. Secondly, the conspicuous success of progressivism, the rout of the Regulars, and in particular the defeat of Taft in Ohio, encouraged the forces of progressive Republicanism in the belief that they could defeat the president for renomination. Thus the election undoubtedly motivated the founding of the National Progressive Republican League a month and a half later. Then too the results of the balloting had thrown the control of the House into Democratic hands and had placed the balance of power in the Senate squarely in possession of the progressives. Both these developments boded ill for the success of the already harassed Taft administration. Finally, the elections effectually silenced for a time the lion of Oyster Bay. With all but two of the men he had spoken for defeated, and temporarily estranged from the party, Roosevelt retired to the seclusion of Sagamore Hill, shattered in prestige and disconsolate of heart. The Roosevelt star had had its first eclipse.

CHAPTER SIX

Progressive Politics

W ITH THE DISASTROUS November elections behind him and the presidential race less than two years away, Taft sought to bring to his strife-ridden party some semblance of harmony. After Congress convened in December of 1910, he invited all the progressive senators, including even the intransigent La Follette, to the White House. He conferred with them about judicial appointments and extended himself in other ways to show that he held no resentment. But his overtures availed him little. One of the keenest political correspondents in Washington noted that while the progressives had all resumed patronage relations with Taft, "they are as much against him as ever and propose to fight his renomination."[1] La Follette's declination of the White House invitation foreshadowed the founding of the National Progressive Republican League late in December.[2]

As if to answer the progressives the president's subsequent annual message to Congress was freighted with conservatism. Its paragraphs arguing against any legislation for readjusting the relations between the business world and government could well have been written by Aldrich. Its proposal to confine federal activities to securing "economy of administration," the "enlargement of opportunities for foreign trade," and the "strengthening of the confidence of capital in domestic investment," were "very satisfactory" to even the stoutest advocate of the old order.[3] The president of the American Iron and Steel Association considered the message

[1] *New York Sun*, December 5, 1910.
[2] *Ibid.*, January 24, 1910.
[3] John D. Ryan to Thomas H. Carter, December 5, 1910, Carter MSS.; *New York Sun*, December 7, 1910.

a "plain bid" for the support "of the business interests" for renomination. That, he thought, would be forthcoming if Taft did not change his mind on the tariff and the "corporation question" in the meantime.[4]

Only one part of the message brought cheer to the progressives. That was the demand for a revision of the tariff, schedule by schedule. But here again the Middle Western block in Congress was to be disappointed; for the tariff measure that the president recommended to Congress on January 21, 1910, was not a revision schedule by schedule, but rather a reciprocity agreement between Canada and the United States.

The history of reciprocity treaties in American tariff practices was an old one. Before the Civil War an agreement existed for ten years between Canada and the United States. Provisions permitting the president to negotiate reciprocity agreements were incorporated into the Dingley Act of 1897, but remained lifeless when the Senate refused to ratify any of McKinley's treaties. During the Roosevelt administration, however, a reciprocity treaty between Cuba and the United States was implemented to the mutual satisfaction of both countries. And when, in the early part of 1910, it appeared that a tariff war between Canada and the United States was imminent, a reciprocity measure was suggested to resolve the difficulty. The president early agreed and in July, 1910, began to stress the benefits of the proposal.[5]

The restoration of international amity was not Taft's only reason for supporting the proposed agreement. Writing to Roosevelt, he argued that the plan would answer the complaints about the high cost of living by reducing the cost of food. It would also open Canadian markets to the manufactured goods of this country, creating a "current of business" between the two nations "which would make Canada only an adjunct of the United States." Moreover, he had always been

[4] J. M. Swank to Joseph B. Foraker, December 10, 1910, Foraker MSS., Cincinnati, Ohio.

[5] *New York Sun*, July 20, 1910.

a "downward revision man" and the arrangement fitted in perfectly with his tariff theories.

The president was aware that the bill would be attacked by agrarian interests. He predicted that it would be extremely unpopular with the lumbering and dairy industries and thought that it might even "break the Republican party for a while." But he believed that he could repair the break and appease the Middle West by subsequently recommending, on the basis of the findings of the tariff board, reductions in the wool, cotton, and other manufacturing schedules of the tariff.[6] Unfortunately for the hapless president, these recommendations were never made until it was far too late to accomplish their purpose. And as for advocating reciprocity with Canada alone, Taft might well have taken heed of his predecessor's warning on the subject. "It is a truism," Roosevelt had written in 1904, "that one man's raw material is another man's finished product, and for Massachusetts to expect Iowa to sanction the tariff on shoes while cutting out the tariff on hides shows a distinctly optimistic frame of mind."[7] Taft, however, went ahead courageously to support reciprocity. As a result he destroyed every chance for unity within his party and made his re-election in 1912 all but impossible.

The negotiations for the treaty were carried on in Washington during the fall of 1910 by two Canadian cabinet ministers and Secretary of State Philander C. Knox. An agreement was reached on January 21, 1911, and was presented to Congress five days later along with a lengthy presidential message which stressed the benefits to be obtained from the cheapening of food and forest products.[8] As introduced into Congress, the treaty placed the following on the free lists of both countries: live animals, poultry, wheat, rye, oats, barley, corn, hay, vegetables, fruits, dairy products, fish of all kinds, lumber not further manufactured than sawed, railroad ties, telephone poles, brass, carbon, cream separators, galvanized

[6] Taft to Roosevelt, January 10, 1911, Roosevelt MSS.
[7] Roosevelt to N. M. Butler, August 13, 1904, in Pringle, *Roosevelt*, 550.
[8] Memorandum, September 27, 1910, Knox MSS.

iron, steel sheets and plates, coke, and iron and steel. In addition, wood pulp was to be admitted free into the United States if the Canadian provinces repealed the existing export limitations upon it. Great reductions were to be made in the rates on farm machinery, wagons, portable engines, band instruments, clocks, watches, plate glass, cement, peanuts, and coal.[9]

The first response to the treaty was a favorable one. Newspapers, gratefully aware of the proposed reduction of the duties on wood pulp denied to them in the Payne-Aldrich rates, were united in their commendation. Papers and periodicals, hitherto utterly hostile to the administration, thought that it was Taft's "first big, broad, brave, right accomplishment."[10] The American Newspaper Publishers Association agreed to distribute propaganda prepared by the administration throughout the country.[11] The Democratic congressional delegation, as anticipated by Taft, almost solidly supported the measure. Even Roosevelt, dubious as he had been about the advisability of reciprocity in his own administration, wrote the president that he thought the proposal was "admirable from every standpoint."[12] The praise from the newspapers and from Roosevelt must have been manna for Taft. Momentarily it seemed as if he had for the first time in his administration scored a political ten-strike.

But Taft, who wanted so much to please, was never to enjoy prolonged public favor as long as he was in the White House. Within a few days a formidable opposition to the reciprocity agreement appeared. The two Pinchots, Senator

[9] *Canadian Reciprocity*, Senate Document No. 787, 61 Congress, 3 Session, 3–9.

[10] *Philadelphia North American*, January 28, 1911; *Kansas City Star*, January 27, 1911; *Des Moines Register and Leader*, February 28, 1911; Norman Hapgood to Roosevelt, February 6, 1911, Roosevelt MSS.

[11] Letters to Philander C. Knox from John Norris, January 16, 1911, and Charles M. Pepper, February 7, 1911, Knox MSS.

[12] Roosevelt to Taft, January 12, 1911, Roosevelt MSS. Roosevelt subsequently, however, changed his mind about reciprocity. In February 1910 when the opposition chorus grew louder each day he found many "jokers" in the bill. By July he felt it had been "very badly drawn" so as to protect the over-protected manufacturer and sacrifice the farmer. In the midst of

Beveridge, Congressman Madison of Kansas, and Van Valkenburg, editor of the *Philadelphia North American*, supported the measure, but the rest of the progressives were against it almost to a man. They maintained that they favored reciprocity in theory, but not the Taft treaty, which would sacrifice the farmer to the city-dweller.[13] This antagonism, after their stand on the Payne-Aldrich tariff bill, exposed them to a charge of inconsistency. Many friends of reciprocity, including Roosevelt, Beveridge, and Congressman Madison, thought they were simply playing politics to embarass the president.[14] That consideration must of course have entered into progressive calculations, but there was also the potent reason that a sizeable body of agrarian opinion was from the first militantly hostile to the proposal.

Whether the majority of farmers were for or against reciprocity is extremely difficult to determine. It is true that the Nebraska Senate unanimously endorsed the treaty.[15] On the other hand, the National Grange and the American Fruit Growers Association both opposed it. The Grange even warned the president that if it were passed they would oppose his re-election.[16] One republican prophet intimated that the president's action would cost him at least a hundred thousand votes in New York state in 1912.[17] At a guess it might be said that the majority of farmers was against the measure. It was difficult to tell the farmer that he would benefit from a tariff reduction after Republican orators had for years nurtured in him the belief that he was one of the direct benefac-

a campaign against Taft a year later Roosevelt was sure the whole scheme was a "sham" concocted by Taft "to buy the support of the press." Roosevelt to William Loeb, Jr., February 3, 1911, to Arthur Lee, July 27, 1911, and to Virgil K. Kellogg, July 17, 1912, Roosevelt MSS.

[13] *New York Sun*, February 12, 1911; *La Follette's Weekly*, August 5, 1911; La Follette, *Autobiography*, 504-505.

[14] E. H. Madison to Roosevelt, February 15, 1911, Roosevelt to E. H. Madison, February 17, 1911, Roosevelt MSS.; Senator Brown to Beveridge, June 29, 1911, in Bowers, *Beveridge*, 411; Roosevelt to O. K. Davis, May 31, 1911, Roosevelt MSS.

[15] *New York Sun*, February 16, 1911.

[16] *New York Times*, May 9, 1911.

[17] J. Sloat Fassett to Thomas H. Carter, April 26, 1911, Carter MSS.

tors of a high tariff. It was not a simple task to convince the farmer that agricultural prices would not decline as a result of the treaty when the president had declared the opposite and when he had only to look at the daily paper to see that the prices of wheat in Winnipeg during the spring and summer were from one to eight cents less than the Minneapolis quotations.[18] The fact that foodstuffs advanced in price on the Chicago market the day after the Canadian defeat of reciprocity was perhaps no mere coincidence.[19]

The saying that politics makes strange bedfellows was never more clearly borne out than in the battle over reciprocity. In addition to the farming elements, a majority of the Stalwart Republicans in the Senate and the House opposed the bill. Much of this Regular opposition was a reflection of economic interests directly involved. Adduced before the Senate Committee on Finance was the fact that the International Paper Company, the National Lumber Association, and other business organizations were militantly supporting the Grange in its fight against reciprocity.[20] Senator Lodge was secretly against the proposal on the ground that it would forever put an end to the deep-sea fishing industry in New England. Maine, viewing a future influx of Canadian potatoes, and Vermont and New Hampshire, fearing the competition in dairy products, were vociferous in their objections.[21]

Suspecting that Canadian reciprocity was only the opening gun of a general war against the high protective policy, the American Protective Tariff League, the American Iron and Steel Association, and the Home Market Club contributed their support to the opposition.[22] They charged Taft with endangering the "greatest teachings of the Civil War" and of "doing his best to convert the Republican party into a free

[18] *Yearbook of the Department of Agriculture*, 1925 (Washington, D. C.), 765–766.

[19] *Chicago Tribune*, September 23, 1911.

[20] *New York Times*, June 1, 1911.

[21] Lodge to Roosevelt, January 28, February 21, 1911, Roosevelt MSS.; *New York Sun*, January 28, 1911.

[22] Some members of Taft's own Cabinet had the same fear. Knox to Charles D. Norton, March 9, 1911, Knox MSS.

trade party." The president of the American Iron and Steel Association wrote that everything possible should be done to sustain the protective policy and to defeat Taft in 1912. James M. Swank then went on to say that with the exception of two of their members the rest "from Judge Gary down" were in accord with his objectives.[23] With the exception of the far-seeing Aldrich, who wrote to Taft that the country was "impelled to make more liberal trade agreements with its American neighbors" by our selfish interests,[24] the Regular Republicans were almost unitedly opposed. In the House Cannon, Dalzell, and Fordney voted against the measure.[25] In the Senate Hale, Gallinger, Smoot, and Frye all co-operated in blocking its passage. In fact, it was declared by one friend of reciprocity that not one Regular in either branch of Congress really favored the measure.[26]

With both the Regular and progressive Republican factions opposed, the reciprocity bill had little chance of success in the Sixty-first Congress. It managed to pass the House without amendment because of the united Democratic support, but was obstructed in the Senate. Reported out of the Senate committee without recommendations, the bill was ignored for weeks. The plan of the anti-reciprocity men was to delay action on all bills until the last few days, when in the legislative log jam they could conveniently kill the measure on the ground that there was not sufficient time to debate the proposal. In the face of the president's threats to call an extra session of Congress, the plan was followed out to the bitter end.[27]

[23] James M. Swank to Foraker, March 29, June 10, 1911, Albert Clark to Swank, March 13, 1911, Albert Brown to Foraker, July 8, 1911, Foraker to Swank, March 16, 1911, Foraker to F. W. Hackett, June 15, 1911, Foraker MSS., Cincinnati, Ohio; Foraker to W. A. Jones, December 9, 1911, Foraker MSS., Library of Congress. There were manufacturers, however, of a different mind. For example, see letter of J. M. Conger to Henry M. Hoyt, November 3, 1910, Knox MSS.
[24] Taft to Knox, March 11, 1911, Knox MSS.; Aldrich to Taft, February 17, 1911, in Stephenson, *Aldrich*, 385.
[25] *Congressional Record*, 62 Congress, 1 Session, vol. 47, pt. 1, p. 395.
[26] E. H. Madison to Roosevelt, February 11, 1911, Roosevelt MSS.
[27] *Des Moines Register and Leader*, March 5, 1911.

The president was not yet beaten. He promptly conferred with both Champ Clark and Oscar W. Underwood, the Democratic powers in the new House, and announced that an extra session would be called in April.[28] The Republican chieftains, who had believed that Taft was making only an idle threat, were stunned by the news. It was inconceivable that a president would call an extra session of Congress against the will of almost every leader of his party, especially when the party would have control of neither house. And when it became known that the president had not secured from the Democratic leaders a promise to limit the business of the session to the passage of the reciprocity measure, anger mounted still higher. An unlimited session would surely bring forth a Democratic-progressive attempt to revise all the schedules of the tariff. Crane, Lodge, Cannon, and Dalzell pleaded with the president to dispel the threat to the protective system. They were joined by thousands of industrial leaders from all parts of the country.[29] But it was all in vain. The unyielding Taft called an extra session of the Sixty-second Congress to convene in the first week of April.

To the Washington observer, accustomed to Republican domination, the new Congress presented many strange sights. For the first time in sixteen years the Democrats were in control of the House.[30] Even more exceptional was the position of Joseph Cannon, now simply a member of the minority party. In his place as leader of the Republicans was Representative Mann of Illinois, and at the Speaker's rostrum Champ Clark of Missouri presided. In the Senate also great changes had taken place. The retirement of Aldrich had marked the passing of the last of the little group of Republican senators who had run the party for so many years. Into retirement with

[28] Charles D. Norton to Philander C. Knox (telegram), March 8, 1911, Knox MSS.; Clark, *My Quarter Century*, 2:7–8; Oscar W. Underwood, *Drifting Sands of Party Politics* (New York, 1928), 166; *Kansas City Star*, March 2, 1911.

[29] *New York Times*, and *Des Moines Register and Leader*, March 3, 4, 1911.

[30] The new House was composed of 228 Democrats and 160 Republicans.

Aldrich had gone Hale, Burrows, Carter, Depew, Flint, Kean Piles, Scott, and Warner. Death had also depleted the ranks of the Republicans. In January, Senator Elkins had died at his home in West Virginia, and the following summer marked the death of William P. Frye. Thus when the Senate convened in April there was hardly a Republican senator, with the exception of Lodge, Root, and Penrose, who had counted for anything in the party councils of the past years. Moreover, the Republican control of the body was a fiction. For with their recent victories the progressives, controlling from ten to fourteen votes, held the balance of power between the evenly divided Democrats and Regular Republicans.[31] The Senate was indeed a "desolate place" for one Republican of the old school who was convinced that in the place of "sincere candid men" there now sat "self-seeking mountebanks engaged in peddling out sophistries to the crowd."[32]

The progressives immediately sought to make their strategic position count. Forty-six nominal Republican congressmen attending a progressive organization meeting in the House declared that thereafter the group would not be bound by the decisions of the Republican caucus. In the Senate the thirteen progressive Republican senators[33] went even further on the road to independence. Meeting before the committee membership was announced, they demanded that they be recognized as a separate minority within the Republican party. Moreover, since their ratio to the Regular Republicans was about one to four, they asked that they be given one-fifth of all the Republican places on the committees. When these surprising requests were denied, they obstructed the election of Senator Gallinger as president pro tempore. Thus

[31] In the Sixty-second Congress the Senate nominally was composed of 41 Democrats and 50 Republicans.

[32] W. O. Bradley to Thomas H. Carter, April 18, 1911, Carter to Elmer Murphy, June 24, 1911, Carter MSS.

[33] La Follette of Wisconsin, Cummins and Kenyon of Iowa, Bristow of Kansas, Brown of Nebraska, Borah of Idaho, Dixon of Montana, Crawford of South Dakota, Gronna of North Dakota, Clapp of Minnesota, Bourne of Oregon, Poindexter of Washington, and Works of California.

at the opening of the Sixty-second Congress there were really three distinct parties in the national legislature. The events of 1912 were already being foreshadowed.[34]

Meanwhile Taft, with an unprecedented show of action, was striking hard for reciprocity. Once more the bill was introduced into the House and once more it was attacked by both progressives and Regular Republicans. As Cannon came to the end of a particularly fiery assault, a strange scene was enacted; two progressive Republicans, Kendall and Pickett of Iowa, rushed down the aisle to grasp Cannon's hand in effusive congratulations.[35] The bill was finally passed, however, on April 21 by a vote of 268 to 89, with 78 of the opposition votes coming from the Republican side of the chamber.[36] Seldom has the Republican party been so divided on a measure. While minority leader Mann was captaining the fight for the proposal, Dalzell, Fordney, the Republican whip Dwight, and Cannon were bending every effort to defeat it. Of the progressives, Cooper, Madison, Murdock, and Kent voted aye, and Lenroot Morris, Prouty, and Kinkaid were opposed.

In the Senate a similar misalliance took place, and the country was treated to the strange spectacle of high-tariff Democrats aligned with low-tariff progressives and "Chinese Wall" Stalwart Republicans. For once Senator La Follette worked hand in glove with the Democratic Senator Bailey and the Stalwart Gallinger and Smoot. But again opposition was futile. The administration succeeded in winning over enough Republican votes to make a majority. The bill was passed on July 22 by a vote of 53 to 27, and thus only needed the president's signature and Canadian approval to become effective.[37] Ironically enough for Taft, who had irreparably

[34] *Des Moines Register and Leader*, April 4, 1911; *New York Times*, April 21, 1911.
[35] *Congressional Record*, 62 Congress, 1 Session, vol. 47, pt. 3, p. 406; *Des Moines Register and Leader*, April 20, 1911.
[36] *Congressional Record*, 62 Congress, 1 Session, vol. 47, pt. 3, p. 559.
[37] Taft to Knox, March 11, 1911, Knox MSS. Of the 27 votes in opposition, 3 were cast by Democrats, and 12 each by Regular and progressive Republicans. *Congressional Record*, 62 Congress, 1 Session, vol. 47, pt. 3, p. 559.

split his party in a desperate effort to get the bill passed, approval by Canada was not forthcoming.

Canadian manufacturing interests and Canadian nationalism leagued together against the measure. They had ample ammunition. For the president had foolishly talked of Canada being "at the parting of the ways"[38] and Champ Clark had urged annexation. Spurred on by breast-beating British imperialists, "Our Lady of the Snows"[39] late in September repudiated reciprocity by defeating the Laurier government which had proposed it. And thus, in the words of Theodore Roosevelt, the "grim comedy" came to an end.[40]

But the unfortunate president had not yet come to the end of the special session's road. Before the reciprocity bill had passed, La Follette was hard at work effecting a Democratic-progressive coalition for the purpose of revising the tariff, schedule by schedule. Then a series of tariff bills was rapidly jammed through the Democratic House. The first of these was the so-called Farmers' Free List bill, which placed on the free list articles purchased by agricultural producers. It was soon followed by acts reducing the duties on the woolen and cotton schedules, the latter reducing the ad valorem average on manufactured cotton goods from 48 to 27 per cent.[41]

When the bills had passed the Senate, after some clever political manipulation by La Follette, the president vetoed all three on the ground that they were not scientific but political. In a speech at Hamilton, Massachusetts, a short time later, Taft amplified his position by declaring that he was aware that tariff revision was vitally needed; but revision should be carried out in a scientific manner and only after the

[38] The Canadian minister of finance later wrote to Secretary Knox that President Taft by his numerous unfortunate utterances had done more than any other man to persuade Canada to vote against the measure. W. S. Fielding to Philander C. Knox, September 29, 1911, Knox MSS.

[39] For a rabid imperialist plea see the poem "Our Lady of the Snows" by Rudyard Kipling.

[40] Roosevelt to Lodge, September 22, 1911, Roosevelt MSS.

[41] *Congressional Record*, 62 Congress, 1 Session, vol. 47, pt. 4, pp. 3584–3585.

tariff board had made recommendations on the subject.[42] With this speech the president walked neatly into a trap, for a damaging question was immediately asked of him. If he was so convinced of the value of the tariff board's scientific rates, why then had he advocated reciprocity without such findings?[43] The progressive answer, of course, was that the president was a foe of all reductions that would in the least hurt the manufacturer, whereas he favored reductions at the expense of the farmer. One progressive senator believed that Taft, by his vetoes, had driven "the last nail in his coffin."[44]

It was during this session of Congress that another determined effort was made by the progressives to pass an enabling resolution calling for the direct election of senators. Many previous attempts had failed. Andrew Johnson in the House, as senator and as president, had persistently advocated the amendment. After 1872 there was scarcely a session of Congress in which such a resolution had not passed the House. But invariably it had met its death in the Senate. By 1910 more than two-thirds of the states had declared for an amendment, and a year later the Senate Judiciary Committee surprisingly reported a resolution favorably to the floor.

Perhaps the one thing that forced consideration of the resolution was the so-called Lorimer affair. In August, 1908, the State of Illinois held a primary election to guide the legislature in choosing a United States senator. In this election William Lorimer was not a candidate. In fact, his name was not mentioned until January, 1909, after the two leading Republican candidates had failed to secure a majority, and it was not until May 13 that he got his first vote. But on the next day, Lorimer, long a questionable figure in Illinois machine politics, received the coveted prize by suddenly obtaining overnight 108 votes, of which 53 were cast by Democratic members.[45]

The sudden shift in both Republican and Democratic

[42] *Outlook*, 99: 53–54 (September 9, 1911).
[43] *Kansas City Star*, August 19, 1911.
[44] Coe I. Crawford to Roosevelt, July 27, 1911, Roosevelt MSS.
[45] *Outlook*, 97: 13 (January 7, 1911).

votes looked suspicious enough to warrant a state investigation. Incontestable evidence was produced at the investigation to show that a slush fund of a hundred thousand dollars had been contributed by large Chicago corporations to aid in the election of Lorimer.[46] That the money had been used in an illegal manner was proved beyond doubt when four Illinois legislators confessed in court that they had received a sizeable sum of money to vote for Lorimer. In return for the money it was understood that the business interests would be amply recompensed. Lorimer, they were told, was the "proper man" to take care of the tariff.[47]

Early in 1910 a progressive-sponsored resolution to inquire into the alleged corruption passed the Senate. The investigating committee, dominated by a Regular Republican majority, reported back to the body in December, 1910. It vindicated Lorimer on the ground that since only seven votes of his majority of fourteen were proved to have been purchased, he had therefore received an untainted majority of seven, and was properly elected.[48]

This subtle reasoning produced a furor in the country. With the encouragement of popular support, the progressive block in the Senate continued its attack on Lorimer and for once they found a willing ally in the president, who felt that the Illinois election should "be stamped with disapproval."[49] But to get action from the Senate was exceedingly difficult, for Lorimer was supported by a solid alliance of "big money" and the Regular machine. Despite the fact that the combined urgings of Taft and Roosevelt won over Root and Lodge, the Senate in a roll call vote on March 1, 1911, declared by a 46 to 40 margin that William Lorimer had been duly elected.

At the same time that the Lorimer matter was being fought

[46] *Election of William Lorimer*, Senate Document No. 484, 62 Congress, 2 Session, 16: 431–436.
[47] *Ibid.*, vol. 18, 2023. Lorimer also had for years been taking care of the Republican fiscal deficit in Illinois. Martin J. Hutchens to Thomas H. Carter, December 14, 1910, Carter MSS.
[48] *Outlook*, 96: 987 (December 31, 1910).
[49] Taft to Roosevelt, January 6, 1911, Roosevelt MSS.

out, the progressives, led by Senator Borah, were urging a resolution seeking the direct election of senators. The Regulars, in turn, sought desperately to defeat the resolution. Led by Root and Lodge, they hammered at the measure with long-winded speeches for a month. Root declared that its passage would destroy states' rights and the federal system, and that the whole amendment was based on the theory that the state governments were too corrupt to make wise choices.[50] Lodge was sure that it would increase corruption a hundredfold, for then the whole electorate instead of the state legislators would be bribed.[51] Senator Heyburn of Idaho excelled in his denunciation of the measure. Stating that the demand for the popular election of senators was an "ignorant demand," he declared that he had no wish for the people's votes, for they had not sent him to the Senate, and that he never wanted to see the day the Constitution was amended.[52]

Despite the oratory it seemed for a while that the measure would pass through a combination of Democratic and progressive votes. But the conservative Republicans had one last card up their sleeve. It was the ace of race prejudice. The Sutherland amendment, which gave the national government the power to alter state election laws, was added to the resolution. This alleged threat to white supremacy in the South alienated enough Democratic senators to defeat the measure when it came to a vote on February 28, 1911.[53]

The Senate's defeat of the direct election measure and its retention of Lorimer led to a fusillade of public criticism. Lodge was excoriated as a "political Ichabod," Root as a man with his face eternally turned to the past. The *Kansas City Star* predicted that soon the majority of the American people would "see much wisdom in the idea lately advanced to abolish the upper House."[54] Popular indignation could not long

[50] *Congressional Record*, 61 Congress, 3 Session, vol. 46, pt. 3, pp. 2241–2246.
[51] Lodge to Roosevelt, February 6, 1911, Roosevelt MSS.
[52] *Congressional Record*, 61 Congress, 3 Session, vol. 46, pt. 3, p. 2768.
[53] *Ibid.*, pt. 4, p. 3639.
[54] *Kansas City Star*, January 21, 1911.

be disregarded. The following year Lorimer was unseated, and the resolution for direct elections passed.

From 1910 to 1912 the struggle between progressive and conservative Republicanism continued. Progressives severely censured the president for vetoing the enabling act to create the states of Arizona and New Mexico. Taft could not stomach the Arizona constitution allowing the recall of judicial officials. He did not mince words in defense of his veto. Branding the scheme as one that would make of justice "legalized terrorism," he declared that "the people at the polls no more than kings upon the throne are fit to pass upon questions involving the judicial interpretation of the law." His distrust of a complete democracy was all too apparent. "The rule of the people," he continued, "would degenerate into anarchy and revert to despotism as the only way of escape,"[55] These unfortunate statements were soon answered by the progressive Republican press. Taft had vetoed more than the recall of judges, they exclaimed. He had vetoed "the basic principles of popular government.[56]

The session was not without its constructive aspects. In fact, discounting the reciprocity bill, the direct elections measure, and a proposal urged by the president to enlarge the powers of the tariff commission, the first session of the Sixty-second Congress was notable for its legislative achievements. Acting upon a report of the Interstate Commerce Commission, Congress passed a parcel post act.[57] It enacted legislation providing for the establishment of the Industrial Bureau and the Children's Bureau. It abolished the manufacturing of phosphorus matches in the United States, provided for an eight-hour day on government projects, amended the Food and Drugs Act and the Alaskan Civil Government Act, and passed a federal corrupt practices bill. Nevertheless, viewed

[55] *New York Times*, August 16, 1911.
[56] *Philadelphia North American*, November 17, 1911; *La Follette's Weekly*, August 26, 1911; *Kansas City Star*, August 16, 1911.
[57] The commission reported that the express companies in 1909 through monopolistic practices had made an average profit of fifty per cent of all invested capital. *Ibid.*, January 17, 1911.

from the standpoint of the president's future, the session was a dismal failure. Canadian reciprocity had incurred for him the enmity of the conservatives, irretrievably lost him the support of the progressive wing, and gained him nothing except the temporary support of the press. His veto of the "popgun" tariff bills had placed him in a position extremely difficult to defend, and his veto of the statehood bill had further convinced the progressive forces that at heart he was a hopeless conservative. All in all, Taft's political position in 1911 would have been much more tenable had he not called Congress into session.

While Taft was slowly digging his own political grave, other forces were seeking to hasten his interment. During the last week of 1910, Senators La Follette and Bourne met with a small group of progressives to draw up a declaration of progressive principles. This manifesto was sent, with an invitation to attend a national conference, to progressive leaders in every state.[58] The meeting, held on January 21, gave birth to the National Progressive Republican League. Organized at the La Follette home, its charter membership embraced senators, six governors, numerous congressmen, and other important non-officeholding progressives.[59] Ostensibly the League was formed to advocate progressive principles. Its official declaration listed five such reforms. But no one doubted that its fundamental *raison d'être* was to defeat Taft for the renomination in 1912. The Regular press immediately recognized this as its purpose and promptly anathematized its founders as "insurrectors," "party wreckers," and "disgruntled rebels."[60]

The League grew rapidly. Even before its official founding

[58] La Follette, *Autobiography*, 494.

[59] The governors were Hiram Johnson of California, McGovern of Wisconsin, Chase S. Osborn of Michigan, William R. Stubbs of Kansas, Chester H. Aldrich of Nebraska, and J. M. Carey of Wyoming. Among other well known charter members were the two Pinchots, James R. Garfield, Louis D. Brandeis, Charles R. Crane, Ray Stannard Baker, Francis J. Heney, Frederic C. Howe, W. S. Uren, and William Allen White.

[60] *New York Sun*, January 23, 24, 1911; *Chicago Inter-Ocean*, January, 24, 1911.

the State Progressive League of Minnesota had been born at a convention in Minneapolis. By March comparable state organizations had been set up in Wisconsin, Michigan, Nebraska, South Dakota, and Washington.[61] Soon the Progressive Federation of Publicists and Editors was organized as an auxiliary "to work for the nomination and election of a Progressive president." Included among its members were Norman Hapgood, editor of *Collier's*, Howard Brubaker, editor of *Success Magazine*, H. K. McClure of *McClure's*, Lincoln Steffens, and others. By the first of April the League with its auxiliaries and local units was a force to be reckoned with.

The guess that the League was little more than a nominating machine was soon confirmed by Senator Bourne. Early in February this one-time golfing companion of Taft ruthlessly attacked the president on the floor of the Senate. Reading the notorious Norton patronage letter, Bourne described Taft's actions as dishonest and corrupt. The senator was obviously making a campaign speech. He was also obviously overlooking the historic principles of patronage disposal, including those applied by Theodore Roosevelt.[62]

Two days later Senator Bourne, speaking in Boston, declared that the next presidential race would be between Governor Woodrow Wilson of New Jersey and Senator La Follette of Wisconsin. Roosevelt, the senator added, apparently as an afterthought, was on trial before the progressives of the country. If Roosevelt produced a program of concrete remedies for the present evils, he might capture the Republican nomination, Bourne intimated.[63] But in the spring of 1911 the National Progressive Republican League was mainly interested in pushing the candidacy of Robert Marion La Follette. By the middle of April it was said that all the progressive senators had agreed to support him, and there were many in Washington who thought that Taft would have some difficulty in obtaining the renomination. La Follette himself,

[61] *La Follette's Weekly*, April 22, 1911.
[62] *Congressional Record*, 61 Congress, 3 Session, vol. 46, pt. 4, p. 3551.
[63] *New York Times*, March 30, 1911.

after making sure of adequate financial support, largely pledged by Charles R. Crane, William Kent, the two Pinchots, and Alfred L. Baker, publicly announced his candidacy on June 17, 1911. With this announcement the campaign of 1912 had begun.[64]

The National Progressive Republican League in the spring of 1911 had one serious defect. It did not have the support of Theodore Roosevelt. From the start every effort was made by the organizers of the League to win that potent name. La Follette, Pinchot, Bourne, and others all besought the Colonel to throw his influence behind the League. "Now, Colonel," La Follette wrote, "can't you consistently give this movement the benefit of your great name and influence?"[65] Roosevelt in January, 1911, was not in the mood to act in any impetuous fashion. Exceedingly wary, he replied to an earlier request from La Follette, asking him to sign the call for the national meeting of the League, in a most ambiguous tone. "I wish I could see you personally," he wrote, "for I am rather doubtful whether it is advisable for me to be one of the signers of such a call. I should like to have gone over it with you."[66]

To understand Roosevelt's attitude properly one must understand the frame of mind in which the previous elections had left him. After encountering the first major defeat of his career he was in the depths of despondency. He truly felt that he was through as a national leader. In fact, he felt he had lost so much influence that although he offered to speak in Idaho for Senator Borah he questioned whether such a speech would help or hurt the Senator.[67]

His melancholy was not lightened by the critical letters that came to him after the election, from both Regular and progressive friends. Letters from ardent progressives were

[64] La Follette, *Autobiography*, 526.

[65] La Follette to Roosevelt, January 19, 1911, December 28, 1910, Roosevelt MSS.

[66] La Follette to Roosevelt, December 28, 1910, Roosevelt to La Follette, December 30, 1910, Roosevelt MSS.

[67] Roosevelt to Borah, January 19, 1911, and to W. D. Foulke, January 2, 1911, Roosevelt MSS.

full of implications that he had been far too conservative, that he was a straddler and had traded with his convictions.[68] Others, from Taft men, accused him of losing the election because he had refused to support the administration. Invariably the letters then went on to intimate that a declaration by Roosevelt of "avowed support" and "cordial endorsement" was but due the president.[69]

Roosevelt still believed that his previous summer's plan of compromise had been the proper one. To his progressive critics he defended his actions in the New York state convention and his support of Lodge by replying that he had "screwed" the New York platform "up to as high a pitch of radicalism as was possible"; and that he had been as radical in the East as he could possibly be without losing the support of the great majority of voters. He then went on to say that the defeat in New York was attributable not to the compromise made but to the fact that "we were too radical"; he implied that to have gone further in a left direction at the time would have been foolish.[70] To his conservative critics he replied with equal heat that the progressives had "a genuine wrong to complain of," and that if he had come out more strongly for Taft the disaster would have been even greater.[71]

Before the beginning of 1911 Roosevelt had little hope for 1912, whichever faction captured the nomination. What might have been feasible in the summer of 1910, he wrote to friends who were neutral in the party struggle, was now impossible. The breach was now too wide, the cleavage far too sharp for a general reconciliation. The Republican party was heading straight toward defeat and not even Roosevelt could stop it. Each side would "have to dree its weird," he sadly opined, before common sense returned. Then and only then

[68] William Kent to Roosevelt, November 18, 1910, Roosevelt MSS. Bonaparte to H. C. Gauss, November 17, 1910, Gauss to Bonaparte November 14, 1910, Bonaparte MSS.

[69] Seth Low to Roosevelt, November 10, 1910, Roosevelt MSS.

[70] Roosevelt to William Allen White, November 11, 17, 1910, and to William Kent, November 28, 1910, Roosevelt MSS.

[71] Roosevelt to Seth Low, November 16, 1910, and to F. S. Oliver, February 8, 1911, Roosevelt MSS.

would it be possible to obtain a Republican working majority.[72]

Until the time that defeat forced mutual concessions from
both sides the administration perhaps "offered a little better
promise for good than anything practical in sight." When
everything was weighed in the balance, the views of the conservatives, Roosevelt felt, were "not quite as erroneous" as
those of the radicals. As for the "ultra radicals" who sought
to defeat Taft for the renomination, they were traveling the
road toward the company of single-taxers and prohibition-
ists. The right thing to do was to renominate Taft and face
defeat, and then reorganize under "some progressive leadership." This from Roosevelt in January, 1911.[73]

Feeling thus, Roosevelt might have openly repudiated the
National Progressive Republican League. He did no such
thing. From reading his voluminous correspondence over the
period, one gets the impression that Roosevelt himself fully
expected to head the reorganization of the party after 1912,
in fact, felt characteristically that he was the one man in the
country to see it through to success. For this reason it would
never do for him to completely alienate either wing of the
party. And so from January to November, 1911, Roosevelt
walked on eggs.

Although he would not join the League, Roosevelt went
out of his way to be cordial to its founders. Early in its career
he wrote both La Follette and Bourne that while he was not
at all decided about the recall, the initiative, and the referendum, he was in complete agreement with the rest of the principles of the League and especially with those enunciated in
the Wisconsin platform. Later he heartily congratulated La
Follette upon his work in the Lorimer affair, characterizing
it as "one of the greatest services that could have been rendered to decent government and good American citizen-

[72] Roosevelt to Robert Bacon, January 2, 1911, and to William Allen
White, January 24, 1911, Roosevelt MSS.
[73] Roosevelt to John C. Greenway, November 21, 1910, and to Theodore
Roosevelt, Jr., January 2, 1911, Roosevelt MSS.

ship."[74] But when the requests for his membership became importunate, Roosevelt shied off. Although he himself knew, he said, that the League was not meant to be an instrument with which to attack Taft, he was sure it would be taken that way. Since he "was very anxious not to appear as going into a movement for the political control of the party," he thought he could better support it from the outside. He did, however, promise that he would "cordially" endorse the League, with certain qualifications, over his own signature.[75]

In the *Outlook* for January 14 Roosevelt kept his promise. "Under the leadership of Senator La Follette," he wrote, "Wisconsin during the last decade, had advanced at least as far as, and probably further than, any other state in securing both genuine popular rule, and the wise use of the collective power of the people." Four months later Roosevelt reiterated his fulsome praise of the Wisconsin Senator in an article entitled "Wisconsin: An Object Lesson for the Rest of the Union."[76]

Battle Bob had never completely trusted Roosevelt. He did not trust him now. Nor was he altogether satisfied with Roosevelt's qualified endorsement. He made some effort to have a personal conference with Roosevelt, but because of the senator's illness the meeting never took place. La Follette did get some idea, however, through the medium of third parties of how Roosevelt felt about contesting Taft's renomination. In March, according to La Follette's *Autobiography*, Roosevelt told various progressives that he did not favor putting up a candidate against Taft, for he felt that 1912 was certain to be a Democratic year.[77] That much would seem to be in harmony with Roosevelt's other correspondence of the period. After his return from his Western trip, though, the trail becomes confused. It is certain that Gilson Gardner visited

[74] Roosevelt to La Follette, January 3, 17, 1910, and to Jonathan Bourne, January 2, 1910, Roosevelt MSS.
[75] Roosevelt to La Follette, January 24, 1910, Roosevelt MSS.
[76] *Outlook*, 97: 59 (January 14, 1911); 98: 143 (May 27, 1911).
[77] La Follette, *Autobiography*, 502–503.

him as La Follette's emissary. It is also relatively certain that he did not get Roosevelt to commit himself during their conference. When Gardner returned to Washington, La Follette announced his candidacy.[78] Later, after Roosevelt precipitately jumped into the presidential race, it was to be freely charged that he had used La Follette as a stalking horse. It has even been suggested that Roosevelt gave La Follette a definite commitment. The charge immediately after the event seemed plausible. Roosevelt's praise of the Wisconsin senator and the timing of his own entrance into the presidential race appeared to substantiate the story. But it was not so. In the spring of 1911 Roosevelt was not thinking of 1912 but rather of 1913 and the years beyond. That was why he could honestly write in June, in reply to La Follette's letter of thanks, that he was happy to express himself in the *Outlook*. "I felt that I owed it to Wisconsin," Roosevelt ended, "and my dear Senator, that I owed it to you."[79]

With his left hand patting the progressives, Roosevelt was equally busy with his right, carrying on a caressing correspondence with Taft. This resumption of relations was initiated by the president, who, in a characteristically generous mood, was willing to forgive and forget. In November, after the sad elections, Taft wrote his former chief an exceedingly cordial letter describing the progress of the Panama Canal. It would be completed, he said graciously, about the first of July 1913, "a date at which both you and I will be private citizens and we can then visit the canal together."[80] Taft followed this overture with even more concrete evidences of his friendship. In December he sent Roosevelt the proof of his annual message, asking him to read it and make suggestions for changes. Later he asked for advice from Oyster Bay on the Japanese question. The president was sure that his secre-

[78] Gilson Gardner papers, cited in Walter F. McCaleb, *Theodore Roosevelt* (New York, 1931), 300–301; see also La Follette, *Autobiography*, 512–513.

[79] La Follette to Roosevelt, June 8, 1911, and Roosevelt's reply, June 13, Roosevelt MSS.

[80] Taft to Roosevelt, November 30, 1910, Roosevelt MSS.

tary of state could benefit from the counsel of one who had "studied the matter with a good deal of care."[81]

Roosevelt did not reject Taft's overtures. He read his message with "great interest" and had nothing to say "save in the way of agreement and commendation." To Taft's inquiries on foreign affairs he replied with an extensive letter of cordial advice.[82] In his first speech after the election Roosevelt heartily commended Taft's selection of a chief justice for the Supreme Court.[83] This literary camaraderie extended over into the first half of the following year. The two men advised with each other on the Lorimer affair, on which they were in substantial agreement, over the president's proposal for reciprocity with Canada, which Roosevelt thought "admirable from every standpoint," over the Far Eastern situation and the Mexican revolution.[84] When the latter seemed to be assuming serious proportions, Roosevelt asked Taft for permission to raise a division of cavalry if it came to war. He was certain he could organize "as formidable a body of horse riflemen . . . as has ever been seen." The president replied that he would be only too glad to conform to Roosevelt's desires if the occasion arose.[85]

Early in June the two men met in Baltimore at a celebration for Cardinal Gibbons, shook hands heartily, whispered together, and at times broke into unrestrained laughter.[86] Then just when it seemed as if the old relationship might be restored, the *rapprochement* came to an abrupt halt. The last correspondence between them for years to be found in the Roosevelt manuscripts is a short note from Taft thanking the Colonel for his gift on the occasion of the president's silver wedding. It was dated June 18, 1911.[87]

[81] Taft to Roosevelt, December 2, 9, 20, 1910, Roosevelt MSS.

[82] Roosevelt to Taft, December 8, 22, 1910, Roosevelt MSS.

[83] *Des Moines Register and Leader*, December 13, 1910.

[84] Taft to Roosevelt, January 6, 10, 17, March 22, 1911, Roosevelt to Taft, January 7, 12, 1911, Roosevelt MSS.

[85] Roosevelt to Taft, March 14, 1911, Taft to Roosevelt, March 22, 1911, Roosevelt MSS.

[86] *New York Times*, June 7, 1911.

[87] Taft to Roosevelt, June 18, 1911, Roosevelt MSS.

One can only conjecture why the relations between the two men cooled so suddenly. Roosevelt had never really forgotten Taft's actions in New York in the summer of 1910. He held Taft responsible for the remarks of the president's associates. He reminded Henry White, who was seeking to draw the two men closer together in March of 1911, that McKinley, Hillis, and other of Taft's associates were occupied even then "in a perfectly dastardly campaign of slander or mendacity" against him and that Taft had not lifted a finger to stop them.[88] Perhaps in June he heard something from the tale-peddling Lodge, who was then, as usual, turning an honest political penny in both camps. Perhaps the Colonel felt that the increasing rumors to the effect that he would support Taft in 1912 ought to be laid once and for all. It may have been more than coincidence that the correspondence between the two stopped just after Roosevelt issued a public statement that he would not be a candidate himself in 1912 and that he would not support any man for the nomination. Certainly Roosevelt's critical articles appearing in the *Outlook* in June and July on the administration's attitude toward the recall in Arizona fostered the estrangement.[89]

But Roosevelt's renewed criticism of the administration was decidedly not an indication, as some seemed to think, that he had changed his mind about 1912. From January, 1911, until the following November there is not one scrap of evidence in his correspondence to support such a conclusion. In March, 1911, while preparing for his transcontinental speaking tour, he declared repeatedly that the trip was the last one of its kind he would ever take.[90] On his return, many ambitious politicians, mistaking his trip for a bid for support, wrote to him offering to build up an organization. He answered each one in the same tone: that he would "under no circumstances" consider the nomination and that he counted

[88] Roosevelt to Henry White, March 5, 1911, Roosevelt MSS.
[89] *New York Times*, June 8, 1911; *Outlook*, 98: 378 (June 24, 1911); 98: 613 (July 22, 1911).
[90] Roosevelt to Hiram Johnson, March 30, 1911, to Arthur Lee, February 2, 1911, and to Taft, April 1, 1911, Roosevelt MSS.

on all his friends to use their energies to stop and not to start such movements.[91]

During the summer and early autumn of 1911 Roosevelt, like the Tar Baby, said nothing. For the next year, he wrote Henry Wallace, he was going to follow the advice once given by a New Bedford whaling master. The captain had told his mate that all he wanted from him "was silence and damned little of that."[92] Accordingly, for the next five months Roosevelt declined all invitations to speak, even on innocuous subjects. As for the race between Taft and La Follette, privately he thought that the progressives were losing ground and that the president was in a stronger position each day. He was highly critical of La Follette for working with the Democrats to pass the "popgun" tariffs and by September was sure that Taft would be renominated on the first ballot.[93]

Roosevelt became even more impatient with La Follette when the senator sponsored a resolution empowering the Clapp committee which was investigating campaign contributions to inquire into the financial transactions between John D. Archbold, George W. Perkins, and Theodore Roosevelt. This did not prevent him, however, from congratulating La Follette on the first chapter of his *Autobiography*, which was then appearing in serial form in a popular periodical.[94]

All through the summer and into the early autumn Roosevelt flirted with both Regulars and progressives. But at the same time he clearly desired the renomination of William Howard Taft. He even defended the president from the more severe of his progressive detractors. When Republicans wrote that they would probably support Woodrow Wilson in 1912, Roosevelt urged them to vote for Taft.[95]

Why in September of 1911 did Roosevelt so earnestly de-

[91] Roosevelt to Frank Knox, May 5, 19, 1911, to E. Mont Reily, June 27, 1911, and to J. C. O'Laughlin, June 25, 1911, Roosevelt MSS.

[92] Roosevelt to Henry C. Wallace, June 27, 1911, Roosevelt MSS.

[93] Roosevelt to Arthur Lee, July 27, 1911, to Lodge, August 22, 1911, and to Benjamin I. Wheeler, August 22, 1911, Roosevelt MSS.

[94] Roosevelt to La Follette, September 29, 1911, Roosevelt MSS.

[95] Roosevelt to William Kent, September 19, 1911, Roosevelt MSS.

sire Taft's renomination? Perhaps the answer lay in his letter to Arthur Lee of a year before. Defeat was in store for any Republican, he wrote, "and therefore for every reason I most earnestly hope to retain sufficient control to make Taft's nomination inevitable."[96] Only after the defeat, Roosevelt continued, would it be possible to reorganize the party under "capable and sane progressive leadership." And throughout the length and breadth of the Republican party who else was there better able to reorganize capably and sanely than Theodore Roosevelt himself?

[96] Roosevelt to Arthur Lee, September 16, November 11, 1910, Roosevelt MSS.

CHAPTER SEVEN

Awaiting the Call of the People

POLITICS WAS IN the air throughout the autumn of
1911. Daily rumors had it that Roosevelt would soon add his
voice to the clamor. And in the middle of September the
president himself set out on a coast-to-coast speaking tour
with the object of feeling the public pulse. If Taft was expecting a burst of enthusiasm in response to his efforts, he was
vastly disappointed. It was a standing joke over the country
that the president had changed his itinerary in the middle of
the tour to include a few Southern states so that he might
thaw out. His mood reflecting the noticeable coldness of his
welcome, Taft became very despondent over his future.
While he was in Denver he publicly admitted that there was
a strong probability of his defeat the following year.[1]

That admission was, to say the least, exceedingly impolitic,
but Taft had every reason to believe, in September and
October of 1911, that it was eminently correct. Labor was
becoming more hostile each day to the administration. The
American Federationist was branding the course of the government as one of "defiant, uncompromising hostility" to
the causes of the American workingman.[2] The congressional
progressives had been alienated beyond all hope of conciliation, and because of Canadian reciprocity a large section of
the farming population had been estranged along with them.
That ill-considered measure incurred the antagonism of the
devotees of high protection, an antagonism that was still
smouldering three months after the issue had been disposed of. "The whole proceeding," wrote Foraker, "indicated that the President deemed to regard himself not as a

[1] *New York Times*, October 6, 1911.
[2] *American Federationist*, 18: 996 (December, 1911).

mere Executive, but as an actual Ruler, whose will must be law."[3]

If Taft had been in any sense a politician, he would have played to the conservative faction in his party in the autumn of 1911. It alone had a disposition to renominate him. But the president remained a jurist in a political office. That was his tragedy. Instead of placating the industrial interests of the nation at this critical time in his career, he drove them almost to the point of personal antagonism by launching out into a crusade for the strict enforcement of the Sherman Anti-Trust Law. At Boise, Idaho, early in October, he warned business to readjust itself to return to a competitive system, and declared that the attorney general was under orders to prosecute without discretion. When bitter objections poured in upon him, he merely gritted his teeth and vowed that the crusade against monopolies would go on "no matter whether we be damned or not."[4] And while Taft was thus verbally defying big business, his attorney general was busy in Washington initiating suit after suit against alleged monopolistic concerns. By the end of the administration the president could rightfully claim that he had done more to enforce the Sherman Law than any of his predecessors, including Roosevelt "the trust buster."

Wall Street was in a psychological panic; the atmosphere around it was blue with pessimism. In unison industry urged the president and the attorney general to desist. Financiers who had recommended Wickersham to Taft now thought of their protégé as "basely ungrateful."[5] The *New York Sun* began a violent attack first on the attorney general and then on the president. Suggesting that George W. Wickersham was doing more to injure the "established institutions of society" than any anarchist who had ever lived, it called

[3] Joseph B. Foraker to W. A. Jones, December 9, 1911, Foraker MSS., Library of Congress. This was an amusing statement in view of Taft's theoretical conviction that presidents should be administrators and not makers of legislative policy.

[4] *New York Sun*, October 6, 20, 1911.

[5] Emanuel Parker to Grenville M. Dodge, January 13, 1912, Dodge MSS.

upon President Taft to dispose of this disturber of business peace. When Taft refused, the *Sun* indicted him along with Wickersham for the cloud resting upon industry and accused him of bringing on a major panic.[6]

With the president under attack by both conservatives and progressives, the politicians began to break for cover. Rumors were plentiful that Postmaster General Hitchcock and George Cortelyou would attempt to nominate a "business candidate" for 1912. Lodge thought that the losses in the November election could be ascribed almost entirely to the desire of the small business man to hit back at Taft for the shock he had given honest business.[7] Almost every political observer agreed that by his anti-trust campaign the president had lost the confidence of the nation's business interests and had imperilled his candidacy for 1912. The anti-Taft campaign sponsored by business was not mere talk. In 1912 Alexander H. Revell, a Chicago merchant who contributed heavily to the Roosevelt campaign, stated that he had "given up Taft" because of his persistent attacks upon legitimate business interests.[8]

While the president was apparently losing his hold on the conservatives, La Follette was leading the progressives in a determined onslaught upon the administration. Supplied with money by Charles R. Crane, the Pinchots, William Kent, Rudolph Spreckels, Alfred P. Baker, and William Flinn, the La Follette organization, which had opened up headquarters in Washington, was keeping as many as fifty clerks busy deluging the country with anti-Taft propaganda.[9]

Despite this activity, however, La Follette apparently was not developing the strength necessary for victory. He did

[6] H. C. Gauss to Bonaparte, January 17, 1911, Bonaparte to Gauss, January 18, 1911, Bonaparte MSS.; *New York Sun,* October 1, 28, 29, 31, 1911.

[7] Lodge to Roosevelt, November 13, 1911, Roosevelt MSS.

[8] Alexander H. Revell to Roosevelt, March 21, 1912, Roosevelt MSS.; Joseph B. Foraker to W. A. Jones, December 9, 1911, Foraker to James Boyle, December 7, 1911, Foraker MSS., Cincinnati, Ohio; Frank Trumbull to Frank A. Vanderlip, October 3, 1911, Dodge MSS.

[9] *La Follette's Weekly,* June 1, 1912; *New York Times,* October 24, 1911.

not, of course, attract any of the conservative support that the administration was alienating. In the eyes of businessmen the senator from Wisconsin was little short of a harbinger of revolution. Furthermore, the La Follette candidacy was not securing the undivided support of the progressives. Many of them, like Beveridge, who refused to sit on a La Follette reception committee in Indiana, preferred to remain strictly neutral.[10] Perhaps they were reticent with a purpose. It was repeatedly said of Beveridge that he was doing the "favorite son stunt," hoping that the "lightning would strike him" as compromise candidate. Other progressives, like Governor W. R. Stubbs of Kansas, would not support La Follette because they felt that he could not possibly win. Governor Stubbs spent most of his energy urging Roosevelt to jump into the fight.[11] Still others, who had committed themselves to the cause of the Wisconsin senator, had little hope for success, and therefore little heart. Cummins thought that it was impossible for La Follette to come to the convention with more than two hundred votes, and Bristow felt that Roosevelt was the only man who could save the party from a smash.[12]

In fact, this progressive disposition to turn to Roosevelt, even while he was vociferously shouting no, ran throughout the country. Both the *Philadelphia North American* and the *Kansas City Star*, two journals that had labored long for the progressive cause, all but ignored the La Follette campaign in the autumn of 1911. Indeed, they did much to harm it by raising the hope, every now and then, that Roosevelt could be induced to run. Within the La Follette organization Gifford Pinchot, Medill McCormick, and Gilson Gardner warned La Follette that if he antagonized Roosevelt they would have to leave him.[13]

---

[10] Bowers, *Beveridge*, 415.

[11] W. R. Stubbs to Roosevelt, December 4, 1911, Roosevelt MSS.

[12] Cummins to Beveridge, July 13, 1911, in Bowers, *Beveridge*, 412; J. B. Bishop to Roosevelt, October 30, 1911, Roosevelt MSS.; Bonaparte to Gauss, February 6, 1912, Bonaparte MSS.

[13] La Follette, *Autobiography*, 545.

As the weeks went by La Follette became painfully aware of the increasing Roosevelt sentiment. When reports drifted into his headquarters that his candidacy was being obstructed by men working for Roosevelt, he assumed that there was a plot within his own organization to turn his strength, once developed, over to the Colonel. It was not long before he thought that actual sabotage was going on within his headquarters. In his *Autobiography*, written in the heat of the campaign, La Follette accused Medill McCormick of willfully changing the wording of printed material in order to commit him to the support of Roosevelt.[14] From these suspicions it was only a mental step to include Roosevelt in the conspiracy. And when James R. Garfield came direct from Oyster Bay in the middle of October to argue against pledging a Chicago progressive conference to La Follette, some of the senator's misgivings did not appear to be groundless.[15]

La Follette may have had some basis for his allegation that there was treachery inside his own organization. But his implication that Roosevelt himself became an early party to it in the hope of advancing his own candidacy cannot be taken very seriously. Up until October Roosevelt was urging the renomination of Taft and would not hear of a movement looking toward his own candidacy. Throughout the summer of 1911, however, it was becoming increasingly difficult for him to support the president. As the days went by he came to differ violently with the actions of the administration. Early in the summer he had been very critical of Taft's Mexican policy.[16] In August he expressed himself as being "extremely indignant" at the president's veto of the Arizona constitution providing for the recall of judges.[17] More irksome by far

[14] *Ibid.*, 555–558.
[15] Roosevelt to W. B. Howland, October 25, 1911, Roosevelt MSS.; *Philadelphia North American*, October 17, 1911; *New York Sun*, October 14, 1911; La Follette, *Autobiography*, 527.
[16] Roosevelt to John C. Greenway, May 12, 1911, Roosevelt MSS.; *Kansas City Star*, July 21, 1911.
[17] Roosevelt to Charles D. Willard, August 18, 1911, Roosevelt MSS.

was the administration's attempt to negotiate blanket arbitration treaties with the several nations for the peaceful settlement of almost all possible international disputes. Roosevelt's overdeveloped sense of nationalism flamed. Then, too, the president's actions were an implicit criticism of Roosevelt's own arbitration treaties negotiated and ratified while he was master of the White House. At any rate, Roosevelt felt that the Taft treaties were "hopelessly wrong." He would not object, he wrote, if only the British Isles were concerned—in fact he was prepared "to have a far closer relationship with the British Empire even than the one involved" —but as for other nations, the proposals were impossible.[18]

Describing the treaties as an outrage, born of some very "sloppy thinking," Roosevelt furiously set about to destroy them.[19] He wrote innumerable letters to Lodge, chairman of the Senate Foreign Relations Committee, corresponded with Root, and indirectly reached Cummins and Borah. His articles appeared in the *Outlook*, and he came very close to insulting the president. An invitation to a citizens' peace dinner, at which Taft was to deliver an address in support of his arbitration scheme, Roosevelt declined in a seven-page public letter. He even censured other men for accepting the invitation, calling them "traitors" to their own principles.[20] Long after the treaties had been properly emasculated, Roosevelt observed that "of all the misconduct of the Administration, no misconduct has been greater than that relating to foreign affairs."[21]

Again in the early autumn of 1911 Roosevelt found himself publicly opposing the White House. But this sharp divergence over policy would in all likelihood have had little political significance had not Taft then egregiously committed the most costly political mistake of his entire career. On the

[18] Roosevelt to Admiral Mahan, August 15, 1911, and to Arthur Lee, August 22, 1911, Roosevelt MSS.

[19] Roosevelt to Lodge, June 19, September 22, December 23, 1911, and to Carter H. Fitz-Hugh, October 31, 1911, Roosevelt MSS.

[20] *New York Times*, December 27, 1911.

[21] Roosevelt to Henry White, October 5, 1912, Roosevelt MSS.

morning of October 27, 1911, the administration announced
that it had initiated a suit against the United States Steel
Corporation for violation of the Sherman Anti-Trust Law. By
that action the president lit the fuse of a powder bag. The
resulting explosion changed the course of American politics.

In the midst of the panic of 1907 two representatives of the
United States Steel Corporation, Judge Elbert H. Gary and
Henry C. Frick, had quietly called on President Roosevelt
early one morning before he had breakfasted. They told him
that the Tennessee Coal and Iron Company had deposited
thousands of its shares of stock in important New York
banks as collateral for loans. The money panic had driven
the market value of these shares far below the total sum of
the loans, and the banks would shortly be forced to pour the
collateral on the open market. The rapid dumping of securities would again send the price of the stock down sharply,
with the result that the banks would fail and the panic thus
be turned into a major financial catastrophe.

To ward off such a smash, Frick and Gary told Roosevelt,
the United States Steel Corporation proposed, from a sense
of public duty, to buy the stock of the Tennessee Coal and
Iron Company from the ailing financial institutions and so
deliver the country from the impending disaster. Stressing
the fact that the motive for their action was not in any sense
dictated by a desire for profit, they intimated that only one
factor held them back. They feared that the government
would prosecute the steel corporation under the Sherman
Act for monopolistic practices. After Roosevelt indicated
that although he could not advise the purchase he did not
feel duty bound to interpose any objections, the deal was
consummated as proposed.[22]

When the panic had spent its force, voices began to be
raised against Roosevelt's action. Opponents of the merger

[22] On January 27, 1917, Richard H. Edmonds, editor of the *Manufac-
turer's Record*, couched a patriotic appeal in an open letter to the United
States Steel Corporation asking the company to develop the Tennessee
Coal and Iron property. Specifically he estimated the size of the iron and

charged that the steel corporation had used the panic as an excuse to gobble up a competitor at a ridiculously low price, that in doing so they had violated the Sherman Anti-Trust Law by effecting a monopoly, and that Roosevelt in tacitly sanctioning the action had been guilty of a serious breach of the law. It followed then, if the allegation were substantiated, that Roosevelt had either been in collusion with the lawbreakers or had been neatly hoaxed. In one case he was made out a rogue, in the other a fool.

Perhaps no allegation incensed Roosevelt more than the charge that he had been dishonest or had been fooled by the purchase of the Tennessee Iron and Coal Company. When the Democrats regained control of the House the Stanley committee began to investigate the steel corporation. Fishing for campaign material, the committee examined the Tennessee Coal and Iron sale and asked Roosevelt to appear before it for questioning. Roosevelt considered the request a sheer piece of effrontery by "dishonest jacks!" But despite the fact that President Taft urged him not to testify, he was so convinced of the falseness of the charge that he appeared before the committee to relate with much emphasis his interpretation of the affair.[23] He was willing to admit in the fall of 1911 that the representatives of the steel corporation probably had other than benevolent motives in absorbing the Tennessee Coal and Iron Company. But that admission did not indicate any subsidence of his flaming anger at the charge that he had acted contrary to the interests of the people at large and to the laws of the nation.[24]

It was natural then that Roosevelt on the morning of

coal deposits in Alabama as being equal to the company's entire holdings in iron and twice that of coal at the time the corporation was formed. Needless to say the panic price paid for the stock of the Tennessee Coal and Iron Company was extremely low.

[23] Roosevelt to James R. Garfield, August 9, 1911, and to Nicholas Longworth, June 19, 1911, Roosevelt MSS.

[24] Roosevelt to Albert H. Waller, August 7, 1911, and to Samuel H. Barker, August 11, 1911, Roosevelt MSS.; *Outlook*, 98: 866 (October 19, 1911).

October 27, 1911, should have had a profound convulsion of feeling about William Howard Taft. On that morning the administration announced that it had initiated suit against the United States Steel Corporation for violation of the Sherman Anti-Trust Law. In its bill of equity the government accused the steel corporation of being a monopoly and charged that it had effected the monopoly in part through the purchase of the Tennessee Coal and Iron Company. The obvious conclusion was that Roosevelt, in permitting the transaction, had been completely duped.[25]

Roosevelt's reaction was as instantaneous as it was violent. Since Taft had been in the Cabinet at the time, Roosevelt exclaimed, his protests should have been made at once, "or else from every consideration of honorable obligation" never under any circumstances afterward. Taft had not even maintained a discreet silence in 1907, Roosevelt wrote, but had actually been "emphatic in his commendation" of the merger. Therefore his present actions were in particularly bad faith and could only be characterized as "small, mean, and foolish."[26] When Secretary of War Stimson went to Oyster Bay a short time later he reported back to Taft that the Colonel "was as hard as nails and utterly implacable" against the administration.[27]

Not long after the government initiated the steel suit, Roosevelt made his public rebuttal in an article in the *Outlook*. He asserted that the administration had not told the whole truth. In hard-hitting and sentient paragraphs he maintained that he had acted in the public interest. He went on to develop a whole theory of industrial regulation and the control of trusts. Describing the efforts of the Taft administration to restore the competitive system by "destruction" of the trusts as "a return to the flintlocks of Washington's Con-

[25] *New York Times*, October 27, 1911.
[26] Roosevelt to Everett P. Wheeler, October 27, 1911, to James R. Garfield, October 31, 1911, to F. C. Saughlin, November 21, 1911, to T. C. Becker, November 25, 1911, and to J. B. Bishop, December 13, 1911, Roosevelt MSS.
[27] Butt, *Taft and Roosevelt*, 2: 811.

tinentals," he advocated in its stead a thoroughgoing regulation by a government body comparable in power to the Interstate Commerce Commission. Along such lines, he wrote, he
would even go so far as to set prices on commodities manufactured by monopolies.[28]

The article, which appeared in mid-November, evoked immediate response in all parts of the country. Business leaders, politicians, judges, and even preachers joined in a debate
on the merits of the plan. In the daily newspapers, in periodicals, and on the floor of Congress the whole problem of
trust regulation was once again the *pièce de résistance* of discussion. A considerable section of the business world, exceedingly weary of the administration's trust prosecutions, rallied
behind Roosevelt's plan. Frank A. Vanderlip, Andrew Carnegie, Elbert Gary, and Grenville M. Dodge were among the
many who publicly commended the article.[29] Roosevelt was
soon to hear from Henry White that his article had created
"a great impression in Wall St. Circles," a sentiment that was
constantly reiterated by his correspondents for weeks after
the article appeared. Even the intransigent Foraker thought
"that regulation and not destruction should be the aim of the
government." To some extent the *Outlook* article regained for
Roosevelt the support of the business interests he had lost at
Osawatomie.[30]

The trust article had one other important effect. Like a
stroke of summer lightning it brought again before the country the possibility of Roosevelt's candidacy. By October
most of the politicians urging Roosevelt into the presidential
race had given up hope. His reaction to the steel suit revital-

[28] Roosevelt, "The Trusts, the People, and the Square Deal," *Outlook*'
99: 649–656 (November 18, 1911).

[29] *Ibid.*, 99: 858 (December 9, 1911); 100: 261 (February 3, 1912). Grenville M. Dodge to Roosevelt, December 1, 1911, Roosevelt MSS.; Charles
J. Bonaparte to H. C. Gauss, November 27, 1911, Bonaparte MSS.

[30] Henry White to Roosevelt, October 16, 1911, Joseph B. Foraker to
W. A. Jones, December 9, 1911, letters to Roosevelt from J. F. Townsend,
November 18, 1911, E. A. Van Valkenburg, November 19, 1911, H. H.
Kohlsaat, November 21, 1911, and Charles A. Prouty, November 3, 1911,
Roosevelt MSS.

ized their efforts. Sensing the temper of the man, they importuned him to answer Taft in the "one most effective way." They agreed with Joseph Bucklin Bishop that the article as a "campaign platform" was "impregnable and powerful." "In my opinion," Bishop said, "the matter has already passed out of your hands. Whether you wish to be the candidate or not does not weigh a particle. The party needs you and will take you willy-nilly."[31] A month later Roosevelt himself thought that his effort in the *Outlook* "was generally accepted as bringing me forward for the Presidential nomination."[32]

Roosevelt was intensely angry at Taft. In August he had confessed that his inactive life at Oyster Bay was beginning to bore him.[33] But he did not jump rashly into the game without weighing for a considerable time the odds of winning and losing. As late as October 20 he predicted that Taft would be nominated on the first ballot.[34] On the day the steel suit was announced, he discussed the political situation at length in a confidential letter to Hiram Johnson. Warning Johnson not to show the letter to anyone he could not trust absolutely, Roosevelt asserted that Taft never thought of, never believed in, nor appreciated the tenets of liberalism, and that as far as he himself was concerned, he could never have any "enthusiasm" for the president again. La Follette had done well in Wisconsin and was constantly doing better in national affairs but he earnestly wished that the senator would make it understood that he did not believe that the majority was always right, nor that crooks and scoundrels did not exist in the ranks of labor as well as in high finance. All in all he thought that Taft would be renominated and indicated that he would support him after the nomination. As for his own candidacy, he felt that he would be woefully weak. "I have no cause to think at the moment that there is any real or widely extended liking for or trust in me among the masses of the people." He would not object to being sacrificed if necessary, but in this

[31] J. B. Bishop to Roosevelt, December 1, 1911, Roosevelt MSS.
[32] Roosevelt to W. B. Howland, December 23, 1912, Roosevelt MSS.
[33] Roosevelt to Sir Cecil Spring Rice, August 22, 1911, Roosevelt MSS.
[34] Roosevelt to J. C. O'Laughlin, October 20, 1911, Roosevelt MSS.

PURSUED

Cartoon by Harding in the *Brooklyn Eagle*, reproduced in the *Literary Digest*, December 9, 1911.

particular case he would have his own throat cut and would damage the progressive cause to boot. That being so, he felt that no one should even ask him to run; he had the "right to ask every friend of mine to do everything possible to prevent not only my nomination, but any movement looking toward my nomination."[35]

But as letters poured in congratulating him on his trust articles, Roosevelt began to change his mind about his own popularity. And as he revised his estimate of his strength he developed a willingness to alter his political plans for the future. Still he did not promise to announce his candidacy. He was not at all sure in November, was not to be sure for weeks, that he had even a fighting chance. With his instinctive dislike of foredoomed causes, he said nothing publicly or privately that would have committed him. He did, however, permit his friends to send up trial balloons and to build up a national organization to work for his nomination. In answer-

[35] Roosevelt to Hiram Johnson, October 27, 1911, Roosevelt MSS.

ing the letters from his personal friends urging his candidacy, Roosevelt no longer in late November asked them to cease their activities, but instead invited them to Oyster Bay for a conference.[36] To a man he scarcely knew, who wrote that he was sending out petitions in Nebraska to put Roosevelt's name on the primary ballot, the Colonel replied that he appreciated the courtesy, but did not want to be a candidate of any sort. But significantly he did not command nor even urge the man to stop his work.[37] Finally, on December 1, 1911, Roosevelt cleared the way for his friends to work for his nomination. In the middle of November an outright endorsement was made at a meeting of the Garfield Republican Club in Toledo. Probably instigated by James R. Garfield and Dan Hanna, the endorsement made the Colonel very "uncomfortable." He hoped that his Ohio friends would make it clear to the La Follette men that no friend of his had anything to do with the matter.[38] Roosevelt's supporters replied that the La Follette men in Ohio, knowing that the senator's chances were small, had agreed to make a progressive campaign against Taft and not for any particular candidate, and that there could be little grounds for misunderstanding. They also added significantly that the only thing that would stop the Roosevelt boom was a final statement from Roosevelt himself, a statement they were sure he should not make. On December 1 Roosevelt gave his approval to the plan.

"All right," he wrote, "take no further action. Well I am inclined now to have but one personal hope and that is a devout wish that for my own personal comfort either Taft or La Follette, or some third party, will develop such overwhelming strength that there will not possibly be any tendency to come to me."[39]

[36] A. P. Moore to Roosevelt, November 22, 1911, Roosevelt to Moore, November 24, 1911, Roosevelt MSS. Moore was editor of the *Pittsburgh Leader*.

[37] John O. Yeiser to Roosevelt, November 23, 1911, Roosevelt to Yeiser, November 23, 1911, Roosevelt MSS.

[38] Roosevelt to Garfield, November 24, 1911, Roosevelt MSS.

[39] Roosevelt to Garfield, December 1, 1911, Roosevelt MSS.

From that day the Roosevelt organization developed rapidly. On December 2 Roosevelt approved an editorial in the *Cleveland Leader* proclaiming that progressives could go forward all over the country confident that if they needed the leadership of Theodore Roosevelt it would be forthcoming.[40] Two days later Major Butt was warned by Alice Roosevelt to get out of his present job and not to wait for the convention or the election.[41] In the meantime the *Cleveland Leader*, the *Toledo Blade*, both papers owned by Mark Hanna's son, the *Pittsburgh Leader*, the *Philadelphia North American*, and the *Kansas City Star* were all urging the renomination of the ex-president. The national Republican committeemen from Ohio, Indiana, and New York openly stated that they were unconditionally for Roosevelt. At the same time that the Colonel was making it known to an increasing audience that he was not a candidate and would even consider it a "personal calamity" if he were nominated, he conceded that "if the American people wish for *their* sake to have me undertake a given job, that is a totally different question."[42] He felt he was not at liberty to shirk plain public duty if such it proved to be. Truly, in the words of William Allen White, the Roosevelt campaign ark was afloat, and the nation began to feel the thrill of life along her keel. By the first week in December Roosevelt was willing if not eager to run if it could be demonstrated that sufficient support was at hand.

In particularizing about another man's motives one takes a long chance whatever the evidence. Human beings have a way of consciously or unconsciously dressing up ordinary emotions for public display in Sunday clothes. And since Roosevelt was a master of the art, one can only guess what forces operated to plunge him into another campaign. Certainly boredom with his private life and his unquestionable

[40] Roosevelt to Dan R. Hanna, December 2, 1911, Roosevelt MSS.

[41] Butt, *Taft and Roosevelt*, 2: 776.

[42] Roosevelt to Walter R. Stubbs, December 4, 1911, to Judge Ben Lindsey, December 5, 1911, to J. B. Bishop, December 13, 1911, to L. B. Hanna, December 13, 1911, and to G. B. Daniels, December 15, 1911, Roosevelt MSS.

desire for place and power were important elements in his decision. But they could hardly have been the only ones, since in the early autumn of 1911 he was willing to await the defeat of Taft before again offering his own name to the nation. Clearly, as ex-Attorney General Bonaparte wrote, with Taft defeated in 1912, the Republican party could nominate but one man in 1916, provided that man desired the nomination.[43] Why then did Roosevelt suddenly choose to enter into the uncertain campaign of 1912? The only logical explanation is that his irritation with Taft, which had been almost continual since 1909, had broken all bounds with the institution of the steel suit. When his answering article in the *Outlook* was nationally acclaimed, he regained the confidence in himself that he had lost in the November elections of 1910. Realizing that his popularity had not ebbed as low as he had thought, he determined to chasten his erstwhile friend for his impudence.

It is probable also that still other elements influenced the Colonel. For one thing, he was certain that Taft would easily defeat La Follette, in which event the prospect for a Republican victory was decidedly not good. And a Democratic victory would be a minor national tragedy. Just a month before he himself began to think about the nomination, Roosevelt wrote Governor Johnson of California that he would support Taft, if nominated, because he felt that the Democratic party was led by either "Bourbon reactionaries," "foolish" radicals, or men like Wilson who were able but insincere and only playing politics for personal advantage.[44] Then, too, Roosevelt was sincerely interested in implementing the series of reforms outlined in his Osawatomie address. He undoubtedly desired office in order to put them into effect because of their inherent justice and to stop the rising tide of radicalism. Finally, it was extremely difficult for him to ignore the call of his political friends who wanted his nomination for its value in obtaining support for local tickets. All these reasons had

[43] Bonaparte to H. C. Gauss, December 20, 1911, Bonaparte MSS.
[44] Roosevelt to Hiram Johnson, October 27, 1911, Roosevelt MSS.

their influence. But one cannot doubt that the steel suit was one of the most influential elements in his ultimate determination to make the race. Otherwise his actions are totally inexplicable.

But not even in the heat of personal resentment was the craftiest politician of the age to be drawn into a hopeless race. Roosevelt was not yet sure that enough financial and popular support would be forthcoming to warrant an outright try for the nomination. Until he was convinced that he could have such support for the asking, he intended to lie low and say nothing. In the first weeks of December he contented himself with holding conferences and reading long state-by-state political reports. Skillfully refusing to make a definitive statement, he held surreptitious meetings with almost every one of the political sages who had written to urge his candidacy.[45] These men in turn left Oyster Bay to work quietly among the politicians and to report back the results. Among the most important of them were J. C. O'Laughlin, chief of the Washington bureau of the *Chicago Tribune*, Frank Knox, at that time chairman of the State Central Committee of Michigan, and William L. Ward, who held the same job in New York.[46]

Daily the reports from these men poured in. State by state, city by city, the situation was analyzed. Often the lights at Oyster Bay burned far into the night as the meaning of each incoming paper was discussed and pondered over. Most of the faithful agreed that the La Follette candidacy was hopeless and that Taft could not be re-elected. But where did that put Roosevelt? Should he run in 1912 or 1916? It was pointed out that if he waited four years a Democratic administration might be successful enough to justify a second term. Then

[45] Roosevelt to Lodge, December 13, 1911, to Frank Knox, December 8, 1911, to J. C. O'Laughlin, December 8, 14, 1911, to James Keeley, December 19, 1911, and to William L. Ward, December 15, 1911, William L. Ward to Roosevelt, December 15, 1911, Roosevelt MSS.

[46] Frank Knox had been a Rough Rider during the Spanish American War. In 1911 he was an ardent supporter of Governor Osborn's liberal administration in Michigan. Norman Beasley, *Frank Knox* (New York, 1936), 55–61. William L. Ward was one of the New York state bosses who had opposed Hughes and Roosevelt in 1910.

there was always the chance that some Republican leader other than Taft would "spring up" to take the nomination. On the other hand, enough Regular Republicans might knife Roosevelt to allow a strong Democrat like Wilson to win in 1912. All these possibilities were gone over a score of times. But in the end the almost inevitable conclusion was reached that Roosevelt could secure the nomination and then whip any Democrat in the field.[47]

Still Roosevelt temporized. He would not stop the efforts of his friends. Neither would he commit himself to running. It was much better to wait and see. He still remembered the dreary days of 1910. But from the optimism around him that autumn Roosevelt began to regain his old buoyancy. He was signally encouraged by the meeting of the Republican National Committee in Washington. There four national committeemen spoke out openly against the renomination of President Taft. A series of riotous public welcomes staged almost everywhere he went heightened his sanguinity. Coming out of a meeting of the overseers of Harvard University, he was met by a crowd of eight thousand who cheered him as the next president.[48] Speedily his mental attitude changed. Whereas in late October he had stated that the masses of the people had no trust in him, by the middle of December he thought that a "revulsion" of public sentiment had occurred.[49] A few days later he was sure that a "good many plain people" were turning "longingly to him as a leader,"[50] and shortly thereafter he conceded that the movement for his nomination was anchored upon a "real popular basis."[51]

Meanwhile the Roosevelt nomination campaign had quietly but surely got underway. In Washington Senators Borah and Dixon were contacted. Extremely enthusiastic, they had telegraphed henchmen in Idaho and Montana to organize local Roosevelt clubs. From New York City came the

[47] November and December, 1911, Roosevelt MSS.
[48] *New York Times*, December 13, 14, 1912.
[49] Roosevelt to Hiram Johnson, October 27, 1911, Roosevelt MSS.
[50] Roosevelt to Henry B. Needham, December 19, 1911, Roosevelt MSS.
[51] Roosevelt to W. B. Howland, December 23, 1911, Roosevelt MSS.

cheering news that the checkbook of George Perkins, a Morgan partner, and the powerful newspapers of Frank Munsey would be at Roosevelt's disposal. From New York, Pennsylvania, Michigan, and Ohio came the promising reports of William L. Ward, Gifford Pinchot, Frank Knox, and James R. Garfield. About this time also Ormsby McHarg, with his highly checkered political career, joined the Roosevelt camp. He at once busied himself in the almost hopeless attempt to win the Southern officeholding Republican group away from the administration.[52]

Everywhere this work had been kept more or less secret. But the plan to develop Roosevelt strength had to be brought out in the open during the meeting of the Ohio Progressive Conference at Columbus on New Year's Day. A few days before the conference La Follette entered the state on a speaking tour. His lieutenants had planned to end his electioneering efforts with a unanimous vote of endorsement by the conference. That would be embarrassing to the Roosevelt men. They would either have to announce their Roosevelt sentiments by voting against La Follette or else be committed by bonds of honor to the senator's candidacy. In the end, before the conference met, the Ohio progressive leaders hit upon a dodging compromise. After a stiff fight led by Garfield, Gifford Pinchot, and Walter Brown, the resolution endorsing La Follette was defeated. In its place the League signified its intention of nominating "a Progressive Republican for Presi-

---

[52] Roosevelt to Ormsby McHarg, December 29, 1911, Roosevelt MSS. McHarg, working through Postmaster General Hitchcock, in 1908 had secured the Southern delegates for Taft. In 1909 he was appointed assistant secretary of commerce and labor, only to be relieved from that position eighteen months later after he had delivered a fiery denunciation of the Roosevelt-Pinchot conservation policy during the Ballinger-Pinchot episode. A short time later he was appointed by the administration to the position of counsel for two Indian tribes at $12,000 a year. Grateful for such benevolence, he had, in the summer of 1910, campaigned against Stimson in New York on the grounds that a vote for Stimson in 1910 would be a vote for Roosevelt in 1912. However, when the new secretary of the interior removed him because of his obvious uselessness to the Indians, he turned against the Taft administration with as much vigor as he had used before in its behalf.

dent, recognizing as fellow Progressives all who hold the principles for which we stand whether they be for the Presidential nomination of Robert M. La Follette or Theodore Roosevelt, or any other Progressive Republican." Roosevelt thought the conference had had a "very satisfactory outcome."[53]

To dissemble their love the Roosevelt progressives explained their action as simply a means to unite all Ohio progressives against Taft. Gifford Pinchot declared afterward that La Follette would be the man nominated by the Republican convention.[54] But politicians everywhere, gray with years of experience, interpreted the affair as a declaration by Roosevelt that he would run if enough support was forthcoming. Within four days after the conference Governors Stubbs of Kansas, Osborn of Michigan, and Glasscock of West Virginia committed themselves publicly to the Roosevelt cause.[55] The press interpreted the Ohio proceedings in the same light. By the middle of December the *New York Times* implied that the La Follette candidacy was being used as just a decoy for Roosevelt. After the Ohio Progressive Conference it asserted that the Colonel's candidacy was one of the most real movements in the entire political scene. Most other astute political observers agreed with Franklin K. Lane that while the Colonel was keeping silent he was a lot like the Negro woman who was "quite willing to be 'foced'."[56]

That the "focing" was almost certain to take place was apparent when at the turn of the year one politician after another announced himself for the nomination of the ex-president. From the East, South, and West they came to enlist in the Roosevelt cause. Some of them, like Everett Colby of New Jersey, Francis J. Heney of San Francisco, and Judge Ben Lindsey of Denver, were sincere liberals, seeing in Roose-

[53] Roosevelt to Garfield, January 4, 1912; *New York Times*, January 2, 1912; La Follette, *Autobiography*, 574.

[54] *New York Times*, January 2, 1912.

[55] William B. Glasscock to Roosevelt, January 1, 1912, Roosevelt MSS.; *Kansas City Star*, January 5, 7, 1912.

[56] *New York Times*, December 13, 1911, January 5, 1912; *The Letters of Franklin K. Lane*, ed. by A. W. Lane and Louise H. Wall (New York, 1922), 84.

velt a chance to elect a progressive. Others, like Pearl Wight of Louisiana, Cecil Lyons of Texas, William Allen White of Kansas, and William R. Nelson of the *Kansas City Star*, were also devoted friends of long standing ready to follow where Roosevelt led. Wight and Lyons, in control of the Republican machines in their respective states, had to risk an already established position in pledging their support. But for the most part, the rest of the men who came to Oyster Bay had less altruistic reasons.

Throughout the autumn of 1911 many Republican officeholders looked ahead to the 1912 elections with dread. They were disturbingly aware that it would be a herculean task to carry local offices for the party if Taft headed the ticket. In the minds of these men the principle of party regularity became subordinate to a desire for survival. "I have nothing against Mr. Taft," wrote a typical officeholder, "except that Mr. Taft cannot carry the state."[57] A great many of them, remembering the plurality of 1904, thought that Roosevelt was the only Republican who could possibly win. What was more to the point, in winning the ex-president would immeasurably aid their own candidacies. Governor Herbert Hadley of Missouri was simply talking their language when he committed himself to Roosevelt. "Under his leadership," Hadley said, "a continuation of Republican administration in Missouri is assured."[58]

Other men, like William Flinn of Pittsburgh, a typical boss without a shred of interest in progressivism as such, saw in the Roosevelt rebellion a chance to upset the reigning machine dynasty in their states and capture it for themselves. Flinn had been ousted from his position in Pennsylvania by Penrose. With Penrose supporting Taft, Flinn first announced that he was for La Follette, but quickly turned to Roosevelt

[57] W. H. Llewellyn to George Curry, April 20, 1912, W. H. Rich to Ormsby McHarg, February 15, 1912, C. J. Bonaparte to Roosevelt, March 16, 1912, Roosevelt MSS.

[58] *St. Louis Globe Democrat*, January 28, 1912; letters to Joseph B. Foraker from M. G. Norton, January 24, 1912, and I. F. Mack, February 4, 1912, Foraker MSS., Cincinnati, Ohio; J. F. Fort to Roosevelt, January 6, 1912, Roosevelt MSS.; *Kansas City Star*, February 19, 1912.

when it became apparent that the chances for success were greater there. Still others, such as Ormsby McHarg, Dan Hanna, and Walter Brown of Ohio, left the Taft administration to support Roosevelt only when they had failed to receive what they considered their due. It was whispered without proof that Walter Brown first offered the support of Hanna and his two newspapers to Taft if the government would drop its indictment against Hanna under the Sherman Law, and turned to Roosevelt only after his offer had been refused.[59]

In January the representatives of big business and high finance came to Roosevelt's support. Many of these industrialists felt that the election of a progressive in 1912 could not very well be avoided. Daniel Willard, president of the Baltimore and Ohio Railroad, spoke their mind when he said that of all the so-called progressives Roosevelt was the safest.[60] Others, representing established monopolies, were irritated at Taft because of his campaign to enforce the Sherman Law. Conversely they were attracted to the Roosevelt scheme of regulation because it offered them the hope that their monopolies would be legally sanctified, at the same time insuring them a fair profit and helping to stifle competition. The Roosevelt type of federal regulation apparently contained little that was obnoxious to George W. Perkins and other representatives of the United States Steel Corporation.[61] Even after Roosevelt's radical Columbus speech twenty per cent of the Republican members of the New York stock exchange selected him as their choice for president.[62]

It was an incongruous company that banded together to nominate Theodore Roosevelt in the first days of the new year. Liberal idealists, fervid friends of the Colonel, self-seek-

[59] Hanna and the attorney general later came to an understanding. Hanna's firm was fined $20,000 and the personal charges against Hanna were dropped. The presiding judge accepted this settlement out of court. Roosevelt to Garfield, December 19, 1911, Roosevelt to Henry L. Stimson, January 19, 26, 1912, Roosevelt MSS.

[60] Daniel Willard to Chase S. Osborn, January 9, 1912, Roosevelt MSS.

[61] *Bankers' Magazine*, 81: 5–6 (July 10, 1912); *Outlook*, 100: 261 (February 3, 1912); D. R. Hanna to Roosevelt, May 24, 1912, Roosevelt MSS.

[62] *Kansas City Star*, February 25, 1912.

ing politicians, and captains of industry with their eye on the economic main chance made up the lot. In the final summing up the first two categories by no means outweighed the last three, either in influence or in numbers.

The main problem before the small inner Roosevelt group was as old as politics. How could they make it appear that the office was seeking the man and not the man the office? In the interests of making black look white J. C. O'Laughlin labored in Washington among senators, congressmen, and national committeemen. Frank Knox was busy with governors and newspaper editors, confidently telling them that Roosevelt would run if he were called upon to do so. Ormsby McHarg was off on a long swing into the West and South, and William L. Ward undertook to win over to the Roosevelt standard the New York Republican bosses who had so bitterly fought him in 1910. The entire movement in the meantime was unified by

IS IT AFTER HIM OR IS HE AFTER IT?

Cartoon by Fox in the *Chicago Evening Post*, reproduced in the *Literary Digest*, February 3, 1912.

frequent conferences, usually held in the houses of mutual friends in New York City to escape detection by newspaper men.[63]

Roosevelt was not content for long to sit back in easy fashion while others were working night and day. Steadily he was drawn into more and more personal activity. At first he confined himself to writing letters of appreciation to the men actively interested in building up an organization. Outside of occasionally sending them newspaper clippings for circulation he did little to aid them personally.[64] However, by the middle of January he had become so interested that he was combing his files for all the names and addresses of men who had offered their support.[65] O'Laughlin, Knox, McHarg, and Ward then wrote each of these correspondents, assuring them that Roosevelt would run and urging them to organize their own localities for him. Roosevelt, while awaiting the call of the people, was not above a little tub-thumping himself. Assured by his actions that the Colonel was in earnest, the inner group refrained from public action no longer. On January 16, 1912, a Roosevelt National Committee was formed in Chicago. A few days later it moved into a suite of rooms at the Congress Hotel.[66]

The success of the movement was obstructed, however, by two elements. In the first place the La Follette candidacy stood squarely in the way. A united reform candidacy offered some hope of success, but certainly a progressivism divided against itself could look for nothing but defeat. Of course it was argued that once the country was assured that Roosevelt would run, most of the La Follette support would quickly turn to him. But such a swapping of horses, especially for those progressive leaders who had committed themselves to

[63] Letters to Roosevelt from Herbert Hadley, January 18, 1912, and William L. Ward, January 6, 1912, Roosevelt MSS.

[64] Roosevelt to James Keeley, January 6, 1912, Roosevelt MSS.

[65] Roosevelt to J. C. O'Laughlin, January 11, 1912, Frank Harper to Frank Knox, January 24, 1912, Roosevelt MSS.

[66] James Keeley to Roosevelt, January 22, 1912, Roosevelt MSS.; *New York Times*, January 29, 30, 1912.

"Battle Bob," could not be so easily or honorably effected. There were a few like Cummins who needed no more justification for their switch than the realistic one of riding the winning horse. But the Pinchots and others found the situation much more difficult. Many of them had signed a memorandum urging La Follette to make the race, and others had unqualifiedly committed themselves to him after his announcement. The problem of squaring their consciences at the same time they appeased their political appetites became more perplexing each day.

The La Follette men flirting with Roosevelt hoped at first that La Follette would agree to a nationwide Roosevelt-La Follette ticket. Under this arrangement the same set of delegates would be placed under both names on the ballot, the delegates being pledged finally to the man who in each state accumulated the greatest number of votes. When La Follette refused even to consider the idea the Pinchots tried to persuade the senator to withdraw. In this they were also unsuccessful.[67] Reduced to near desperation, many of the men backing La Follette then proceeded to play a double game. The Pinchots, William Flinn, and Medill McCormick, while campaigning for the senator during January, were secretly contributing to the Roosevelt war chest.[68] Governor Robert S. Vessey of South Dakota and Congressman Charles A. Lindbergh of Minnesota let Roosevelt know that although they were working for La Follette the support they developed could easily be turned elsewhere. "There will be nothing," wrote Governor Vessey, "to interfere with our cooperating with other States that are standing for a Progressive Republican candidate for President that has the confidence of the people."[69]

Still, to avoid public embarrassment the abrupt change could scarcely be made without some reason. As the days

[67] Roosevelt MSS., January, 1912; La Follette, *Autobiography*, 597–598.
[68] Pringle, *Roosevelt*, 554.
[69] Robert S. Vessey to Herbert S. Hadley, January 30, 1912, and to Roosevelt, January 30, 1912, Charles A. Lindbergh to Roosevelt, February 13, 1912, Roosevelt MSS.

went by without an incident, La Follette's summer soldiers became increasingly uncomfortable. The senator's unfortunate address in Philadelphia on February 2 came as a providential blessing to many a sorely agitated politician. Just ten days before, La Follette had delivered a masterful speech at Carnegie Hall in New York.[70] But in Philadelphia, talking before the periodical publishers, sick at heart because of an ailing daughter and the fickleness of his supporters, he broke down to deliver a confused and most impolitic harangue. Speaking on the power of organized economic groups, he came very close to indicting the press of the country as their tool. He repeated many portions of the speech and wandered aimlessly for at least an hour. Compared with the crisp address of Woodrow Wilson, who had preceded him, the speech was a poor one indeed. As the senator finished he sank back in his chair apparently exhausted.[71]

Before dawn the next morning an age-old cry resounded: *Le roi est mort, vive le roi.* With indecent haste the Pinchots, Medill McCormick, William Flinn, and many others transferred their fealty to Roosevelt. Without waiting to find out the exact state of La Follette's health they precipitately announced that because of his physical incapacity they would now support the ex-president. The story was even circulated that the La Follette headquarters itself had announced his withdrawal. The actual announcement from the senator's headquarters simply stated that because of overwork he was ill and would cancel his engagements for the next two weeks. But by the time that it had been made clear that there would be no withdrawal, the damage had been done. Most of La Follette's prominent supporters had turned to Roosevelt.[72]

As a result of the wholesale transfer, charges of apostasy flew. La Follette accused Roosevelt of using him to cover up his own ambitious plans. La Follette's manager was even more

[70] *New York Times,* January 23, 1912.

[71] *Philadelphia North American,* February 3, 1912; Henry Beech Needham to Roosevelt, February 6, 1912, Roosevelt MSS.

[72] *New York Sun,* February 4, 6, 1912; *New York Times,* February 5, 6, 1912.

direct. "Roosevelt has betrayed La Follette," Hauser charged, "and is a traitor to the Progressive cause."[73] Whatever the outward appearances seemed to indicate at the time, this much is certain: there is not a shred of evidence that Roosevelt ever definitely promised to support La Follette for the nomination. On the contrary, there is ample evidence to indicate that Roosevelt preferred Taft to La Follette.[74]

Not as much can be said for the Pinchots, Cummins, and McCormick. In spite of their later explanation that their promise to see the fight through had applied only to the cause and not to the man, there can be little doubt that they broke faith with La Follette. And in breaking faith with the man the Pinchots, who were no doubt acting from the sincerest motives, unwittingly broke faith with the cause. For in the end Roosevelt was to be largely responsible for the destruction of progressivism in the Republican party.

The political situation, wrote Charles J. Bonaparte to H. C. Gauss on February 19, 1912, "has been slightly clarified by Pinchot's abandonment of La Follette, but inasmuch as the latter's candidacy never seemed to me serious . . . this action of the ex-Forester tends to remove only a minor complication." With the problem of La Follette removed, there remained in January of 1912 one major obstruction to the successful building up of a Roosevelt organization. Throughout the country the party placemen, ward heelers, and precinct nurses, whose support was necessary to control local constituencies, were exceedingly loath to commit themselves without definite knowledge of Roosevelt's intentions. Fearing that the renomination of Taft would mean defeat, many of them were quite willing to risk their places in the Taft administration if they were certain that Roosevelt would run. In that event they had visions of continued emoluments for four more years. They were not, however, to be weaned away from the pap they had upon a mere supposition. Accordingly, Roosevelt was swamped with agonizing letters beseeching

[73] *New York Sun,* February 15, 1912.
[74] Roosevelt to Gilson Gardner, February 20, 1912, Roosevelt MSS.

him to make a public announcement. Henry Adams noted that the Colonel's would-be followers were "squirming like a skinned eel," not knowing what to do.[75]

To make an announcement that he would accept the nomination was not at all to Roosevelt's liking. The public would regard it as an admission that he was ambitiously seeking a third term and it would place dangerous ammunition in the hands of his opponents. It is quite likely that Roosevelt was attempting, not without success, to assuage his own conscience by convincing himself that his candidacy was a response to public demand. At any rate the pressure upon him for a declaration made him very "uncomfortable." He sought to meet the situation by writing a sixteen-page letter to Frank Munsey. He would not be a candidate, he said. He was not interested in holding office, but if the nomination were offered to him as a result of an overwhelming demand from the masses he would accept it as a public duty. "Before I speak," he ended, "there should be some tangible evidence that such is the case."[76] He then sent copies of the letter to all the men who were pressing him to define his position.

It was soon evident, however, that the Munsey letter did not satisfy the harassed politicians. Prompt action was imperative for other reasons as well. In answer to the rising tide of Roosevelt sentiment the administration was already actively engaged in marshalling support for renomination. Taft was determined to beat Roosevelt in the national convention and had already ordered all state conventions to be held as early as possible. By that action he hoped to pledge a majority of the delegates before the Roosevelt organization could make an impression on the country.[77]

[75] Henry Adams to Elizabeth Cameron, February 25, 1912, in Henry Adams, *Letters*, 586; letters to Roosevelt from Chase S. Osborn, January 12, 1912, A. P. Moore, January 25, 1912, Franklin Fort, January 30, 1912, and W. R. Nelson, January 26, 1912, E. W. Sims to J. F. Bass, February 13, 1912, Roosevelt MSS.

[76] Roosevelt to Frank Munsey, January 16, 1912, Roosevelt MSS.

[77] Herbert S. Hadley to Roosevelt, January 16, 1912, Roosevelt MSS.; *Kansas City Star*, January 11, 1912; Butt, *Taft and Roosevelt*, 2: 814.

The pressure of his own supporters and the activities of the opposition forced Roosevelt to make the grave decision. Even at that late hour some of his friends advised him to wait until 1916. But the majority convinced him that there was a real popular demand for his nomination. And Roosevelt finally agreed with Mark Sullivan that the time to set a setting hen was when the hen wanted to set. "There was no use in sitting back and waiting for another year when somebody entirely different might do best as a leader," he wrote afterward. So while protesting to all his friends that he had very little chance of success, he proceeded to cross the Rubicon. Happily, at the same time, he thought of a way to extricate himself from an embarrassing situation.[78]

On January 12, 1912, Roosevelt hit upon the idea of introducing his candidacy by replying to a joint letter of invitation from the four governors who had been urging him to make the race. With this in mind he sent Frank Knox to Governors Glasscock of West Virginia, Bass of New Hampshire, Hadley of Missouri, and Stubbs of Kansas to discuss the "shape in which to put my statement if I do speak."[79] The plan was almost discarded when news of it leaked out. But after two other Republican governors, Osborn of Michigan and Aldrich of Nebraska, agreed to join in the demand for Roosevelt, he decided to go ahead.

When the contents of the Munsey letter became known, Roosevelt received many letters of protest from his conservative friends. They feared, with reason, that this announcement was but the prelude to an all-out struggle within the party. Elihu Root, knowing his Theodore, was painfully aware that if Roosevelt were awaiting the call of the people, a peremptory demand would not be long in materializing. And he was alarmed at the prospect. "No thirsty sinner ever took a

[78] Herbert S. Hadley to Roosevelt, January 16, 18, 1912, Roosevelt to Walter R. Stubbs, January 22, 1912, to Hadley, January 18, 1912, and to R. H. M. Ferguson, March 26, 1912, Roosevelt MSS.
[79] Roosevelt to Walter R. Stubbs, January 18, 1912, to Robert Bass, January 20, 1912, to W. E. Glasscock, January 20, 1912, and to Herbert S. Hadley, January 20, 1912, Roosevelt MSS.

pledge," he wrote Roosevelt, "which was harder for him to keep than it will be for you to maintain this position." Astutely Root went on to predict that Roosevelt would inevitably be drawn into a personal contest with Taft like a "common or garden variety" of presidential candidate. The result of that, Root thought, would be catastrophic. Neither Roosevelt nor Taft would win the election. The Republican party would be irreparably damaged. And the consequences to Roosevelt's future and to his "position in history" would be injurious beyond thought. "No friend and no number of friends," Root concluded, "had any right to ask such sacrifice."[80]

Many other friends of bygone days joined Root in his protest. H. H. Kohlsaat, Nicholas Longworth, and Andrew Carnegie were but a few. But Roosevelt was adamant. He acted not for personal reasons, he replied to Root, but to champion "the interests of the people as a whole," interests which Taft did not "understand" or to which he was actively "hostile." "If I were longer doubtful, I would telegraph you to come and talk with me," he wrote his son-in-law, Nicholas Longworth, "but it would not be of any use now, Nick. I have got to come out."[81]

At a meeting in Chicago on February 10, 1912, eight Republican governors met with fifty-six delegates from thirty states to form a nationwide permanent organization. A National Executive Committee of seven, state chairmen, and state committees were selected.[82] A more important result of the conclave was the issuance of the canned declaration for the Colonel, which for the most part had been prepared in Washington by J. C. O'Laughlin. Roosevelt, who privately thought the statement of the governors "admirable," told the press after the meeting that he would answer the round-

[80] Elihu Root to Roosevelt, February 12, 1912, Roosevelt MSS.

[81] Roosevelt to Root, February 14, 1912, and to Nicholas Longworth, February 13, 1912, Roosevelt MSS.; Andrew Carnegie to Roosevelt, March 1, 1912, Carnegie MSS.

[82] Herbert S. Hadley to Roosevelt, February 11, 1912, Roosevelt MSS.; *New York Sun*, February 11, 1910.

robin letter within a few days after his Columbus speech.[83]

The Columbus speech, delivered before the Ohio Constitutional Convention during the last week in February, was at once perhaps the most sincere and the most disastrous of all Roosevelt's public addresses. Certainly it came very close to expressing Roosevelt's real attitude toward many public questions. It also revealed the large kernel of compromise at the center of his character. Prepared weeks in advance, the manuscript had been sent to most of his important backers for their criticism. In particular, the Colonel was anxious to obtain the reactions of the more conservative of his supporters. Almost to a man they attacked the Taft administration's rigid endorsement of the Sherman Law, and advised Roosevelt to stress the fact that his scheme of federal control and regulation would make for a period of business peace, prosperity, and stability. They counseled him also to abstain from anything that would agitate the business world. They assured him that such a course would result in a wave of support as well as contributions from the more prosperous economic groups.[84]

A most interesting reply came from Frank Munsey, the newspaper publisher. In one of his mercurial moods Munsey savagely attacked the competitive system. From his observations, he wrote, the American state had to swing away from its "vaunted Republicanism" toward a more "parental guardianship of the people." The people increasingly needed "the sustaining and guiding hand of the state." "It is the work of the state," Munsey concluded, "to think for the people and plan for the people—to teach them how to do, what to do, and to sustain them in the doing." Scarcely fifty years separated that doctrine from the Gettysburg Address. Idealogically measured, the two were centuries apart.[85]

[83] Roosevelt to Robert Bass, February 13, 1912, Roosevelt MSS.; *New York Times*, February 11, 1912.

[84] Letters to Roosevelt from W. L. Ward, February 8, 1912, Alexander H. Revell, March 21, 1912, and Frank A. Munsey, February 13, 1912, Roosevelt MSS.

[85] Frank A. Munsey to Roosevelt, February 13, 1912, Roosevelt MSS.

Roosevelt considered all the suggestions while preparing the last draft of his speech. He adopted many of them. "I am trying to put the business part of it so as to convey the ideas you have conveyed in your letter," he wrote to William A. Ward. At the same time he invited Ward and Lucius Littauer, a friend of ex-Speaker Cannon, to confer with him in a final examination of the entire manuscript.[86] When it was finished, Roosevelt, at least, thought that it took a middle-of-the-road position. In answer to letters of objection that the speech was not radical enough he replied that he had consciously worked for a moderate position. His qualifications, he observed, were along the lines of Lincoln's. If his speech did not suit the mind of the country, his leadership then was useless. For then "the demand is for a man who shall go to one of two extremes, both dangerous to the welfare of our people."[87] Only a month later Roosevelt wrote to an English friend that he belonged neither to the extremists of reaction nor to those of progress but rather was allied spiritually with Lincoln, Chatham, the Whigs of the Reform Bill, and Macaulay.[88]

Certainly the speech Roosevelt delivered at Columbus, Ohio, on February 21, 1912, except for one particular was nothing if not moderate. True, he adhered to the policies enunciated at Osawatomie, but so qualified were his assertions, and so studded was the speech with assurances to the business world, that he might have won over a great portion of conservative Republicans if he had not also included his plan for the democratization of the judiciary. His scheme, however, for the recall of state judicial decisions alienated most of that element.

Much ink has been spilled over the question why Roosevelt, usually the skillful politician, made such an egregious mistake. Some historians have attributed it to his long ab-

---

[86] Roosevelt to W. L. Ward, February 9, 1912, Roosevelt MSS. Littauer was an important New York glove manufacturer. Cannon's fight for high rates on gloves in the Payne-Aldrich schedules was in part influenced by the relationship between the two men.

[87] Roosevelt to Amos Pinchot, February 15, 1912, Roosevelt MSS.

[88] Roosevelt to J. St. Loe Strachey, March 20, 1912, Roosevelt MSS.

sence from public life and the consequent failure of his political touch. Probably it was not so much the loss of his political skill as his fidelity to his own program that led Roosevelt into this attack upon the judiciary. In 1911 he was acutely aware of the nation's social unbalance. He sincerely believed that comprehensive legislative corrections should, and in fact must, be made quickly. He was interested in steering the country into a path between what he called the "sinister reactionaries" and "the furies of discontent."[89]

To stem the ever ascending tide of Socialism, to prevent the election of a Democratic William Jennings Bryan, or to frustrate the splitting off from the Republican party of a new radical party, Roosevelt was willing to go far to the left. But he felt that no comprehensive program of reform could be achieved unless the nation's courts were first curbed. Throughout his presidency Roosevelt had disliked the essentially autocratic American judiciary with its expanding quasi-executive and legislative powers. Several times during those years the judiciary had failed to concur with him. Moreover, it was during these very years that the nation's courts were shaping the federal and the several state constitutions into an almost impenetrable barrier against social legislation. And as a wave of criticism arose, Roosevelt was prompt to agree with Franklin K. Lane that the country would have to satisfy the common man's sense of justice, or worse things than the recall of judges would come to pass.[90]

Nor was this estimation of public opinion radically at fault. Organized labor, frustrated by interpretations of the courts, was hostile to the whole judicial hierarchy. Moving more slowly but in the same direction was the great body of progressive opinion throughout the nation. By the end of the decade reforming journals were lashing at the courts for their conservative findings. With ridicule humorous *Life* was serving the same cause. Liberal judges themselves were out-

[89] *Ibid.*
[90] Franklin K. Lane to Albert Shaw, April 30, 1912, in Lane, *Letters*, 97.

spoken in their criticism of their colleagues. Justice John M.
Harlan of the Supreme Court created a national stir in 1910
by stating in a minority decision that the business interests of
the country were constantly changing the constitution to
their liking by simply bringing a case to court for judicial interpretation.[91]

In June of 1911, after the New York courts had held a
workingmen's compensation act invalid, Roosevelt wrote
that if he had his way he would remove every man on the
bench responsible for that decision. Such men were socially
"unfit" for their position.[92] Later he spoke of the judiciary as
"absolutely reactionary" and described its course over a
twenty-five-year period as one calculated "almost to bar the
path to industrial, economic, and social reform."[93] Just a
week before his Columbus speech, in a long confidential letter, he spoke his mind without reserve on the subject of the
courts. Many of the state courts, he believed, were doing
more harm to "honest citizenship and the spirit of orderly
living" than any dishonest legislature had ever done. The
federal judiciary was different. "I do not believe we have ever
had a corrupt judge on the Supreme Court." But there was
Taney, who had been a far worse influence than a president
like Buchanan. In his own time, Roosevelt stated, he had
seen well-meaning judges "whose presence upon the Supreme
Court was a menace to the welfare of the nation." "They
should not have been left there a day," he snapped.[94]

The plan for the recall of state judicial decisions was first
outlined in one of Roosevelt's numerous articles in the *Out-*

[91] *Kansas City Star*, May 21, 1911; *Philadelphia North American*, December 16, 1911; *Life*, 59: 56 (January 4, 1912); Jacob Treeber to Roosevelt, February 22, 1912, Roosevelt MSS.; Walter Clark, "Aaron's Rod; or
Government by Federal Judges," *Arena*, 38: 479 (November, 1907). Robert
M. La Follette at Carnegie Hall in New York City advocated that popular
recall be extended to include Supreme Court judges.

[92] Roosevelt to C. D. Willard, June 20, 1911, Roosevelt MSS.

[93] Roosevelt to Hiram Johnson, October 27, 1911, and to Herbert Croly,
February 29, 1912, Roosevelt MSS.

[94] Roosevelt to Henry L. Stimson, February 5, 1912, Roosevelt MSS.

look.[95] Conservative reaction was immediate. Vested privilege, assailed for a half century by Greenbackers, Grangers, and Populists, had found protection in the Republican party and the courts. Now with the Grand Old Party threatened by a progressive palace revolution the big propertied interests of the nation found their only cover in the courts. Fervently they agreed with Senator Carter that the courts were "the sheet-anchor of the Republic."[96] The president himself bitterly answered Roosevelt's attack on the sacred cow of conservatism. "Such extremists," he declared, "would hurry us into a condition which would find no parallel except in the French Revolution or in that bubbling anarchy that once characterized the South American Republics. Such extremists are not progressive,—they are political emotionalists or neurotics."[97]

Neither the realization that his court scheme was politi-

[95] Theodore Roosevelt, "Judges and Progress," *Outlook*, 100: 42 (January 6, 1912).

[96] Carter to Charles G. Burk, July 2, 1910, Carter MSS. Carter, many times a millionaire, should have known whereof he spoke. He had opportunities to select federal judges in Montana. In 1911 at the resignation of federal district judge Carl Rasch an appointment was made with the closest collaboration of O. M. Lanstrum, chairman of the Republican State Committee and John D. Ryan, of the Anaconda Copper Company. In the tri-cornered correspondence which took place between Washington, D. C., New York City, and Butte, Montana, there were many references to the searching investigations being carried on into the "character," politics and economic views of the candidates. One Democrat was considered but Senator Carter was assured that he had always been "an anti-Bryan democrat" and never had been a "radical." However, his name was dropped when it was considered his appointment "will hurt President W. H. Taft, Senator T. H. Carter and the Company." Finally a list of Republican preferences was made out which was sent first to John D. Ryan in New York City and only later to Senator Thomas H. Carter. Eloquent and appealing was the description of one of the leading candidates "that whilest we know that —— is not hostile to any of the large interests in the State, his appointment would not be unsatisfactory to the other interests . . . ." John D. Ryan's secretary to Thomas H. Carter, September 9, 1911, J. C. Morony to John D. Ryan, September 8, 1911 (copy of telegram), Milton S. Gunn to Carter, September 4, 1911, O. M. Lanstrum to Carter, September 12, 1911, Carter to Charles D. Hilles, September 7, 1911, Carter MSS.

[97] *New York Sun*, February 13, 1912.

cally dangerous nor the pressure of his political advisors moved Roosevelt to cease his advocacy of the reform. In his Columbus address he spoke out plainly and courageously for the recall of state judicial decisions. "The judges have decided every which way, and it is foolish to talk of the sanctity of judge-made law which half of the judges strongly denounce," he exclaimed in its defense.[98] That bold statement impaired considerably Roosevelt's chances of securing the nomination. For by attacking American judicial institutions he alienated the conservative wing of his party, which might have supported him for the sake of a possible victory. Outside the party organization he had also estranged the great industrial interests, which had at least toyed with the idea of supporting him because of his opposition to the administration's trust policy. But now that he had questioned the sanctity of the judicial doctrines, that possibility was gone. The date and contents of a letter from W. L. Ward to Frank Harper, Roosevelt's secretary, a few days after the Ohio speech may not have been merely coincidental. "Tell the Colonel to cancel the du Pont engagement that he made for three o'clock Friday at the Union League Club," Ward wrote. "The opposition have secured du Pont through Hitchcock. He does not talk right."[99]

More disappointing news came in from standpat politicians. James E. Watson, the militant foe of Beveridge in Indiana, called at Oyster Bay to request that he be released from his promise to support Roosevelt.[100] Other Stalwarts like ex-Congressman Peter Hepburn who had intended to back the Colonel were of the same mind.[101] "Before Roosevelt made his Columbus speech I thought if he became a candidate, he would be nominated. After he made that speech

[98] *New York Times*, February 22, 1912. Roosevelt had made one concession. He limited his scheme to state courts and was silent about the federal judiciary.

[99] W. L. Ward to Roosevelt, February 29, 1912, Roosevelt MSS. See also a letter from Bonaparte to Gauss, March 16, 1912, Bonaparte MSS.

[100] Watson, *As I Knew Them*, 147–148.

[101] John E. Briggs, *William Peters Hepburn* (Iowa City, Iowa, 1909), 335.

President Taft seemed to be far more popular than he has ever been," observed ex-Senator Foraker.[102] Even Henry Cabot Lodge, who probably was indebted to Roosevelt for his re-election to the Senate in 1911, now wrote his lifelong friend that they would have to part political company. And although Lodge tearfully stated in his letter that he could "not think of supporting anyone else," he was soon secretly at work building up a nation-wide organization to fight the recall of judicial decisions.[103]

After the presentation of the recall plan in the Ohio speech the conservative press was beside itself with rage. "A charter of demagogy," "Mr. Roosevelt's formal invitation of anarchy," a "proposal of revolution"—these were but a few of the many caustic phrases they applied to it.[104] Far more restrained but almost as critical in their implications were the comments of many of Roosevelt's supporters. Ex-Governor E. C. Stokes of New Jersey, Senators Dixon, Borah, and Cummins, ex-Governor Herbert S. Hadley, and William D. Foulke were all for various reasons opposed to the recall of judges.[105] Borah's blunt comment that the recall of judicial decisions was "bosh" was probably the sincere feeling of many. Quite a few, however, were indignant because Roosevelt by his "crazy plan" had seriously disturbed a perfectly assured situation.[106] Only the radicals in the Roosevelt camp, like Senator Bristow and Governor Stubbs of Kansas, were delighted with the speech.[107]

[102] Joseph B. Foraker to J. K. Hamilton, April 22, 1912, Foraker MSS., Cincinnati, Ohio.
[103] Lodge to Roosevelt, February 28, 1912, Roosevelt MSS.; Lodge to Foraker, July 11, 1912, Foraker to Jacob H. Gallinger, March 25, 1911, Gallinger to Foraker, March 31, 1912, Foraker MSS., Cincinnati, Ohio.
[104] *New York World, New York Sun,* and *New York Times,* February 22, 1912.
[105] Letters to Roosevelt from Herbert S. Hadley, March 3, 1912, W. D. Foulke, March 17, 1912, Oscar S. Straus, March 7, 1912, and O. K. Davis, March 10, 1912, Roosevelt MSS.
[106] E. C. Stokes to Roosevelt, February 27, 1912, Roosevelt MSS.; Charles J. Bonaparte to H. C. Gauss, March 16, 22, 1912, Bonaparte MSS.
[107] J. L. Bristow to Roosevelt, February 23, 1912, Roosevelt MSS.

But the die had been cast. Had he wanted to, Roosevelt could not have backed out of the race at that time. Such a thought, however, was farthest from his mind. With the old ringing militancy and with the old happy phrasing, he had declared before the Columbus speech, "My hat is in the ring." Three days later in a letter to the eight governors he announced his intention to do battle for the Republican nomination.

CHAPTER EIGHT

Old Friends are Friends No Longer

ROOSEVELT'S announcement of his candidacy signaled the opening of a four months' campaign of invective. Certain that once in power the Colonel would attempt to transform his revolutionary New Nationalism into federal statutes, conservative editors spewed venom at every opportunity. The Roosevelt camp parried all charges with as good as they received. And with Taft attacking both La Follette and Roosevelt, who were just as busy maligning each other, the whole affair degenerated into a saturnalia of scurrility.

Characterizing Roosevelt's entrance into the race as a "vulgar" and "boorish" display of political apostasy, one conservative journalist designated him as the first "liar" who had sat in the White House.[1] Even the temperate *Springfield Republican* predicted that the country was in for a period of bitter strife and turmoil until the new "Caesar" gained control of the government again.[2] Joining with the press in the chorus of opprobrium were individuals. W. W. Howard, a supreme court justice of the state of New York, with a nice judicial impartiality characterized Roosevelt as a creature with the "daring of a madman" and the "instincts of a beast." The Republican state chairman of New York described the Colonel and his adherents as "followers of Aaron Burr" and a pack of "disordered minds." The dignified president of Columbia University contented himself with "Cossacks," "itin-

[1] *New York Times*, February 26, 1912; *New York Sun*, February 26, 1912.
[2] *Springfield Republican*, February 26, 1912.

erant political patent medicine men," and "sandlot orators."[3]

Taft himself for once in his life was not too reluctant to trade in personalities instead of issues. He began by attacking Roosevelt's theories of government as "crude" and "revolutionary," but soon turned his charges into more personal channels. At Boston, two months after he had called Roosevelt a neurotic, he declared that the Colonel had been unfaithful to a friendship and described his whole campaign as one based upon an ugly appeal to discontent and class hatred.[4]

Meanwhile administration men were diligently searching the entire Roosevelt record for other damaging evidence. On April 24 the House of Representatives called for the executive papers pertaining to the sudden cancellation of the International Harvester suit of 1907. After the papers had been supplied, the air became laden with charges that Roosevelt had bargained illicitly with the Harvester company. To help substantiate the accusation Taft subsequently published a letter from Roosevelt to Attorney General Bonaparte requesting that the suit be discontinued.[5] When Roosevelt in a heated reply stated that Taft had agreed to the discontinuance in a Cabinet meeting, the president, Senator Root, and Secretary of Agriculture Wilson denied in a published statement that the subject had ever been discussed in the Cabinet.[6] Later the United States attorney who had been in charge of the suit testified that Bonaparte had believed the company guilty and had ordered the proceedings quashed only after Cyrus McCormick and George Perkins had held a conference with Roosevelt.[7] This selfsame George Perkins,

[3] *New York Times*, February 28, April 10, May 17, 1912.
[4] *Ibid.*, April 26, 1912.   [5] *Ibid.*, April 25, 1912.
[6] *Ibid.*, April 27, 1912.
[7] Roosevelt and Bonaparte agreed in 1912 that the suit had been stopped in order to give Herbert Knox Smith, head of the Bureau of Corporations, a chance to proceed with the investigation of the company which he had started a year before, and which would have been automatically halted

the Taft men pointed out, was now the largest contributor to the Roosevelt campaign fund.[8]

Once again the old story of the connection between Roosevelt, Harriman, and campaign contributions in the 1904 campaign was raked over. Roosevelt's phrase, "We are practical men," again made the press streamers. At the same time a whispering campaign informed everyone willing to listen that Roosevelt was either continually drunk or crazy and probably both. "If Roosevelt don't quit drinking he won't last until the campaign is over," the *Denver Post* reported an authoritative speaker as saying.[9] While Roosevelt was thus attacked by the conservatives, the La Follette forces were accusing him of being a tool of the money power.[10]

Caught in the crossfire of criticism, the Colonel replied with vigor. Taft he branded as a colleague in perfidy with Senator Lorimer and George Cox of Cincinnati. He accused him of acquiescing in the "scandalous abuse" of federal patronage and declared that it was an odious shame for such a "government by corporation attorneys" to talk about bargains.[11] Stung by the president's Boston address, in which Taft had said that most of the Roosevelt leaders were nothing if not bosses, Roosevelt replied the next day at Worcester. In a hissing diatribe he accused the president of having "been disloyal to every canon of decency and fair play" and described the tactics of the Taft supporters as having "been foul to the verge of indecency." Altogether Taft's actions, Roosevelt claimed, constituted "the crookedest kind of a crooked deal."[12] Afterward the Colonel expressed himself as extremely satisfied with his effort at Worcester. "I am glad

had the suit not been discontinued. They both agreed that the matter had been discussed in a Cabinet meeting and that Taft had consented to the delay. Bonaparte to Roosevelt, March 6, 1912, Roosevelt to Bonaparte, April 30, 1912, Bonaparte to Elliot H. Goodwin, May 8, 1912, Bonaparte MSS.

[8] *Cincinnati Times Star*, May 11, 1912; *New York Sun*, May 19, 1912.
[9] April 28, 1912.
[10] *La Follette's Weekly*, April 13, 1912.
[11] *New York Times*, April 1, 10, 11, 1912.
[12] *Ibid.*, April 27, 1912.

you liked the way I answered Taft," he wrote to O. K. Davis. "I then practically dropped him partly because I think stamping on a man I have knocked down is both useless and discourteous."[13]

Meanwhile a nationwide Roosevelt organization had been feverishly constructed. William Loeb, Roosevelt's former secretary, seemed to be the general choice for captain of the campaign, and Loeb had indicated his willingness to accept the position. But Roosevelt, on the ground that Loeb was not well-to-do and would need the position he held in the Taft administration, refused his offer of support.[14] Truman H. Newberry of Michigan, whose money would have been quite "advantageous," was considered for a while but finally dropped because of his inability to make friends.[15] At length Joseph M. Dixon of Montana, an able, widely acquainted, and likeable senator, was chosen. Before long headquarters were set up in New York City and a National Executive Committee selected, which included, besides Dixon, William L. Ward, Roosevelt's personal representative, Frank Knox, Walter Brown, Cecil Lyon, William Flinn, O. K. Davis, Alexander Revell, and Edwin W. Sims. In Chicago a Western group was organized with Truman Newberry as head.[16] Soon thereafter a press bureau and other subsidiary organizations were formed. Among these were the United States Progressive Federation, the National Progressive Italian American League, the American Progressive German Alliance, and numerous other linguistic groups, including even such small racial minorities as the Lithuanians, Hungarians, and Syrians. Altogether it was a most impressive collection.[17]

Despite this imposing political architecture, there was from the first much inefficiency and friction within the Roosevelt

[13] April 28, 1912, Roosevelt MSS.
[14] Roosevelt to William Loeb, February 17, 1912, and to Robert Bass, February 15, 1912, Roosevelt MSS.
[15] Roosevelt to J. C. O'Laughlin, February 12, 1912, Roosevelt MSS.
[16] Roosevelt to Truman H. Newberry, February 20, 1912, Roosevelt MSS.
[17] From a typewritten memorandum in the Roosevelt MSS.

organization. For one thing, in the entire structure there were few experienced politicians. Again and again Roosevelt complained bitterly of the need for tested leaders.[18] Ridiculous and costly mistakes were numerous. Roosevelt himself was continually forced to plan and administer bothersome details. In the propaganda and publicity fields he was virtually his own manager.

Another thing that made for trouble was the almost constant personal warfare within the organization. As each subleader, with an eye to future favors, attempted to gain as much personal prestige as possible, the welfare of the candidate was often overlooked. From such pulling and hauling sharp personal animosities soon arose. A painful lack of cooperation between the New York, Washington, and Chicago offices was immediately apparent.[19] Knox became suspicious of Revell, Munsey thought that Knox should take more direction from headquarters than he was inclined to do. W. L. Ward was certain that Munsey was "crazy"; he claimed he could not even hold an intelligent conversation with the newspaper publisher. Numerous other complaints were sent to Roosevelt about Medill McCormick, Herbert Hadley, and Joseph M. Dixon.[20] A series of conferences was held at Washington to allocate the authority of each of these would-be king-makers. And while many of the quarrels were successfully composed, there continued to be a good deal of friction throughout the campaign.

Another early rift in the organization, one that continued to grow, was the inner feud between the idealists and the practical politicians. From time to time the expressions of Gifford Pinchot and Lincoln Steffens did not at all agree with

[18] Roosevelt to J. C. O'Laughlin, February 8, 1912, and to Matthew Hale, March 5, 1912, Herbert S. Hadley to Edwin W. Sims (copy), February 19, 1912, Roosevelt MSS.

[19] E. W. Sims to Roosevelt, March 16, 19, 1912, Roosevelt to Sims, March 16, 1912, Roosevelt MSS.

[20] Letters to Frank Harper from W. L. Ward, February 22, 1912, and E. Mont Reily, March 12, 1912, Frank A. Munsey to Roosevelt, March 15, 1912, Roosevelt MSS.

the politicians' conception of expediency and caused severe anguish in the breasts of William L. Ward, William Flinn, and Walter Brown. When one of the practical men expressed the double desire "to kill Lincoln Steffens" and "bottle up Pinchot," Roosevelt indicated that he was agreeable at least to the first part of the suggestion.[21]

As time went on the so-called "moonbeamers"[22] were periodically surprised and irritated by the influence these "practical men" exerted over Roosevelt. In particular they resented the power of George Perkins and Frank Munsey. However, had it not been for these two it is doubtful whether there would have been a Roosevelt candidacy in 1912. For Perkins and Munsey supplied most of the sinews of war, and Roosevelt was always aware that in politics lady victory was almost invariably on the side of the larger bank balances. As it was, the Roosevelt organization was well supplied with money. A final reckoning of prenomination expenditures by the Clapp committee indicated that Roosevelt had spent more than any presidential candidate.[23] In the fight to win delegates in New York City, where sixty thousand dollars was spent, Perkins and Munsey each contributed fifteen thousand dollars. Apropos of these contributions *Life* observed that there were some great opportunities in the Roosevelt camp "for several practical malefactors of great wealth," if they guaranteed not to save their letters and if they applied at the back door.[24] This financial advantage somewhat offset Roosevelt's lack of press support. For with the exception of the Munsey papers, the five journals owned by John C. Shaffer of Chicago, the *Chicago Tribune*, the *Philadelphia North American*, the *New York Evening Mail*, and the *Kansas City Star*, precious few newspapers supported him.

If the jealousies and the overlapping of authority in the up-

[21] Roosevelt to J. C. O'Laughlin, February 12, 1912, Roosevelt MSS.
[22] The term was Frank Munsey's.
[23] The figures were: Roosevelt $611,118, Taft $499,527, Wilson $219,104, Harmon $150,496, and Underwood $52,000. *New York Times*, October 15, 1912.
[24] *Life*, 59: 583 (March 21, 1912).

per reaches of the Roosevelt organization sometimes resulted in near chaos, the situation in the local and state structures was infinitely worse. Because the movement was new, there was little established authority. In each state dozens of men laid claim to the top positions in the local and state organizations. Their battle for the plums was often as bitter as that against the opposition, if not more so. Thus in Oklahoma two Roosevelt leaders, backed by two rival organizations, locked horns in a struggle for a place on the National Committee. It was not until a special representative from the national headquarters intervened that they turned their energies to nominating Roosevelt.[25] And since the situation in Oklahoma was typical of the whole organization, much time and energy went into untangling these local snarls.

Meanwhile Taft was straining every effort to secure his own renomination. By the first week in February it was noted that in the Southern states a political organization was being built up that for purposes of discipline and precision of movement seemed to be perfect.[26] With ruthless political realism William B. McKinley, at the head of the Taft forces, combed Dixie for Roosevelt men and then proceeded to dismiss them at once. On February 6 Cecil Lyons, Republican state chairman of Texas, was summarily removed from his position as patronage adviser. From that day on, for a federal employee to reveal that he was for Roosevelt meant that he lost his position.[27] Local postmasters were bluntly told that if they did not bring a Taft delegation to the state convention they would not be reappointed. The postmaster at Hastings, Oklahoma, was informed by J. A. Harriss, chairman of the State Republican Central Committee of Oklahoma, that the postal department had reported the Hastings office in an unsatis-

[25] E. Mont Reily to Frank Harper, March 10, 1912, Harper to E. E. Perry, March (?), 1912, Roosevelt MSS.

[26] *New York Sun*, February 4, 1912.

[27] Sloan Simpson to Roosevelt, February 7, 1912, Cecil Lyons to Ormsby McHarg, February 15, 1912, Oscar R. Hundley to Ormsby McHarg, February 8, 1912, John Allison to Roosevelt, May 29, 1912, Roosevelt MSS.; William D. Foulke to H. Goodwin, February 3, 1912, Foulke MSS.

factory condition at the last inspection. "I hope that you have your office in first class condition,"the letter continued, "and will continue to have it so. If you will bring a delegation to the state and district conventions instructed for Taft and Harriss I will see that you are reappointed."[28]

The strategy of the Taft forces throughout the South was to hold state conventions before the Roosevelt men could organize their followers. Each state chairman was ordered from Washington to hold conventions and to select delegates months before the usual time.[29] In the face of these thorough preparations Roosevelt's lieutenants were rather dubious about their ability to win any delegates from Dixie. Roosevelt felt that in view of the "rotten boroughs" they could do little or nothing there.[30] But there was always the hope that with Cecil Lyons and Pearl Wight, Republican chairmen of Texas and Louisiana, standing openly for the Colonel, at least a few delegates could be picked up. There was also the possibility that many job-hungry Southern Republicans, fearing the defeat of Taft, would finally swing to Roosevelt as the only Republican who could win. At any rate, Ormsby McHarg during January, February, and March spent most of his time in the Southern states, trying by one means or another to swing them over into the Roosevelt column. To supplement this work the Roosevelt faction in the Senate started to investigate the use of patronage in the section and to block all appointments of a political nature.[31]

But by February 6 it was obvious that these tactics alone would fail of their purpose. On that date the first state convention to select delegates organized a solid Taft delegation in Florida. With the temporary organization in their control, the Taft men straightway proceeded to settle most of the contested delegations in favor of the president. Whereupon the Roosevelt men walked in a body from the hall, held

[28] J. A. Harriss to N. S. Figley, February 17, 1912, original in Roosevelt MSS.

[29] Pearl Wight to Joseph M. Dixon, April 17, 1912, Roosevelt MSS.

[30] Roosevelt to D. R. Hanna, February 29, 1912, Roosevelt MSS.

[31] Roosevelt to Ormsby McHarg, March 4, 1912, Roosevelt MSS.

a second convention, and nominated a contesting delegation of Roosevelt men.[32] Fearing that the Florida results would be duplicated in almost every Southern state, and apprehensive that such a large total of early instructed delegates for Taft would influence subsequent Northern conventions, McHarg decided to contest the results of all Southern conventions irrespective of the merits of the case. From almost every state in the South the Taft delegates, most of whom were unquestionably legally selected, were contested by Roosevelt bolters. And while the procedure may have slightly helped the Roosevelt cause in the North, as a whole the policy was to be a disastrous one.

In the North and West the Roosevelt leaders were far more hopeful of success. Believing that the rank and file of Northern Republicans were indisputably for the Colonel, the Roosevelt men aimed to secure there the selection of convention delegates by direct vote of the people. At this time the direct primary was used to select delegates in only six states. Accordingly the Roosevelt headquarters publicly challenged the Taft forces to a trial of strength by means of the direct primaries in every state of the union.[33] As was to be expected, Taft refused to change the rules while the game was in progress. Consequently many Northern state legislatures fought fiercely over the question of adopting the direct primaries. In the end, Massachusetts, Pennsylvania, Illinois, Maryland, Ohio, and South Dakota adopted the device. With the six states in which the system was already in operation, this made a sizable block of normal Republican states from which a popular referendum could be obtained.

Meanwhile Roosevelt had personally assumed the burden of another campaign. At first he had planned to make only a few speeches, perhaps one in every state,[34] and to let his subordinates handle the rest of the task of gathering delegates. But as plaintive calls for help and dire predictions came to

[32] *New York Times*, February 7, 1912.
[33] *Ibid.*, March 6, 1912.
[34] Roosevelt to Moses E. Clapp, March 14, 1912, and to Matthew Hale, March 8, 1912, Roosevelt MSS.

him, the restless Roosevelt found himself unable to resist the urge to action. From the first of April until June he waged one of the most strenuous campaigns in American political history. Invading every important state and speaking as often as ten times a day, he set a pace which even his indefatigable vigor could not sustain. Finally he had to warn his headquarters that his schedule in Kansas and Nebraska must not be repeated if his voice was not to give out completely.[35]

Throughout his campaign speeches Roosevelt, taking Munsey's advice, sought to win back the confidence of the business world. Frequently he alluded to his plan for stabilizing business prosperity as one that was essentially regulatory and not destructive of interstate industry.[36] He wrote conservatively toned articles for the *Outlook*, defining his position on the relation of business and government. When his stand on the reciprocity measure was used against him in the Northwest, he confessed that he had changed his mind and that for the future he was against any sort of Canadian reciprocity.[37] He did not, however, accept the advice of another of his moneyed backers, Lucius Littauer, who urged him to endorse an "adequate tarriff" as opposed to Taft's stand for downward revision.[38] Much to his credit, neither did he sing low on his program of social reform or precipitately drop his scheme to reform the judiciary. In a fighting speech before the Massachusetts legislature he defended the judiciary reform on the ground that it gave back to the people the right to direct their own destinies. "If that is revolution, make the most of it," he ended.[39]

At the same time that Roosevelt was continuing the somewhat uneven tenor of his progressive ways, President Taft's public utterances became increasingly conservative. He repeatedly attacked Roosevelt's stand on the initiative and

[35] Roosevelt to O. K. Davis, April 20, 1912, Roosevelt MSS.
[36] Frank A. Munsey to Roosevelt, March 1, 13, 1912, Roosevelt to Munsey, March 12, 1912, Roosevelt MSS.
[37] *New York Times*, April 9, 1912.
[38] Lucius N. Littauer to Roosevelt, March 6, 1912, Roosevelt MSS.
[39] *New York Times*, February 27, 1912.

recall, and even damned the direct primary with faint praise.[40] He opposed the Roosevelt scheme for government regulation and adhered to the old percolator theory of economics, so well beloved by the defenders of the status quo. The economic need of the country, according to Taft, was not innovation nor yet agitation, but rather a period of governmental somnolence during which those who had capital to invest would again gain confidence in the industrial and financial future. Following a return of such "quiet confidence" capital would be invested in a bewildering number of enterprises, from which in turn would flow more jobs, higher wages, and greater happiness for all.[41] Roosevelt answered with a stream of sarcasm, branding the president as an outright reactionary who by his do-nothing policy would lead the country straight into financial and industrial chaos.

Being the national champion of progressivism, however, did not prevent Roosevelt from accepting the support of some of the most notorious machine politicians in the country. In fact, much of Roosevelt's strength came from the most conservative of Republican leaders. While disagreeing with his advanced professions, they supported him either with a view to capturing the Republican state machinery or because they felt that his leadership would materially aid their own candidacies. Roosevelt in turn did not pledge them to his political views. All he asked of them was their support. He interposed no objections to a deal in Indiana arranged by Frank Knox. There, in consideration for a place on the Roosevelt National Committee and the promise of Roosevelt's future support, C. H. Campbell, long a leading member of the standpat Fairbanks-Keating-Watson machine, promised to divert part of the convention to the Roosevelt ticket. When Beveridge and Campbell appeared on the same platform, many a Hoosier found it hard to believe his eyes.[42]

No state, however, proved the ancient saw about politics

[40] *Kansas City Star*, March 18, 1912.

[41] *Ibid.*, March 8, 1912.

[42] Undated memorandum, Roosevelt MSS.; Bonaparte to E. H. Goodwin, April (?), 1912, Bonaparte MSS.

and strange bedfellows better than did North Dakota. Long before 1912 Senator Gronna had been in the vanguard of the progressive fight within the state. One of his chief opponents had been the Stalwart Congressman Hanna. When La Follette announced his candidacy for the presidency in 1911, Senator Gronna promptly threw the support of the North Dakota progressive organization behind him. Later when Roosevelt entered the race, Congressman Hanna and the Stalwart wing of the party at once fell in behind him. Shortly thereafter Hanna ran for the governorship. Thus in North Dakota a victory for Roosevelt meant the defeat of the progressive movement. It was significant of the political temper of the state that La Follette carried it easily over the Roosevelt-Stalwart alliance.[43]

The fight to obtain delegates in each state was nearing the point of explosion. Knowing that in some localities there would be an attempt to win by strong-arm methods, Roosevelt wrote his state lieutenants to be firm and to fight fire with fire. "I hope that you will not permit them to override you," he wrote Truman Newberry. "Michigan is with us just as much as Illinois is and if they try any strong-arm tactics make it evident that we can stand Rough House quite as well as they can."[44] To John C. Greenway, one of his representatives in Arizona, he went further. Judging from Oyster Bay that all the contested Roosevelt delegates were rightfully entitled to their seats, he advised Greenway, in the event his men were unjustly unseated, to maintain their rights even if they had to fight for them.[45]

In temper the conventions themselves lived up to expectations. The pattern for many of them was foreshadowed by the conduct and the tone of the Missouri district conventions meeting early in March. Fist fights and mob action were a

---

[43] R. W. Farrar to Ormsby McHarg, February 24, 1912, letters to Roosevelt from C. A. Lindbergh, March 7, 1912, and Thomas Thorson, March 21, 1912, Roosevelt MSS.

[44] Roosevelt to Truman Newberry, April (?), 1912 (telegram), Roosevelt MSS.

[45] Roosevelt to John C. Greenway, May 31, 1912, Roosevelt MSS.

part of almost every one of them. In one of the meetings so many of the members were equipped with baseball bats that it became known over the state as the "ball bat convention."[46] Perhaps the wildest scenes, however, were those that took place at the Oklahoma state convention. A few hours before the meeting a subcommittee of the State Central Committee ordered that two hundred contested Roosevelt delegates be unseated. Whereupon the Roosevelt leaders marshalled all their delegates, rushed past the doorkeepers, and took possession of the convention hall. The following convention, which lasted all day and until four o'clock the next morning, was carried on in the best Western tradition. Mass gun play was momentarily expected. One man dropped dead from excitement; three more were carried out after personal encounters. Before the convention opened the Roosevelt leaders had warned the Taft man presiding that if he attempted any chicanery he would not walk out of the convention hall alive. To emphasize the point still further a Roosevelt disciple, it was reported, stood behind the chairman all during the convention with his hand on a gun "ready for an emergency."[47]

In many other states the conventions split wide open to select two sets of delegates. At the Michigan meeting at Bay City rational procedure was impossible. Despite the presence of state troops, a mass fight broke out on the platform when a Taft man threw a football block into a Roosevelt speaker. Refusing to give his scheduled keynote address, Beveridge left the hall in the midst of the uproar. Shortly thereafter the convention, unable to agree on anything, split in half and elected two chairmen. Then amid the wildest disorder and violence both conventions, from the same platform, simultaneously went through the motions of selecting two sets of delegates.[48]

[46] William T. Miller, *Progressive Movement in Missouri* (Columbia, Missouri, 1928), 88–90.

[47] Unsigned memorandum, March 17, 1912, Roosevelt MSS.; *Kansas City Star*, March 14, 1912.

[48] *New York Times*, April 12, 1912; Beasley, *Frank Knox*, 77–80.

During March and the first part of April it looked as though the president would win the nomination with but negligible opposition. Besides the solid South, the important states of New York, Indiana, Michigan, and Kentucky selected Taft delegates. The president then followed up these victories by shading Roosevelt slightly in the Massachusetts primary. In the Middle West, where Roosevelt was thought to be strongest, he lost the North Dakota primary to La Follette by a margin of almost two to one. Altogether the first two months of the race gave little cheer to the Roosevelt followers. True, in almost every case Roosevelt charged the Taft organization with "bare faced fraud" in the conduct of the contests, but in the eyes of the country such charges were unimpressive as compared with the Taft totals of pledged delegates. Charles J. Bonaparte, viewing the results, felt that a Roosevelt victory was scarcely more than a "forlorn hope."[49]

About the middle of April, however, the fortunes of the game began to turn. On April 9 Roosevelt won the Illinois direct primary by a margin of more than two to one. A few days later in Pennsylvania the Flinn machine, in utterly routing the Penrose organization, won most of the nominations for state offices and contributed sixty-five pledged delegates to the Roosevelt cause.[50] From then on until the middle of May almost every week witnessed a Roosevelt victory somewhere in the country. In short order California, Minnesota, Nebraska, Maryland, and South Dakota followed one another into the Roosevelt column. Day by day the total number of delegates opposed to the renomination of the president mounted until by mid-May Roosevelt's chances of winning the nomination appeared excellent. With the increase in the Roosevelt totals there was a corresponding rise of temper among his opponents. Taft, while campaigning in Maryland, minced no words in describing his former friend as the associate of the most venal of political bosses and as

[49] Bonaparte to Joseph M. Dixon, April 27, 1912, Bonaparte MSS.
[50] *New York Times*, April 15, 1912.

the protégé of crooked high finance. His campaign manager, McKinley, openly accused Roosevelt of buying his majority in Baltimore.

With the Ohio primary the drama reached a climax. Each side recognized that a victory in Ohio would be of tremendous value, not only because of its heavy quota of delegates but also because it was the home state of the president. Ohio's denial of Taft, it was thought, would be almost the equivalent of a national repudiation. Both sides veritably poured campaign orators into the state. A week before the primary President Taft left Washington for his home state accompanied by a battery of orators, including Cabinet officers, United States senators and representatives, and governors.[51] The next day Roosevelt, Bonaparte, ex-Senator Beveridge, Senators Poindexter and Clapp, Governor Stubbs, Garfield, and Congressman Murdock, followed the president.[52] During the next week Roosevelt traveled eighteen hundred miles in the state to give some ninety scheduled speeches. Taft covered even more territory and spoke more often. With their special cars chasing each other across the state, both men, worked up to the highest pitch of intensity, relieved their emotions with a constant flow of abuse against each other.

At Cambridge, Taft set off the personal fireworks by designating Roosevelt as a "dangerous egotist," a "demagogue," and a "flatterer of the people." "I hate a flatterer," he ended. "I like a man to tell the truth."[53] The next day Roosevelt returned the compliments by describing the president as a "puzzlewit" and a "fathead" who had an intellect a little short of a guinea pig's.[54] From that time on, while the country at large alternately cheered, booed, and otherwise had the time of its life, the two candidates, like street urchins, tossed at each other such imprecations as "honeyfugler," "demagogue," "hypocrite," "apostate," "Jacobin," and

[51] *New York Sun*, May 14, 1912.
[52] *New York Times*, May 13, 1912; *New York Sun*, May 14, 1912.
[53] *Cleveland Plain Dealer*, May 14, 1912.
[54] *Ibid.*, May 15, 16, 1912.

"brawler."[55] To further complicate matters, La Follette entered the state on May 17. Rapidly getting into the swing of the Ohio campaign, he launched charges at both Roosevelt and Taft in his first address at Bowling Green. In no other campaign perhaps have three candidates engaged in such a back-alley fight as did Roosevelt, Taft, and La Follette in Ohio. One evening at Steubenville the two private cars of Roosevelt and Taft stood side by side, and hopeful onlookers expected a street fight. But both men refused to recognize the presence of the other, and by morning the cordial friends of but four years back had gone their separate ways.

The result in Ohio was a complete victory for Roosevelt. Winning the state by a sizeable majority over both Taft and La Follette, he captured every district delegate.[56] Many politicians, including Taft men and Democrats, were now willing to concede that Roosevelt would win the nomination.[57] The results in New Jersey the following week, reproducing those in Ohio, strengthened this feeling. Even the pessimistic Roosevelt, who had felt from the start that there was little chance of victory, now admitted that he was "reasonably sure" of controlling the convention.[58]

By the end of the first week in June, however, with all the delegates selected, no one knew for certain who would control the convention. For of the eleven hundred legal delegates over one-third were contested. And since Taft controlled the National Republican Committee, whose duty it was to hear the contest and make up the temporary roll, Roosevelt's supposition that he would dominate the body was somewhat ill-

[55] *Cleveland Leader*, May 13, 14, 15, 16, 1912; *Cleveland Plain Dealer*, May 14, 15, 16, 1912.

[56] The final vote stood Roosevelt 165,809, Taft 118,362, La Follette, 15,570.

[57] Letters to Roosevelt from Frank Munsey, May 15, 1912, and Nicholas Longworth, May 27, 1912, Roosevelt MSS.; Bonaparte to H. C. Gauss, May 16, 1912, Bonaparte MSS.; Woodrow Wilson to Mrs. Reed, May 26, 1912, in Baker, *Woodrow Wilson*, 2: 316; Edward M. House to Charles A. Culberson, May 1, 1912, in Morris R. Werner, *Bryan* (New York, 1929), 178; *New York Sun*, May 24, 1912; *Brooklyn Eagle*, May 7, 1912.

[58] Roosevelt to Joseph M. Dixon, May 23, 1912, and to William E. Glasscock, May 28, 1912, Roosevelt MSS.

founded. Not in doubt, however, was the fact that Roosevelt was the popular choice of Republicans for the nomination. From the thirteen states where the rank and file of Republicans had voted, La Follette received thirty-six delegates, Taft forty-eight, and Roosevelt two hundred and seventy-eight. Moreover, in the popular vote Roosevelt had received an absolute majority over La Follette and Taft and had polled a half million more votes than the president.[59] It was true that Roosevelt was proportionately stronger in the states having direct primaries, for the question of adopting them was squarely at issue between the Republican candidates. But the overwhelming results of the primaries and the figures of numerous newspaper polls prove that Roosevelt, in the face of Taft's use of patronage, and in the face of the powerful organization of a dominant party, was the actual choice of the majority of Republicans. Of that there can be little doubt.[60]

The results of the primaries proved one other thing. Since the Radicals of Lincoln's day had transformed the high tenets of Republicanism from a defense of personal rights into a defense of property, the Republican party had been traditionally the party of conservatism. But the figures of the 1912 primaries pointed unerringly to the fact that at that time the great mass of Republican voters were progressive—progressive enough to strike at the courts, to believe in the New Nationalism, and to support Robert Marion La Follette. For every vote that Taft received Roosevelt and La Follette together obtained two. And thus the toil of years by the apostles of progressivism within the Republican party had begun to bear fruit.

[59] The totals for the states were La Follette 351,043, Taft 761,716, Roosevelt 1,157,397.

[60] Moreover, most of the Roosevelt strength was in traditional Republican states, while a good many of Taft's votes came from states almost certain to be Democratic in the elections.

CHAPTER NINE

"We Stand at Armageddon"

BY THE END OF THE first week in June, 1912, Roosevelt had received an indisputable majority of the votes cast in the Republican primary elections over the country. But that did not mean he could be sure of being nominated at the Chicago convention. For Taft, adding the 254 contested delegates to his totals, had an actual majority of the seats in the nominating body. Roosevelt needed forty or fifty of the disputed delegates to block the renomination of Taft and a score more to win.

To the more naive followers of Roosevelt it seemed certain that he could win at least seventy of these contests and thus insure his nomination. Hardened politicians, however, shook their heads. In the first place, many of the Roosevelt contests were admittedly spurious. Secondly, all the contests were to be decided by the National Republican Committee. Now this body was nothing if not partisan in 1912. Selected in 1908, its members had been chosen from loyal Taft supporters. They had continued in their offices in the intervening years only by grace of the administration. Consequently with few exceptions the committee was unqualifiedly for Taft's renomination. By all party precedents they could then be expected to ignore all questions of morality and devote themselves entirely to the task of accrediting enough of the disputed Taft delegates to insure his renomination. No one was more painfully aware of this prospect than were the Roosevelt managers.[1]

The committee, which convened on June 7 for a hectic two weeks' session, was the object of national attention. Upon its

[1] Cecil Lyons to Ormsby McHarg, February 15, 1912, Herbert S. Hadley to Dixon, May 29, 1912, Roosevelt MSS.

decisions, in all probability, the outcome of the nomination rested. Into its deliberations Roosevelt sent some of his most formidable and skillful fighters. The combative Governor Stubbs of Kansas, the vice-hunting Francis J. Heney of California, and the square-jawed, bespectacled William Flinn, boss of Pittsburgh and a keen student of the under-the-surface politics, were added by means of proxies to the regular Roosevelt leaders in the body, Senator William E. Borah and Frank B. Kellogg. But on the Taft side were men just as resolute. The soft-spoken Murray Crane of Massachusetts and Congressman William B. McKinley, supported by an overwhelming majority of votes in the committee, never once wavered throughout the long sessions.

Generally little pretense was made of hearing all the evidence before a decision was made. In many disputes each side presented masses of affidavits, and in the half hour given to each side to state its case a fair determination of the evidence was impossible. Beyond this was the fact that a just decision would have entailed investigation of the proceedings of the numerous district and county conventions. That was obviously an impossible task. Therefore some of the decisions would have been open to question regardless of whom they favored.[2]

In all there were 254 contested seats. In many cases a decision was easily reached. Especially in the South, where delegates had been selected before the Roosevelt organization had been perfected, Ormsby McHarg had subsequently instigated spurious contests that even the Roosevelt men admitted were not tenable. And there can be little doubt that McHarg's manufactured claims, originally made to bolster the confidence of the Roosevelt forces in the North, became a great liability. For the public, who had been given to understand that the claims were valid, were amazed to find Roosevelt's own men on the committee voting against them. Hoaxed by some of the Roosevelt contests, they were inclined to suspect the rest.

[2] *New York Sun*, June 10, 12, 1912; *New York World*, June 11, 12, 1912.

Probably about one hundred Roosevelt contests deserved a thorough examination. From the investigations of these contests it was obvious that the committee as a whole was less interested in justice than in seating enough delegates pledged to Taft to insure his renomination. In the case of Indiana the committee admitted that the primary had been marked by many irregularities, but decided that since the president had received an unmistakable majority in the vote it would be a "farce" to question its results.[3] However, with respect to Washington, where the results of the primary had been overwhelmingly for Roosevelt, the committee reversed itself and declared that because of the irregularities it would abide by the action of the regular Republican organization in the state, which had given the delegates to Taft. Texas had no primary. There the National Committee rejected the results of the convention on the ground that the selection of delegates had been dictated by the Roosevelt-dominated state committee and that it was necessary to remove boss rule and restore a measure of self-control.[4]

Of the 254 contested seats, 235 were awarded to Taft and only 19 to Roosevelt. And although there is much room for argument, it would seem that Roosevelt had a right to at least thirty more delegates than he received. Elihu Root felt privately that in a minority of cases there was certainly a basis "for honest differences of opinion."[5] A friend of La Follette's, however, who was in no way biased toward Roosevelt's cause, thought he should have received about fifty of the contested seats, which agrees roughly with the figures Borah and Hadley prepared after they had parted political company with Roosevelt.[6] Thirty additional votes would not have given Roosevelt a majority of the convention. But the loss of thirty votes would have been a serious blow to Taft's

[3] *Kansas City Star*, June 11, 1912.

[4] *New York Sun*, June 11, 12, 13, 1912; Victor Rosewater, *Backstage in 1912* (Philadelphia, 1932), 109.

[5] Elihu Root to Grenville M. Dodge, July 5, 1912, Dodge MSS.

[6] Gilbert E. Roe, "The Truth about the Contests," *La Follette's Weekly*, July 20, 27, August 3, 1912.

hopes. For with the addition of the delegates for Cummins and a few for La Follette, Roosevelt would have been able to dictate the organization of the convention and to block Taft's victory on the first ballot.[7] The result, considering the temper of the convention, would have been the nomination of a compromise candidate or, more likely, of Roosevelt himself. Thus Taft secured the nomination by manipulation. In another sense he defeated Roosevelt by making use of the practices by which most presidents are made. These were precisely the tactics that Theodore Roosevelt had used in 1908 to nominate William Howard Taft. "In the pre Convention campaign of 1908 the conventions in the Southern states were unquestionably 'run' in Taft's interest by Federal office holders," wrote the fair-minded Bonaparte in 1912.[8]

The Roosevelt men did not take defeat sitting down. Tumult and near riot punctuated almost every session of the National Committee. When it announced its decision on the Kentucky contests, the Roosevelt leaders hurled the lie direct across the floor and charged outright robbery.[9] Francis J. Heney observed once, after vainly trying to get the floor, that no one would be recognized "but a hand-picked, machine-made crook."[10] Several times during the sessions actual physical encounters almost broke up the meetings. Outside, the Roosevelt forces, sensing the outcome, launched a national campaign to discredit the body's findings. No words were too sharp for their purpose. One of the most stinging jeremiads ever to be issued from a national headquarters came from the Roosevelt offices after the committee awarded two California delegates to Taft:

The saturnalia of fraud and larceny now in progress under the auspices of the National Committee took on new repulsiveness today with the announcement of the committee's action in the case

[7] In the first test of strength over the temporary chairmanship the vote stood 558 for the Taft candidate to 502 for the Roosevelt man. Thus a shift of 29 votes would have resulted in a Roosevelt victory.

[8] Bonaparte to Elliot H. Goodwin, April 17, 1912, Bonaparte MSS.

[9] *New York Times*, June 12, 1912.

[10] Rosewater, *Backstage*, 130.

of California. It was thought that the limit of folly and indecency had already been reached by this doomed and passion-drunk committee which in the last four days have issued the party's credentials to bogus delegates, reeling with fraud and straight from the cesspools of Southern corruption.

Hitherto it was supposed that the National Committee was content with the political emoluments of pocket-picking and porch-climbing. Today, however, they essayed the role of the apache and the garroteer.[11]

Time and time again the progressive forces pointed out how inequitable was the basis for the election of delegates. It was reiterated in the progressive press that Florida, Louisiana, Mississippi, and South Carolina together had cast less than 34,000 votes for the Republican nominee in 1908, yet they were as instrumental in choosing the Republican candidate as were Kansas, Connecticut, New Hampshire, Oregon, and West Virginia with their 550,000 Republican votes. Ironically enough for Roosevelt, it had been his influence four years before that had defeated a motion more closely apportioning the number of Republican delegates in a state to the number of Republican votes.[12]

The Taft people countered with a similar barrage of abuse. As mutual recrimination increased, the tempers on both sides became shorter, until by convention time many feared that the nominating body would be terminated not by the orderly process of nomination, but in a vicious physical mass struggle between the inflamed partisans. The *New York Sun* even went so far as to predict the death of the Republican party when the Roosevelt forces, "carrying sealed orders to draw the sword or the club or the revolver," saw they were beaten and resorted to violence.[13]

Meanwhile behind the scenes in the Roosevelt headquarters a most important decision had to be made. Late in May the Taft forces had selected Elihu Root as their candidate

[11] *New York Times,* June 13, 1912.
[12] Watson, *As I Knew Them,* 129.
[13] *New York Sun,* June 19, 1912.

for both the temporary and the permanent chairmanship. No wiser choice could have been made. Cool, astute, and a master of parliamentary and convention procedure, the senator from New York would rule with an experienced hand. There was little chance that even the most militant minority could secure any advantages by parliamentary stratagems with Root presiding. Moreover, he was the one man in the opposition whom Roosevelt could not very well attack. For in better days Roosevelt had held him up to the public view as the most able and most virtuous of American statesmen, a man *sans peur et sans reproche.*

Some in the Roosevelt inner circle felt that it would be unwise to oppose Root, but the Colonel thought otherwise.[14] At first he offered Governor Hadley the honor. When Hadley, for reasons of his own, exhibited a reluctance to accept, Governor McGovern of Wisconsin became his choice. With a Wisconsin progressive as chairman Roosevelt thought the split in the progressive ranks might be healed.[15] So shortly before the opening day of the convention he announced that he would contest the selection of his former friend and associate for the temporary chairmanship. It was true, the announcement ran, that Root had "rendered distinguished services" in the past, but now that he had become the "representative of reaction" there was nothing left to do but oppose him.[16] And thus Root followed in the wake of Taft, Lodge, and many another. The threads of friendship were fast snapping. Where once Roosevelt had stood at the head of this little group of the party, he was now the object of their attacks. Gone was the old hearty cooperation, gone the old camaraderie.

But Roosevelt's loss of personal friends was perhaps compensated for by the almost consecrated homage he got from the commonalty of his followers. To the men within the ranks

[14] Roosevelt to Dixon, May 23, 1912, and to Hadley, May 24, 1912, Hadley to Roosevelt, June 13, 1912, Roosevelt MSS.

[15] Roosevelt to Dixon, May 25, 1912, Roosevelt MSS.

[16] *Philadelphia North American*, June 4, 1912.

of Republicanism who had long joyfully supported him, to the crusaders among them, the starry-eyed liberals, Roosevelt was now something more than a revered political leader. He was gradually becoming a minor deity. The man who had promised so much for so long, but who had always fallen short of their expectations, had now finally and without reservation declared himself their champion. He had thrown the spear that knew no brother straight at the heart of reaction, and they repaid him with a devotion approaching idolatry. Nowhere was this more apparent than on the faces and in the actions of the Roosevelt delegates streaming into Chicago. Even among the Taft leaders this religious spirit did not go unnoticed.[17]

If the devotion the Roosevelt followers bestowed upon their leader was unusual, their feeling toward his opponents was no less intense. Worked up to a high emotional pitch by the inflammatory messages issued from the Roosevelt headquarters,[18] some of the delegates arrived in Chicago more eager to crack heads than to cast ballots. As many a Taft delegate arrived in much the same humor, affairs of mutual obligation were soon arranged. In the bars, hotels, and in the streets fist fights were common; these were usually started by the Roosevelt men, who greeted the sight of a Taft badge with yells of "robber" and "thief."[19] When the convention was about to open, wild rumors echoed by the newspapers were circulated. It was noised that the Roosevelt men were going to rush the convention hall and then refuse to admit Taft delegates, that the Roosevelt delegates from Oklahoma were all armed with six-shooters to see that their candidate got his just due. Even the *New York Times* was prepared to believe that the Roosevelt men would stop at nothing short of assault and burglary to gain their ends.[20] Mr. Dooley predicted that the convention would be "a combynation iv th'

[17] Watson, *As I Knew Them*, 160.
[18] *Philadelphia North American*, June 15, 16, 17, 18, 1912.
[19] *New York Times*, June 18, 1912.
[20] *Ibid.*, *New York Sun*, June 18, 1912; Arthur W. Dunn, *From Harrison*

Chicago fire, Saint Bartholomew's massacree, the battle iv th' Boyne, th' life iv Jessie James, an' th' night iv th' big wind." When asked if he were going he replied: "Iv coarse I'm goin'! I haven't missed a riot in this neighborhood in forty years, an' onless I'm deceived by the venal Republican press this wan will rejoice the heart, as Hogan says."[21]

To heighten the intensity of passion, Roosevelt himself came to the convention city. A week before he had not planned to attend in person, but had finally responded to the pleas of most of his lieutenants. He arrived in Chicago on June 15 and at once took over the direct command of his forces. At the Chicago Auditorium on the night before the convention he addressed his followers in a speech wrought of passion. To a crowd of five thousand in the hall and to thousands more jammed into the streets Roosevelt served notice that he would not be bound by the convention if the seventy-six delegates whose seats were contested were allowed to take part in organizing the body. He charged Taft and the Regular Republican organization with almost every kind of theft known to the statute books. Amid the wild cheers of the half hysterical crowd he ended with dramatic climax, "We stand at Armageddon, and we battle for the Lord."[22]

Considering the fact that Taft had a majority in the convention, if the Credentials Committee agreed with the actions of the National Committee on the matter of contested seats, some observers viewed Roosevelt's trip to Chicago as the last action of a desperate man. But others were not so sure of victory for the president, even granting that he would win all the contested seats. For one thing, it was obvious that Taft inspired in the delegates pledged to him no such loyalty as animated the Roosevelt men. In many a state convention, as in Iowa, the Regular leaders had secured Taft pledges only by exerting pressure. Now they very much feared that their

to Harding (New York, 1922), 2:178; Solomon B. Griffin, *People and Politics* (Boston, 1923), 441.

[21] *Kansas City Star*, June 16, 1912.
[22] *New York Times*, June 18, 1912.

forces might "disintegrate" before the time came to select a candidate. As a matter of record, almost daily before the convention opened some Taft delegate from here or there announced that he could no longer vote for the president and would accordingly cast his ballot for Roosevelt.[23]

Moreover, no one was certain that the sixty-six Negro delegates pledged to the president would remain loyal. A swing by even a portion of the colored delegates would change the complexion of the whole convention. The Roosevelt national colored headquarters in Chicago was bringing pressure to bear upon each of them, attempting to persuade them by one means or another to change their allegiances.[24] Each side hired detectives to guard against bribery, and each side accused the other of corruption.[25]

When the convention met on Tuesday, June 18, scarcely a seat in the building was vacant. The entire hall was pervaded by a sullen bitterness and hostility that foreshadowed the tumult to come. In fact, from the sound of the opening gavel to the moment of adjournment the body was in an almost constant state of disorder. Scarcely a speaker for either side was heard for long. Many simply had to stop speaking when the hisses and yells swelled into a roar against which a single throat was impotent. As passions ran high, actual fights broke out. One observer counted five in the last three hours of the convention.[26]

No sooner had the convention formally opened than Governor Hadley, floor leader of the Roosevelt forces, introduced a motion to substitute some seventy Roosevelt delegates for the Taft delegates whom the National Committee had placed on the temporary roll. But after a few minutes of caustic debate, Victor Rosewater, acting chairman of the National Committee, ruled the motion out of order, and the convention went on to select the temporary chairman.

[23] *Kansas City Star*, June 8, 1912; *New York Sun*, January 17, 1912.
[24] A. L. Williams to Roosevelt, June 11, 1912, Roosevelt MSS.
[25] *New York Times*, June 17, 18, 1912; *New York Sun*, June 14, 1912.
[26] *New York Times*, June 25, 1912.

Over the objections of La Follette, Governor McGovern of Wisconsin was nominated for the permanent chairmanship. In the battle between Senator Root and Governor McGovern pandemonium really broke loose. The nominating and seconding speeches for Root were all but drowned out by the cries of "liar," "thief," and "swindler" from the Roosevelt men on the floor. The Taft men reciprocated. At one point Francis J. Heney stopped short on the rostrum to point at a Colorado member of the National Committee and remark that the only difference between him and Abe Ruef of California was that Ruef had been in the penitentiary the preceding week, whereas the Coloradan had helped to make the temporary roll. The convention almost broke up then and there.[27] Nor did the tumult die down when it was learned that Root had beaten McGovern 558 to 502. In the first test vote the Taft forces had secured twenty-nine more than a bare majority, giving them control of the organization.

Root had no sooner finished his keynote speech than Governor Hadley once more offered his motion to substitute the names of seventy-odd Roosevelt delegates for as many Taft delegates who were voting on the points at issue. In the ensuing debate the convention once again showed its ugly humor. With the exception of Hadley scarcely one of the speakers was able to make himself heard beyond the platform. Some of them, after uttering a few sentences, simply gave up the attempt and sat down, ridiculed by laughter and hoarse shouts.[28] When order was partially restored, Hadley's motion was referred to the Committee on Credentials. Another Roosevelt motion, offered by Governor Charles S. Deneen of Illinois, which would have barred the contested delegates from voting on any of the contests, was, however, voted down on the floor after Root had pointed out that such practices would permit any minority to control any body by simply contesting enough of their opponents' seats.[29]

[27] *Philadelphia North American*, June 19, 1912.
[28] *New York Sun*, June 20, 1912.
[29] The motion lost 564 to 540. Thus the Taft forces on this ballot had a

Meanwhile the battle for control shifted to the Committee on Resolutions, where the permanent roll of the convention was to be adopted. The Roosevelt forces had as little hope of success there as they had had in the National Committee. Senators Root, Penrose, and Crane had selected its membership with infinite pains,[30] as was patent at the first meeting of the committee. The Taft majority quickly proposed that a maximum of ten minutes be given each side to state its case for a given contest and that no evidence be presented that had not been laid before the National Committee. In the uproar that followed Roosevelt was misinformed that these proposals had been adopted. By telephone he ordered his men to bolt the committee. By the time the bolters reached the Roosevelt headquarters in the Congress Hotel a movement was already under way for the Colonel's separate nomination by a convention to be held in Orchestra Hall.[31]

This action was stopped, however, when it became known that the Committee on Credentials had made concessions to meet Roosevelt's objections. But although the Roosevelt men went back, it was clear that they could expect nothing more than a recapitulation of the National Committee's decisions. This made the hopelessness of the Colonel's cause obvious. Faced with the fact that the Old Guard would neither surrender nor die, Roosevelt called together all his delegates late that night. The purpose of the meeting was not publicly announced, but it was understood that the decision to bolt or not to bolt would be made.

The members of the Roosevelt inner council did not seriously question which decision would finally be made. For the Colonel had come to Chicago firmly convinced that he was the choice of the masses of the Republican party. He had come determined to be nominated. He had long since de-

majority of 24 votes. A switch by 13 delegates would have been disastrous for the president.

[30] Watson, *As I Knew Them*, 149.

[31] *New York Times, New York World*, June 21, 1912; Davis, *Released for Publication*, 300.

cided that if he were counted out he would lead a bolting faction out of the party, provided, of course, that enough support was at hand when the critical hour came. Several times in the weeks from March through May he had stated that he would not be content to sit back and watch the bosses of the party nominate his adversary if it were evident from their votes that it was he the masses wanted.[32] In letters to friends he mentioned the possibility of an "independent candidacy."[33] In the first week of June his daughter Alice realized that if he lost the nomination, he would run on an independent ticket.[34]

At the convention, even before the opening session, many of the Roosevelt men were speculating about a new third party.[35] The talk was encouraged when the California and Pennsylvania delegations passed resolutions empowering their leaders to take any action necessary to secure the submission of Roosevelt's name as a presidential nominee.[36] Even before the Credentials Committee had met, a strong minority in the Roosevelt forces was ready and willing to leave the old party. The actions of the committee during the morning and afternoon of Wednesday, June 20, served to increase this element.

But when the Roosevelt chieftains met that night it was evident that many were decidedly opposed to leaving the party. Most of the men who controlled the Regular Republican organization in their home states and most of those who were standing for election argued against it. Governors Stubbs of Kansas, Aldrich of Nebraska, Hadley of Missouri, Glasscock of West Virginia, and Deneen of Illinois all raised stout objections.[37] On the other hand, most of the leaders who had little at stake at home, all the radicals, and a great

[32] *New York Times*, March 28, April 9, 1912.
[33] Roosevelt to Bradley Gilman, May 10, 1912, Roosevelt to Sidney Brooks, June 4, 1912, Roosevelt MSS.
[34] Longworth, *Crowded Hours*, 196.
[35] *Kansas City Star*, June 16, 1912; *New York Times*, June 13, 1912.
[36] *Kansas City Star*, June 15, 1912; *New York Sun*, June 20, 1912; Harold Howland, *Theodore Roosevelt and His Times* (New Haven, 1921), 220.
[37] *New York Times*, June 21, 1912.

majority of the rank and file of the delegates were solidly in favor of a bolt.

Evident though it was that he would be given enough personal support to make a respectable showing, the cagey Roosevelt still had to be assured of adequate financial backing before committing himself to an independent candidacy. This important question was finally settled in one of the inner rooms of the Roosevelt headquarters long after the general meeting had disbanded. There Roosevelt, Munsey, and Perkins held a momentous conference until the early morning hours. In the end Munsey, the millionaire newspaper owner, Perkins, director of the United States Steel Corporation, the International Harvester Company, and closely affiliated with the house of Morgan, promised their financial support. With their quiet assurance, "Colonel, we will see you through," the Progressive party, dedicated to the task of national social therapy, was conceived.[38]

Late that afternoon Roosevelt announced that there would probably be a new national nominating convention. He would accept either the nomination from the "honestly elected" majority of the Republican convention, he declared, or a nomination made by such progressives as would gather together to form a new party based on progressive principles.[39] That the first alternative would never occur was apparent when the convention met on the same day to accept in full the report of the Committee on Credentials. To this flouting of his claims Roosevelt replied next morning in no uncertain terms. Shortly after the Republican convention opened on Saturday Henry J. Allen of Kansas rose to read Roosevelt's message to his pledged delegates. Chronicling the alleged thefts and frauds of the convention, Roosevelt charged that as made up the body could not claim to represent the voters of the Republican party. He ended with the hope that none of the Roosevelt delegates would take any further part in its deliberations.

[38] Bowers, *Beveridge*, 419–420; *New York Times*, June 21, 1912.
[39] *New York Sun*, June 21, 1912.

With the split in the party a reality and almost certain defeat ahead, there was much talk that Saturday morning of a compromise candidate whose nomination would reunite the shattered organization. Such talk was not new. Weeks before, after Roosevelt had won the contest for delegates in Pennsylvania, Ohio, and Illinois, many Taft men high in the hierarchy of Republicanism felt that the president could not be elected; some of them wished that a way could be found to nominate Charles Evans Hughes.[40] Even after the convention had convened this hope was not altogether abandoned. Three times William Barnes, the Republican boss of New York, approached Senator Borah with the suggestion that he take second place to Hughes on a compromise ticket.[41] The question whether it would not be advisable to nominate a third candidate was even seriously discussed among the little group of men who were steering the convention for Taft.[42]

Over in the Roosevelt camp almost as much thought was directed to compromise. The names of Cummins and Borah were constantly being suggested. But the most consideration was given to Governor Hadley of Missouri, the man James E. Watson had named to the Taft supporters. Hadley, although a reform governor, had never been tarred with the same ultra-progressive brush as had La Follette, Cummins, and Borah. Hence his candidacy would not have been altogether displeasing to the conservatives. He had become exceedingly popular with the convention. Tall, handsome, mellow-voiced, and impartial in manner, he was the one Roosevelt leader to whom the body of delegates would listen without interruption. In fact, on the second day of the convention both the Roosevelt and the Taft delegates joined together for once during that hectic and bitter week to give him a twenty-minute demonstration of approval.[43]

There is no doubt that Hadley was approached by various

---

[40] Frank Trumbull to Grenville M. Dodge, April 28, 1912, Dodge MSS.; *New York Times*, April 11, May 23, 1912; *New York Sun*, June 21, 1912.

[41] Claudius O. Johnson, *Borah of Idaho* (New York, 1936), 139.

[42] Watson, *As I Knew Them*, 180–181.

[43] *Kansas City Star*, June 19, 1912.

Taft leaders with the suggestion that he might be nominated
if Roosevelt would agree. After the convention Hadley himself said that the Taft men had promised to seat the Roosevelt
delegates from Washington and Texas if Roosevelt would
concur in the nomination of someone other than himself.[44]
What authority the Taft men had to make the offer is uncertain, as was their ability to carry it through. At any rate, the
whole plan was nullified by Roosevelt's attitude. For when
Hadley went to see him about the proposal, the Colonel made
it clear that he would consider no compromise until the
seventy-two contesting Roosevelt delegates were placed on
the convention roll. If the delegates were seated he promised
to stay in the convention and abide by its choice: "I stated
. . . if that were done I would gladly work and support the
man whom the convention chose to nominate, and if he were
not Mr. Taft that I would gladly support his nomination."
This of course applied to Governor Hadley and Senator
Cummins.[45]

The Taft men, naturally, refused the offer. There was little
question who would be nominated once the seventy-two
Roosevelt delegates were seated. Hadley, feeling that Roosevelt was opposed to any choice other than himself, likewise
refused to carry on the negotiations. Roosevelt later claimed
that by this time he was not interested in nominating himself
or any particular man. He was simply interested in a thorough "purging" of the dishonest roll.[46] Perhaps Roosevelt,
one of his most ardent admirers states, was a "visionary" in
1912, more interested in the honesty of the convention roll
than in the choice of the body, and could have had the nomination had he remained and sanctioned what he thought to be
dishonesty.[47] But the facts clearly indicate that the Colonel

[44] *Ibid.*, June 27, 1912; Rosewater, *Backstage*, 180 *passim;* Frederick S.
Wood, *Roosevelt As We Knew Him* (Chicago, 1927), 266–269; Davis,
Released for Publication, 302–305.

[45] Roosevelt to Paul A. Ewart, July 5, 1912, Roosevelt MSS.; Rosewater,
Backstage, 179.

[46] Roosevelt to James M. Pierce, July 9, 1912, and to Paul A. Ewart,
July 5, 1912, Roosevelt MSS.

[47] William Allen White, *Masks in a Pageant* (New York, 1928), 341.

would have tolerated no nomination but his own.[48] Certainly his public statements before the convention met, to the effect that no one should dare mention a compromise candidate, the plans to bolt which he had made before the convention convened, and his position when a compromise was suggested all point to that conclusion. At least it agrees with a statement made by Roosevelt's secretary before the convention. Roosevelt, he wrote, had asked him to state that he would "never under any circumstances compromise or agree to any compromise candidate."[49]

Roosevelt's uncompromising spirit gladdened the hearts of at least some Republicans. For not a few stout conservatives strongly felt that the Roosevelt split was a godsend. As W. P. Hepburn pointed out, it would do away with "the guerillas and insurgents" within the ranks and once again restore the party to the old conservative basis.[50] It lifted the dreadful fear that the party machinery might one day fall entirely into the hands of the radical faction. Hepburn was quite right. For with the Roosevelt secession radicalism as a potent force within the Republican party was dead for at least thirty years. And in turn it lay with Roosevelt either to nourish or to destroy the ex-Republican progressivism which had in the previous decade flourished like a green bay tree.

Meanwhile the National Republican Convention had wound up its business. On Saturday morning, with a bit of old-fashioned oratory, a small-town Ohio newspaper editor, Warren Gamaliel Harding, presented the name of William Howard Taft. After the subsequent nomination of La Follette and a dreary round of monotonous seconding speeches, the first and only nominating ballot was taken. Amid jeers and catcalls from every part of the hall it was announced that Taft, by virtue of the 561 votes cast for him as against

[48] Pringle, *Roosevelt*, 564.
[49] Frank Harper to John C. Greenway, May 10, 1912, Roosevelt MSS.
[50] W. T. Hepburn to Hepburn Chamberlain, June 25, 1912, in Briggs, *Hepburn*, 338; Leo Rothschild to Beveridge, July 3, 1912, in Bowers, *Beveridge*, 422; *New York Sun*, June 21, 1912; Charles J. Bonaparte to E. C. Carrington, June 12, 1912, Bonaparte MSS.

107 for Roosevelt and 41 for La Follette, had been renominated as the party's choice.[51] The announcement also indicated that 344 of the delegates had refused to vote. Thus three-fourths of the Roosevelt delegates signified by their silence that they had ceased to be Republicans.

The renomination of Taft accomplished, there remained only the tasks of selecting a vice-presidential candidate and adopting a platform. Both were routine matters. "Sunny Jim" Sherman, a typical Republican vice-president, was renominated, and a typical Republican platform was adopted. Conservative throughout, it carried the usual platitudinous wishes for the betterment of farmer and laborer, ignored the Payne-Aldrich tariff except to mention that some duties were too high, neatly dodged the Aldrich central bank plan, and contained a militant paragraph against all proposals to lessen the power of the courts. Scarcely one of its clauses betrayed any impact of progressivism upon traditional Republican doctrines.

Its work done, the convention adjourned and most of the delegates prepared to go home. The closing minutes were marked by none of the noisy, hilarious jubilance of a united and confident party. Instead all was confusion, bitterness, and gloom.[52] Almost to a man the delegates knew that without Roosevelt's active support Taft's candidacy was hopeless. The future must have appeared even more lugubrious to the homeward bound when they reflected that even then Roosevelt was at work perfecting an organization whose main object was to defeat and smash the old Republican party.

On Saturday afternoon it was announced from the Roosevelt headquarters that a new party would be formed that night at Orchestra Hall. As the time for the meeting approached, the crowd around the building grew larger with the minutes. The California delegation headed by Governor Johnson and the representatives from Pennsylvania, Illinois, Ohio, Nebraska, Minnesota, Kansas, and New Jersey, states

[51] Cummins received 17 and Hughes 2.
[52] *Kansas City Star*, June 22, 1912.

that had formed the bedrock basis of the old Republicanism, seemed to have come almost to a man. Governor Johnson opened the meeting with a fighting speech to an already half-hysterical throng. And then after a series of jeremiads against the convention at the Coliseum, Theodore Roosevelt himself was escorted into the hall. Restlessly shifting from one leg to the other on the platform, Roosevelt renounced his Republicanism. With narrowed eyes and snapping jaws, he proclaimed that he would accept the nomination of a new progressive party if it were made by a convention regularly called and regularly elected. From the answering roar which fairly shook the building there could be little doubt that a new party would be organized.[53]

It has been much debated why Roosevelt undertook the fight when it was fairly obvious that it would prove to be a losing one. He himself conceded that.[54] Many have pointed out that if Roosevelt had accepted the convention results, Taft would certainly have been defeated in the election. Four years later, in 1916, Roosevelt as the leader of the party's progressive faction could have had the nomination without opposition. And surely Roosevelt himself thought of that possibility in 1912. What then explains his actions in bolting the party? Perhaps, as has been suggested, he acted rashly in the heat of his anger and later regretted that he had done so. Borah felt that had the matter rested for a day or two longer the Progressive party would never have been born.[55] But there was something in Roosevelt's character that probably dictated that he continue the battle with Taft to the finish. Beyond question Roosevelt thought of himself as robbed and publicly humiliated by Taft. To have quit then after the first skirmish would have been, in his own words, an "avowal of weakness." "I wish to Heaven I was not in this fight," he wrote to Ambassador Jusserand, "and I am in it

[53] *New York Times, New York Sun,* and *New York World,* June 22, 23, 1912.
[54] Roosevelt to William D. Foulke, July 1, 1912, and to Paul A. Ewart, July 5, 1912, Roosevelt MSS.
[55] Johnson, *Borah,* 140.

only on the principle, in the long run a sound one, that I would rather take a thrashing than be quiet under such a kicking."[56]

Beyond this personal consideration, Roosevelt in June of 1912 may have held secret hope of victory. He had been told by some of his leaders that the masses of the Republican party would stand by him even if he were to bolt.[57] Moreover, the Democratic convention had yet to meet, and no one knew what William Jennings Bryan and his thousands of followers would do if the Democrats chose a conservative. Bryan had already suggested that Roosevelt would win if the Baltimore convention chose a man opposed to progressive principles. Roosevelt and Bryan badges made their appearance in Chicago, and one of the Roosevelt leaders later wrote that Bryan had confessed that he would support the Progressive ticket if the liberals were ignored at Baltimore.[58] If Woodrow Wilson had not been nominated at Baltimore, perhaps the final result would have been different.

Roosevelt in 1912, at least in his own idiom, was sincerely interested in advancing and implementing a progressive program. If that were not true, a man of Roosevelt's political genius would hardly have included the proposals for court reform in his unfortunate Columbus speech. And though one may question whether he really believed that the alternative to a progressive program was "a general smash up of our civilization," there can be no doubt that he was terribly in earnest in advocating his "New Nationalism."[59] At any rate, with his speech before the assembled crowd at Orchestra Hall, Roosevelt had advanced to a point from which there was no turning back. He had promised to run as an independent. And, knowing Roosevelt, the country looked forward to a hard-fisted campaign with no holds barred.

[56] Roosevelt to Chase S. Osborn, June 28, 1912, to Jusserand, July 3, 1912, to Brooks Adams, June 27, 1912, and to W. F. Cochran, July 16, 1912, Roosevelt MSS.
[57] Letters to Roosevelt from Frank A. Munsey, April 12, 1912, Arthur D. Hill, May 29, 1912, and J. A. Arthur, June 8, 1912, Roosevelt MSS.
[58] *New York World*, June 22, 1912; *New York Times*, June 26, 1912; Davis, *Released for Publication*, 316.
[59] Roosevelt to Rider Haggard, June 28, 1912, Roosevelt MSS.

CHAPTER TEN

Floodtide

AFTER THE Republican convention Roosevelt and his lieutenants kept an anxious eye on Baltimore. There the Democrats, jubilant over the breach in the opposition, were meeting to select their own candidate. And when after a long struggle Woodrow Wilson, a recent convert to progressivism, emerged victorious, the chances for a Roosevelt victory diminished perceptibly. Both Roosevelt and his chief supporters admitted that. After Baltimore, Roosevelt wrote a friend that had Wilson been nominated before the Chicago convention, he would not have remained in the fight.[1] In other letters Roosevelt, surprisingly open-minded about an opponent, described Wilson as an able man who would make an "excellent" president albeit he was no "Nationalist."[2] The Baltimore platform, however, was a different matter. Perhaps Roosevelt was not entirely wrong when he said it was not progressive at all but rather an expression of "rural toryism."[3]

In announcing the formation of a new Progressive party at Chicago Roosevelt had undoubtedly counted upon the continued support of most of the progressive Republicans who had worked for his nomination. The following weeks, however, revealed that assumption to have been a grave miscalculation. After his return home Governor Hadley wrote Roosevelt that he could not join the new movement. Progressive control of Missouri was only possible, he said, by his

[1] Roosevelt to Alford W. Cooley, July 10, 1912, to Arthur Lee, August 14, 1912, and to John F. Bass, July 2, 1912, Roosevelt MSS.
[2] Roosevelt to Chase S. Osborn, July 5, 1912, and to Horace Plunkett, August 3, 1912, Roosevelt MSS.
[3] Roosevelt to Plunkett, August 3, 1912, Roosevelt MSS.

remaining in the Republican party. Within two weeks Roosevelt heard substantially the same bad news from six of the seven governors who had signed the round-robin letter back in February. Of the original seven only Hiram Johnson of California stood by.[4]

To many progressive Republicans apparently a family quarrel was one thing, a divorce quite another. Of the progressive Republican senators, La Follette, Works of California, Gronna of North Dakota, Brown of Nebraska, and Nelson of Minnesota declared themselves against Roosevelt; and Borah of Idaho, Bourne of Oregon, Crawford of South Dakota, and Cummins and Kenyon of Iowa announced that although they were for him as against Taft, they were not for the third party. Thus of all the men who had formed the progressive Republican nucleus in the Senate only Poindexter, Beveridge, Dixon, Bristow, and Clapp lent their names to the new progressivism.[5] And of these Beveridge, Bristow, and Clapp deliberated at length before announcing their new allegiance. To make matters worse, three progressive Republican senators, La Follette, Gronna, and Works, were supporting Wilson.[6]

"What a miserable showing some of the so-called Progressive leaders have made," Roosevelt complained. "They represent nothing but mere sound and fury. A year or two ago, when it was merely a question of loud words, they were claiming to be much further advanced than I was, but they have not the heart for a fight, and the minute they were up against deeds instead of words, they quit forthwith."[7]

Perhaps by the first week in July Roosevelt was already

[4] Herbert S. Hadley to Roosevelt, June 25, July 5, 1912, Roosevelt MSS.; *New York Times,* July 22, 27, 1912. With few exceptions most of the "practical politicians" supporting Roosevelt's nomination also decided to stay with the Republican party. William L. Ward and Ormsby McHarg deserted Roosevelt within a few days after the Republican convention. William L. Ward to Roosevelt, June 25, 1912, Roosevelt MSS.

[5] *New York Sun,* July 31, 1912.

[6] *New York Times,* July 8, October 14, 1912; *New York Sun,* July 14, 1912; *La Follette's Weekly,* November 2, 1912.

[7] Roosevelt to J. C. O'Laughlin, July 9, 1912, Roosevelt MSS.

regretting his rash actions of June. But there was little to do now but go on. Accordingly a committee was set up to organize the new party. Two weeks later Senator Dixon issued a call to the people at large to meet in convention at Chicago on August 5 to organize a new progressive party erected on non-sectional lines "so that the people may be served in sincerity and truth by an organization unfettered by obligations to conflicting interests."[8] Among the more prominent names attached to the document were those of Hiram Johnson, Ben B. Lindsey, Julian Harris, Medill McCormick, Charles J. Bonaparte, William R. Nelson, Joseph M. Dixon, George L. Record, James R. Garfield, and Miles Poindexter.

Before the convention met the Roosevelt general staff had to decide some very perplexing and important questions. The first of these concerned presidential electors. Many of the states had chosen their electors by direct primaries before the Republican convention met. The result was that many men designated as Republican electors were actually Roosevelt supporters. About one hundred of them announced in July that they would cast their vote for Roosevelt even if the Taft ticket won in their states.[9] To add to the problem a definite movement to compromise on the electoral tickets was being led by Governor Hadley and William Flinn. Hadley proposed to place the same electors under both Taft's and Roosevelt's names with the understanding that in each state they would vote for the man having the highest total of votes.[10]

At first Roosevelt declared that he would accept the votes of any Republican electors selected by state primaries even though their states went to Taft in November. Accordingly he urged them all to resist the pressure on them to resign. "I hold that I am in honor and honesty entitled to the vote of every elector nominated by the people through their pri-

[8] *New York Times*, July 8, 1912.
[9] *New York Sun*, July 11, 1912.
[10] Letters to Roosevelt from William Flinn, July 17, 1912, and Herbert S. Hadley, July 18, 1912, Roosevelt MSS.; *New York Times*, July 16, 1912.

maries," he wrote to one such elector, "and that Mr. Taft is entitled to the votes of those electors nominated by Barnes, Penrose, Guggenheim, and Company."[11] But here Roosevelt was obviously inconsistent. He had left the Republican party. And he very shortly learned that as the country's most outspoken champion of the eighth commandment he was particularly vulnerable in claiming things not his own. Short and to the point was a current *New York Times* rhyme:

> What matter if I lose a state
> Provided I can confiscate
> My adversary's delegate?
> Thou Shalt Not Steal!
>
> That's very true, but then you see,
> The text does not apply to me;
> It's written most explicitly
> *Thou* Shalt Not Steal.[12]

Roosevelt very soon changed his mind about the whole subject.

Both Taft and Roosevelt refused to have anything to do with the proposal for identical electors. Declaring that he would rather see the Democrats than Flinn in control of Pennsylvania, Penrose started suit to oust the Roosevelt Republican electors in Pennsylvania. His lead was soon followed in all parts of the country. Aware that under such an arrangement he could expect no Democratic votes, Roosevelt was equally against it. He regarded Taft as a recipient of a swindled nomination. He would not consent to do anything that would appear as though he were joining with the president. "I won't go into a friendly contest with a pickpocket as to which of us shall keep *my* watch which *he* stole," he wrote.[13] And that was that.

A far more serious problem threatened stillbirth to the Progressive party. That was the moot question whether an entire ticket should be run in every state. The question was

[11] Roosevelt to Joseph R. Baldwin, July 12, 1912, Roosevelt MSS.
[12] George B. Morewood in the *New York Times*, July 17, 1912.
[13] Roosevelt to E. A. Van Valkenburg, July 16, 1912, Roosevelt MSS.

fundamental to the whole future of the party. Not to campaign for Progressive senators, representatives, governors, and other local offices would be tantamount to admitting that the aim of the party was to elect Roosevelt and nothing more. No national political party can endure unless it is supported by local offices. William Flinn frankly admitted that he had little faith in the permanent existence of the Progressive party when he advanced a plan to support Roosevelt nationally and the Republican ticket locally.[14]

Flinn's proposal was to place the names of all Republican candidates on both the Taft and Roosevelt electoral tickets, provided such candidates accepted three propositions. First, they would not oppose Roosevelt in the presidential campaign. Second, they would agree to vote for Roosevelt for president if the election was thrown into the House of Representatives and the Roosevelt vote in their respective districts or states was larger than that for Taft. Third, if Roosevelt polled more votes in their districts or states than Taft they would subsequently be known as Progressive Republican members of Congress.[15] Flinn pointed out, as did others, that the plan would insure Republican control of Pennsylvania, Ohio, and Illinois, where a split in Republican ranks would almost inevitably result in defeat. The plan would also, it was argued, remove the danger of defeat for progressive Republicans who in Iowa, Kansas, and Nebraska had captured the state Republican machinery.

The proposal was applauded by those who were more interested in the holding of offices, or in Republicanism, or in the personal fortunes of Theodore Roosevelt than they were in progressivism. William Flinn, Frank Knox, Medill McCormick, and Governor Stubbs backed the move.[16] In addition, progressive Republicans who had not joined the third-party movement, including Governor Hadley and Senators Borah

[14] William Flinn to Roosevelt, July 17, 1912, Roosevelt MSS.
[15] William Flinn to Frank Garrecht, August 10, 1912 (copy), Roosevelt MSS.
[16] Medill McCormick to Roosevelt, July 25, 1912, Roosevelt MSS.; Beasley, *Knox*, 83–85.

and Cummins, heartily supported it. They wrote to Roosevelt that a third party in their state would mean their defeat and thus a progressive defeat.[17]

On the other hand, the radical wing of the Progressive party almost to a man opposed the coalition scheme. They argued that in Pennsylvania Roosevelt would be, at least in the public mind, openly bargaining with Penrose and his gang of reactionaries. Moreover, such a move would make their organization look like a mere schismatic fragment of the old Republican party having no goal other than victory. Such a position, they pointed out, would alienate any Democratic support and thus make a bipartisan progressive movement impossible.

In this struggle between the conservative politicians and the radicals in his organization, Roosevelt was for once disposed to align himself with the radicals. For one reason or another he preferred to see a complete state and national ticket put into the fight wherever that was possible.[18] But throughout July he was at his wit's end to know what to do in Iowa and Kansas. There progressive Republicans, who were in complete control of the state Republican machinery, were ready to support his candidacy but not at the price of leaving the Republican party. In the end he decided on only one hard and fast principle. He would insist upon a third party ticket in every state where the Republican nominees were not prepared individually and collectively to support his candidacy and oppose Taft's.[19] Thus in Pennsylvania, Michigan, Missouri, and Illinois a third state ticket was prepared against the objections of Flinn, Knox, Hadley, and McCormick. Later, however, he accepted the proposal of Governor Stubbs in Kansas to support the Roosevelt ticket nationally without leaving the Republican party.[20]

[17] Herbert S. Hadley to Roosevelt, July 29, 1912, Roosevelt to Nicholas Longworth, August 3, 1912, Roosevelt MSS.

[18] Roosevelt to William H. Prendergast, June 25, 1912, and to Hadley, July 23, 1912, Roosevelt MSS.

[19] Roosevelt to Hadley, July 15, 1912, and to Robert Bass, July 17, 1912, Roosevelt MSS.

[20] *New York Sun*, July 9, 1912.

But even this connection with the old Republican party hurt Roosevelt's chances in the election. As some of his supporters observed, their organization was "too highly colored with former Republicans" to attract any great measure of Democratic support.[21] Caught between the two sharp horns of a dilemma, the only suggestion Roosevelt had to offer was that in as many states as possible a Democrat or two be nominated for important offices.[22] However, the nomination of a Democrat for a principal office was a rare occurrence, and this undoubtedly predisposed progressive Democrats to shy away from the Progressive party in November.

Whatever the sentiments of the Democrats, there was no doubt of the attitude of the thousand and some gathered in Chicago on August 5, 1912, to attend the first national Progressive convention. Stamped on their faces was an earnestness that often suggested fanaticism. From every part of America they came, with the reverential air of the consecrated. Strikingly absent were the crowds of "plug-uglies," ward bosses, and other avaricious specimens of the lower depths of politics which customarily swarm around a national convention. In their place was a group of well-dressed, serious citizens with the respectability of Sunday school superintendents. In fact, this was less a political convention than an assemblage of crusaders. To such a group had Peter the Hermit preached, and to such an audience had Garrison's *Liberator* thundered some seventy years before.

The tone of the body was in keeping with the character of its membership. There was little of the blaring brass bands or the noisy claques that punctuate the usual convention. The solemn gravity "was striking and impressive." All through the convention the delegates listened to the speakers with rapt faces. With each emotion-laden hour dedicated to social justice the delegates became more intense. Here and there both men and women were seen wiping tears from their

[21] R. W. Childs to Roosevelt, August 15, 1912, Roosevelt MSS.

[22] Roosevelt to Arthur D. Hill, July 18, 1912, and to James P. Magenes, July 18, 1912, Roosevelt MSS.

eyes. And as the body reached the peaks of emotionalism it broke forth in the swelling strains of a hymn.

The moose has left the wooded hill; his call rings through the land.
It's a summons to the young and strong to join with willing hand:
To fight for right and country; to strike down a robber band,
And we'll go marching on.[23]

This was, indeed, progressivism militant. But when the convention roll was called some significant absences were noted. Missing were the dead Dolliver and Senator Cummins, who had made the creed of progressivism dominant in Iowa. Absent too were William E. Borah and George Norris, who had led the progressive fight in Congress for years. But most conspicuous was the absence in this gathering of the liberal clans of Robert Marion La Follette, one of the very fathers of progressivism.

As if to balance these missing faces there were new leaders at Chicago—new and also strange leaders, at least for a reform gathering. Standing out among the other delegates were the two, George W. Perkins and Frank Munsey, whose money and support had made the Progressive party possible. Certainly their progressivism was at best of questionable character, and if there is any truth to the old saw that he who feeds a political party directs its policies, then the Progressive party faced an inevitable internal conflict. Side by side with the ardent devotees of reform at Chicago stood also the old-line bosses Flinn, Walter Brown, and Dan Hanna, who had already given evidence of their disbelief in the permanence of a reforming party. So little faith did Charles J. Bonaparte have in Flinn's political integrity that he had advised against making him a member of the National Municipal League.[24] But even with such incongruities, the great gathering at Chicago was a monumental tribute to the spirit

[23] *Chicago Tribune, New York Times,* and *New York World,* August 5, 6, 1912; *New York Sun, Philadelphia North American,* and *Kansas City Star,* August 6, 1912.
[24] Bonaparte to Clinton R. Woodruff, November 22, 1912, Bonaparte MSS.

of reform and social consciousness that had been sweeping the country for a decade. It was also a testament of the faith of millions in the leadership of Theodore Roosevelt.

The convention opened with the keynote address of ex-Senator Beveridge of Indiana. Never did Beveridge arouse more enthusiasm. With phrases reminiscent of Robert Ingersoll the one-time boy orator from Indiana fired the vast crowd with a religious passion. Running the gamut of social causes, he called for a national policy of "social brotherhood as against savage individualism." Beveridge inveighed against the "invisible government," economic in character, which he maintained permeated every fiber and dictated every policy of the two old major parties. Such invisible government must be destroyed before true reform could be accomplished. As he spoke his closing words, "Mine eyes have seen the glory of the coming of the Lord," the delegates again burst out with the stirring cadences of the "Battle Hymn of the Republic."[25]

Not until the next day, however, did the convention reach its most feverish peak. It was then that Theodore Roosevelt first walked into the hall to give what he termed his "Confession of Faith." As he stood on the platform in the old familiar attitude, his body swaying with delight, his left hand in his pocket and his right vigorously waving a reply, fifteen thousand people roared their welcome. For fifty-two minutes, wildly waving red bandanas, they cheered him as they had never cheered anyone else. Here were no claques, no artificial demonstration sustained by artificial devices. None were needed. Men and women simply stood on their feet for an hour to welcome a man because they liked him and believed in him. When Roosevelt himself finally sought to stop the demonstration, the crowd once more broke into song:

> *Thou wilt not cower in the dust,*
> *Roosevelt, O Roosevelt!*
> *Thy gleaming sword shall never rust,*
> *Roosevelt, O Roosevelt!*[26]

[25] *New York Times*, August 6, 1912.
[26] *Chicago Tribune, New York Sun*, and *New York Times*, August 7, 1912.

Just what went on behind the Colonel's snapping eyes during that uproarious welcome only he knew. But a press correspondent noted that as the vast crowd again and again broke into a fervent hymn, his face took on a look of bewilderment. That look, the newspaperman later wrote, was a token of Roosevelt's inability to understand the temper of his audience. "They were crusaders; he was not."[27] But if Roosevelt was unable to identify himself spiritually with the crowd before him, he at least fulfilled most of their expectations as a leader. Realizing that he could expect no support from conservatives, Roosevelt made a direct bid in his Confession of Faith for almost every radical and reform group in the nation. "If your friend does not think my speech . . . radical enough, then I do not know what radicalism is," he wrote.[28] And in truth, perhaps, never before in the history of the country had a major candidate for president given a speech demanding such sweeping changes.

Roosevelt began, as could be expected, with a blast at the two old parties, which were nothing more than "husks" with no "real souls within" but "divided on artificial lines, boss ridden, and privilege controlled." "Democrats and Republicans alike," he continued, "represent government of the needy many by professional politicians in the interests of the rich few." With that opening he turned his attention to his old enemy, the courts. "The American people, and not the courts are to determine their own fundamental policies," he fairly hissed as the crowd roared its approval. "The people themselves must be the ultimate makers of their own Constitution, and where their agents differ in their interpretations of the Constitution, the people themselves should be given the chance . . . to settle what interpretation it is that their representatives shall thereafter adopt as binding."

The second half of the speech was given over to the advocacy of a long list of specific reforms. In turn Roosevelt endorsed the direct election of United States senators, preferential primaries in presidential years, an efficient corrupt

27 *New York Times*, August 7, 1912.
28 Roosevelt to Gilson Gardner, August 3, 1912, Roosevelt MSS.

practices act, the short ballot, the initiative, referendum, and recall, the publication of primary and election expenditures, woman suffrage, the recall of state judicial decisions, and the simplification of the process of amending the Constitution. To control rapacious industry Roosevelt advocated a national industrial commission to regulate all interstate industry, a Federal Securities Commission to supervise the issuance of all securities, a land monopoly tax, a permanent tariff commission, an immediate revision of the tariff schedules in favor of the employee and the consumer, and government ownership of Alaskan railroads. Nor were the underprivileged forgotten. A more stringent pure food law, a minimum wage and maximum hour provision, unemployment insurance and old age pensions, abolition of child labor and laws for the protection of women engaged in industry were all demanded in this sweeping charter of reform.[29]

As Roosevelt closed his speech with an invitation to all men of good will to join his ranks in battling for the Lord, a great roar of approval swept over the auditorium. Most of the delegates had come to Chicago expecting just such a speech and would have been disappointed with any less progressive utterance. Later Roosevelt wrote to a friend that for once he had said the things that were "deepest" in his heart and that he had believed he would never get a chance to say.[30] Surprisingly enough, both Perkins and Munsey approved of the speech. From London Munsey wrote that the Confession of Faith was an exceedingly progressive document. "In this respect it goes far, but in no sense reaches a disturbing point. And while splendidly progressive it is, at the same time, amply conservative and sound."[31]

But if Roosevelt's speech evoked unanimous approval, other proceedings of the convention were less conducive to harmony. In the following days at least two major conflicts broke out into the open, threatening the success of the party

[29] *Chicago Tribune*, August 7, 1912.

[30] Roosevelt to Charles D. Willard, August 15, 1912, Roosevelt MSS.

[31] Roosevelt to Frank A. Munsey, August 2, 1912, Munsey to Roosevelt, August 16, 1912, Roosevelt MSS.

in November. The first was over the question of Progressive policy toward the Negro in the South. The advancing industrialization of the South had alienated a good many men of property from the Democratic party. They liked neither its low tariff doctrines nor the control of William Jennings Bryan over the party machinery. But they had never completely broken from the party because the only alternative had been "black Republicanism"; on election day their racial prejudices had usually won out over their changing economic doctrines. With the birth of a new party devoted to protection and untainted by any odor of carpet-baggers, scalawags, and Negro legislatures, a change of political affiliation became easier. Hopefully the Roosevelt organization started to organize a lily-white party in the South to destroy the Democratic monopoly.[32]

Within the ranks of the Progressive party, however, there were strong objections to the plan. In the first place, the reform wing of the party had a definite strain of the old Garrisonianism of Lincoln's day which sincerely wished to see the Southern Negro emancipated politically. In that vein F. L. Luther, president of Trinity College, protested violently against the scheme.[33] More practical Northern Progressives asked how the policy would affect Negro votes in their own states. For despite the Brownsville episode many Northern Negroes, attracted by the Progressives' championship of the underprivileged, were supporting the new party. In fact, Roosevelt's victory over Taft in the Maryland primaries was largely attributable to the support of the Negroes. Would they continue their support if the political rights of their Southern brothers were overlooked? That was a vexing question.[34]

[32] Letters to Roosevelt from J. C. Pritchard, December 7, 1911, and George L. Wise, June 29, 1912, A. M. Beatty to George W. Perkins, April 27, 1912, Roosevelt MSS. Cf. George E. Mowry, "The South and the Progressive Lily White Party of 1912," *Journal of Southern History*, 6: 237–247 (May, 1940).

[33] F. L. Luther to Roosevelt, August 8, 1912, Roosevelt MSS.

[34] Bonaparte to Isaiah Mitchell, March 23, 1912, and to C. G. Kidder, October 30, 1912, Bonaparte MSS.

The question had to be answered once and for all late in July. At that time three Progressive state conventions in the South split over the question of the color line and elected contesting delegations. In all three cases there was no doubt that the Negroes had been deprived of their rights in the traditional fashion. The Florida white delegates candidly admitted that they had prevented regularly elected Negro delegates from taking their seats.[35] When both sides besought Roosevelt to support their respective contestants, he dictated the policy of his party in a long public letter to Julian Harris.

Hoping to retain the support of the colored voters of the North, Roosevelt argued that North and South had quite different race problems. In the North many Negroes were educated and deserving men. They had, he said, a long history of political action singularly free from corruption and venality. Therefore he had encouraged his party leaders north of the Ohio River to take the Negro in on the same terms with the white man. In the South, however, despite forty-five years of experimentation with racial equality within the party structure, Republicans had succeeded only in making themselves a minority party, in forcing every white man of character into the Democratic party, and in corrupting instead of helping the Negro. There was only one thing to do. "I earnestly believe," Roosevelt said, "that by appealing to the best white men of the South . . . and by frankly putting the movement into their hands from the outset we shall create a situation by which the colored man of the South will ultimately get justice as it is not possible for them to get justice if we are to continue and perpetuate the present conditions."[36]

When the provisional Progressive National Committee met just before the opening of the convention, it clearly had

[35] *Official Minutes of the (Provisional) Progressive National Committee*, 95, 101, 212–213, Roosevelt MSS.; *New York Times*, July 25, 26, 1912; *New York Sun*, July 25, 26, 1912.

[36] Roosevelt to Julian Harris, August 1, 1912, and to Bradley Gilman, July 24, 1912, Roosevelt MSS.

no choice but to follow Roosevelt's lead. After some spirited debates the committee passed the Heney motion permitting each state organization to determine the legality of its own contests. A motion signifying the committee's concurrence with Roosevelt's letter to Julian Harris was also carried.[37] But of course the matter did not stop there. Protestations against the letter from disappointed Negro supporters were plentiful. Although Roosevelt worked hard and long, he failed to disabuse both the Northern and the Southern Negro of the idea that social justice, even in the Progressive party, stopped short at the color line.[38]

A far more serious quarrel, which eventually drew in most of the leaders of the party, was one over the platform; in the end it went far to encompass the destruction of the organization. The dispute originated in part over the notorious disappearance of the anti-trust plank from the platform during the course of the convention. But the quarrel had a far more fundamental basis. Essentially it was a struggle for control between two groups in the party with conflicting ideologies. In another sense it was a struggle between nineteenth- and twentieth-century liberalism.

At one pole in this battle for factional supremacy stood George W. Perkins, financier of the party, a man whose expressed economic and social views coincided very closely with those of Roosevelt. For years prior to 1912 Perkins had attacked the theory behind anti-trust legislation. Intimately connected with the House of Morgan, Perkins advocated government regulation instead of government destruction. By 1912 he was advocating a federal regulatory body, similar in scope to the Interstate Commerce Commission, with the power to set prices on industrial goods. He closely concurred —vocally at least—in Roosevelt's desire to extend the regulative power of the federal government to protect the more

[37] *Official Minutes of the (Provisional) Progressive National Committee*, 12–50, 51–55, 214, 265, Roosevelt MSS.
[38] Louis Edelman to Roosevelt, August 6, 1912, Roosevelt to Floyd DuBois, August 26, 1912, Roosevelt MSS.; *New York Times*, August 6, 25, 1912.

submerged portions of the country's population from the ravages of industrial capitalism. Thus Perkins and Roosevelt stood together as exponents of a new paternalism which took sharp issue with historic individualism.

Many Progressives, however, still believed that a restoration of competition was possible and desirable. Most of these men came from west of the Appalachians. When they learned before the convention that Roosevelt opposed the inclusion of an anti-trust plank in the platform, they sent hot letters of protest to Oyster Bay. "Many Progressives contend for a restoration of competition, believing that it would be better for the country and more conducive to industrial progress," argued Senator Bristow.[39] Cummins, Clapp, Borah, and many others agreed with him. Not a few important leaders of the party doubly distrusted the scheme for the regulation of business, especially when it came from the lips of Perkins. They doubted Perkins' progressivism and his fair intent. They disliked his power in the party. They feared that his gospel of regulation was the scheme of financial titans to get a strangle hold on the government. Voicing these apprehensions, Bristow asked Roosevelt, "In this scheme of regulation is there not a grave danger that 'big business' will more likely control the government than the government controlling big business?"[40]

This questioning of Perkins' regulatory doctrines and of their ultimate purpose crystallized into frank suspicion during the convention. Before the convention met Roosevelt had stated that he would continue to oppose the anti-trust proposal. In the Committee on Resolutions, however, a plank endorsing and strengthening the Sherman Law was passed after a sharp struggle. In part the statement read: "We favor strengthening the Sherman law by prohibiting agreements to divide territory or limit output; refusing to sell to customers who buy from business rivals; to sell below cost in certain areas while maintaining high prices in other places; using the

[39] Joseph L. Bristow to Roosevelt, July 15, 1912, Roosevelt MSS.
[40] Bristow to Roosevelt, July 15, 1912, Roosevelt MSS.

power of transportation to aid or injure special business concerns; and other unfair trade practices."[41]

After the resolution had been adopted it was carried upstairs, where Roosevelt, Perkins, and Beveridge were engaged in supervising the work of the committee below. At once a debate started over Perkins' objections to the anti-trust section. Roosevelt later wrote that he had concurred with Perkins, but that they had both objected not to the endorsement of the anti-trust law but rather to the listing of prohibited practices on the ground that they would weaken the law. This defensive statement, however, did not coincide with either Roosevelt's previous or his subsequent statements on the Sherman Act. At any rate, the whole plank endorsing the act and not merely the enumeration of the specific practices was stricken out and sent back to the committee below. Just what happened in the lower room when the committee considered the revision is uncertain. Most of those present later remembered that the committee disapproved of striking out the clause and re-adopted it as it had been written originally. Roosevelt himself admitted later that such action had probably been taken inadvertently, although at the time he was told by Senator Dixon that the committee had approved the revised platform.[42]

The next day William Draper Lewis, in presenting the platform to the convention, included both the endorsement of the Sherman Law and the list of undesirable practices. As he did so, Perkins excitedly got to his feet. "That does not belong in the platform. We cut it out last night," he shouted to Amos Pinchot as he hurriedly left the hall. A conference of the party leaders was called at once. Roosevelt instructed O. K. Davis, secretary of the party, to delete the paragraph dealing with the Sherman Law. According, the platform was printed by the newspapers and later for campaign distribu-

[41] Bowers, *Beveridge*, 431–432.
[42] Roosevelt to Amos Pinchot, December 5, 1912, and to George L. Record, December 13, 1912, Henry F. Cochems to Roosevelt, November 16, 1912, Roosevelt MSS.

tion without mentioning the Sherman Anti-Trust Law.[43] And thus the Progressive party opened itself to the campaign charge of attempting to legalize monopoly.

The omission of the Sherman plank was immediately denounced by many members of the party. Irately they charged that Perkins was responsible for the surreptitious guillotining. They had strongly protested against Perkins' connection with the party from the very beginning, and now their objections crystallized into rebellion. When the Progressive National Committee met, these men, led by William Allen White, the two Pinchots, and Meyer Lissner, tried to prevent the selection of Perkins as its chairman. But the financial godfather of the party, supported by Roosevelt, was too strong for them: after hours of debate he was duly elected. Later the committee even increased his power by authorizing Roosevelt and him to select the rest of the National Executive Committee. Momentarily after this setback the opposition to Perkins waned. But when the story of the anti-trust episode was noised around, all the misgivings returned. For the sake of unity during the campaign the opposition to Perkins remained silent. But silence emphatically did not give consent.[44]

On the rest of the platform there was little disagreement. Long ago the leaders of the party had indicated their desires to Roosevelt. And since there was little hope of attracting any measure of conservative support, Roosevelt accepted most of the suggestions. He did not, however, consent to Gifford Pinchot's proposals for an immediate national workingmen's compensation act and the creation of a department of social welfare, or to a curious plan to prevent the exportation of raw materials. Neither would he accept a suggestion by

[43] Roosevelt to Amos Pinchot, December 5, 1912, and to George L. Record, December 13, 1912, Roosevelt MSS.; Bowers, *Beveridge*, 440; O. K. Davis, *Released for Publication*, 329–334.

[44] *Official Minutes of the Progressive National Committee*, 2; Meyer Lissner to George W. Perkins, August 5, 1912 (copy), Roosevelt MSS.; Bowers, *Beveridge*, 440; O. K. Davis, *Released for Publication*, 337–339.

William Rockhill Nelson for the socialization of lawyers.[45] In the end, with a few exceptions, the platform closely followed the lines Roosevelt had laid down in his Confession of Faith. Altogether it was perhaps the most radical platform any major party had yet presented to the electorate. Eugene V. Debs remarked succinctly that the Progressives' bandanas had replaced the red flag of socialism.[46]

Now the convention had only to nominate the president and vice-president before adjourning. And since Roosevelt had selected Governor Johnson of California as a running mate, the nominations were reduced to mere formalities. At seven o'clock on Wednesday, August 7, Senator Beveridge, competing with the wild cheers of the delegates, announced that Theodore Roosevelt and Hiram Johnson had been nominated. Shortly thereafter, Roosevelt and Johnson appeared before the convention. Introduced by Beveridge, Roosevelt received a demonstration such as few men have ever evoked. As he stepped forward to speak after the riotous acclaim had died, the convention to a man broke out into the fervent "Battle Hymn of the Republic." Only in song could that sincere group of men and women indicate just how much and how far they trusted their leader.

Roosevelt was visibly shaken. In the deep silence that followed his voice trembled and for once he could find no words. "I come forward," he said simply, "to thank you from the bottom of my heart for the great honor you have conferred on me and to say that of course I accept."

A few minutes later the convention adjourned on a typical note. After the notification speeches were over, the whole body of delegates burst into song. And as the last chords of the Doxology faded away, Chairman Beveridge let his gavel fall. The first national convention of the Progressive party was at an end.[47]

[45] J. Franklin Fort to Roosevelt, July 29, 1912, Roosevelt to William Rockhill Nelson, July 30, 1912, Roosevelt MSS.
[46] *New York Times*, August 14, 1912.
[47] *Chicago Tribune*, August 8, 1912.

The campaign that followed was a stormy one. Almost before the convention had got under way the first salvo of sharp criticism had been fired. Before it ended the floodgates of denunciation were wide open. The members of the new party were described as "liars," "thieves," and "besmirchers of honest men." Roosevelt was depicted as a "political anti Christ" whose swollen and prurient ambition had led him beyond the moral law, and whose promises were as false as a dicer's oaths. The platform of the new party, according to the conservative press, was not an orderly program of reform but a long wild call to revolt. The Confession of Faith, screamed the *New York Sun*, "is a manifesto of revolution. It is a program of wild and dangerous changes. It proposes popular nullification of the Constitution. It proposes state socialism."[48]

President Taft, at least, added little to the heat of the campaign. In accordance with his announcement early in July that under no conditions would he campaign actively, he confined his efforts to a moderate acceptance speech and two or three dignified public letters. In these few efforts Taft reconciled his political position with his own true philosophical bent. For deep underneath he had always been a conservative. For a while in the first decade of the century, under the spell of the restless Roosevelt, he had thought of himself as a progressive and had even accepted the succession with the sincere intention of making advances on Roosevelt's liberal beginnings. But faced with the reality of office and with a widening fissure between conservative and progressive in his party, he had gradually found his true political level. Once there, he saw, perhaps to his surprise, clustered around him the Aldriches of the Republican party and not the Dollivers or the La Follettes.

Taft's campaign utterances of 1912 might well have come from the lips of Aldrich. In his acceptance speech on August 1 he deplored the reign of "sensational journalism" and the unrest of the people. He feared that social justice as then in-

[48] *New York Sun, New York Times,* and *New York Herald,* August 7, 1912.

terpreted simply meant a "false division of property" which would approximate socialism. He denounced the recall of judges, the limitation of the power to grant injunctions, and trial by jury in contempt cases as vicious examples of class legislation designed to protect the lawless.[49] His later written views approached toryism. For in defending the high protective tariff, in calling for measures to restore business confidence, and in his allusions to the law of supply and demand as it worked its inevitable way on the labor market, the president was simply repeating the fifty-year-old shibboleths of organized reaction.[50]

In contrast to Taft, Roosevelt soon swung into a strenuous campaign of electioneering. Although he fully expected to lose the election and faced reluctantly the arduous labors of the campaign, he stuck at it with all his old vigor.[51] A fortnight after his initial August campaign in New England he was in the Middle West. Two weeks later he was on the Pacific Coast, and by September 24 he was again in the Corn Belt. After a ten-day swing into the South he once again invaded the Northwest. While speaking in Milwaukee on October 14 he was shot by an insane man. From then until the last of October he rested, recovering from his wound.

As in the past Roosevelt's journeys through the country had been triumphal as a Roman warrior's. This was not the Roosevelt of 1900, for the years had left their mark. He was a bit slower in movement now, heavy around the waist; gray touched his temples. But he had lost none of his old power to attract the multitude. If anything, his manifest sincerity in 1912 and his ostensible abandonment of opportunism engendered even more devotion. At the opening of the campaign ten thousand people jammed the railroad station at Providence, Rhode Island, to welcome him. That night at Infantry Hall, with seats selling for a dollar apiece, thousands of people had to be turned away.[52] When he visited Los Angeles the entire city turned out. Business closed down, traffic was

[49] *New York Times*, August 2, 1912.   [50] *Ibid.*, October 7, 1912.
[51] Roosevelt to Arthur Lee, August 14, 1912, Roosevelt MSS.
[52] *New York Times*, August 16, 1912.

completely stopped, and two hundred thousand people lined the streets to cheer him as he rode from the station.[53]

Nor did the election lack the dramatic and the spectacular with which Roosevelt always managed to surround himself. The country grinned when it heard that "Teddy" had climbed over a tender into the engine of a transcontinental express to run the train for a space and jar the passengers off their seats.[54] Even his enemies admired the mettle he displayed at Milwaukee when he insisted on continuing his speech after being dangerously wounded. Everyone applauded his magnanimity in protecting the would-be assassin from the fury of the bystanders. "Stand back. Don't hurt the man," he had shouted as the crowd rushed to avenge the deed.[55] Even with a bullet in his breast he could savor the drama, and his mind shrewdly dictated the best histrionic tactics. He clutched a bloody handkerchief, held up for all to see. A month later Roosevelt wrote to Earl Grey with revealing candor: "I would not have objected to the man's being killed at the very instant, but I did not deem it wise or proper that he should be killed before my eyes if I was going to recover."[56]

Throughout the campaign Roosevelt scarcely mentioned the president but centered most of his remarks on Woodrow Wilson. Setting aside his old weapons of irony and sharp sarcasm, he attacked his Democratic opponent with a gentle but devastating ridicule. Against the polished and literary phrases of his adversary, Roosevelt at least held his own. It was difficult for him to answer Wilson's charge that his election would mean the rule of United States Steel Corporation through the mediation of Perkins.[57] Troublesome also was the prediction that the election of a Progressive president would cause legislative chaos, since the Congress would be Democratic or Republican. The renewed inquiry into corpor-

[53] *Kansas City Star*, September 16, 1912.
[54] *New York Times*, September 9, 1912.
[55] *Ibid.*, October 15, 1912.
[56] November 15, 1912, Roosevelt MSS.
[57] *New York World*, October 9, 1912.

ate campaign contributions of 1904 may possibly have lost Roosevelt considerable support. Wilson scored heavily also when he attacked Roosevelt's faith in high protection. But in the polemics over two divergent philosophies of government Roosevelt was calling the tune of the times.

Espousing the tenets of Jeffersonian liberalism, Wilson had leveled one attack after another at the Rooseveltian concept of a master state almost without limit in its power to direct the economic life of the nation. He maintained that freedom of industrial activity was necessary for a healthy economic life. Roosevelt's program of regulation would inevitably lead to governmental sanctification of exploiting monopolies. What was needed was not the regulation of industrial combines but their dissolution under the Sherman Law and the restoration of a competitive basis. Such a bureaucratic state as Roosevelt envisaged would put an end to human liberty. "The history of liberty," remarked Wilson with his usual felicity, "is the history of the limitation of governmental power."[58]

Roosevelt, designating such doctrines as "rural toryism" and their author as a sincere doctrinaire who delighted in professorial rhetoric, replied that such a description was true of governments up until the advent of democracy, but not thereafter. For what have the people to fear, he asked, from a strong government which is in turn controlled by the people? If Wilson's doctrine meant anything, it meant "that every law for the promotion of social and industrial justice which has been put upon the statute books ought to be repealed."[59]

But Roosevelt's most effective answer to his critics was in his last speech before sixteen thousand people jammed into Madison Square Garden. Leaving a sickbed to deliver it, he made in this redefinition of his principles his greatest speech of the campaign and one of the finest of his whole political career. As he stood on the platform men noticed that this was

[58] *New York Times*, September 16, 1912.
[59] *New York Sun*, September 16, 1912.

a new Roosevelt. For once he immediately tried to stop the cheering, which lasted, despite his efforts, for forty-five minutes. He used none of the old sarcasm or the belligerent personal attacks, and the pronoun *we* took the place of the overworked *I*.

"We are for human rights and we intend to work for them," he said in answer to the charges that the New Nationalism would lead straight to autocracy. "Where they can be best obtained by the application of the doctrine of states' rights, then we are for states' rights. Where in order to obtain them, it is necessary to invoke the power of the Nation, then we shall invoke to its uttermost limits that mighty power. We are for liberty. But we are for the liberty of the oppressed, and not for the liberty of the oppressor to oppress the weak and to bind the burdens on the shoulders of the heavy laden. It is idle to ask us not to exercise the powers of government when only by that power of the government can we curb the greed that sits in the high places, when only by the exercise of the government can we exalt the lowly and give heart to the humble and downtrodden."

And then in the last moments of the campaign Roosevelt took occasion to fire one more explosive shot at his old enemy the courts. "We stand for the Constitution, but we will not consent to make of the Constitution a fetich for the protection of fossilized wrong," he exclaimed. "We recognize in neither court, nor Congress, nor President, any divine right to override the will of the people."[60]

As election day neared it was obvious that the real race would be between Roosevelt and Wilson. Taft could expect little support from the reforming members of the Republican party. Moreover, the president had alienated a large block of conservative supporters. Many industrial leaders who had voted the Republican ticket for years agreed with James M. Swank, president of the American Iron and Steel Association, that the president's tariff and trusts views were heretical.[61]

[60] *New York Times*, October 31, 1912.
[61] James M. Swank to Joseph B. Foraker, May 15, 1912, Foraker to

For once a Republican administration was having a difficult time in collecting enough money to finance an election. When asked to contribute, H. C. Frick answered that he would give almost any amount to insure the success of the Republican party but that he did not care to contribute to this campaign because the administration "utterly failed to treat many of its warmest friends fairly."[62]

As Taft's defeat became more patent with the days, so-called sober conservatism, fearing a Roosevelt victory, dipped its pen in hysterical and malicious abuse. Branding Roosevelt as the American Mahdi and his followers as wild dervishes, the *New York Sun* predicted that once Roosevelt gained the White House he would never depart. "As the Emperor Sigismund was above grammar, so is Theodore Rex above recall, except that of his promises and his principles."[63] The *New York World* joined in the chorus by predicting that a second term would lead to a third, and a third straight to a tyrant.[64] *Harper's Weekly* had long before warned the country that Roosevelt's election would be followed within ten years by a bloody revolution and the subsequent rule of a despot.[65] But the depths of scurrility and foolishness were plumbed by George Harvey in an editorial entitled "Roosevelt or the Republic." "Roosevelt was the first President," it began, "whose chief personal characteristic was mendacity, the first to glory in duplicity, the first braggart, the first bully, the first betrayer of a friend who ever occupied the White House." From there it went on with equally bitter adjectives, referring to Roosevelt's "perpetual lying," his "shameless treatment of helpless women," and his willingness to grind the American people under the iron boot. "It is not the foreign war," the editorial concluded, "so com-

J. G. Schurman, November 19, 1912, Foraker MSS., Library of Congress; *Washington Post*, August 18, 1912.

[62] Henry C. Frick to Charles D. Hilles, November 2, 1912, in George Harvey, *Henry Clay Frick* (New York, 1928), 310.

[63] *New York Sun*, September 25, 1912.

[64] *New York World*, November 2, 1912.

[65] *Harper's Weekly*, June 1, 1912.

monly anticipated as a consequence of Roosevelt's accession to the dizzy height of unrestrained authority that makes for dread; it is the civil strife that would almost inevitably ensue from patriotic resistance to usurpation by a half mad genius at the head of the proletariat."[66]

Those unreasoning charges might well have remained unwritten; for a Roosevelt victory was next to impossible. Since Wilson's nomination precluded any great migration of progressives from the Democratic party, Roosevelt had to depend upon the support of Republican progressives. They were not enough. Beyond that, traditional progressivism in the Republican party, unlike the make-up of the Democratic party, had always flourished in the agrarian sections of the country. There Roosevelt was handicapped by the fact that many of the progressive Republican leaders in the western sections of the country were either opposed to him or were content in giving him meager support from outside the ranks of the Progressive party.

Roosevelt's paternalistic philosophy of government was not agrarian but urban in its appeal. A high protective tariff, the regulation of industrial monopolies, the long list of labor reforms, offered little to the farmer. In fact the New Nationalism, in almost every instance, was the antithesis of the physiocratic, low-tariff, trust-busting doctrines of the farming West. It is little wonder then that in the eighteen largest cities of the country Roosevelt polled a considerably greater proportion of the total vote than he did throughout the agricultural regions.[67] He was supported in the West not because of his New Nationalism but in spite of it.

Other factors stood in the way of a Roosevelt victory. Thanks to the party's "lily white" tag many Northern Negroes were alienated. The absence from the platform of an anti-trust plank antagonized not only farmers but many city

---

[66] *North American Review*, 195: 433–438 (October 12, 1912).

[67] In the eighteen largest cities of the country Roosevelt obtained thirty-five per cent of the total vote, Wilson forty-one, and Taft twenty-three, whereas in the country at large Roosevelt received twenty-five per cent, Wilson forty-five, and Taft twenty-five.

dwellers who believed in the competitive system. Roosevelt's strict conservation views hurt his cause in the Far West, he was told after the election.[68] Then perhaps most important of all was the lack of a smoothly running organization. Built up hurriedly in the space of four months it was woefully inadequate in efficiency and strength. No party has since the Federalists won its first contest in a national election, and the Progressive party was no exception to the rule.

In the November election Roosevelt at least achieved his desire to defeat Taft. By count Roosevelt received 4,126,020 votes to Taft's 3,483,922, obtained eighty-eight electoral votes to Taft's eight, and was second in twenty-three states while the President ran second in seventeen.[69] Wilson, obtaining only forty-five per cent of the total vote, was handsomely elected. Armageddon had been fought, but the Lord had forgotten.

Roosevelt later wrote to Henry White that "it was a phenomenal thing to bring the new party into second place and to beat out the Republicans."[70] Certainly Roosevelt's personal achievement, obtained without the support of either major party's organization, constituted an enduring testament to his own personal popularity. But a more searching analysis of the election figures fails to bear out his statement that he had brought his party into second place. Instead it appeared from the returns that there was little to the Progressive party save Roosevelt. Despite the fact that the Progressives ran a full national ticket in the majority of the states, they captured only one governorship and elected only a dozen or so congressmen. The results in the minor state and local contests were even more grave for the future of the party. Of the thousands of contests for local offices the Progressives succeeded in winning only about 250. These local results showed that with few exceptions the Progressives

[68] Fred H. Blum to Roosevelt, November 7, 1912, Roosevelt MSS.

[69] Roosevelt carried Pennsylvania, Michigan, Minnesota, South Dakota, Washington, and California, while Taft won only Vermont and Utah.

[70] Roosevelt to Henry White, November (?), 1912, in Nevins, *Henry White*, 315.

hopelessly trailed both their Republican and Democratic opponents. For example, in twenty-two states where Progressives ran for the governorship their combined vote totalled twenty-one per cent less than Roosevelt's total for the same states. In Massachusetts the combined vote for Progressive congressmen totalled thirty-seven per cent less than Roosevelt's figure. In other places the disparity was greater.

This condition of affairs presented an alarming problem indeed to the Progressive party. It is a maxim of politics that a national party lives through the medium of its local office-holders. Without the pecuniary rewards accruing from such petty offices, the courthouse politician, whose hand is necessary to maintain a permanent organization, soon finds other fields for his endeavors. No one realized this danger more than Roosevelt himself. And while he agreed with Garfield that the party had been permanently established, he was exceedingly fearful that the disintegrating force of four years without the sustenance of office would so debilitate the Progressive state organizations that by 1916 it would be a party in name only. "The danger in sight is exactly as you place it," he wrote to Robert Bass, "namely, that we may lose ground in the state elections during the next two or three years. We must do our best to strengthen our local organization."[71]

The danger was not only that the Progressive party would disintegrate but that the whole progressive movement within the Republican party, built up slowly through a decade, would perish with it. Upon Roosevelt rested the full responsibility for the future of Republican progressivism, whether it would grow in its new environment to a dominant place in national life or would languish and finally expire. He had led a good many of the progressive leaders out of the Republican party just at a time when they had threatened to control it. Now sapped of its reforming element, the party of Lincoln was overwhelmingly conservative and was destined to remain so for years. After 1912 there could be no turning back. For

[71] Roosevelt to Seth Bullock, November 12, 1912, and to Robert Bass, November 12, 1912, Roosevelt MSS.

by their desertion the Progressive chieftains had irretrievably lost their power within the party structure. If the former Republican progressivism was to be a vital national force after 1912, it must be through independent political action.

In November of 1912 the future of that permanent action was not at all clear. Judged by the elections there was no denying that the old progressivism had lost ground. Stubbs, Dixon, Bourne, Beveridge, all of them once powerful figures in the nation, had been beaten. In addition the results of the election in Iowa, Kansas, Nebraska, and New Hampshire, states where progressivism had once been the dominant political factor, left either the Democrats or the conservative Republican faction in control. Even Roosevelt admitted that the first result of the great departure had ended in disaster. "We must face the fact," he wrote, "that our cutting loose from the Republican party was followed by disaster to the Progressive cause in most of the states where it won two years ago."[72]

Already conservative Republicans, despite the November losses, were chortling with glee over the results. Already predictions were being made that the discredited Progressives would soon seek to reunite with the Republican party on any terms. That reunion, according to ex-Senator Foraker, would take place under a leadership "of all who believe in the protective tariff policies, with enough protection to protect, and of all who believe in our representative form of government, without any of the socialistic vagaries that are being put forward in the name of progressiveness to first modify, then ultimately destroy our Institutions."[73]

Of course, such predictions in 1912 were merely the result of wishful thinking. From the vantage point of 1912 no man could predict with certainty the future of Progressivism. At that stage of its development its fate simply lay in the lap of time and in the strong but nervous hands of Theodore Roosevelt.

[72] Roosevelt to Gifford Pinchot, November 13, 1912, Roosevelt MSS.
[73] Joseph B. Foraker to J. G. Schurman, November 19, 1912, H. M. Clark to Foraker, December 7, 1912, Foraker MSS., Library of Congress.

CHAPTER ELEVEN

Division and Defeat

IN THE GRAY November days of 1912 Taft was still in the White House, a defeated man. Woodrow Wilson, eager and confident, was clearing up unfinished business at Trenton, New Jersey. At Oyster Bay Theodore Roosevelt was writing his reminiscences. Retrospection is sometimes an anodyne against the present. Often a man looks backward when he can no longer face the tomorrows with certainty. Roosevelt's preoccupation with his autobiography undoubtedly said volumes more for the future of the Progressive party than his letters and conversations. Roosevelt would not admit for two years that the Progressive party was through as a successful organization. The nearest he came to that in 1912 was to write close confidants that the future of the party lay not with its friends but with the Democrats in Washington. Perhaps the crazy-quilted Democratic party, compounded of Tammanyites, conservative Southerners, and Bryan-Wilson men, would split wide open in attempting to make good its progressive promises. Only then would there be much of a chance.[1]

But that pessimistic statement was written to a very, very few. For Roosevelt could not afford so quickly to dash the hopes of millions of his followers who had left the Republican party at his call, and who were even then gathering in Chicago to lay a permanent basis for a great party enduringly dedicated to reform. He had led them into the struggle; his was the obligation to lead them further—at least for a while.

However reluctantly, Roosevelt went to the Progressive conference that opened in Chicago on December 9. There the

[1] Roosevelt to Pearl Wight, December 23, 1912, and to Arthur Lee, December 31, 1912, Roosevelt MSS.

fifteen hundred eager delegates gathered at the La Salle Hotel, representing every state in the Union, perhaps helped him momentarily to regain his old enthusiasm. His opening speech with its outright reaffirmation of the 1912 program, its caustic indictment of the judiciary, and its resounding demand for a permanent party, was typically Rooseveltian. Once again the thrusting head, the waving hands, the whistling staccato sentences awakened the old response. The November defeat, the wrangle over the trust plank, the bitterness against George Perkins had temporarily vanished. Militantly the delegates accepted a plan for a permanent organization with headquarters at both New York and Washington, D. C. Yearly financial quotas were set for every state in the union, a sum of $148,000 a year proposed for organizational and publicity purposes. And after waves of emotional oratory, the delegates left Chicago convinced of victory in 1916. "The conference at Chicago was a wonderful success," wrote Miles Poindexter.[2]

No such spirit of unity, however, characterized the early relations of the small Progressive group of eighteen or nineteen members in Congress. Called together by Woodrow Wilson to revise the tariff, the Sixty-third Congress met on April 7, 1913. Previous to the opening, James R. Mann, Republican leader, had promised the Progressives membership on the committees of the House.[3] Convening in a caucus open to the public, the Progressive congressional delegation selected Victor Murdock of Kansas as their leader and nominee for speaker. A general program of social legislation was unanimously agreed upon and sent to the National Legislative Committee for confirmation and drafting. "If we are to survive," Roosevelt had written a Progressive member of Con-

[2] *Kansas City Star*, December 9, 1912; Miles Poindexter to Roosevelt, December 16, 1912, Roosevelt MSS.

[3] The number of Progressive congressmen in 1913 is not clear. Some men were elected in 1912 on a fusion ticket and afterwards styled themselves progressive Republicans. The *American Yearbook* for 1913 lists nine Progressives and seven progressive Republicans. At the first Progressive Congressional Conference fourteen members of the House appeared. Perhaps all but one of these could properly be called Progressives. There was one Progressive senator, Miles Poindexter, from Washington, in 1913.

gress, "we must act together,"[4] a statement which the recipient undoubtedly understood to mean that party policy would be dictated from Oyster Bay. It was for that purpose that the National Legislative Committee had been organized. But the hopes for unity and singleness of command were soon dissipated. As an organ of revolt the Progressive party had mainly attracted the rebels of politics. Never amenable to the old party's rules, they could scarcely be expected to submit tamely to this even more rigid discipline.[5] And yet Roosevelt was right. If they dispersed their energies, so small a group could hope for nothing but oblivion. Moreover, the Progressive congressional delegation, in order to convince the public of its right to exist, had to distinguish itself from both the Democrats and Republicans. It could not vote with the opposition nor could it afford to vote consistently with a reforming Democratic administration. The Progressive chance lay in the hope of an administration frustrated by its own supporters or in the possibility that Wilson "would take the reactionary instead of the Progressive side."[6]

Unfortunately for Progressive purposes, Woodrow Wilson, using a judicious mixture of political pap and high-minded persuasion, half led, half coerced the unstable Democratic party to enact what has been called "the most remarkable program of national legislation" passed since 1865.[7] Where the rough and tumble Cleveland had twice failed to induce a Democratic Congress to revise the tariff downward, this ex-professor from Princeton signed the Underwood bill, incorporating the first important tariff reduction since the Civil

[4] Roosevelt to W. H. Hinebaugh, March 19, 1913, Roosevelt MSS.

[5] Outside this inclination for independent action the Progressive congressmen were little different from their Republican and Democratic colleagues. The thirteen comprised eight lawyers, two newspaper editors, one businessman, a dentist, and a college professor. Ten of them had been practising politicians holding local and state offices before 1912. Ten eventually returned to the Republican party and held some office after their Progressive interlude. In career and ability, as a group, they ran true to the congressional pattern.

[6] Memorandum in Roosevelt MSS., January 8, 1913.

[7] Charles A. and Mary Beard, *The Rise of American Civilization* (New York, 1937), 2: 606.

War. Thereafter in quick succession followed the Federal Reserve Act, the Clayton amendment to the Sherman Anti-Trust Act, the La Follette's Seamen's bill, a child-labor enactment, and the creation of the Federal Trade Commission.

Such was the record of Wilson's first four years, a record worthy of any reformer and a record exceedingly embarrassing to the Progressive party. Wilson had stolen its thunder and much of its excuse for being. Oyster Bay, instead of being elated over Wilson's mistakes in domestic policy, was increasingly vexed at his successes.

Roosevelt was even more vexed at his own Progressives. Long before the Underwood bill came to a vote, Progressive leaders, seeking the unity which Roosevelt had called so essential, had decided upon a party line. According to the dictum from Oyster Bay, Progressive congressmen were to vote neither for nor against but simply "present" to emphasize the party's demand for "scientific" tariff-making by a commission. However, the moment the plan was expounded to the faithful, rebellion broke out. On the final vote in the House four Progressive votes were registered for the bill, the rest against it.[8] The Progressive "sheep" had become "goats" and they remained goats as long as they were in Congress, some voting for, some against each piece of major legislation.[9]

Troubles gathered thick over Sagamore Hill. It had been expected that many former insurgent Republicans would desert the old party when it was clear that the Progressive party was to be a permanent organization. After the Chicago conference much time and effort was spent in suing for their affection. The cheer and good-fellowship of Oyster Bay was extended particularly to Borah, Norris, Bristow, Hadley, Kenyon, and Cummins. But coolness supplanted coyness as time went on and none of them accepted. Some had scruples about missing "even one session of the Senate," others were

[8] Melville C. Kelley and A. R. Rupley of Pennsylvania, James W. Bryan of Washington, and John I. Nolan of California.

[9] O. K. Davis, *Released for Publication*, 409–411; Roosevelt to Victor Murdock, May 13, 1913, Roosevelt MSS.; *New York Times*, May 9, 1913.

too busy, and all of them were a little "skittish." Finally in May, 1913, when Governor Hadley and Senator Cummins organized a conference at Chicago of thirty-eight progressive Republicans to liberalize the party, the courtship came to an abrupt end. That autumn Cummins was in Maine supporting Republican candidates, and his old comrade of Payne-Aldrich days, Beveridge, was answering from an opposing stump. And as so often happens when friends quarrel, affection turned to aversion. Progressive Republicans to George Perkins became "cowardly straddlers" who were happy with you one moment "and reaching for your ribs with a knife the next." As if to reply, Herbert S. Hadley candidly wrote Roosevelt that the actions of the Progressives were killing the chance for liberal action within the Republican party.[10]

To make matters worse, out in the country during 1913 the Progressive machine, hurriedly built in 1912, was sadly falling apart. Jobs and money, the two lubricants needed for any political machine, were lacking. In the exuberance of the campaign, the National Committee had managed to collect and spend almost three-quarters of a million, but defeat brought financial stringency. With the exception of Perkins, who, along with Frank Munsey, had contributed the greater part of the 1912 funds, the Progressive party had few rich philanthropists willing to subsidize a losing cause. By January, 1913, the Progressive News Service was on the point of discontinuing its publications for lack of the five hundred dollars needed to buy a multigraphing machine. One year later the *Progressive Bulletin* also died of anemia. Most of the other bureaus and services so bravely proposed by the first party conference had long since ceased to operate.[11]

Meanwhile leaders of state and local machines were beseeching the national offices for nonexistent subsidies. The invariable reply that the National Finance Committee expected

[10] Letters to Roosevelt from Joseph M. Dixon, February 7, 1913, and Herbert S. Hadley, September 4, 1913, Roosevelt MSS.; Bowers, *Beveridge*, 448; George W. Perkins to Bonaparte, March 3, 1914, Bonaparte MSS.
[11] Reports of the Executive Committee of the Progressive Party, December 19, 1912, January 24, 1914, typewritten mss., Roosevelt MSS.

each local unit of the party to finance itself did not help to assuage harassed local leaders. Moreover, for every job the Progressive party had to give there were thousands of claimants instead of the usual hundreds. From every state desperate telegrams and letters asking for the loaves and fishes of politics came into Oyster Bay. When jobs were not forthcoming, cries that the Progressives "failed to recognize the true virtue of 'helping your friends' " were numerous.[12] "Running a motor without oil a very difficult process," tersely reported one henchman to Oyster Bay after a Progressive defeat in a congressional election early in 1913.[13]

To add to the early woes of the Progressive party some of the generals as well as the privates began to desert the ranks. Frank A. Munsey, the multimillionaire publisher, had been one of the godfathers of the Progressive party. A staunch admirer of Roosevelt, he had, in a moment of mingled indignation and enthusiasm, promised financial support to the new party in 1912. Throughout the campaign he had liberally opened his editorial pages and his purse in Roosevelt's service. But Munsey had never felt at home in the Progressive party. Its reforming spirit was alien to his nature. As owner of magazines, newspapers, and chain grocery stores, he was by station and temperament a business man devoted to contemporary business ideals. The principles of the Republican party in 1912, he later confessed, had thoroughly satisfied him. By January of 1913 he felt that he had enough of promoting "uplift" and of "climbing up moonbeams"; the time had come to reunite with the Republican party.[14] In the February issue of his magazine Munsey proposed an amalgamation of the Progressive and Republican parties.[15]

Desperately the remaining leaders of the Progressive party, who had learned of the article only after it was well on

[12] Letters to Roosevelt from Francis W. Bird, February 5, 1913, and Timothy L. Woodruff, January 24, 1913, Miles Poindexter to George W. Perkins, July 25, 1914, Roosevelt MSS.
[13] Charles H. Thompson to Roosevelt, April 8, 1913, Roosevelt MSS.
[14] Charles J. Bonaparte to Roosevelt, February 15, 1913, Roosevelt MSS.
[15] "A Scheme of Political Amalgamation," *Munsey's Magazine*, 48: 729–733.

its way to publication, sought to undo the damage. Roosevelt announced publicly that he was unalterably opposed to the scheme, and a determined effort was made to dissuade Munsey from pushing his proposal farther. But the publisher continued to spread his doctrine of amalgamation. And when the Progressive party continued to receive his plan with coolness, he launched an attack upon his associates of 1912: "This reform idea has so possessed the thought of the new party, and the spirit of uplift and idealism has so dominated it, that the bread and butter issue has been largely obscured."[16] Whereupon Mr. Munsey went to the heart of at least one part of the "bread and butter" issue by intimating to Beveridge that there was very little money in the Progressive party "save in the pockets of a very few, and the few will not feel called upon to fight another campaign alone."[17]

Thus the fat was in the fire. For no one could expect the smaller men in the party to stay put when its leaders, and especially those who supplied the sinews of politics, were suggesting their own departure. Moreover, by October, 1913, the Democratic party, with the aid of some Progressive votes, had effected a sweeping reduction in the tariff. What specific glue has held the Democratic party together in recent American history is still something of a mystery. But Republican cohesiveness, after the slavery issue waned, has come, if from any one thing, from the mucilage of the high protective tariff. Now when Progressive protectionists perceived that the Underwood desecration was a result of 1912, they began to repent of their hasty action. "This situation . . . only means that we will keep the Democrats in power, damn them," wrote Dan Hanna; "they will ruin not only the farmer but everything that has been built up under a protective tariff."[18] Soon this lesser son of a mightier father was preaching amalgamation through his newspapers. From then

---

[16] "Amalgamation No. 3," *ibid.*, 49: 14–21.

[17] Frank Munsey to Beveridge, February 3, 1913, in Bowers, *Beveridge*, 441–442.

[18] Dan R. Hanna to Roosevelt, April 28, 1913, and letter dated 1913, Roosevelt MSS.

on until the autumn of 1914 reports of further desertions poured into the party's central headquarters. The retreat from Armageddon was at full gallop.

The Progressive party, however, despite all its losses, still represented in 1914 a considerable wedge of political strength. Theodore Roosevelt, Hiram Johnson, Miles Poindexter, Albert J. Beveridge, Gifford and Amos Pinchot, Medill McCormick, John Parker of Louisiana, Walter Brown of Ohio, and William Flinn of Pennsylvania, together with their following, could be expected to drum up from two to four million votes in any presidential election. That total, of course, was not enough for a Progressive victory. But if it were held together, some sudden whirl of the political wheel might make it the nucleus of such a victory. Beyond that the trading value of two to four million votes in American politics has never been infinitesimal. Roosevelt was too good a politician to discount either possibility. As early as January, 1913, while he was publicly opposing Munsey's amalgamation plan, he was privately speculating on the probability of its success "a year or two hence."[19]

The remnants of the party had to be kept together, however, if either course was to be pursued. Throughout the four years from 1912 to 1916 this became increasingly more difficult as the party leadership split into two violently opposing sections over the personality of Perkins and his place in the determination of party policy.

From an office boy at the age of fifteen, George Walbridge Perkins had become an executive of the New York Life Insurance Company. Typifying the growing financial control of American industry, he was made a partner of J. P. Morgan and Company, where he aided in the organization of the International Harvester and the Northern Securities combines. By 1908, as a member of the Morgan firm, a director of the Harvester Company, the United States Steel Corporation, and many less potent combines, he personified what the Pujo Committee was later to call the money trust.

[19] Roosevelt to P. V. Bunn. January 17, 1913, Roosevelt MSS.

The short-statured Perkins was possessed of an amiable nature and a kindly disposition. Possibly inheriting some of his father's public spirit, he early pointed the way to the development of welfare capitalism by inaugurating in the steel corporation a plan whereby employees could purchase the company's stock at less than market prices. Perkins was also interested in public charities and parks. But throughout the period he was most concerned over the trust-busting proclivities of the progressive movement. Believing that the combination movement in industry was inevitable and beneficial, he was inalterably opposed to the anti-trust crusade. In lieu of the Sherman Law he proposed a federal business commission with power to charter interstate and international enterprises. In formulating a code of business conduct, this commission was to have authority to investigate any and all records of private business and to exercise control over the issuance of industrial securities.[20] It might suspend the charter of a company found guilty of wrongdoing, and initiate criminal procedure against the management. Whatever else Perkins may have been, he was sensitive to the need of some public control over business life, a point of view exceptional for the industrialists of his age. And some of his proposals at least were prophetic of the future.

The dissolution in 1904 of Perkins' own creation, the Northern Securities Company, convinced him of the necessity of public action and education. When in 1910 Roosevelt included in his New Nationalism a proposal to substitute regulation for dissolution Perkins became a firm supporter of the ex-president.[21] And undoubtedly Taft's actions against the Steel and Harvester corporations was a prime factor in his willingness to join and finance the Bull Moose crusade.

During the campaign of 1912 Perkins contributed over a quarter million dollars to the party funds[22] and continued to

[20] George W. Perkins memorandum, May 22, 1915, Roosevelt MSS.

[21] George W. Perkins to William H. Childs, October 29, 1915, Roosevelt MSS.

[22] *New York Times*, November 26, 1912.

be no less liberal thereafter. In 1914 the Progressive party was able to balance its books solely because of his advances. When a bond issue for a new Eastern Progressive newspaper failed to sell, Perkins personally subscribed for the entire issue of thirty thousand dollars.[23] His open purse, his manifest executive ability, and his business connections made him Roosevelt's choice for chairman of the party's National Executive Committee, an office that enabled him to exert a preponderating influence over party policy. He was consulted on every move, and his views weighed heavily in every party council. It was Perkins who was largely responsible for the abandonment of the trust plank in the 1912 platform. And after it was later reinserted by majority will, Perkins continued to assail the Sherman Law on the stump and even in the official party press.

But from the start Perkins was distrusted by a large number of Progressive leaders. His connections with Morgan and the Harvester and Steel corporations made him suspect in the country west of the Hudson, which was traditionally against whatever Wall Street was for. His attacks on the Sherman Law intensified the opposition. Much of the strength of the Progressive party lay in the Middle and the Far West, and this was precisely where the Sherman Law was most venerated.

Moreover, even in the East, among the more radical members of the party who agreed with Roosevelt's trust-regulating policy, there was considerable distrust of Perkins. J. P. Morgan and the steel corporation represented perfectly the forces they had been fighting against for years. They opposed the Sherman Law not because of its deleterious effects on business but because it had failed to curb the activities of just the people whom Perkins represented. Were not his proposals, they asked themselves, a scheme to destroy the Sherman Law without putting anything effective in its place? If

[23] Typewritten report of the Executive Committee of the Progressive Party, April 13, 1914, and George W. Perkins to Roosevelt, May 2, 1913, Roosevelt MSS.

George Perkins had a hand in the outcome, would not the regulated also be the regulators?

For the sake of unity the opposition to Perkins was temporarily stilled during the campaign. But under the surface the hostility to him increased, if anything, as the months went by. His habit of deciding party affairs without consulting other leaders incensed many of the Western leaders of the party. Senator Joseph M. Dixon, who as chairman of the National Committee should have directed the campaign, was at times completely ignored in the determination of party strategy. Dixon became so unhappy over his ambiguous position that at one point in the campaign he was on the point of resigning and going home to Montana.[24]

When once the election was over, all the pent-up opposition to Perkins found expression in the demand that he resign his office. Amos and Gifford Pinchot, Dixon, and John Parker of Louisiana led the movement. William Allen White, Hiram Johnson, Raymond Robins, and Medill McCormick gave it their support. Many of the post-election diagnoses that Roosevelt received placed the blame for the defeat squarely on Perkins' shoulders. His connection with the missing trust plan, his affiliation with Wall Street, his positions with the Steel and Harvester trusts all had discredited the party among the masses of the people, Roosevelt was told. If the party were ever to be victorious, it must command the support of the millions of farmers and laborers. And that, according to these correspondents, was impossible so long as George Perkins retained his present position in the organization. These "radicals," as Roosevelt styled them, then went on to demand that the trust plank be reinserted in the platform, that Perkins be removed from his office, and that to emphasize the new direction of the party its principles be made even more progressive than the platform of 1912. The objectors then carefully added that they had no intention of running Perkins out of the party. If he cared to continue his

[24] Medill McCormick to Roosevelt, November 18, 1912, Henry F. Cochems to Roosevelt, November 23, 1912, Roosevelt MSS.

financial contributions after his wings were clipped, they would be more than welcome.[25]

Roosevelt saw that unless this anti-Perkins movement was stopped, the party might break into fragments. Prior to the Chicago conference he attempted simultaneously to defend Perkins and to appease the opposition. To the removal of Perkins he was violently opposed. The failure of the party, he intimated, had been mainly due to the want of organizing ability and money. Perkins had supplied the most of both: "If we had lost his very great organizing ability, his devoted zeal and the money which he so generously gave . . . I think our whole campaign would have gone to pieces." His reaction to the proposal for a more radical party program was that the Progressives had no excuse for existing except as a radical party, but he wanted to keep it as the party of sane and tempered radicalism "such as that of Abraham Lincoln." He would agree, however, to the reinsertion of the anti-trust plank at the Chicago conference.[26]

Roosevelt's answers, however, did not satisfy the two Pinchots and the other leaders of the anti-Perkins drive. As their insistence drove him almost to the point of distraction, Roosevelt became heartily disgusted with this "advanced radical element." These "extremists were doing their best to break up the party by attacking the moderate men." At the Chicago conference he refused to talk with them.[27]

Forced by Roosevelt's position to retire from the party or to continue and accept the leadership of Perkins, the rebellious group were for the most part silent at Chicago. As a sop to their feelings the anti-trust plank was reinserted in the platform. But their one indirect attempt to cripple Perkins by removing the national offices of the party to Washington,

[25] Letters to Roosevelt from Medill McCormick, November 18, 1912, Henry F. Cochems, November 29, 1912, and Arthur D. Hill, November 29, 1912, Roosevelt MSS.

[26] Roosevelt to Gifford Pinchot, November 13, 1912, and to Amos Pinchot, December 5, 1912, Roosevelt MSS.

[27] Roosevelt to R. H. M. Ferguson, December 10, 1912, and to Kermit Roosevelt, December 3, 1912, Roosevelt MSS.; Bowers, *Beveridge*, 439.

D. C., was beaten by a substantial majority. For every practical purpose Perkins came away from Chicago second only to Roosevelt in command of the party. Just how securely he was in the saddle is indicated by a motion passed at a subsequent meeting of the National Executive Committee empowering him at any time to issue statements on any matter in the name of the committee.[28]

Perkins must have interpreted his victory at Chicago as a party vote of confidence in his ideas as well as in his person. For despite the conference action on the anti-trust plank he continued and even increased his assaults on the Sherman Law. Thereafter in almost every issue of the *Progressive Bulletin*, the official party organ, was found either an attack on trust-busting or an encomium on the blessings of big business. The Harvester Company was held up as an example of a benevolent corporation in the copy for June, 1913. A month later an article appeared concerning the Standard Oil Company's great gifts to the country; the issue of March 7, 1914, featured Perkins' reply to Senator Borah's attack on the United States Steel Corporation. The prosecution of the steel corporation, a model employer according to Perkins, would result in a national calamity for labor as well as the country at large.[29] Not confining his views to the party press, Perkins in public addresses defended J. P. Morgan, E. H. Harriman, and other "men of imagination" as wise and benevolent leaders in the march of industry. "You don't know the views Mr. Morgan had toward labor. I do and I know that there was never a man in a place of big responsibility toward labor who was a better friend of the workingman."[30]

To the leaders of the Progressive left wing these business homilies from the party's spokesman constituted treason. All through 1913 they wrote one another in protest. Once Amos

---

[28] Minutes of the Progressive National Committee, December 11, 1912; *New York Times*, December 12, 1912; Minutes of the Progressive National Executive Committee, May 24, 1913.

[29] *Progressive Bulletin*, June, July, 1913, March 7, 1914.

[30] *New York Times*, April 12, 1915.

"FOR WE STAND AT ARMAGEDDON AND
WE BATTLE FOR THE LORD"
Cartoon by Kirby in the *New York World*, reproduced
in the *Literary Digest*, June 20, 1914.

Pinchot and ex-Senator Dixon, chairman of the National
Committee, were on the point of a public protest. They were
held back only by the argument that after accepting Perkins'
money in the 1912 campaign this action would be one of
rankest ingratitude. By May of 1914, however, Amos Pinchot
could restrain himself no longer. In a letter to Senator Dixon,
copies of which he sent to every member of the National
Committee, Pinchot charged that Perkins had perverted the
original purpose of the Progressive party, that he was a friend
of the trusts and the foe of unorganized labor. "To talk
against monopoly," Pinchot continued, "to place the words
'Social and Industrial Justice' on our banner, and then to
hand over this banner to a man who has been monopoly's ar-

dent supporter and one of the most distinguished opponents of social and industrial justice . . . is, in my opinion, a handicap to the party, and a fraud on the public." Pinchot concluded from these facts that for the good of the party Perkins' resignation was necessary.[31] Three weeks later a part of Pinchot's letter found its way into public print, and the whole country was apprised of the family quarrel. Meanwhile, although regretting the unfortunate publicity, other party leaders were actively supporting the movement. Medill McCormick, Raymond Robins, and Meyer Lissner, among others, wrote Roosevelt that they agreed with the purpose of Pinchot's letter if not with its spirit.[32]

Upon his return from his son's wedding in Spain, Roosevelt gave vent to his indignation over the whole movement and his rage at Amos Pinchot. Belligerently he announced that if Perkins was forced from the party he would also leave. Soon afterward he made it clear that Perkins was to be left in his office. That statement effectively stopped any further organized opposition until after 1916. But Amos Pinchot would not be stilled. He continued to make the charge that Perkins had corrupted the party. Finally in the waning days of the 1916 campaign Pinchot made the specific indictment in a published statement that all of Perkins' machinations had had the complete approval of Theodore Roosevelt and thus the Colonel was directly responsible for the degeneration of a great cause. Roosevelt's reaction was swift. In a final letter concluding the political friendship Roosevelt wrote: "When I spoke of the Progressive party as having a lunatic fringe, I specifically had you in mind."[33]

But Roosevelt's indignation and personal recrimination

[31] Amos Pinchot to Joseph M. Dixon, May 22, 1914, in *Literary Digest*, December 5, 1914.
[32] Letters to Roosevelt from Medill McCormick, June 22, 1914, Raymond Robins, August 3, 1914, and Meyer Lissner, December 3, 1914, Roosevelt MSS.
[33] *New York Sun*, November 22, 1914; *New York Times*, August 18, 1915; Roosevelt to Amos Pinchot, November 3, 1916, Roosevelt MSS.

was not the only result of Pinchot's charges and defection. The episode served to bring the latent hostility to Perkins within the party to the surface. And although it was suppressed for a while by Roosevelt, it continued to flourish underneath. Never again was Perkins fully trusted by a large group in the party. More significantly, a portion of that distrust was aimed at Perkins' defender, Theodore Roosevelt. The army of reform had become skeptical of its leaders.

This public washing of Progressive linen was unfortunately timed. It came just as the congressional campaign of 1914 was getting under way, a campaign for which Roosevelt had little heart. He had no hope of victory for the Progressive party, and to him victory was the wine of life. The few by-elections in 1913 indicated that unless an unexpected shift occurred, Progressive strength was steadily diminishing. Moreover, the exponent of the strenuous life was growing old. The active years in the White House, the hunting trips, the expeditions to Africa and South America were beginning to leave their marks. At least Roosevelt thought they were. Twice during the summer of 1914, in the midst of a mental depression brought on by a lingering jungle fever contracted on the "River of Doubt," he wrote to friends, "I am now an old man." What mental anguish must have preceded that confession.[34]

When Roosevelt left for Spain early in June without voluntarily sending a message of cheer to party leaders, the *Nation* quoted: "He left full soon on the first of June, But bade the rest keep fighting."[35] But the ex-president had little thought of evading the campaign upon his return. True, he had been spending much thought on the prospects of the party, and had about concluded that it had little future as a separate entity. For the first time since 1912 phrases prophetic of what was to come crept into his correspondence with closest in-

[34] Roosevelt to Leonard D. Wood, June 26, 1914, and to John Willis, September 5, 1914, Roosevelt MSS.
[35] June, 1914, 98: 655.

timates. "We must, as you say, amalgamate or fuse with some body of men. Permanently there is only room for two national parties in this country." But those sentiments were not yet to be conveyed to all the faithful; the time was not ripe. And so upon returning from abroad he again stoutly proclaimed his unyielding allegiance to the party and predicted victory in November.[36]

In launching the campaign of 1914 most Progressives sought to take up where they had left off in 1912. The call for reform resounded from the hustings, descriptions of pelf were vividly drawn, the manipulators of politics came in for a proper anathematizing. If there was something less than the old fever it was still the old crusade. But for all of that, something was wrong. The more acute spirits sensed from the first that their captain without consultation had subtly changed his sailing orders. That was apparent in Roosevelt's first major political speech since 1912.

Speaking at Pittsburgh on the last of June, he concentrated his efforts, first, upon a prosperity and protection argument worthy of McKinley and, secondly, upon a biting criticism of the Democratic trust program.[37] There was little mention of the New Nationalism; there was no criticism of the Republican party save for William Barnes and Boies Penrose; there was praise for the nation's industrialists. The next day the *New York Times* noted that Roosevelt without saying a specific word had adroitly moved toward a Republican reunion in 1916.[38]

Soon after his Pittsburgh speech Roosevelt took a more tangible step in the same direction. While he was in Spain a group of New York leaders seeking a winning state ticket had attempted to draft the ex-president to run for governor.

[36] Roosevelt to Raymond Robins, August 12, 1914, and to Alexander P. Moore, July 10, 1914, Roosevelt MSS.

[37] Upon the subject of industrial combinations Roosevelt virtually repeated what Perkins had been publishing in the *Progressive Bulletin.*

[38] *New York Times*, July 1, 1914. "The almost unanimous opinion of the business district approves the Pittsburgh speech—moderately, heartily or enthusiastically, according to temperament." Medill McCormick to Roosevelt, July 3, 1914, Roosevelt MSS.

Firmly declining upon his return, Roosevelt startled a good many of his followers by suggesting that a victory could be won only by combining with the progressive Republican element in the state. He then proposed that the Progressives nominate Harvey D. Hinman, one of Charles E. Hughes's old supporters, who appeared to be the most probable Republican nominee. And after silencing the opposition of the Progressive majority Roosevelt offered the honor to Hinman provided he would run on the Progressive ticket if he failed to capture the Republican nomination. In the end, after a month's delay, Hinman refused the condition, and the Colonel announced that the Progressive party would nominate and run its own candidate. The Hinman episode gave heart to the fusionist faction in the Progressive party. Severely criticized before, they now felt they had Roosevelt's blessing. And as a result, in almost every state a minority of the party demanded, and in some places obtained, a combined ticket. In the New York state elections fusion candidates were offered in fourteen assembly districts.[39]

To men like Hiram Johnson, William Allen White, John Parker, and Albert J. Beveridge, who despite reverses wished to continue the Progressive party as a permanent and separate organization, Roosevelt's New York actions were dismaying. They saw in them a retreat from the party's advanced doctrines and possibly an indication that the leader who had led them into the wilderness might now be on the point of forsaking them. Moreover, for those who were running for office in 1914, the attempted New York fusion diminished their chance in the November elections. It gave their Republican opponents ground for their triumphant claim that this was the last confession of a dying party and that the electorate would soon administer extreme unction. A vote for the Progressive party was therefore a lost vote. Indignantly the opponents of fusion expressed their sentiments. A not uninfluential member of the party suggested that the National Committee be called together to censor the

New York action. A peremptory demand came from Beveridge that Roosevelt do "one or two definite things" in Indiana "in order to make up in a very small way for the large handicap" Roosevelt had placed upon him. And even the faithful Bonaparte suggested to Perkins that Roosevelt ought to speak to his people immediately "to explain his policy in the present campaign, for they do not understand it and are getting restless."[40]

Roosevelt described the actions to censor him as "preposterously foolish."[41] He was desperately tired and more than a little disgusted. After the fusion plan had been discarded in New York, Roosevelt had to promise to spend all of October campaigning in the state before a suitable Progressive candidate could be persuaded to make the race for governor. In addition he was pressed to come to almost every state in the Union, and despite his reluctance to make a "cartail campaign," he spoke almost daily from August to November. At the same time he was always aware of the hopelessness of his actions. Poor crowds—only twenty-five hundred turned out to hear him in Boston—the general lack of spirit, and his good political sense told him that disaster loomed ahead. He wrote to the governor general of Australia that he was "finishing a hopeless campaign." And to O. K. Davis he declared during the last hours of the campaign that he had paid all his political debts and would soon be out of politics for good and all. "I have done everything this fall that everybody has wanted. This election makes me an absolutely free man. Thereafter I am going to say and do just what I damned please."[42]

Roosevelt was right. November did bring disaster to the Progressive party. Making every effort to rehabilitate itself, the party had run its ablest men. Albert J. Beveridge, Gifford Pinchot, Raymond Robins, James R. Garfield, Victor Murdock, Henry J. Allen, Bainbridge Colby, Francis J. Heney,

[40] Beveridge to Perkins, August 10, 1914, Roosevelt MSS.; Bonaparte to Perkins, August 18, 1914, Bonaparte MSS.

[41] Roosevelt to Henry Wallace, August 13, 1914, Roosevelt MSS.

[42] Roosevelt to Sir Ronald Ferguson, November 5, 1914, Roosevelt MSS.; Davis, *Released for Publication*, 441.

and Hiram Johnson headed up the various state tickets. Yet every one of them lost except Johnson.

To make matters worse, most of the Old Guard defeated in 1912 had been returned victorious. Uncle Joe Cannon, William B. McKinley, Nicholas Longworth, and Charles Curtis re-entered Congress to join Penrose, Gallinger, Lodge, and Smoot in preserving complete conservative control of the Grand Old Party. When the election returns of 1914 were totaled, the future shade of Warren Gamaliel Harding stalked into the White House.

The total Democratic and Republican votes cast throughout the nation was each estimated to be in excess of six million, whereas the Progressive total had fallen below two million. Only one Progressive was left in the House of Representatives. The party had disintegrated and the Roosevelt revolt was almost over. Scanning the election returns, William Howard Taft wrote to his former secretary of state: "I hope the late election satisfied your desires. I am able to endure it with Christian resignation."[43]

[43] Taft to Philander C. Knox, November 17, 1914, Knox MSS.

CHAPTER TWELVE

Wilson and War

THE CATACLYSM was just about what I had expected it to be," wrote Theodore Roosevelt on the morning after the elections of 1914. But expectation of the disaster did little to soften its reality after it came. In the gloom of total defeat during the early November days Roosevelt momentarily lost his political touch. He was ready to retire permanently from politics. The Progressive party, he felt, had not been the young Republican party born again but the hopelessly defeated and forgotten Free-Soil party. In a historical mood Roosevelt argued that it would have been better for the cause and the man to have remained with Webster in the old Whig party until the Republican party was firmly established than to have joined Sumner in the ephemeral Free-Soil organization. "I should suppose," he wrote to his son, "that the Progressive party now would probably disband."[1]

Roosevelt could think of many reasons for the Progressive defeat. The Progressive leadership had been a little too lofty in morals and in aim for the average man. The movement and the party had in the course of time attracted to it emotionalists and cranks of a modified I.W.W. sort. When he himself had been president he had succeeded in keeping it a sane and constructive movement. But after that it had grown every which way under the leadership of men like La Follette, Wilson, and Bryan, until the public unconsciously connected it with the "lunatic fringe" in politics. The American system was a two-party system, and the average American citizen was either a Democrat or a Republican, requiring no

[1] Roosevelt to Archie Roosevelt, November 7, 1914, to Kermit Roosevelt, November 11, 1914, and to Arthur D. Hill, November 9, 1914, Roosevelt MSS.

more reason for being than the members of the blue or green faction of the Byzantine Circus. But the fundamental trouble in 1914, Roosevelt thought, was that the people were tired of reform. Other explanations of the debacle were scattered through dozens of letters, but he never failed to assert that a conservative reaction from the progressive movement had set in. For twelve years after he had started the movement by settling the anthracite coal strike in 1902, Roosevelt wrote, a great wave of reform spirit had rolled over the country. Now it was rapidly subsiding, as was witnessed by the overwhelming defeat of reform legislation in the state elections of 1914. Five states had soundly defeated women's suffrage. The initiative referendum and recall had lost wherever it was voted upon. Even progressive Wisconsin had turned its back upon progress. The dog had "returned to its vomit!" The great masses of people, Roosevelt believed, no longer cared for political "fair play and decency."[2]

This personal feeling that the progressive movement was dying in the inevitable flux of politics was a conviction to which Roosevelt held tenaciously. It was to color and partially explain his political course during the next few years. But during the week after the elections Roosevelt changed his mind about the advisability of putting the party permanently to sleep. The perspective of a few days restored some of his buoyancy and most of his old political acumen, and he realized the trading value of even two million votes. Certainly if the party were to evaporate entirely the Republican directorate would have the Bull Moose leaders at their mercy. Perhaps, after all, the party, if it continued to exist, could demand a price in the 1916 elections. And if that race were close, the price might be a high one. Much could happen in the next two years. As one of Roosevelt's close advisers remarked, to blow up the boat and immediately enlist elsewhere seemed premature; to tie up the boat and wait for the tide seemed to be good sense.

[2] Roosevelt to William Allen White, November 7, 1914, and to James R. Garfield, November 9, 1914, Roosevelt MSS.; Roosevelt to Charles J. Bonaparte, Bonaparte MSS.

A Progressive conference was called to meet in early December in Chicago. Long before that meeting the party heads had agreed in the face of some opposition that the 1912 platform was to be quietly forgotten, that the meeting should be devoted almost entirely to the problem of keeping the organization alive, and that Roosevelt's name should be introduced as little as possible. For the present the Colonel would adopt a policy of "silence and sit tight." He was not going to Chicago. He did not even want to write a letter to E. A. Van Valkenburg to bring him over to support the program of throttling the 1912 platform, a program with which Roosevelt momentarily agreed. It was in his judgment not only inadvisable but rather worse than useless for him to discuss the matter even in a private letter to a long-time friend and supporter.[3]

The conference, attended by representatives from thirty-five states, more or less smoothly adopted the prearranged program. The National Committee was instructed to meet no later than January 15, 1916, for the purpose of calling a national nominating convention. The members of the party throughout the country were exhorted to maintain their ranks. A statement prepared by William Allen White and Chester Rowell was made public. This attracted widespread attention, chiefly for what it did not say. Nowhere in the document were the social planks of 1912 mentioned; instead it was largely given over to an attack on the Simmons-Underwood tariff and a demand for a bill prepared by a tariff commission. Important opposition to the abandonment of the great reform program arose within the party. The Progressive county committee of New York labelled it an official "asphyxiation" of the party, and numerous individuals wrote to Roosevelt and Perkins to protest. Though Roosevelt conceded that perhaps the step had been a mistake, he made no attempt to change the findings of the conference. Meanwhile Perkins, in a circular letter to all Progressive leaders, inti-

[3] Roosevelt to Charles J. Bonaparte, November 19, 1914, and to George W. Perkins, memorandum, November 23, 1914, Roosevelt MSS.

mated that the Rowell-White statement had been unanimously approved by the Chicago meeting. And thus the final chapter to the Armageddon of 1912 had been written. The Progressive hosts had not only lost the battle; their captains had now enlisted on the other side.[4]

After the congressional elections Roosevelt had stated that "silence and sit tight" would be his policy, but the essence of his being was hardly adapted either to silence or to sitting tight. Particularly when he was irritated, silence was the last thing Roosevelt's temperament could achieve. And Roosevelt had been mightily irritated at Woodrow Wilson all through the spring and summer of 1914. In May of that year William Jennings Bryan as secretary of state announced that he had negotiated a treaty with Colombia which provided that the United States apologize for her part in the Panama revolution and pay an indemnity of twenty-five million dollars. This direct criticism of what Roosevelt considered to be the greatest feat of his administration made him hopping mad. Moreover, Roosevelt had opposed Taft's arbitration treaties as limiting the sovereignty of the United States and perhaps as an indirect criticism of the treaties signed in his own administration. Now Bryan was attempting to promulgate his "cooling off" treaties, which went even further than those proposed by Taft. Roosevelt, ever quick on the trigger in dealing with small nations, had deplored Taft's "flabby" Mexican policy. Wilson's was worse. In April when American troops took the town of Vera Cruz to prevent the Mexican dictator Huerta from securing foreign arms, the Colonel was hopeful of a "strong" policy. When the president, accepting the mediation of the ABC powers, withdrew the armed forces, Roosevelt's hopes were dashed and his disgust for Wilson increased. But of all things that tempered his attitude toward Wilson and his foreign policy, the most important by far must have been the

[4] Minutes of the Executive Committee, November 6, December 2, 1914, E. A. Van Valkenberg to Perkins, December 6, 1914, and Roosevelt to Van Valkenberg, December 11, 1914, Roosevelt MSS.; *New York Times*, December 1, 1914; Perkins to Bonaparte *et al.*, December 7, 1914, and William Dudley Foulke to Bonaparte, December 24, 1914, Bonaparte MSS.

Colombia episode. Before and after 1914 nothing aroused his anger so quickly as the charge that his actions in Panama had been a little less than honorable. No other charge inspired him to quite so self-righteous, quite so sulphurous a rebuttal. In the amalgam of his later hate for Wilson, a hate which at times was altogether unreasoning, the Colombia episode remained one of the chief ingredients. It was partly responsible for his demand for war, partly responsible for his actions in 1916.[5]

Roosevelt attacked Wilson's foreign policy at the first opportunity in the campaign of 1914. Heavily sarcastic, he described the administration's Mexican policy as one of "mushy amiability."[6] In his last article as associate editor of the *Outlook* he said he had no choice but to make war on an administration whose foreign policy had "meant the abandonment of the interest and honor of America." For the rest of the campaign he was strangely silent on the subject.[7]

The reason for this silence appears in his letters. After his first attacks on Wilson's foreign policy the men for whom he was campaigning objected. Wilson's peace policy with Mexico was popular, they said, and any attack on that policy would lose instead of win them votes. Roosevelt capitulated. "I told my friends that as I was doing what I could for them this Fall I should not make an attack which they thought would hurt them but that after the election I should smite the administration with a heavy hand."[8]

His hands tied by his own party, Roosevelt through the summer and fall was kept informed of the Mexican situation largely through letters from Senators Henry Cabot Lodge and Albert B. Fall. This interchange with the senator from New Mexico was the beginning of a friendship with the central figure of the future Teapot Dome affair that was to last until Roosevelt's death. It was a strange friendship indeed for

[5] Roosevelt to Perkins, memorandum, November 23, 1914, Roosevelt MSS.

[6] *New York Times*, June 25, 1914.

[7] *Outlook*, July 11, 1914.

[8] Roosevelt to Henry C. Lodge, December 8, 1914, Roosevelt MSS.

the crusader of 1912, but in the autumn of 1914 Roosevelt was setting out on strange paths.[9] When the campaign was over, Roosevelt kept his promise to assail Wilson's Mexican policy. In an article for the *New York Times*, laden with denunciations of the anti-clerical Mexican régime well calculated to stir up the American Catholic Church, he stated categorically that the American government should have recognized Huerta or at once announced a protectorate of the whole of Mexico.[10]

But before the Colonel had even written this article, his attention had fastened on a far greater quarrel and perhaps a greater issue. For in the early days of August the thread of peace drawn taut since Sarajevo had snapped, and once again Europe was at war. And by December the struggle which in July seemed of so little concern to America was already having serious repercussions in Congress, in the nation's industrial and financial institutions, and throughout the country at large. By that time the president had issued his appeal for neutrality of mind as well as act; the American government had instructed domestic financial institutions not to make loans to belligerents; Senator Hitchcock of Nebraska had introduced in Congress an embargo forbidding the shipment of arms and munitions to any warring power. By that time also the New York banks had succeeded in getting a revision of policy permitting them to make short-time loans to the Allies; an investigation had been demanded into the state of preparedness; the American Navy and American Security leagues had called for an increase of the American army to two million men and of the navy to twenty-four battleships. President Wilson had in turn assured the nation's people in his December message to Congress that our defenses were adequate and that there was no need to turn the country into an armed camp. The president of Columbia University had concurred by publicly stating that all the hysterical propaganda for preparedness might be traced "to a single inspiring

[9] Roosevelt to Albert B. Fall, December 8, 1914, Roosevelt MSS.
[10] *New York Times*, December 6, 1914.

source which had a business interest in preparedness."[11] By December issues revolving about the war had already been joined and the lines were forming fast.

Theodore Roosevelt was busy campaigning when the World War broke out in Europe. For over a week he remained silent on the great conflict. When he did speak publicly on August 5 he simply suggested that all Americans would support any public man who would try to preserve the country's honor and interests during the war period. There was not the faintest touch of partisanship for either side of the struggle. Privately he wrote that unfortunately the war was really inevitable and that each side from its own standpoint was right under the existing conditions of international relations. International law was beside the mark because there was no real homologue between national and international law. The power that made the first assault might in reality be acting on the defensive. The treaties guaranteeing the neutrality of Luxemburg and Belgium had seemingly been violated by Germany even before the fighting began. But, Roosevelt continued, "I am not prepared to say that in dire need the statesmen of a nation are not obliged to disregard any treaty if keeping it may mean the most serious jeopardy to the nation."[12] In the *Outlook* he emphasized that he was not taking a stand at that time on the treaty violations. "When giants are engaged in a death wrestle," he wrote, "as they reel to and fro they are certain to trample on whomever gets in the way of either." In August Roosevelt was not too much disturbed about the violations of Belgium.[13]

Three weeks later, however, after a Belgium mission had visited the United States, he had shifted ground. For while he still thought it possible to defend sincerely the position of either side in the war, one thing was evident and that was the complete innocence of Belgium. "If treaties are ever to amount to anything," he wrote, "then some efficient way

---

[11] *Ibid.*, December 10, 1914.
[12] Roosevelt to Hugo Münsterburg, August 8, 1914, Roosevelt MSS.
[13] *Outlook*, August 22, 1914.

must be designed for preventing the recurrence of the thing that has happened to Belgium." Moreover, a peace which left Belgium's wrongs unredressed "would not be a real peace."[14] And of course a redressing of Belgium's wrongs would mean some penalties against Germany even though Roosevelt insisted at the time that he was not passing judgment on that country one way or another.

But sympathy with Belgium, Roosevelt felt, should not in any way affect the international policy of this country. It was certainly eminently desirable that we remain entirely neutral, and nothing but urgent need would warrant breaking our neutrality. And then Roosevelt wrote a sentence that was to rise up to plague him later. "We have not the smallest responsibility," he wrote in the *Outlook*, "for what has befallen her." The only responsibility this country had was to profit by the example of Belgium. For it was manifest that pacifists were living in a fool's paradise. Treaties obviously afforded no protection unless armed force was behind them. The first duty of this country was to strengthen its defenses and the second to work for a world league backed by force.[15]

Thus until the middle of September Roosevelt had not publicly or in his correspondence said one positive word indicating his opinion on the war guilt unless his reference to the innocence of Belgium can be regarded as an indictment of Germany. But during the next two weeks Roosevelt rapidly aligned himself with the Allied cause. On October 3 he wrote the British ambassador Spring-Rice that had he been president at the outbreak of the war he would have accepted the Hague treaties guaranteeing Belgium's neutrality as a "serious" obligation upon all the signatory powers. He would have called on all neutral nations to aid the United States in enforcing them.[16] This statement was of course in direct contradiction to his earlier pronouncements upon America's ob-

[14] Roosevelt to Count Albert Apponyi, September 17, 1914, Roosevelt MSS.; *Outlook*, 108: 169–178 (September 23, 1914).

[15] *Ibid*. This was the first time that Roosevelt had mentioned a world league since his speech at Christiania in 1910.

[16] Roosevelt to Cecil Spring-Rice, October 3, 1914, Roosevelt MSS.

ligations. Had this doctrine been applied by the president it undoubtedly would have meant war with Germany.

In ten days Roosevelt had changed from an isolationist to an interventionist. And from then on his mind hardened rapidly on the issue. By the beginning of the new year he was convinced that the guilt for the war was entirely Germany's. Six months later he wrote an English friend that had he been president "in my judgment we would now have been fighting beside you."[17]

Meanwhile Roosevelt's attitude toward the Wilson-Bryan policy of neutrality became more wrathful with each passing day. Characterizing it as both stupid and timid, he considered it a policy unworthy of a great state. It was not even pure neutrality, he thought, but a tacit acceptance of international wrongdoing and hence unneutral toward the powers that were in the right. All in all, it clearly indicated the administration's utter incapacity to direct the nation's destiny in a time of international crisis. Some of Wilson's actions, Roosevelt believed, might be interpreted as pro-German. But that was too much even for an Englishman at war. Sir Edward Grey objected that both the president and Ambassador Page "had been strictly correct" in their international dealings.[18]

What explains this complete reversal of Roosevelt in less than a month? Other men before and after Roosevelt have shifted their ground completely on more stable issues than foreign policy, but seldom so decisively and so suddenly. Most of them have required months instead of days to make the mental transition.

The explanation probably lies in a multiplicity of factors. Certainly in the curious compound of Roosevelt's character the warrior strain was always close to the surface. Action had always been more natural than reflection. As an adolescent he had been ready to duel for the favor of a young lady, as a young man he had ridden off to Cuba with the gaiety

---

[17] Roosevelt to Arthur Lee, June 17, 1915, Roosevelt MSS.
[18] Confidential source.

and gusto of a Jeb Stuart riding to the North with roses in his hair. Twice between 1911 and 1914 he had talked about raising a troop of mounted infantry to invade Mexico, and when no war eventuated he substituted the Brazilian jungles for a human enemy. The bald fact was that Roosevelt liked war—its noise, its smoke, its action were a part of his soul. War made heroes, and Roosevelt had to be a hero. Had he been a nobody in a country village he would certainly have been a member of the volunteer fire department.

As an emotionalist Roosevelt had to take sides on any question. Every fiber of his being was partisan. During his presidency he had been suspicious of the actions of both England and Germany, but of the two he preferred England. Germany's policy of expansion had been more disquieting to the United States than England's policy of holding what she already had. Roosevelt's foreign friends, the people with whom he regularly corresponded, were English. Then too, from the viewpoint of 1914 Germany was undeniably the aggressor.

Early in November of 1914 a New York paper predicted that Roosevelt would seek to mend his political fortunes on the issues of preparedness and the war.[19] Roosevelt had certainly reached a political impasse. Progressivism, he thought, had run its course. The country was turning conservative, and in such a political atmosphere the Progressive party was doomed. To return to the Republican party with his hands empty of voters would have meant oblivion. What Roosevelt needed in 1914 to repair his prestige was an issue that would attract the non-partisan support of millions of his fellow Americans and particularly of his one-time fellow Republicans. For that purpose the war was heaven-sent.

Looking back, the pieces of the puzzle fall together very nicely. But was the completed picture chance or was it preconceived by one of the most astute political minds of the century? Unfortunately for the historian very few men, even in their most intimate moments, would confess to such cold

[19] *New York Times*, November 10, 1914.

practical causation for their actions, granted that they were aware of it. Most men would succeed in deluding even themselves. And as self-delusion over an unhappy memory came easily to Roosevelt, there can be no proof either way. Three facts are relevant. Roosevelt had given up hope for the Progressive party before the election of 1914. He sensed the national swing to conservatism, and before the European war started had indicated his plan to attack the administration's foreign policy. He was still politically ambitious.

One other factor remains: Roosevelt's hatred of Wilson. The two had little in common. Democrat and Republican, introvert and extrovert, scholar and activist, idealist and pragmatist, they were made of different clay. Both, however, were the religious descendants of John Calvin; both were certain they were of the elect and spoke with divine authority. In addition, Woodrow Wilson had presumed to be the progressive leader in the year that Roosevelt had chosen to lead the reforming hosts, and Wilson had won the election. Thereafter the successful translation of the New Freedom from theory to legislative fact had done much to destroy any chance of success the Progressive party might have had. Yet all that might have been passed over, if not forgiven, in Oyster Bay, had not Wilson committed the unforgivable. By suggesting that reparations be paid to Colombia he was officially acknowledging that Roosevelt had been guilty of bad international manners in the Panama incident. And in 1914, if one accepted the Wilson interpretation, the parallel between Belgium and Panama was too close to make the subject completely academic. William Howard Taft had once questioned the actions and the motives of his predecessor in a suit against the United States Steel Corporation and had been roughly handled for his pains. Wilson's slip was to receive no less attention than Taft's. Eventually Roosevelt was to forget the first slight because of the second. By December, 1914, Roosevelt was charging that Wilson and Bryan were the worst leaders the country had ever had. "I really believe," he wrote, "that I would rather have Murphy, Penrose or Barnes as the standard bearer of this nation."[20]

Such was the probable mixture of motives that impelled Roosevelt in his war policy. Which was the most important no man can decide with certainty. But it is probable that Roosevelt would have been on the Allied side from the beginning whoever lived in the White House and whatever the administration's policy. He would certainly have been for sweeping enlargements of this country's defense forces. For Roosevelt was first of all a sincere patriot. But his patriotism and his bias for the Allies do not explain his emotional intensity in hurrying America into the war. That can only be construed in the light of his burning aversion for Wilson.

The thing was double-edged. His hatred of Wilson made him more pro-Ally, and his Allied bias furnished fuel for that hatred. At any rate, his convictions about the war were soon beyond the point of argument. England and France were "standing for humanity and civilization"; Germany fought for the forces of evil.[21] By the spring of 1915 Roosevelt was swallowing and reprinting all of the common run of atrocity stories. After the *Lusitania* was torpedoed on May 7, he was ready to believe almost anything of the German nation. "The American who defends the action taken against Belgium, or who fails to condemn it," he wrote in October of 1915, "is unworthy to live in a free country, or to associate with men of lofty soul and generous temper." The first German crime of "unforgiveable treachery" had led to every "succeeding infamy from terrorism and indiscriminant slaughter on land to massacre of non-combatants at sea."[22]

This being his point of view, Roosevelt naturally had no sympathy with a policy of neutrality. America had been guilty of condoning a crime by its "recreant silence" after

[20] Roosevelt to Henry C. Lodge, December 8, 1914, in Lodge, *Letters*, 2: 450.
[21] Roosevelt, "International Duty and Hyphenated Americanism," *Metropolitan*, 42: 2–8 (October; 1915).
[22] *Ibid.*, sentence transposed.

Germany's violation of the Hague treaty, to which the United States was a signatory. We could make amends for our reprehensible conduct only by positive action in the future. The United States had the right to sell arms and munitions to both sides, but it was immoral to help Germany win, whereas it was "highly moral" to aid the Allies.[23]

On those who did not see eye to eye with him Roosevelt did not spare the lash. He dismissed the pacificists and "the peace-at-any-price" men by shouting that they had done more harm to this country "than all the crookedness in business and politics combined."[24] Many of his opponents, he intimated, were American citizens of German birth who were attempting to bring about an order of "unadulterated mischief and evil to the United States." These hyphenates were stirring up labor trouble in the United States and were organizing to formulate the foreign policy of the United States in the interest of certain belligerent nations. He accused members of Congress of being in touch with the embassies of foreign nations and of carrying on activities in the interest of those nations.[25] Calling for "Straight United States," Roosevelt branded as outrageous any action designed to shape American policy to favor a foreign power.[26] Whereupon he privately urged the English government to recall Lord Bryce, who was in this country interpreting England's position to the American public. The great Englishman was far too impartial for Roosevelt. "I had hoped that Lord Bryce would make an argument to America that could tend to clarify the American sentiment and put it on the side of the Allies and against Germany," he wrote a friend who was departing for England, "but I really think now that the best thing he can do is not to open his mouth again."[27]

But people who did not care to fight, Americans of German

[23] *Ibid.*

[24] Roosevelt, "Peace Insurance by Preparedness," *Metropolitan*, 42: 10–12 (August, 1915).

[25] Roosevelt, "The Need of Preparedness," *Metropolitan*, 41:14–16 (April, 1915).

[26] *Ibid.; New York Times*, October 13, 1915.

[27] Roosevelt to Robert Bacon, March 29, 1915, Roosevelt MSS.

extraction, and more or less objective Englishmen were all of secondary importance to Roosevelt. His first concern was the hesitant administration and its policy. And for the rest of his life he became its self-appointed scourge. Through the monthly issues of the *Metropolitan* magazine, which had signed him up in December of 1914 to write a minimum of fifty thousand words a year for twenty-five thousand dollars, on the stump, and in private letters, he unceasingly castigated the president. A Cato crying of Carthage could have been no more zealous, no more persistent.

After the sinking of the *Lusitania* Roosevelt demanded that the American government prohibit all commerce with Germany at once and in turn encourage intercourse with England and France.[28] When Wilson refused to follow the suggestion and insisted upon writing notes of protest, Roosevelt's contempt was boundless. In an address delivered at the Plattsburg training camp by invitation of Major General Leonard Wood, he condemned the official policy of "elocution as a substitute for action," charged that the administration had done nothing for the defense of the nation, and inferred that it was high time that the country put a wrong president right. When subsequently the secretary of war officially reprimanded Wood for permitting Roosevelt to make a political speech at a training camp, the Colonel labelled the action as "buffoonery."[29]

One of Roosevelt's points Wilson answered directly in his annual address to Congress on December 8, 1915, by proposing to increase the standing army to about 140,000 men, with a supplementary "Continental" enlisted force of 400,000 men. He further proposed that the navy be increased so that by 1921 the fleet would consist of twenty-seven battleships and their necessary complements. Roosevelt's name was not mentioned in the speech, but the discerning saw in one of its paragraphs a reprimand directed toward Oyster Bay. Wilson had been speaking of the alien troublemakers of the country. "Some men among us," he said, "have so far forgotten them-

[28] *New York Times*, May 12, 1915.
[29] *Ibid.*, August 26, 27, 28, 1915.

selves and their honor as citizens as to put their passionate sympathy with one or the other side in the great European conflict above their regard for the peace and dignity of the United States." In doing so, the president added, they also preached and practised disloyalty.[30]

What Roosevelt thought of being classed with disloyal aliens was never set down, but it can be gauged from his reaction to the message. Privately he felt that the administration was "all wrong on the navy" and "ninety-five per cent wrong on the army." Publicly he criticized the plan as offering no encouragement to industrial preparedness. The continental army idea was a farce; what was needed was conscription. As for the rest of the president's elocution, it was that of a "Byzantine logothete."[31] From the epithet historical Roosevelt soon descended to downright malevolence. Before the end of January, 1916, he had called Wilson a Micawber, characterized his policy as one of "sordid baseness," and spoken of his "dishonorable conduct."[32]

Privately Roosevelt had begun, as early as the spring of 1915, to doubt the personal and public honesty of the administration leaders. In January the malevolent Lodge, always ready to believe the worst of the opposition, wrote to his friend that the desire behind the administration's ship purchase bill was not to aid the Germans but something much worse. William Gibbs McAdoo, he stated, was a friend of Kuhn, Loeb and Company, who were in turn connected with German shipping lines. "The indications all point to a job," ran Lodge's accusation, "in which McAdoo and some other of the President's close friends are involved."[33] Soon Roosevelt was writing that Wilson and the men around him had utterly failed in their duty to their country, partly from timidity and folly, partly from even worse unspecified

[30] *Ibid.*, December 8, 1915.
[31] Roosevelt to Lodge, February 4, 1916, Roosevelt MSS.; *New York Times*, December 8, 1915.
[32] *Ibid.*, January 31, 1916.
[33] Henry C. Lodge to Roosevelt, January 15, 1915, Roosevelt MSS.

causes.[34] At the same time he was charging that the administration's neutrality policy was a blind behind which Wilson and his friends were really seeking to aid the Central Powers. "With great dexterity and adroitness" they had done all that they could "to influence American public opinion against the Allies and in favor of Germany." All of this, Roosevelt ended, in the face of "our duty to England."[35]

War and its accompanying hysteria often does strange things to the human being. Sometimes it drains away the dross, sometimes reason and perspective. Upon Roosevelt's character it seemed to operate both ways simultaneously. The great war summoned up in him a shining spirit of sacrifice and patriotism; at the same time it stripped him of his sense of proportion and fairness. Woodrow Wilson was not only an American in 1915 but he was, if anything, pro-English. And yet he engendered only hatred and suspicion in Roosevelt's soul. This animosity grew as the months passed until it reached the point of mental aberration. It was Roosevelt against Wilson; immemorial right against irremediable wrong. For one of Roosevelt's friends to defend Wilson's policy was to be disloyal to their friendship. In that sense only was there a grain of truth in Franklin K. Lane's observation that Roosevelt "hates Wilson so, that he has lost his mind."[36]

[34] Roosevelt to Mrs. Cornelius Vanderbilt, 1915 (no other date), Roosevelt MSS.

[35] Roosevelt to St. Loe Strachey, March 25, 1915, Roosevelt MSS.

[36] Herbert Croly to Roosevelt, January 11, 1915, Roosevelt MSS.; Lane, *Letters*, 188.

CHAPTER THIRTEEN

New Directions

BETWEEN 1914 and the date of America's entrance into
the World War, Roosevelt focussed most of his interventionist criticism upon the Wilson administration. But neither the
Republican party nor his own Progressive organization wholly
supported his position. In fact, some of the most militant
opposition to any American entanglement in European affairs
was voiced by Progressives. Leaders of the Roosevelt movement, which had served as a magnet for many footloose reformers and idealists in the country, were to find, as Wilson
and a second Roosevelt found later, that many people with
these convictions do not at once jump for a gun in times of
international stress. Humanitarianism and war's barbarism
are at antipodal poles of social action. Moreover, the reformers of 1914, remembering the Civil War, had reason to
fear that a wave of militarism in the country would set back
social progress for a generation. As for the Progressive party,
there may have been some truth in Roosevelt's own explanation of its bent toward peace. The party, according to its
founder, had attracted large numbers of German-Americans
because they could understand better than native Americans
the industrial and economic programs of the Progressives.[1]
Whatever the reason, there were countless party members
who agreed with Albert J. Beveridge, Amos Pinchot, and
Jane Addams that America should stick to her own domestic
knitting and leave international military crusades alone.

To Roosevelt such sentiments were treasonable to the
party and to himself. For the out-and-out anti-militarists
like Amos Pinchot and Jane Addams he had nothing but

[1] Roosevelt to H. C. Lodge, February 4, 1916, and to Winston Churchill,
undated, Roosevelt MSS.

scorn and anger. When asked to take part in welcoming Jane Addams and her companions back from her peace trip to Europe, he exploded, "They have not shown the smallest particle of courage; and all their work has been done to advance the cause of international cowardice; and anyone who greets them or applauds them is actively engaged in advancing that cause."[2]

The Colonel kept his peace with Beveridge, who was explaining the war as a natural European development born of the industrial revolution, but the old cordiality between the two men had disappeared. Privately Roosevelt thought of him as pro-German: "The editorials of *Collier's* cordially back up Wilson and Bryan and make Beveridge's articles the greatest display feature of the magazine; and therefore the whole to me is pro-German and anti-ally."[3]

As time went on, Roosevelt was increasingly impressed with the strength of the anti-war wing of the Progressive party. On a trip to the West he found that the two leading anti-preparedness papers on the coast were Progressive papers. And at the same time he heard that large sections of the party were deserting him on the war issue. Finally he came to agree with Henry Cabot Lodge "that the worst crowd we have to deal with is the progressive senators and their followers."[4]

As he withdrew from the "reforming crowd" because of its anti-war and preparedness feelings, Roosevelt became increasingly congenial with the supporters of the status quo in domestic politics. As the country's leading advocate of preparedness it was natural for him to cooperate with the many patriotic organizations that had been formed throughout the nation. Though the conservative elements had no monopoly on patriotism, they were in almost complete control of the so-called patriotic organizations. Names like J. P. Morgan, Perry Belmont, Henry C. Frick, George R. Sheldon, Robert

[2] Roosevelt to Henry Green, July 2, 1915, Roosevelt MSS.
[3] Roosevelt to Gifford Pinchot, March 29, 1915, and to William Dudley Foulke, December 2, 1914, Roosevelt MSS.
[4] Roosevelt to Henry C. Lodge, February 4, 1916, Roosevelt MSS.

Bacon, and Samuel Insull appeared frequently in the lists of the boards of directors and heaviest contributors to the Navy League of the United States, the National Security League, the American Defense Society, the American Legion, and the National Society for the Advancement of Patriotic Education. At least seven of the directors of the Navy League in 1915 were in some way connected with the firm of J. P. Morgan and Company. On the national committee of the National Defense Society, which combined in its platform a proposal for universal military service and a demand for government cooperation with business, were the chief executives of nine of the nation's leading industrial and financial institutions.

Roosevelt had a successful politician's happy faculty of meeting prize fighters and poets, stevedores and statesmen, on their own level. Mirrorlike, his basic nature was inclined to reflect the color of his surroundings. While leading the drive for national preparedness and friendship with the Allies, he saw less of his reforming friends and more of his one-time conservative foes, and inevitably his opinion of the latter began to change. He acquired "respect" for Perry Belmont. He had dinner with Frick, Gary, and other tycoons and liked them. His estimation of their political counterparts likewise changed. Names long absent from his correspondence and his appointment book began to reappear. Here was a cordial letter to Senator Smoot of Utah, there an exchange of views with ex-senators Crane of Massachusetts and Aldrich of Rhode Island. For three years the letters between Nahant and Oyster Bay had been short and non-political; now they were filled with long discussions of the shortcomings and knavery of the opposition. Throughout 1915 the men of great wealth were slowly changing their spots, were being transfigured from malefactors to benefactors, and the 1912 charges of thievery against the Republican directorate were becoming perceptibly blurred.[5]

[5] Roosevelt to Elbert H. Gary, June 5, 1915, to Joseph B. Bishop, May 14, 1915, and to Reed Smoot, August 1, 1915, letters to Roosevelt from

If Roosevelt was changing his mind about the conservatives, they too seemed to be experiencing something of a conversion. There were, of course, those who still remembered Armageddon with bitterness and muttered about the eternal damnation of apostasy. But others were apparently willing to forgive and forget. In October, 1915, the *Republican National Magazine* carried articles by James R. Mann, Charles W. Fairbanks, and Myron T. Herrick which approached the subject of Theodore Roosevelt with a gentleness of spirit that did not go unnoticed by either the Progressives or the Republicans. Some of the Progressives were frankly suspicious that Roosevelt was already making plans to combine with the Republicans in 1916 whatever the cost to the Progressive party and to Progressive politicians.[6]

They were at least partially right. For as early as a year before the presidential nominations, Roosevelt had made up his mind that barring a political upheaval there should be no Progressive ticket in 1916. His one aim throughout the two years before the election was to remove Wilson from the presidency, and that could scarcely be done by a divided Republican party. Week in and week out he preached this to his friends with an eloquent persistence. In international affairs Wilson and Bryan were "more dangerous than Murphy or Sullivan or Barnes and Penrose."[7] He would vote to put in even a man like Root rather "than to continue Bryan and Wilson at the head of the government." If the Republicans did worse than that he would "go fishing." Only if the Republicans nominated Taft would he cast a "conscience vote" for a third candidate and that with no intention of electing the man or of founding a third party. These sentiments he made known not only to his Progressive intimates but even to men in the Republican party. He was trying, he wrote to Henry Cabot Lodge, to get all the Progressives back of the

Frederick Hale, March 8, 1915, and Albert B. Fall, December 21, 1915, Roosevelt MSS.

[6] *New York Times*, October 10, 1915.

[7] Roosevelt to Raymond Robins, June 3, 1915, Roosevelt MSS.

Republican party in their fight to drive Wilson and Bryan from power.[8]

Throughout the summer of 1915 and into the autumn Roosevelt was busy taking political soundings and discussing the availability of various Republican hopefuls. His letters to Lodge, Nicholas Longworth, and Medill McCormick were studded with speculations about high-ranking Republicans. Personal messages were exchanged between the Colonel and Boies Penrose, the Pennsylvania representative extraordinary of standpatism. Senators Fall and Borah were consulted. But for the talk, little or nothing was decided.[9] Roosevelt made it clear that he could in no way support Taft. Knox, he felt, had been defending hyphenated Americans too much. John W. Weeks was too conservative. Theodore E. Burton, excluded because of his position on national defense, was a less desirable candidate than Root. However, Root was unavailable because the Progressives would not vote for him; he would be a splendid choice for secretary of state in the new Cabinet. Hiram Johnson would be fine, but Roosevelt was sure the Republicans would not accept him. Perhaps Albert B. Cummins, Herbert S. Hadley, or Charles Evans Hughes would be the man. Of the three, Roosevelt temporarily seemed to prefer Hadley, though he did "not like his attitude at all in 1912."[10]

All this might suggest that Roosevelt had no personal ambitions in the 1916 elections and was mainly interested in settling upon a man that both Republicans and Progressives could support. Such was far from the truth. Ambition was a part of the man's inner core, and the desire to reside at 1700 Pennsylvania Avenue again was always with him. "Perhaps you won't misunderstand me," he wrote in February, 1915,

[8] Roosevelt to Gifford Pinchot, March 29, 1915, to Raymond Robins, August 6, 1915, and to Henry C. Lodge, undated, Roosevelt MSS.

[9] Roosevelt to Henry C. Lodge, November 27, 1915, and to Nicholas Longworth, November 8, 1915, Roosevelt MSS.

[10] Roosevelt to Charles G. Washburn, June 23, 1915, to Nicholas Longworth, June 4, 1915, to Angus McSween, November 27, 1915, to Lodge,

"when I say that I wish I were at the head of affairs just to deal with Mexico and this whole European business."[11] His confidant, a hardheaded newspaperman who knew Roosevelt quite well, probably understood perfectly. Roosevelt had written far too many letters explaining at far too great a length why he could not get the Republican nomination and why, if he should get it, he would be defeated, to mislead any of his really close admirers. He was out to defeat Wilson first. If by some hook or crook he were the man to do it, so much the better. But it would have to be done on the Republican ticket without Progressive opposition, and in the summer and fall of 1915 Roosevelt saw only a faint hope of securing the Republican nomination. "It is my deliberate judgment that if the Republicans are ever found to entertain the thought of nominating me next year, it will be because they know they will be defeated under me . . . thereby not only smashing the Progressives but definitely getting rid of me and enthroning standpatism in the Republican party."[12] Thus he was willing to talk of others and, in the event the lightning did not strike him, secure the best compromise he could get from the rulers of the Republican party.

To realize these purposes by means of practical politics was difficult. First Roosevelt had to have something to bargain with when convention time approached. So by all odds the Progressive party must be held together as a unit. On the other hand, the Progressive leaders must not be too aloof and stir up more hostility among the Republicans. Some spirit of a willingness to compromise needed to be evident. And yet that could not be too obvious lest the rank and file of the party, sensing the final outcome, return to the Republican party before the propitious moment. Moreover, it would be most convenient for Roosevelt's own personal candidacy

December 7, 1915, to Longworth, November 8, 1914, to George E. Miller, December 27, 1915, and to Hiram Johnson, December 26, 1915, Roosevelt MSS.

[11] Roosevelt to Calvin O'Laughlin, February (?), 1915, Roosevelt MSS.
[12] Roosevelt to George W. Perkins, September 3, 1915, Roosevelt MSS.

if some trusted friend could be found within the Republican party. In short, the game was to pursue without seeming to, with the general objective of being pursued.

On the surface the moves of that game were likely to appear contradictory. In the summer and fall of 1915 it seemed as though the remaining part of the Progressive party was leaderless and moving in twenty different directions. Roosevelt, while knifing Wilson and hammering for preparedness, was discreetly silent on politics. George Perkins, on the contrary, was straining every faculty to prevent desertions from the party in New York and elsewhere.[13] Meanwhile many of the professional politicians of the party had announced their return to Republicanism and were busy carrying on extended correspondence with Oyster Bay. Men like Medill McCormick and Senator Poindexter could possibly be of great use in the Republican party if a Roosevelt boom ever seriously got started there. When asked publicly about the movement back to the Republican party, Roosevelt advised the Progressives to stay put, but was noticeably mild in his comments upon the already departed. "It has been fine of them to have made the great fight that they have made during the past three years for Progressive principles, and I am sure they are acting conscientiously," Roosevelt remarked.[14]

In mid-July it was decided at a Progressive conference in New York to allow the party in each state to determine for itself whether to run local tickets in 1915 or to fuse with the Republicans. Under no circumstances, however, was the party to disband or sacrifice its identity. Even before this time Roosevelt had written his party chieftains that common action with the Republicans in those states where it was possible might be the best course for the immediate future.[15] Beveridge, who had suspected the drift of affairs since the summer of 1914, took these actions as final evidence that the

[13] *New York Times*, August 6, 1915; George W. Perkins to J. A. H. Hopkins, August 9, October 2, 1915, Roosevelt MSS.

[14] *New York Times*, August 3, 1915, Roosevelt MSS.

[15] Roosevelt to Gifford Pinchot, June 1, 1915, and to Medill McCormick, June 10, 1915, Roosevelt MSS.

Colonel was ready to go back to the old party "on his own terms and in his own interest." Beveridge was not alone in this judgment. "It is very evident," William Howard Taft reflected, "that T.R. is taking a running jump back into the party."[16]

Early in September, possibly under the retrospective influence of autumn, Roosevelt wrote Perkins a letter that followed a previous pattern. Certainly his advice to Perkins not to do or say anything which might be interpreted by his Republican friends as a play for the Republican nomination rings a familiar tone. Only four years ago he had written just such letters filled with the same admonitions and the same reasons therefor. It had been perfectly evident to him then, as it was now, that the people were tired of his leadership, that they were against his policies and resented him personally, and that his political star had set for an indeterminate time.[17] In the autumn of 1911 he had changed his mind in the space of three months. In 1915 and 1916 the process was to take longer, but in the end the conversion was to occur again. Whether by Roosevelt's own direction or by that of the Progressive chieftains, a national poll, starting in early November, was taken of most of the important state Progressive leaders in the country. They were asked two questions by Meyer Lissner, head of the Progressive party machine in California. How many Progressives had gone back to the Republican party and *what chance did the Progressives have of controlling the selection of delegates in the next Republican national convention?* The answers to those delicate questions were all carefully forwarded to Roosevelt and by a five to four margin they indicated a belief that Roosevelt could secure the state delegations if he wanted to.[18]

Meanwhile George W. Perkins had left New York for a

[16] Bowers, *Beveridge*, 485–486; Taft to Helen H. Taft, April 10, 1915, in Pringle, *Taft*, 2: 889.

[17] Roosevelt to George W. Perkins, September 3, 1915, Roosevelt MSS.

[18] The replies to Lissner's questions were dated from November 15 to November 17. Copies of the original are to be found in the Roosevelt MSS.

swing through the Middle West and South to sample opinion and to attend Progressive meetings in those sections. There is some evidence that Perkins was not confining his politicing to the Progressive party. One former Progressive, at that time a Republican, wrote Roosevelt protesting against Perkins' inept plan to capture the Republican delegation in Michigan and Indiana. "Borah can do more in the open," Medill McCormick observed, "than Perkins can do underground."[19] But the financial godfather of the party, oblivious to or unimpressed with such criticism, sent back an optimistic report on his travels. The people of the nation were disturbed about the lack of preparedness, he found, as they had not been since the days of the Civil War. By next year the party lines would be wiped out and the people would be looking "for the man who is best equipped to do their work for them."[20]

Was Roosevelt interested? Not in so many words did he say so, but there were many indications that he was. Apparently he asked Lodge whether in his opinion he stood any chance of being nominated by the Republican party. Lodge replied in a vein calculated at once to mollify and to discourage. He would like nothing better than to see Roosevelt become president again, but he doubted that it would be possible "under the existing circumstances." In this situation the only thing for them both to do, since their first duty was to the country, was "to remove this administration from power." That could only be accomplished if both the Progressive and Republican party would combine upon a candidate acceptable to both. Two days later in another long letter Lodge said he believed Hughes was that man, for there was less opposition to him from all elements in both parties.[21]

In July of 1915, while talking to reporters at Portland, Oregon, Roosevelt had stated that if the Republicans should

[19] Letters to Roosevelt from Herbert S. Hadley, November 23, 1915, and Medill McCormick, November 24, 1915, Roosevelt MSS.; George W. Perkins to Charles S. Bonaparte, November 23, 1915, Bonaparte MSS.
[20] George W. Perkins to Roosevelt, December 3, 1915, Roosevelt MSS.
[21] Henry C. Lodge to Roosevelt, December 2, 1915, Roosevelt MSS.

nominate Justice Hughes for president, "it would be proper for us to support him. Our progressive idea could be embraced in such a candidacy."[22] Now four months later in conceding Hughes's availability he had some mental reservations: "There is, however, a considerable feeling that it is not wise to establish a very bad precedent and take a candidate from the Supreme Court."[23] Such protective reverence for the highest judicial body in the nation from a confirmed breaker of precedents and a man who had been consistently hostile to the Court must have been a source of worry to the masters of the Republican party. Had they known that the Progressive National Executive Committee had decided not to put Roosevelt's name into the Republican primaries, they would have regained their peace of mind.[24] But a Roosevelt letter of December 21, 1915, would have raised their fears once more. "You are entirely right in your statement that it would be useless to precipitate an open fight again," that significant document began. Roosevelt by all odds did not want to give "the entirely erroneous impression" that he was receptively a candidate. He would be gratified, however, if it could be made known that there was a "growth of sentiment in favor of my ideas and of what I stand for." Perhaps the best thing to do at the time was "to encourage that growth of sentiment." But for an open declaration—no. "I have had enough of announcing unalterable decisions in public," he had ruefully written some time before.[25]

As the new year of 1916 opened, future events were casting their shadows across the United States. The Allied cause to which this country was already so deeply committed emotionally looked none too bright. The British were just withdrawing from the blood-soaked Gallipoli Peninsula, and Eng-

---

[22] *New York Times*, July 20, 1915.

[23] Roosevelt to Henry C. Lodge, December 17, 1915, in Lodge, *Correspondence*, 2: 468.

[24] Typewritten Minutes of the Executive Committee of the Progressive National Committee, November 30, 1915, Roosevelt MSS.

[25] Roosevelt to Frank Knox, December 21, 1915, and to Raymond Robins, June 3, 1915, Roosevelt MSS.

WITHOUT MOVING THE HAT
Cartoon by Harding in the *Brooklyn Eagle*, reproduced in the
Literary Digest, January 8, 1916.

land had enacted its first compulsory military service law.
To the south of the Rio Grande the Mexican situation gave
every indication of an impending explosion. On January 10
nineteen United States citizens were taken from a Mexican
train and murdered. A week later Theodore Roosevelt's
friend, Major General Leonard Wood, in testifying before a
Senate committee, called for compulsory service as the only
way to build an army adequate for protection in a warring
world.

In such an atmosphere the Progressive National Committee met on January 11 to map fateful plans for the future.
Already the inner directorate of the party had agreed to hold
the Progressive convention simultaneously with the Republican meeting. And despite widespread disapproval of the
plan they were determined to bind the committee to that

course. Medill McCormick, Charles J. Bonaparte, Roosevelt's old attorney general, Albert J. Beveridge, and Matthew Hale of Maine, among others, had registered strong protests, but the die had been cast with Roosevelt's approval, and so the committee agreed. Explaining the action to the public, George Perkins declared that he was hoping that the Progressive and the Republican parties would agree on a candidate and "it will not necessarily have to be the Colonel."[26]

The public statement issued by the committee was a further bid for reconciliation. Reaffirming in one sentence the Progressive principles of 1912 as vital to the national well-being, the document then ran on for two pages, denouncing the conduct of foreign affairs by the Wilson administration. The party sought "leadership for Americanism" and pledged itself earnestly to work with the Republicans "to choose the same standard bearer and the same principles." In conclusion it assured the Progressive faithful that their leaders would not surrender Progressive principles to the party bosses.[27]

After reading the statement, however, some members of the party wanted to know what principles were left to surrender. The incorrigible New Jersey reformer, George L. Record, referring to the slighting of the 1912 program, labelled the committee action as "the most cynical and contemptible abandonment of principles by so-called leaders" that this country had ever witnessed. As if to give point to some of Record's criticism the deep-dyed Republican *New York Sun* rejoiced that "a platform could be drafted in harmony with Republican principles and traditions in which virtually every paragraph of the statement issued at Chicago might be included. And after reading the report even the

[26] George W. Perkins to Meyer Lissner, November 16, 1915, letters to Roosevelt from Medill McCormick, December 29, 1915, and to Perkins, January 19, 1916, and typewritten Minutes of the Progressive National Committee, January 11, 1916, Roosevelt MSS.; Albert J. Beveridge to John C. Schaeffer, December 23, 1915, in Bowers, *Beveridge*, 481; Charles J. Bonaparte to Roosevelt, January 2, 1916, and to N. Winslow Williams, January 3, 1916, Bonaparte MSS.

[27] Minutes of the Progressive National Committee, January 11, 1916, Roosevelt MSS.

most cautious commentators concluded that the Bull Moose was shedding his progressive antlers.[28]

Why had the inner circle of the party decided upon the simultaneous convention plan? No reasons are given in the Roosevelt manuscripts. Years later O. K. Davis, the party secretary, wrote that it was done to confuse the Republicans about the real Progressive intentions and to mislead them into the belief "that the Colonel would accept another Progressive nomination, which they knew would be tantamount to insuring the re-election of President Wilson."[29] In the face of such a possibility those in control of the Republican party might be more ready to negotiate a bargain. At best they might even accept Roosevelt; at worst a Republican in whom Roosevelt had confidence. In addition, a simultaneous convention offered the best chance to quell dissidence in the Progressive party. In a convention previous or subsequent to the Republican gathering, the delegates might get out of hand and insist upon a separate nomination. They might disregard their leaders if Roosevelt should refuse the honor, perhaps even nominate another man.

At the same time that the Progressive party was striking out in new directions, its leader was also shifting his sails. Back in the summer of 1914 Roosevelt had explained the lack of party success in terms of the nation's disposition, after a decade of liberalism, to turn conservative and have done with reformers. Since that time his utterances, public and private, had become increasingly conservative. As he became more interested in rearmament he rapidly forgot the promises of 1912. To that extent the January statement of the Progressive party simply reflected Roosevelt's own changing mental bent.

This change in Roosevelt was apparent as early as the opening of 1915, and by September he was writing in the *Metropolitan* magazine that "the very worst policy that can

[28] *Nation*, January 27, 1916; *New York Sun*, January 12, 13, 1916; *New York Times*, January 12, 1916; George W. Perkins to J. A. H. Hopkins, January 21, 1916, Roosevelt MSS.

[29] O. K. Davis, *Released for Publication*, 448–449.

be pursued by this nation is a policy of harassing and jeopardizing business so as to impoverish and damage it." For, Roosevelt continued, no great industrial well being could come unless big business prospered. In the same year he wrote confidentially of Nelson W. Aldrich's contribution to public life. On the whole Aldrich "was a much better man from the standpoint of the country at large" than La Follette. A few months later he observed that the Socialist papers were without exception the most mendacious and sensational papers" in the country, and muckrakers were more "conscienceless and more indifferent to truth" than any save a very few of the capitalists. These opinions, of course, were held by many honest and intelligent men in 1915, but they sounded strange indeed coming from the expounder of the New Nationalism.[30]

Throughout the new year of 1916 Roosevelt continued judiciously to mix preparedness and conservatism. He defended the munition-makers and their huge profits[31] on the ground that they were doing infinitely more for the country than their critics were. The men calling for government ownership were not in earnest but were merely seeking "an excuse to divert the controversy from preparedness." On January 6, at a meeting of the National Defense League, he demanded a conscripted army of over two million and a navy of at least forty-eight dreadnaughts.[32]

There was no question in Roosevelt's mind now but that the "dreadful, the unspeakably hideous, outrages" committed against the Belgians were done at the "express command of the German government." In a world where such

[30] Roosevelt, "Encourage Business and Control It," *Metropolitan*, 42: 10–11, 74; Roosevelt to Winston Churchill, August 4, 1915, and to Charles G. Washburn, March 31, 1915, Roosevelt MSS.

[31] The net earnings of the E. I. du Pont de Nemours and Company increased from $5,603,153 in 1914 to $57,840,758 in 1915. After fixed charges were deducted a balance of $55,542,275 was available for distribution to stockholders, a sum equalling 94 per cent of the value of the company's common stock. *New York Sun*, February 27, 1916.

[32] Roosevelt to William Hard, January 11, 1916, Roosevelt MSS.; *New York Sun*, January 6, 1916.

deeds were daily occurrences it "was of no use talking about reform and social justice" until the country was able to protect itself from outside attack. In building up an adequate war machine the cooperation of industry was one of the first essentials. England had been weak in industrial preparedness in that she had no machinery "by which industry could be mobilized and the good will of labor mobilized, and the ill will of the refractory among *laboring men* and among all other classes repressed."[33]

In an article, "Fear God and Take Your Own Part," which appeared in the March 1916 issue of the *Metropolitan*, Roosevelt summed up his ideas on the relationship between business and government in the new world. It is noteworthy that he started off by an attack upon demagogues as enemies of social progress. Still consistent, however, with a part of his 1912 program, he advocated controlled cooperation in place of competition. But it was to be a mild, benevolent control and a rational one, not by the states but by the national government in the interest of greater "efficiency along German lines." Too much of the regulating in the past had been by demagogues or by heedless politicians interested in their own monetary or political success, so that the very name regulation "had become an offence and an abomination to many honest business men."

One main effort of the reformers, Roosevelt continued, had been to punish the railroads for their past sin of over-capitalization. Since the past criminals could not be reached, the legislation rested most heavily upon innocent people. The new regulation he was proposing provided "certain types of public service and certain types of action toward . . . employees," but it also guaranteed "*as a first charge a certain minimum profit to the investor.*" In fact, any regulation, whether in the interest of the public, of labor, or of the

[33] Roosevelt, "Awake and Prepare," *Metropolitan*, 43:12–13, 70–72 (February, 1916); "America First, a Phrase or a Fact," *ibid.*, 43:12–13 (January, 1916); "Fear God and Take Your Own Part," *ibid.*, 43:11–12 (March, 1916).

farmer, which failed to leave business a "reasonable profit" created a situation "far more intolerable than that which it endeavored to remedy." No government commission was worth its salt, said Roosevelt in conclusion, that did not stand "unflinchingly against any popular clamor which prevents the corporation from getting ample profit."[34]

Right up to convention time Roosevelt continued to hammer out his views along these lines. Gone was the 1912 song of the dispossessed. Gone was the emphasis upon the evil deeds of the malefactors of great wealth. "New times demand new issues and new men." Roosevelt was listening now to the Perkinses, the Garys, the Whitneys, the Belmonts. And in a speech in early June he came close to repeating their advice verbatim. Late in 1915 he had received letters from George W. Perkins and certain other people urging a "nationalization" of business. "The best side of Germany's so-called culture," according to Perkins, was the way that she had "taken care of her working classes while at the same time taking care of her business interests." "You know that Germany in securing its foreign trade," the financier continued, "sends out its corporations with National existence backed up with National help and prestige. How can our corporations hope to get anywhere in the future international struggle with only the backing of a state?" Another friend put the idea more bluntly in asking for national incorporation of all business. "As our investments flow into foreign countries where they must be backed, if necessary, by the military power of the country, this becomes imperative." And Roosevelt apparently accepted this synthesis of industrial nationalism, for in his last speech before the June conventions at Newark he called for an "Americanization of our industries" with which to confront Europe after the war. Thus Roosevelt's regulatory master state was not only to secure for industry "ample" domestic profits but was from time to time to make its diplomatic and military power felt abroad in their inter-

[34] *Ibid.*, 11–12, 70.

est. Philander C. Knox's concept of a Latin-American dollar diplomacy had been swept to the ends of the world.[35]

"There is a good deal of T. R. sentiment, some of it in rather unexpected places," Charles J. Bonaparte noted to a friend early in 1916. A little later Lincoln Steffens was writing that "Wall Street is for T. R."[36] This statement was too sweeping, but there was more than one grain of truth in it. For increasingly as Roosevelt had swung to the right, the men of property had become more friendly. During the progressive years of the Colonel's career Wall Street letterheads appeared only rarely in his incoming mail; after the great conversion they came in sizeable numbers. Wooed by the enticing combination of patriotism and conservatism, financiers and industrialists wrote not only to admire but in many instances to support this former pariah. By March Joseph H. Choate could raise a great cheer in a Wall Street gathering by mentioning the name of Roosevelt. By May twenty-five hundred "Pilgrims" led by the presidents of the Lackawanna Steel Company, the Central Trust Company of New York, and the Casualty Company of America could trudge the dusty road to Oyster Bay to pay homage to a great patriot. A short time before, thirteen Detroit industrialists, officials of the Timkin Axle and the Chalmers, Cadillac, Paige, and Hudson motor companies, signed a petition pledging their support to him for the presidency.[37]

Where such "safe men" led, the conservative press could follow. Calling Roosevelt a remarkable man who had early seen the needs of his country, the *Bankers' Magazine* prophesied that either he or Hughes would be the Republican nominee. The *New York Sun* added its voice of approval in May and in the same month the *New York Tribune* editorially pledged its support. But the clearest admission of conserva-

[35] George W. Perkins to Roosevelt, November 29, 1915, Roosevelt MSS.; *New York Times*, June 2, 1916.

[36] Charles J. Bonaparte to H. C. Gauss, January 11, 1916, Bonaparte MSS.; Steffens, *Letters*, 1: 373.

[37] *New York Times*, March 25, May 27, 1916; Petition from Detroit Manufacturers, May 22, 1916, Roosevelt MSS.

tive support for the returning prodigal was made by George Harvey. He who had written the scurrilous editorial against the Roosevelt "pretensions" of 1912 was now full of heroic praise. The first "cheat" and the first "liar" who had ever occupied the White House was now the "First Citizen of the Republic," and Harvey with all solemnity proposed him as the Republican nominee. Time and politics are the great mollifiers.[38]

Superficially it might appear that Roosevelt had cut his new conservative, patriotic clothing to recapture the public eye, to regain lost support and possibly the presidency. But that is only a half-truth. The ex-president had always been a patriot and a fiery nationalist. Had the call to arms in 1916 been less popular, he would have acted no differently. His conservatism may have been another matter. He had sensed the drift of public opinion to the right and he was drifting with it. What else would a good practising politician who wanted office—oh so badly—do? Besides, Wilson was by common acclaim the first progressive of the country, and could a Roosevelt be second in anything—even in progressivism? The function of an opposition is to oppose.

No one in the country was watching the political jigsaw puzzle of 1916 with a keener eye than Theodore Roosevelt himself. He was aware of every piece that fell into its niche, aware of every piece that had to be discarded. And when the murky picture cleared somewhat in the first month of the year, he was convinced that there was chance to be nominated on both Republican and Progressive tickets. Not a good one, by a long shot, but one worth taking tentatively. But there would be no campaign from a Pullman car this time, no entering into primaries, no noise, no name-calling. There had been enough of that in 1912. He would not even think of taking the nomination, he wrote to Lodge, if it meant manipulation which would suggest that he was merely

[38] *Bankers' Magazine*, 92: 329 (March, 1916). *New York Sun*, May 20, 31, 1916; *New York Times*, April 14, 1916; George Harvey, *North American Review*, 203: 333, 337 (March, 1916), 20414 (June, 1916).

seeking personal aggrandizement. He would not accept unless there was a popular feeling on party and patriotic grounds that he must be nominated. Moreover, he would not accept if the country wanted "safety first." "Unless the country is somewhere near a mood of at least half-heroism it would be useless to nominate me."[39]

Roosevelt's statement of Lodge on the first of February was intended only for his ears and those of a few friends. But word of the Colonel's receptiveness soon spread, despite the fact that he had ordered his name taken off a Republican primary ballot in Michigan. A week after the Lodge letter the *New York Times* editorialized that Roosevelt was willing to take a third cup of coffee. In a signed statement on March 9 Roosevelt himself admitted as much. While he was on a visit to Trinidad his name had been placed on the Massachusetts Republican primary ballot by a few ill-advised well-wishers. Declining the dubious honor by public declaration from the coast of South America, Roosevelt wrote that he was interested in political principles and not in political fortunes. "I will not enter into any fight for the nomination," he continued, "and I will not permit any factional fight to be made in my behalf. Indeed I will go further and say that it will be a mistake to nominate me unless the country has in its mood something of the heroic."[40] Barkis was willing to accept, but Barkis would not woo—at least not openly.

Two weeks later Roosevelt was told by a congress of Progressives headed by George W. Perkins that the country was definitely in a heroic mood. Meanwhile William Howard Taft, nobler in defeat than he had ever been in the presidency, renounced all ambitions for 1916. "I will positively not be a candidate for the Presidency," he stated. "Even if I am nominated unanimously I will not be a candidate."[41]

Roosevelt was in a difficult position. Either he had to make a straight-out fight for the nomination and incur all the lia-

[39] Roosevelt to Henry C. Lodge, February 4, 1916, in Lodge, *Letters*, 2: 479–480.
[40] *New York Times*, February 9, March 10, 1916.
[41] *Ibid.*, December 24, 1915.

WILSON IS **NOT** HEROIC
HUGHES IS **NOT** HEROIC
ROOT IS **NOT** HEROIC

I AM HEROIC

(PERKINS IS HEROIC TOO)

3RD TERM

Cartoon in the *New York World*, reproduced in the *Review of Reviews*, May, 1916, referring to Roosevelt's statement that the country should not turn to him unless it was in a heroic mood.

bilities of such a move or he had to resort to subterranean methods and run without appearing to do so. Both plans had "grave disadvantages," but the latter, he thought, was "infinitely better."[42] And along that line the strategy of subterfuge was planned.

The existing organization of the Progressive party was to be maintained. State conventions to nominate delegates to the national nominating convention were to be held. But all of these were to go to Chicago uninstructed for any man, although most of the delegates were told that they would "probably" have a chance to support Roosevelt in the autumn. Meanwhile every effort was to be made by the state machines to pick "safe" men as delegates, men who would not, as Roosevelt phrased it, "go off into a mass of resolutions about social and industrial justice" to which no one

[42] Roosevelt to A. P. Gardner, April 22, 1916, Roosevelt MSS.

would pay any attention and which "would merely damage the cause." Demos must and should speak correctly.[43]

In California and wherever else the Progressives had a chance to capture the delegation to the Republican convention, they were to rejoin the old party immediately. "I do wish," Roosevelt wrote, "that the hard and fast Progressives of California would go right into this Republican contest." And so in California under the sponsorship of Progressive leaders a list of "United Republican" delegates was entered in the Republican primaries. "I hope," Meyer Lissner wrote Roosevelt, "you may see the Republican and Progressive delegates march up Michigan avenue under one flag."[44]

Where there was no chance that Lissner's hopes would be realized a trade with Republican state leaders seeking office might result in the selection of a Republican delegation partly in favor of the Colonel's cause. After some correspondence between George W. Perkins and Charles J. Bonaparte, a Republican candidate for the senatorship in Maryland was assured that if part of the Republican delegation to Chicago were favorable to Roosevelt there would in all likelihood be no Progressive nomination against him in the fall. As it later developed there was trouble about the number of Roosevelt supporters the delegation should include. Apparently four were offered; Bonaparte and Perkins wanted the entire sixteen.[45] Less trouble materialized in Missouri. There, stated Herbert S. Hadley, the progressive Republican ex-governor, "about two-thirds" at the Republican state convention would be "all right."[46]

As early as January emissaries were sent into the Southern states to insure that the minds of the Republican organization would "not be foreclosed against future develop-

[43] *New York Times*, May 7, 1916; Roosevelt to Dwight B. Heard, April 17, 1916, Roosevelt MSS.

[44] Roosevelt to Hiram Johnson, April 8, 1916, Meyer Lissner to Roosevelt, April 16, 1916, Roosevelt MSS.

[45] Bonaparte to Perkins, March 3, April 3, 1916, Bonaparte MSS.

[46] Herbert S. Hadley to Albert Dexter Nortoni, April 10, 1916, copy in Roosevelt MSS.

"ALAS POOR YORICK"
Cartoon by Cesare in the *New York Sun*, reproduced in the
Literary Digest, April 22, 1916.

ments."[47] In February Perkins had a long conference with
Boies Penrose. And to the surprise of many people and the
apprehension of some Progressives, Roosevelt went to the
home of Robert Bacon in April, where he talked with Elihu
Root and Henry Cabot Lodge. The erstwhile friends and
bitter enemies had conferred on defense matters and not on
politics, Roosevelt said as he was leaving the conference.
But Perkins, to quiet the suspicion of a deal, immediately
telephoned Bonaparte that the meeting had been arranged
"to heal up some soreness which had existed for some time
and which tended to interfere with plans adopted at the
headquarters." Root remembered afterward that all the conferees had "cussed out" Wilson at length, and it was not long
until Roosevelt was sending Root advance copies of his
speeches for criticism.[48]

[47] Letters to John W. McGrath from Medill McCormick, January 17,
1916, and Henry S. Jackson, Roosevelt MSS. McGrath was Roosevelt's
private secretary.
[48] Henry Clay Frick to Philander C. Knox (telegram), February 15,

In February Roosevelt had written an English friend that he had little chance of being nominated. By April, though, he had changed his mind, perhaps on the basis of the exploratory work done in both the Progressive and the Republican party. He had come to feel that there was a "real movement" to nominate him because he was the only man who had stood up "openly against" Wilson. In another month he was sure that he was the popular choice of "the rank and file of the Republican voters," although, he hastened to add, his nomination was very unlikely because the convention at Chicago would be controlled by a set of "machine masters."[49] Where democracy called, however, Roosevelt would follow. He soon announced that he was not seeking the nomination and that he wanted no votes from the hyphenates.

From that time on the machine to nominate Roosevelt by indirection was thrown into high gear. In circles inside the Republican party where Roosevelt and Perkins had little entree, William Loeb was set to work.[50] Negotiations were carried on with the hierarchy of the Catholic Church, who, it was hoped, would impress upon the Republican leaders the information that Roosevelt had not lost any of his Catholic following in the country. According to Lincoln Steffens even Robert La Follette was approached to see if he would support Roosevelt in Chicago.[51]

Promises were made to the defense societies; Republicans were assured that they would be welcome at the plum tree if Roosevelt were nominated and elected. To one skeptical member of the Republican convention Roosevelt wrote, "If a cut is to be healed it must be healed to the bone." The Colonel then went on to say that if he were nominated it would be with the determination to "treat the past as completely past and to give absolutely fair play to all my sup-

1916, Knox MSS.; Charles J. Bonaparte to N. Winslow Williams, April 10, 1916, Bonaparte MSS.; Jessup, *Root*, 2: 344, 350.

[49] Roosevelt to Arthur Lee, February 18, 1916, to F. S. Oliver, April 7, 1916, and to Charley (Charles G. Washburn ?), May 6, 1916, Roosevelt MSS.

[50] Roosevelt to George W. Perkins, May 13, 1916, Roosevelt MSS.

[51] Steffens, *Letters*, 1: 371.

porters."[52] In a published letter Perkins denied that he wanted to become the new secretary of the treasury. Then lest a widespread "misapprehension" that Roosevelt would lead the country into war gain currency, a prepared denial was inserted in the *Saturday Evening Post.*[53]

"That Roosevelt Non-Partisan League is all right!" Roosevelt wrote to George von L. Meyer on May 10, 1916. And soon the secretary of the navy in Roosevelt's cabinet was chairman of a non-partisan group of New York and Boston businessmen working for Roosevelt's nomination in the Republican convention. It never lacked funds. Clarence McKay furnished space for headquarters in his telegraph building. John S. Miller and Ogden Armour were among its Chicago officers. The automobile executive crowd in Detroit vigorously supported the League, and among its adherents in the Republican national convention was Alfred I. du Pont of Delaware. Obviously, as George von L. Meyer wrote, the businessmen were "awakening to the seriousness of the situation."[54] For Roosevelt the League and his candidacy were now synonymous with patriotism. Thanking the men who were responsible for the opening of the League's Chicago offices, he congratulated the great Middle West of Abraham Lincoln and Ulysses Grant, which "now takes the lead in the movement for genuine Americanism and for national preparedness without which Americanism would be an empty boast."[55]

The Middle West, however, had not achieved that state of grace without aid. A month before convention time Roosevelt noted that according to all reports the Middle West was against them. He "was going to try to rouse them up."[56] Speaking at Chicago before the Bar Association, he went all

[52] Roosevelt to Charles S. Thompson, May 4, 1916, and to Foster U. Brown, May 10, 1916, Roosevelt MSS.

[53] *Philadelphia North American*, May 6, 1912; George W. Perkins to Charles J. Bonaparte, May 6, 1916, Bonaparte MSS.

[54] George von L. Meyer to Roosevelt, June 2, 1916, Roosevelt MSS.

[55] Roosevelt to Edward C. Larned (telegram), May 15, 1916, Roosevelt MSS.

[56] Roosevelt to Meyer Lissner, April 22, 1916, Roosevelt MSS.

out for national preparedness. And undoubtedly the ovation he received, during which men climbed on chairs and "fairly shrieked their approval," inspired him to do a little more "rousing" in that section just a week before the opening of the Republican national convention. In this swing through the hinterland, Roosevelt never once mentioned his candidacy. There were only two issues, he told crowds in Detroit and Kansas City, preparedness and Americanism. In Kansas City fifty thousand voices cheered him at the railroad station, and a knife was thrown at him as he rode in an automobile. As Roosevelt belabored pacificism and the hyphenates, demanded universal service, and condemned Wilson's foreign policy, the campaign that was not a campaign came to an end. [57]

[57] *New York Times*, April 22, 30, May 1, 20, 31, 1916.

CHAPTER FOURTEEN

"The Country Wasn't in a Heroic Mood"

WHY ROOSEVELT thought he had a chance at the Republican nomination of 1916 is still a mystery. Perhaps his many conferences with Boies Penrose and the senator's willingness to cooperate in Pennsylvania had fostered the hope. Perhaps Henry Cabot Lodge was deliberately misleading him for his own purposes. It may be that Roosevelt's great desire for the office created a momentary blind spot.[1] But in fact he had no chance. The masters of the Republican party went to Chicago with one determination: to stop the nomination of Roosevelt at any cost. For that no price was too high.[2]

The instructions of the Republican state conventions to their delegates had one refrain: vote for a "tried" or a "good" Republican. Obviously this was pointed at Oyster Bay. So was the reorganization of the Republican National Committee in March. When the efforts of the conservative directorate to unseat the liberal Frank P. Woods of Iowa as chairman failed, they achieved their purpose by making William B. McKinley of Illinois chairman of the Executive Committee and depriving Woods of most of his power. Thereafter Warren G. Harding was carefully chosen to be the temporary chairman of the convention, his chief qualifications being his singleminded devotion to Republican orthodoxy and his remarkable pair of lungs.[3]

[1] Charles J. Bonaparte thought "his very good friends" who had made "great personal sacrifices for him in the past" were responsible for his state of mind. Bonaparte to George A. Pearre, June 15, 1916, Bonaparte MSS.

[2] Nicholas Murray Butler, *Across the Busy Years* (New York, 1939), 247.

[3] *New York Times*, March 30, April 8, 9, May 5, 1916.

Left to themselves the controlling standpat element in the party would have nominated Elihu Root, Charles W. Fairbanks, or Theodore E. Burton, but they feared that none of these men would be acceptable to either the liberals in the Republican party or the Progressives. For victory the support of both elements was essential. And so the name of Charles Evans Hughes had been proposed, argued over, and reluctantly accepted by many.

Hughes had certain qualifications. On the Supreme Court bench he had made few political enemies, and even the politicians could not say where he stood on the matter of war and peace. He was able and honest. In the past he had sometimes looked like a reformer, and his nomination might be the best way to stop Roosevelt and to invite fusion. True, he would have been relished more by the Republican hierarchy if he had been less independent and more of a good fellow. But Paris was worth a mass and Washington a quasi-liberal, even a frigid one. The word went out that no one wanted Hughes, but everyone was for him. At convention time he had twice as many pledged delegates as his nearest competitor, and many more had indicated that they would cast their ballots for him if it was for the good of the party.

The Republican and Progressive conventions opened in an America alarmed and apprehensive of the future. The great European struggle which had already engulfed so much of the world seemed to be drawing nearer with every passing week. In April of 1916 Captain Franz von Papen of the German diplomatic staff had been indicted by a federal grand jury for an attempt to destroy the Welland Canal. In the same month the government threatened to sever diplomatic relations with Germany unless her submarine warfare were immediately abandoned. Even as the conventions met, the regular army and the state militia were massed on the Mexican border in answer to an ultimatum by the Carranza government. Simultaneously the Senate and the House were considering the largest naval and army appropriation bills in the history of the country.

A marrow-chilling rain fell upon Chicago as the conventions opened at the Auditorium theater and at the Coliseum. Somehow the mood of the two gatherings seemed to reflect the elements. Observers noted that the usual boisterous spirit was missing from the Republican body. Perhaps the leading candidate had left his impress upon the delegates; perhaps it was the condition of world affairs.[4]

Over at the Auditorium, where the Progressives had met four years before in a wave of crusading zeal, there was now uncertainty and distrust. Few of those present knew where their leaders were taking them. Their chieftains had assured them as late as the first of June that the Progressive party would not abandon its fundamental principles of popular rule and reform. But then there were the conferences that Roosevelt and Perkins had had with Root, Penrose, George B. Cortelyou, and Charles D. Hillis. What could one make of that? Had Roosevelt captured the old enemies of 1912 or had they captured him? The cynical Bonaparte thought he knew and was doubtful whether he ought to go to Chicago. He was ready to nominate Roosevelt and thus re-elect Wilson, he wrote to Perkins. He was ready to dissolve the party if Roosevelt would not run or if he could not win the Republican nomination, but he had no intention of taking part in the nomination or the endorsement of any Republican.[5]

This spirit of distrust cropped out in a meeting of the National Committee the day before the convention met. When objection arose to a motion expressing "perfect and absolute confidence" in the party's Executive Committee the motion was tabled.[6] The next day more suspicion was aroused when Perkins announced that the party would not make its nominations at once but would await Republican action. The delegates cheered when Victor Murdock, chairman of the National Committee, objected that the committee had made no such agreement.[7] But the destinies of the Progressive

[4] *Chicago Tribune*, June 9, 1916.

[5] Charles J. Bonaparte to George W. Perkins, May 23, 1916, Bonaparte MSS.

[6] Typewritten Minutes of the National Committee, June 5, 1916, Roosevelt MSS.

[7] *New York Times*, June 6, 1916.

party were not in the hands of its National Committee. George W. Perkins and Theodore Roosevelt were making most of its policies.

Roosevelt had not come to Chicago, but a private telephone connected his house at Oyster Bay with both the Progressive and Republican bodies. At all hours of the day and night the Colonel consulted with Perkins. Together they planned the strategy of the one convention and kept a sharp eye on the developments of the other. That they had tight control of the Progressive convention was manifest from the first turbulent session until a weary gavel pounded out its disheartening *sine die*. It was manifest when the platforms of the two parties were announced: the two were almost identical except for the Progressive universal service proposal which Henry Cabot Lodge could not get his fellow Republicans to accept. The similarity was no mere chance. Lodge, chairman of the Republican Resolutions Committee, and William Draper Lewis, chairman of the Progressive body, probably had conferred with that in mind. "Dean Lewis and I agreed," Lodge wrote Roosevelt, "that we could stand equally well on each other's platforms."[8] Lodge was right. The few social reforms mentioned in the Progressive platform of 1916 were relegated to an insignificant paragraph. The rest of the document was divided between praise for a high protective tariff, specific demands for national defense, and essays on foreign policy and patriotism for the benefit of an erring Wilson and his Democrats.

The platform was adopted smoothly enough except for the defeated prohibition resolution, but throughout the rest of the convention Perkins' control was constantly endangered. At the opening session three distinct groups had made their appearance. The first, consisting of a small minority of practising politicians led by Walter Brown of Ohio and William Flinn of Pennsylvania, wanted to go back to the Republican party and support whatever choice it might make. A second group of Roosevelt's close associates who supported Perkins' control of the convention wanted to bargain with the Re-

[8] Henry C. Lodge to Roosevelt, June 14, 1916, Roosevelt MSS.

publicans to the bitter end in the hope of a double Roosevelt
nomination as their first choice and a "preparedness man"
with progressive leanings as their second. The third group,
headed by Hiram Johnson, John Parker of Louisiana, and
Victor Murdock, opposed to Roosevelt's recent conservative,
nationalist bent, apparently had the support of a majority
of the delegates. They wished to preserve the party with a
prompt nomination and permit the Republicans to do what
they would.

The struggle between this last group and the convention
leaders broke into the open during the first session on Wednesday. Even before the keynote speech, demands for an
immediate nomination were made from the floor. The next
day, when it became known that Perkins advocated appointment of a conference committee to sit with the Republicans,
the delegates yelled wildly for Roosevelt. Some semblance of
order was eventually restored by Perkins and Raymond Robins. But not for long. When James R. Garfield moved to
appoint a committee to confer with Republican representatives, bedlam was again unleashed. The delegates roared their
disapproval and demanded a speech from Murdock or Parker.
The disorder increased when Murdock rose to his feet and
asked whether the convention belonged to a little coterie and
whether the delegates proposed to get down on their knees
to the bandits of 1912. He then asked the delegates whether
they wanted to nominate Theodore Roosevelt, and men
popped up all over the floor to carry out the suggestion. But
the chair recognized a delegate from Missouri, who read a
letter carefully prepared in advance by Roosevelt asking the
delegates to cooperate with the Republican convention. A
hush fell over the body, and with the radicals momentarily
quelled the motion was put to a vote and won. The conference committee, carefully selected to include representatives
of the rebel group, was made up of George W. Perkins,
Hiram Johnson, Horace S. Wilkerson, Charles J. Bonaparte,
and John Parker.[9]

Shortly afterward at the Progressives' request the Repub-

[9] *Chicago Tribune*, June 9, 1916; *New York Times*, June 9, 1916.

licans appointed a similar group. Unanimously they selected Murray Crane, Reed Smoot, William E. Borah, A. R. Johnson, and Nicholas Murray Butler. Regulars all except Borah, there was little hope for Roosevelt in that roster of names. When the two groups met that night at the Chicago Club, scarcely a man was present who had not just four years before delivered himself of some choice epithets in appraisal of the other side. But now all was dignified as the Progressive committeemen opened the conference with a two-hour joint argument for the nomination of Roosevelt. Unanimously the Republican members replied that under no circumstances could their convention be forced into accepting Roosevelt and asked the Progressives for a second choice. Stating that they were not prepared to consider a second choice, the Progressives asked the Republicans to suggest a name. When the Republican members refused to do so in advance of the balloting, the committee adjourned, at three o'clock Friday morning.[10]

When the Progressive convention met on Friday morning after the bootless all-night conference, they were in an ugly mood. With deep suspicion of their leaders, they heard the report of the conference committee in silence and at its end moved forward to nominate Roosevelt. Hisses from the floor answered Perkins' plea to have faith for twenty-four hours more. Had it not been for a long wrangle over the prohibition plank in the platform they might have acted despite Perkins. As it was, the convention sat the entire day fretfully listening to the reports coming from the Republican meeting with rebellion in their hearts. When they adjourned for dinner they learned that Roosevelt, despite all his rosy promises, had obtained only a scattering vote in the first two ballots of the Republican convention. Hughes had led the first ballot with $253\frac{1}{2}$ votes; Roosevelt trailed in seventh place with 65 votes. On the second Hughes had a total of $328\frac{1}{2}$ and Roosevelt 81.

[10] Charles J. Bonaparte to Roosevelt, June 13, 1916, to George A. Pearre, June 15, 1916, and to Clinton R. Woodruff, June 16, 1916, Bonaparte MSS.; Butler, *Across the Busy Years*, 258–264.

The Progressive convention met at eight-thirty that night after hearing the bad news from the Republican meeting. A great shout rose up from the delegates: "Why not Why not Why not nominate him now?" Raymond Robins attempted to quiet the body in vain. In the end only Hiram Johnson succeeded in quelling what was to Charles J. Bonaparte an obvious determination to nominate Roosevelt and be done with bargaining. But even as the fiery leader from California stopped the movement for an immediate nomination, he made it plain that he had no sympathy with the Roosevelt-Perkins strategy of "stall and dicker." He was not in accord, he explained, with those who would have the Progressives sit at the feet of Smoot and Crane and bargain with the very men who had robbed them in 1912. He would be for an immediate nomination if that were not against the expressed desires of Roosevelt. Even so, he demanded the right to protest "against what's been done today and tonight with the Progressive party." "In the end," he assured the delegates, "after taking a moral bath we'll stand together again and act like men united to fight and preserve the Progressive Party of America." The speech was ample evidence that Johnson was mad clear through.[11]

By nine o'clock on the night of Friday, June 9, after the two Republican ballots, several things were obvious. First, Roosevelt had little chance, if any, of capturing the Republican nomination; secondly, unless the two conventions came to some agreement it appeared that Charles Evans Hughes would win the prize in short order. In fact, the fear that this would be the outcome of the next ballot had led to the adjournment of the Republican convention so that the two conference committees might meet again. When the conferees met at eleven that night the Progressives reiterated that Roosevelt was their only suggestion, and the Republicans that their convention would not accept the Colonel under any circumstances. Pressed for an alternative, the Republicans reluctantly offered the name of Justice Hughes, adding that three of their five members were opposed to his nomina-

[11] *Chicago Tribune*, June 10, 1916; *New York Times*, June 10, 1916.

tion. The Progressive members declined to receive a suggestion that was not unanimously supported and thus at three o'clock on Saturday morning the committee adjourned again.

It was during these early morning hours that Roosevelt made a last attempt to influence the Republican nomination. He talked directly over the telephone with Nicholas Murray Butler of the Republican conference committee and asked him, first, whether he stood any chance of a Republican nomination. Butler replied no. Roosevelt then asked for suggestions. Butler, having conferred with other Republican leaders, promptly named Elihu Root, Philander C. Knox, and Charles W. Fairbanks in the order given. To each Roosevelt found objection and in turn proposed the names of Major General Leonard Wood and Henry Cabot Lodge. Butler replied that under the conditions Wood was impossible, but that he would talk over the possibility of Lodge with other Republican leaders. Later that morning both conventions received Roosevelt's telegraphic recommendation of Lodge as a man "of the broadest national spirit" and one of the "staunchest fighters for different measures of economic reform in the direction of justice."[12]

To all but the blind Roosevelt's early morning actions were a portent of what was to follow. The Progressive party was Roosevelt, and Roosevelt was the Progressive party. If his name was not to be considered by the Republicans, there was no use mentioning any other Progressive even for reasons of courtesy. Hiram Johnson might measure up to many men's presidential specifications in 1920, but not to Roosevelt's in 1916, regardless of past professions.[13] As for the rest, they were only little men with duties to perform; they could not expect their names to be in the lights even as a kind gesture from a chief they had served long and well. But the crowning blow to Progressive ambition, principle, and pride must have been the sardonic nomination of Henry Cabot Lodge. He whose only political accomplishment had been to remain in office, he whose frosty breath had been blown against every

[12] Butler, *Across the Busy Years*, 269–271.
[13] Roosevelt had not mentioned Johnson as a possible candidate since

important progressive measure for two decades, was now to be traded for the life of the Progressive party. It was enough to bring a gleam to the eye of the sacred codfish and to make men despair.

Promptly at nine Saturday morning the conference committee of the two conventions met for its last session. Previously three members of the Progressive committee, after much debate, had agreed to suggest Lodge's name to the Republicans, but only as Roosevelt's proposal and not as their own. The other two members, Hiram Johnson and John Parker, had walked out of the session in disgust and had refused to participate further in the deliberations. Once the full committee met, however, the Republicans announced that their unanimous choice for a compromise candidate was Charles Evans Hughes. With the understanding that Justice Hughes's name would be presented to the Progressive convention, the body broke up.[14]

Before that took place, a series of feverish meetings were held between Progressive leaders. Charles J. Bonaparte had carried to Chicago a letter previously prepared by Roosevelt, the purpose of which was to ward off by its publication the possibility of a Hughes nomination. The wording was so evasive, however, that Bonaparte thought its publication at that late hour would be useless. The one thing which might stop Hughes's nomination, the ex-attorney general thought, was an "unequivocal and unqualified condemnation" by Roosevelt. When it was established that Oyster Bay was unwilling to go that far, the convention was called into session to act upon Roosevelt's and the Republican suggestions.[15]

On Saturday morning when George W. Perkins rose to report the conference committee's actions to the Progressive convention, he was faced by a hostile crowd of delegates. His long report was punctuated by hisses and cries of "sit down." When he suggested Lodge or Hughes as possible candidates

his remarks in the autumn of 1915. Perhaps the California Senator's views on foreign policy were responsible for Roosevelt's silence in 1916.

[14] Bonaparte to Roosevelt, June 13, 1916, and to George A. Pearre, June 15, 1916, Bonaparte MSS.

[15] Bonaparte to Roosevelt, June 12, 1916, Bonaparte MSS.

loud agonizing "no's" echoed through the hall. After the report was finished the suggestions were immediately tabled. Perkins now moved that the convention suspend deliberation until the Republicans had made their choice. Howls of disapproval tore the air. John Parker demanded Roosevelt's immediate nomination. In the midst of the ensuing uproar it was decided simply to suspend action until the Republicans started to ballot. In two minutes word of the balloting came by telephone, and just ninety seconds later Bainbridge Colby had made the nominating speech for Theodore Roosevelt. At that point Perkins tried to stop the proceedings once more, but this time the delegates would not listen. He was shouted down as he started to speak, and finally withdrew from the rostrum waving his hands above him. At 12:37, just three minutes after the Republicans had nominated Hughes, the chair announced that Roosevelt had been nominated unanimously for a second time. As the convention recessed for lunch, there were few men as unpopular in that body as the party's financial godfather, George W. Perkins.[16]

On Saturday afternoon the convention had scarcely nominated John M. Parker for the vice-presidency when a telegram arrived from Theodore Roosevelt: "I am very grateful for the honor you confer upon me. I cannot accept it at this time. I do not know the attitude of the candidate of the Republican party toward the vital questions of the day. Therefore if you desire an immediate decision, I must decline the nomination; but if you prefer, I suggest that my conditional refusal to run be placed in the hands of the Progressive National Committee." If the committee could be satisfied with Mr. Hughes's statements, Roosevelt went on, they could accept his refusal as definite. If they were not satisfied, they could confer with him to "determine on what action we may severally deem appropriate to meet the needs of the country."[17]

[16] *Chicago Tribune, New York Times*, June 11, 1916.

[17] Typewritten memorandum, Roosevelt MSS. It should be noted that Roosevelt did *not* promise to run even in the event that Mr. Hughes's statements displeased him.

Dumbly the convention listened to the message, only half appreciating its true meaning. As Charles Bonaparte wrote later, it was not until after the convention that many delegates comprehended its significance.[18] At the moment, the majority voted to refer the matter to the National Committee as Roosevelt had asked.[19] But many did so with misgivings, and some were frankly hostile. A significant cheer rose from the convention when Victor Murdock rose to castigate its leaders for using the "old political tricks" to keep the body from acting on its convictions, and again when he pointed out that William Jennings Bryan and Henry Ford might be persuaded to run independently. But at five o'clock the convention came to its disheartening end without further action. While the band played "America" weary delegates tramped to the door. Four years before they had rushed home happily to announce the coming of a new political Messiah. Now in the warm June evening, above the shuffling of tired feet, distinct mutterings of "apostate" and "running out"[20] were audible. As Bronson Cutting noted, most of the delegates were going home "with the conviction that they had been betrayed."

It is obvious from Roosevelt's correspondence that he thought he had some small chance of winning the nominations from both conventions. He had resolved not to run on a third-term ticket alone unless perhaps the character of the Republican nomination forced him to do so to maintain his self-respect. More specifically, he had perhaps decided in advance with the knowledge of several leading Progressives that he would not accept a nomination against Charles Evans Hughes.[21] But that information was not conveyed to the

[18] Bonaparte to Roosevelt, June 13, 1916, Bonaparte MSS.

[19] That night in a stormy session the National Committee accepted the responsibility to fill or *not* to fill vacancies in the ticket. It was further agreed that the committee after conferring with Roosevelt would meet again on June 26 to determine the "acceptability" of Charles Evans Hughes. Minutes of the National Committee, June 10, 1916; Matthew Hale to Roosevelt, June 13, 1916, Roosevelt MSS.

[20] *New York Times*, June 11, 1916.

[21] Roosevelt to Arthur Leland, June 7, 1916, Meyer Lissner to Roose-

mass of Progressives. The plan was to leave them in the dark and barter to the last. If Roosevelt could not be nominated perhaps he could secure a progressive Republican committed to preparedness.

The Progressive convention was to be used as a stalking and a trading horse. The major problem there was how to keep the delegates quiet and how to prevent them from flying off at a tangent to divide the Republican strength in the autumn elections. For that reason the nomination was held off to the very end. For that reason, too, Roosevelt's refusal on Saturday was conditional, although he knew at the time that he would not run. His remark to New York reporters after he had sent the telegram that he was "out of politics" is added evidence.[22] It was clear that Charles Evans Hughes would not have polled a majority of the Progressive delegation at any time in the convention.[23] By referring Roosevelt's provisional declination to the National Committee and getting the delegates home, the chance of a major rebellion against the preconceived strategy was measurably lessened.

The Progressive party had ostensibly been organized to protest in the name of popular rule against a bossed convention. Ironically its last official gathering was not only completely bossed but also continually deceived. Looking back in 1917, one of the men who participated in that deception, as if to ask for absolution, described the whole proceedings as "outrageous chicanery." There was this difference. In 1912 boss rule impaired the fortunes of Roosevelt; in 1916 Roosevelt was doing the bossing.[24]

"Well, the country wasn't in a heroic mood," Theodore

velt, April 15, 1916, Roosevelt MSS.; O. K. Davis, *Released for Publication*, 449. There is some evidence to suggest that a few Republicans had also been told of this resolve. J. A. H. Hopkins to Roosevelt, July 11, 1916, Roosevelt MSS.

[22] *New York Times*, June 11, 1916.

[23] It was Bonaparte's estimate that nine-tenths of the delegates would have voted against him.

[24] A more charitable view would argue that Roosevelt was positive that Wilson's policy was sacrificing the welfare of the nation and was ready in the national interest to defeat him at all costs.

Roosevelt wrote his sister after the conventions had adjourned. "We are passing through a thick streak of yellow in
our national life."[25] Obviously Roosevelt, though he intended
to support Hughes, was not happy in mid-June about the
results at Chicago. He was convinced, he wrote a friend
abroad, that had he been nominated he would have been
elected because the country "recognized him as the real opponent of Wilson." The Republican convention had stub-
bornly refused to recognize that salient fact because, as he
explained, besides his own supporters and a few others there
was not a man there who was not "dominated by his basest
self interest."[26]

It was hard to be counted out upon such grounds, and it
would have been hard to work up any enthusiasm for the
winner of such a battle even if one had liked him in the past.
Between Roosevelt and Hughes no love had ever been lost.
Personally the two men were miles apart, and in 1910 the
Supreme Court justice had fallen squarely athwart the Colonel's wrath. He was a good governor, had been an able
judge, and was personally a man of his word. To all of that
Roosevelt agreed. "At the worst" he would "do better than
Wilson."[27] There was the added consideration that Roosevelt, as presidents go, was yet a young man and would still
be young in 1920. Not that Roosevelt ever wrote or spoke of
1920 in 1916, but some of his confidants pointed out that
Hughes and Fairbanks might very well lose, and if they did
there was not much question who would be the party's nominee in 1920. For these reasons one could become reconciled
after a little time, even though one wished that the "bearded
iceberg" had acted differently "so as to enable us to put more
heart in the campaign for him."[28]

Reconciliation, however, came harder to many Progressives than to Roosevelt, and for some it was impossible. Even

[25] Roosevelt to Anna R. Cowles, June 16, 1916, in *Letters from Theodore
Roosevelt to Anna Roosevelt Cowles, 1870–1918* (New York, 1924), 308.
[26] Roosevelt to Sir Arthur Lee, August 11, 1916, Roosevelt MSS.
[27] Roosevelt to James Bryce, June 19, 1916, Roosevelt MSS.
[28] Roosevelt to W. A. Wadsworth, June 23, 1916, Roosevelt MSS.

before the National Committee met to define the position of the party some of the former Democrats had announced that they were supporting Woodrow Wilson. Others, like Victor Murdock, who started on a trip to China, gave indication that they were retiring from politics. That a few men should openly desert was to be expected, but what worried Roosevelt and Perkins was the extent of the rebellion in the rest of the Progressive ranks. Hiram Johnson, William Allen White, John Parker, Bainbridge Colby, Bronson Cutting, Albert J. Beveridge, and even Charles J. Bonaparte were all acting queerly. White had written for publication that Perkins had purchased title to the party and that Roosevelt had acknowledged that title. Governor Johnson was making it plain that he did not even wish to confer with Roosevelt. And Bonaparte had told Roosevelt that he too might have to vote for Wilson. The dissenters of smaller stature in the party were less reticent and freely called ugly names.[29]

Confronted with such widespread displeasure, Roosevelt and Perkins worked hard before the National Committee met to persuade a majority of its members to embalm the party and accept Hughes. Conferences were held at Oyster Bay and with Hughes, long letters of explanation were sent out from national headquarters, and proxies of would-be absent committeemen were directed into the hands of congenial men.[30]

The session of the National Committee which opened at Chicago on June 26 to decide the fate of the party, was a long and turbulent one. On the night of the twenty-fifth an informal conference was held at Perkins' headquarters in the Blackstone Hotel to win over the dissenters. Until nearly one o'clock in the morning the group listened to Perkins, Raymond Robins, Chester Rowell, and others report on their conferences with the Republican candidate. But when the

[29] *Nation*, 102:636 (June 15, 1916); letters to Roosevelt from John Parker, June 16, 1916, and Bronson M. Cutting, June 11, 1916, Roosevelt MSS.; Charles J. Bonaparte to George R. Gaither, June 22, 1916, Bonaparte MSS.

[30] George W. Perkins to all Progressive state chairmen, June 24, 1916. Roosevelt MSS.

committee met it became apparent that a sizeable group was still unconvinced that the party should support Hughes. When a proposal of the Perkins faction to make the deliberations secret was put to a vote, fifteen members, including the chairman, Matthew Hale from Massachusetts, walked out and consented to return only when an open meeting was promised. When the meeting was resumed, Roosevelt's long statement of his reasons for supporting Hughes was read. After a long adjournment, during which the Perkins forces planned their attack, a motion was made to substitute Victor Murdock for Theodore Roosevelt at the head of the Progressive ticket. Immediately a violent and impassioned debate broke out in which the lie direct was passed between Bainbridge Colby and Raymond Robins. But the committee had been organized well, and the motion was defeated 32 to 15. Thereafter the Roosevelt forces, by the same margin, pledged the party to Hughes.[31]

The committee's action at Chicago was probably supported, however reluctantly, by a majority of the Progressives throughout the country. But after the Blackstone meeting loud and pressing opposition was heard, opposition so insistent that Progressive headquarters found it expedient to instruct the party's state chairmen to let a "cooling off" period elapse before holding state conventions. Even then the action of the National Committee was stoutly repudiated in many states, and the name of Roosevelt roundly abused.[32]

Some of the dissident members of the party, disheartened by the events of June, simply planned quietly to vote for Wilson. Other diehards, however, insisted upon keeping the party alive and tilting "at windmills under a wild sky." Led by Matthew Hale, Bainbridge Colby, and John Parker, they held a convention at Indianapolis in early August, where representatives of seventeen states branded Roosevelt as a

[31] Dwight B. Heard to Roosevelt, June 27, 1916, Roosevelt MSS.; Winslow N. Williams to Charles J. Bonaparte, July 1, 1916, Bonaparte MSS.; *New York Times*, June 27, 1916; *New Orleans Times Picayune*, August 2, 1916.

[32] Charles J. Bonaparte to Winslow N. Williams, July 24, 1916, and to George W. Perkins, September 28, 1916, Bonaparte MSS.

traitor and determined to run Parker as the Progressive vice-presidential candidate.[33] In addition, in some states, as in New York, remnants of the party repudiating Roosevelt and Perkins selected a full state ticket for the autumn elections. But the scattering support they obtained convinced even these unyielding souls, and the rebels never met again. They did, however, almost as a body support the Democratic ticket in the autumn elections.[34]

Originally it had been in the minds of Roosevelt and Perkins to keep the Progressive organization, if not the whole party, alive through the elections of 1916. After the results of November were in, such an organization might prove useful in bargaining with the Republican party for places in the party organization and in maneuvering for 1920. But the actions of the rebels and the diversion of the old organization to Woodrow Wilson in many places changed Roosevelt's mind. "I do not believe in maintaining the Progressive organization in the various states," he wrote on July 5. "They have become small derelict parties of the kind that are the natural prey of cheap crooks, and of those cranks whose crankiness has in it something sinister."[35] It was a proper note on which to end. In 1912 Roosevelt had breathed life into the Progressive party by inveighing against crookedness. He laid the chill hand of death upon it in 1916 for the same reason.

The rest of Roosevelt's summer was busy. The job of persuading Progressives to cast their lot with Hughes was beset with difficulties, as Roosevelt pointed out to the Republican campaign manager.[36] There were questions to be answered, speeches to be made, letters to be written. What could one say to the editor of the *Philadelphia North American* when he asked Roosevelt for some compelling reasons why Progressives should support Hughes? "We confess," Van Valken-

[33] *New Orleans Times Picayune*, August 4, 1916.
[34] Eleven of the nineteen members of the Progressive platform committee of 1912 signed a statement in support of Woodrow Wilson. *New York Times*. November 1, 1916.
[35] Roosevelt to William Dudley Foulke, July 5, 1916, Roosevelt MSS.
[36] Roosevelt to William R. Willcox, August 8, 1916, Roosevelt MSS.

berg had written, "that as we contemplate the task before us, we make the perturbing discovery, after careful scrutiny of the facts, that convincing arguments do not come readily to mind."[37]

As the summer and the campaign wore on, the relations between the Republicans and the cooperating Progressives had to be defined. The membership of the campaign committee was decided upon without too much friction, but in most other matters the recently acquired bonds of matrimony rested none too easily on either party. First Raymond Robins was angered at the actions of the Old Guard in Illinois. Trouble broke out in Maine which almost induced the Progressives to repudiate the union. A major split did occur in California. Everywhere personal quarrels arose which Roosevelt did his best to compromise and settle without hurting the cause. It was distasteful and thankless work.

With most of his old fire Roosevelt shouldered the drudgery of campaigning, this time for another man and without hope of a personal victory. In attacking Wilson throughout the East, he spent most of his time on the administration's foreign policy. If the president had acted with courage, Roosevelt declared, there would have been no invasion of Belgium, no destruction of neutral property and lives, and no threat to the peace of the United States. As for Mexico, we should have intervened, as McKinley had intervened in Cuba, to restore order and stable government.[38] In fact, Roosevelt thumped so hard for a "strong" foreign policy that some of his new Republican friends urged him to go a little slower lest he alienate the votes of the more peaceful sections of the electorate. For that reason he was used mainly in the more belligerent East and was carefully kept out of some states where it was thought "he would probably do more harm than good."[39]

The campaign of 1916, with the exception of the issues re-

[37] E. A. Van Valkenberg to Roosevelt, August 24, 1916, Roosevelt MSS.
[38] *New York Times*, October 29, 1916.
[39] John Weeks to Charles G. Washburn, September 21, 1916, Roosevelt MSS.

volving around the Adamson Act and the administration's record was fought mainly on the grounds of foreign policy. There Wilson had the advantage. True, he had alienated some pro-German Americans, but thus far he had kept the country out of war. His opponent, Charles Evans Hughes, although most of his statements were moderate, left an impression upon the country, perhaps because of his association with Roosevelt, that his election would endanger the peace. At any rate, the Republican candidate carried the most pro-war section of the country, the industrial East, with the exception of New Hampshire and Ohio. Wilson, on the other hand, had in addition to the border states and the solid South, the electoral votes of most of the trans-Mississippi West, where women were more influential in politics and the section as a whole more pacifically inclined. By carrying the normally Republican states of California, Washington, Utah, and North Dakota, some of which not even Bryan had captured in 1896, the Democratic candidate won a very slight majority of the electoral college and the control of both houses of Congress.

Traditional interpretation has it that Wilson won the West because of his stand upon the European war. It might also be said that Hughes lost the West because he failed to win the support of the erstwhile Progressives. In five of eight customarily Republican states in the West the total vote for Hughes was much less than the combined vote for Taft and Roosevelt in 1912. More striking was the Republican candidate's loss of both Washington and California, states which the Progressives had carried in the preceding election. Had Hughes carried California he would have won the election. And there is little doubt that in California Progressive resentment at Hughes helped to spell disaster for the Republican party.

All the relevant facts in the historic California incident of 1916 may never be known, so complex were the issues and so bewildering were and are men's motives. Ancient grudges, the desperate try at the main chance, personalities, politics, and haphazard coincidence all played their part. The story began in 1910 when Hiram Johnson, running as a progressive Republican, won the governorship in the face of every effort of the old California state machine, which in popular tradition at least had regularly represented the best interests of the Southern Pacific Railroad and allied economic nterests. For eight years thereafter the progressive Republicans, and after 1912 the Progressive party, had controlled the state. With the return of Roosevelt to the Republican party in 1916, the standpat element in the state, welcoming the promise of morning after the long officeless night, planned a wholesale removal of Progressives in state offices from Johnson down.

For Hiram Johnson the summer of 1916 was a winter of discontent. Comfortably supported by a dominant Progressive party, he had watched Roosevelt and Perkins at Chicago destroy that party. It was no secret that he had aspirations for the senatorship and perhaps even a higher office at a later date. Roosevelt had seriously impaired his chances for the first and apparently had not even conceded his availability for the second. So wroth was he that on a trip East after the Progressive convention he made it plain to Roosevelt that temporarily at least he found his company most uncongenial.[40]

But office is the bread of politics and a man must live. So on an Eastern trip Chester Rowell, the California Progressive state chairman, met with the Republican steering committee to talk over the California senatorship. He returned West with what he believed was a promise that the committee would support Johnson for the Senate even to the extent of enlisting the aid of Hughes. That had been agreed to, apparently, even by Boies Penrose.[41] A short time later Hiram Johnson announced that he would stand for the senatorship in both the Progressive and the Republican primaries. He had no opposition in the Progressive lists, but two good Republi-

[40] Roosevelt to Chester H. Rowell, August 23, 1916, Roosevelt MSS.

[41] It should be pointed out that this promise may not have included support in the primary but only in the election in the event Johnson won the primary. Confidential sources in the possession of the author.

cans had already entered the race, both satisfactory to the state machine.

After eight years without political pap the hungry Republicans in California saw Johnson's announcement as a brazen attempt to steal what they felt was honorably theirs. Righteously indignant, William H. Crocker and Francis V. Keesling, the regnant standpatters, soon managed to obtain the withdrawal of one of the Republican candidates so as to concentrate all conservative Republican strength behind Willis H. Booth and defeat the interloper Johnson. With that move the political fat began to fry.

Into that sizzling situation stepped the cold, dignified Republican candidate for president, Charles Evans Hughes, who had little genius for solving the personal problems of politics and whose main efforts at conciliation had been by judicial mandate. Hughes was scheduled to make a campaign tour of the state just ten days before the explosive primary came to its conclusion with the balloting. William H. Crocker, the Republican National committeeman, had asked him to delay his trip until after the nomination, but the suggestion was rejected. Perhaps Hughes considered a last-minute change in his itinerary as too undignified and as smacking too much of petty politics; and perhaps his refusal to countenance a strategic delay cost him the election.

Hughes's ill-timed arrival in California posed a delicate problem of strategy. The ex-Progressives, on the ground that they were the majority party, were asking the candidate to signify his choice of Johnson. The Regular leaders, on the other hand, were making it known that they might knife the entire ticket in the fall if Johnson won the nomination. Representatives from both factions were invited to a conference, but Crocker refused to meet with an ex-Progressive. When the Hughes entourage arrived at the California line, it was met by a delegation representing the Regular Republican organization, which surrounded him at every moment of his California tour. True, Rowell and other Progressives accompanied him also, but the local arrangements were entirely in the hands of the Regulars. Meanwhile Johnson was in the southern part of the state on a speaking tour. Apparently there was no direct communication between Johnson and Hughes. No invitation to accompany the candidate's party was either issued or asked for. Hughes sought to solve the delicate situation by remarking at San Francisco that he had "no concern" with local differences.[42]

On August 20, just a few days before Hughes left the state, he stopped for an hour's rest in the Victoria Hotel at Long Beach, where Hiram Johnson was also spending the Sabbath. Johnson kept to his room, though he was aware of Hughes's presence. Unfortunately the fact that Johnson was a guest in the hotel was kept from Hughes by the little group of Regular Republicans surrounding him and he did not learn of it until late in the day, after he had gone to Los Angeles. Immediately he sent his train manager and Keesling, Republican State Central Committee chairman, back to Long Beach to make amends for the unwitting slight. They did little, however, to patch up the misunderstanding. The proposal that Johnson introduce the presidential candidate in Sacramento was vetoed by Keesling, and Johnson rejected all other suggestions for a public gesture of mutual good will. In the end Hughes left the state without exchanging a word with the California Achilles.[43]

A little more than a week later, on August 29, Governor Johnson won in both the Progressive and Republican primaries, carrying the latter by 20,000 votes. From that time on the party and the presidential candidate needed Hiram Johnson far more than Johnson needed them. During the weeks before the election Johnson worked hard for the success of the national ticket. But the "sullen resentment" that had been created in the minds of California Progressives could not be erased by a few weeks of oratory.[44] In November

[42] *New York Times*, August 19, 1916; Pringle, *Taft*, 2: 896, 900.

[43] Letters to Roosevelt from Meyer Lissner, August 28, September 1, 1916, and Benjamin I. Wheeler, November 21, 1916, Roosevelt MSS.

[44] Perhaps a Roosevelt speaking tour of the state might have compensated for the Hughes trip. Roosevelt considered such a venture but he

Johnson was elected to the Senate over his Democratic opponent by 300,000 votes. The presidential vote was so close, however, that returns from every election district in the state had to be counted before the result was certain. The rest of the nation had counted their ballots, and the final decision clearly depended upon California. For two days the uncertainty prevailed. Then Hughes lost the state to Wilson and so lost the presidency by four thousand votes.[45]

Thus the last act of the Progressive party in a national election was, like its first, a negative one. It had never known victory, but it had twice helped to defeat the Republican party. Created by Roosevelt to defeat Taft, it had died by defeating its creator. A tragic cycle completed—perhaps. In December Roosevelt was moaning that the country was running neck and neck with the Chinese as "the greatest of yellow nations." That was the patriot speaking. But then again he was making plans to hunt devilfish.[46] In the Hughes catastrophe of 1916 did he see personal success in 1920? No one will ever know for certain. For the question is not answered in his manuscripts.

found his visit "would be objectionable." Significantly Hiram Johnson had not replied to Roosevelt's telegram of congratulations on his primary victory. Roosevelt to Meyer Lissner, September 14, 1916, and to Edwin T. Earl, November 1, 1916, Roosevelt MSS.

[45] There were, of course, many other weighty factors in Hughes's loss of California. Johnson and the Progressive party had enjoyed the wholehearted support of labor in the state, and California labor in 1916 was decidedly pro-Wilson for more reasons than Hughes's act in crossing a picket line in California. In addition the state, in terms of 1941, was largely non-interventionist, a sentiment upon which both Johnson and Wilson capitalized. But the vote was so close in the state that despite these potent factors Hughes probably would have won had he not alienated many Progressives.

[46] Roosevelt to Hugh D. Wise, December 18, 1916, and to Russell J. Coles, November 2, 1916, Roosevelt MSS.

CHAPTER FIFTEEN

The Final Years

THE TIME had now come for the ex-Progressives to make their peace. After the election a few of them joined the Democrats. Others continued to support the National Progressive party which had split away from Roosevelt after the Chicago convention.[1] But by far the greater number of them were ready to re-enter the Republican party. On December 5, 1916, at Chicago, Chester Rowell, Gifford Pinchot, Raymond Robins, William Allen White, Harold Ickes, and James R. Garfield announced their formal reconversion to orthodox Republicanism. The Republican party, their combined statement read in part, can "best secure" liberal action. To convert that wishful thought into reality the six rebels piously asked that the Republican National Executive Committee be reorganized to include ten members of the Old Guard and six ex-Progressives.[2]

The Republican answer was prompt and plain. In a January meeting the Executive Committee restored its old membership and elected the strong conservative John T. Adams of Iowa as vice-chairman to "aid" the more progressive Willcox. Obviously the committeemen knew a dead horse when they saw one. The action served to shelve William R. Willcox, Hughes's campaign manager, and to announce the terms on which the Progressive rebels would be taken back into the party. From all except Roosevelt unconditional surrender was expected.

[1] Led by Victor Murdock and Matthew Hale, the National Progressive party held its last convention in April, 1917 at St. Louis. There it amalgamated with the Prohibition party and disappeared from history. *St. Louis Daily Globe Democrat*, April 14, 15, 1917.
[2] *Chicago Tribune*, December 6, 1916.

It was verily a bitter drink for independent men. The three ex-Progressive members of the committee protested strongly against the action. A threat was made to revive the Progressive party and fight the congressional election of 1918.[3] George W. Perkins set about planning a general conference at Chicago of all "liberals" opposed to Wilson.[4]

But to back these threats the ex-Progressives held only a political popgun. None knew better than the Republican chieftains that the proceedings of the summer and fall of 1916 had broken the Progressive party into impotent remnants. As for Perkins, he had lost his influence with even those remnants. Some of the ex-Progressives were willing to have a conference, but almost to a man they refused to have anything to do with one called by Perkins.[5] Apparently even Roosevelt had lost faith in the financier, for he admitted that the last thing he wanted was to have Perkins' name associated with a factional political meeting. He had told Perkins exactly that, he wrote, "for the fifteenth or twentieth millionth time."[6] From that time on Perkins' name gradually disappeared from Roosevelt's correspondence, and by the end of 1918 Roosevelt had other political advisers.[7] The proposed "liberal" convention never took place, John T. Adams kept his job, and the more literary ex-Progressives turned to writing articles on "How to Make the Republican Party Progressive."[8]

But there was small chance of making the Republican party progressive after 1916. Roosevelt, it was clear, had determined to support the party whatever its domestic principles. "I don't want to be a mugwump creature," he had written in December, 1916. He promised to keep on fighting for the things in which he believed, but the experiences of

[3] *New York Times*, January 17, 19, 1917.
[4] George W. Perkins to Charles J. Bonaparte, February 2, 3, 1917, Bonaparte MSS.
[5] Roosevelt MSS., January, February, 1917.
[6] Roosevelt to William Allen White, February 17, 1917, Roosevelt MSS.
[7] See Leary, *Talks with T.R.*, 78–82.
[8] Harold Ickes, *New Republic*, 9: 330 (January 20, 1917).

1916 had left him a little dubious of most of his ex-Progressive friends. For those who had supported Wilson he had nothing but contempt. They had no right to call themselves Progressives; they were simply "assistant Democrats." With La Follette, Capper, and the other "progressive pacificists" in the Republican party, he wrote, he had nothing in common.[9] In fact, as the European war loomed ever larger in his thoughts, he increasingly regretted his onetime associates, who, with few exceptions were spiritually more akin to Wilson on the intervention issue than to their former chief. The Progressives in this country, Roosevelt lamented to Lodge, had paralleled their brothers in England. There the ordinary domestic liberal, with the exception of Lloyd George, had become "an utterly hopeless nuisance because of his incredible silliness in foreign affairs." In Roosevelt's estimation, apparently, Kellogg and Poindexter were the only "sound" Progressives.[10]

At any rate, at the beginning of 1917 Roosevelt showed a disinclination even to meet with his former political associates. He was against any kind of a conference. And in particular he was opposed to having one called by an officer of the late Progressive party. That party and every vestige of it, he felt, "ought to be disbanded throughout the union."[11]

Domestic politics, in fact, scarcely concerned Roosevelt in the first half of 1917. There were bigger and much more important events in the air. In January the German government notified the State Department that unrestricted submarine warfare against neutral shipping would be resumed. On February 3 President Wilson announced that the German ambassador had been given his passport. Less than a month later the Zimmerman telegram proposing an alliance between Mexico and Germany if the United States entered the war was intercepted and published. On March 12 an American

[9] Roosevelt to William Allen White, December 2, 5, 1916, Roosevelt MSS.
[10] Roosevelt to Lodge, March 18, 1917, in Lodge, *Correspondence*, 2: 503–504.
[11] Roosevelt to William Allen White, December 2, 1916, Roosevelt MSS.

merchant ship was sunk without warning. Swiftly events were pushing Wilson toward a war the country did not want.

Since the campaign of 1916 Roosevelt had advocated just one public policy. That was war, immediate and total war, with Germany. Throughout January and February after the president's "peace without victory" speech Roosevelt was desperately afraid that Wilson would not declare war "under any circumstances." And as the president patiently and hopefully played out his final fateful cards, Roosevelt, long incensed with Wilson and the peace men, became overwrought. Wilson was "yellow" clear through, he thought, and would "accept any insult or injury from the hands of a fighting man." La Follette was an "unhung traitor" who should be hanged forthwith if war finally came.[12]

Roosevelt used vicious words lightly in 1917. His mind was on more than words. For his greatest personal wish was for action, action with the Allies on the Western front. Long before the sands of peace had run out he was formulating plans to lead a group of fighting men across the Atlantic. The dreams were thoroughly characteristic. Perhaps they originated from a nostalgia for youth and the brave days of Kettle Hill. Perhaps Roosevelt remembered the New York governorship and looked forward to the White House in 1920 as a fitting reward for a returned hero. But in all probability he wanted to go solely because he was Roosevelt. Having always lusted for action, he could not now sit through a war writing and making speeches. Especially in this war, which he so sincerely believed in and which he must have considered peculiarly his, he had to be in the midst of the waving flags, the noise, and the terrible drama. That was the place for the young in spirit.

But there was a hitch. To go he must obtain permission of Newton D. Baker, secretary of war. And that meant in effect getting permission of Woodrow Wilson, the man he despised and whom he had so cruelly criticized. Roosevelt

[12] Roosevelt to Henry Cabot Lodge, February 20, 1917, and to Chester H. Rowell, December 12, 1917, Roosevelt MSS.

was a proud man who must have found galling the thought of asking Wilson for a favor. His earnestness withered away his pride, however, and by February, 1917, he had written Baker asking permission to raise a division of infantry and cavalry.[13] The most he could do for his country, he wrote William Allen White, was to die in a "reasonably honorable fashion at the head of my division." As an afterthought he added that he did not intend to die if it could be "legitimately avoided."[14]

Then followed a long interchange of letters with the secretary of war. Roosevelt was more than polite. And as time went on he became more modest in his desires, even offering at last to serve as an under officer in his proposed division. Baker was cold and abrupt, promising nothing. After the declaration of war Roosevelt went to Washington to talk with the president and the secretary of war personally. The answer was the same, and Roosevelt went back to Oyster Bay with rage in his heart.[15]

It was a terrible blow to Roosevelt, one that he perhaps did not deserve. Yet Wilson was probably right in his decision. If Roosevelt had gone to France it is quite possible that he would have hindered more than helped. But a war without Roosevelt did violence to an American legend. Wilson the historian should have recognized that.

In his last years Roosevelt was as unfair as any man consumed with anger can be. He would not hear a good word said for the president. Wilson was "exceedingly base" and his soul was "rotten through and through," he wrote a friend who had mildly defended the president. Nor could Roosevelt find any merit in any of Wilson's appointments, even when they happened to be ex-supporters and Progressives. Denman, an "active pro-German," was "morally unfit" for his job. Bainbridge Colby had not a single qualification for his place. Neither had Walter Lippman. Felix Frankfurter,

[13] Roosevelt to Newton D. Baker, February 2, 1917, Roosevelt MSS.
[14] Roosevelt to William Allen White, February 17, 1917, Roosevelt MSS.
[15] Leary, *Talks With T.R.*, 93–99.

whom Roosevelt had once described as one of the brains of his generation, would do brilliantly in certain places, but he was an "absurd misfit" in the position he held.[16]

In such a mood Roosevelt was willing to cooperate with almost anyone who for any reason opposed the president and his ideas. Henry Cabot Lodge, narrowly partisan and personally jealous of Wilson, was regularly filling Roosevelt's ears with his song of hate. General Leonard Wood, an old comrade of the Cuban days, furnished tales of the mismanagement of the army. Francis R. Welsh of Philadelphia, who was working hard to save the country from "bolshevism, Townley, Gompers, and other anarchists with whom Wilson was in league" was also a frequent correspondent.[17] The names of John T. King of Connecticut, Albert B. Fall of New Mexico, James E. Watson, and even Joseph B. Foraker showed up in Roosevelt's daily mail. Stalwarts all, Roosevelt's new-found friends contributed little to an objective view toward the administration. By the end of 1918 Roosevelt was writing seriously that casualty reports had not been published in full because "it is assumed that two-third[s] of them are Republicans."[18]

Still, Roosevelt's last years were not wholly spent in bitter contemplation of another's direction of a war that by all the rules of his reasoning should have been his to run. There was the happier side of renewing old friendships that had been consumed in the fiery campaign of 1912. For years the names of Taft and Root had been absent from Roosevelt's correspondence. Now in 1918 they reappeared. Drawn together by their common opposition to the president, the three again found comfort, if not the old comradeship, in each other.

Roosevelt had met and talked with both Taft and Root during the campaign of 1916. But those meetings had been

[16] Roosevelt to William Allen White, January 10, 1918, and to Lodge, August 15, 1917, Roosevelt MSS.

[17] Letters to Roosevelt from Lodge, April 23, September 17, 1917, and Leonard E. Wood, October 29, 1918, Roosevelt to Francis R. Welsh, June 1, 24, July 8, 1918, Roosevelt MSS.

[18] Roosevelt to Lodge, November 27, 1918, Roosevelt MSS.

political and without warmth. In the early part of 1917 Taft
made reconciliation impossible by his defense of the world
league.[19] But as the crucial congressional elections of 1918
neared and Taft became more hostile to the administration,
the way was opened for an understanding. In March Roosevelt sent a copy of the speech he was to deliver at the Maine
Republican convention to both Taft and Root, inviting their
comments. Their replies were soothing. Root liked the speech
"very much" and Taft was glad to note that Roosevelt had
spoken of "the failure of labor with proper condemnation."[20]

Roosevelt had not thought of attending the New York Republican state convention in midsummer. But hearing that
Root and Taft were attending, he wrote that "of course he
would go."[21] A month later Taft wrote a characteristic letter.
It was Roosevelt's duty, the ex-president said, to run for
governor of New York, and if Roosevelt felt inclined to do so
he could make the letter public.[22] It was not in Taft's nature
to carry a grudge to the grave. After eight long years it was
once more "Dear Will" and "My dear Theodore."

Roosevelt had one great ambition in the summer of 1918.
That was to defeat Woodrow Wilson by electing a Republican Congress which, in Taft's words, would "supply the de-
ficiencies of . . . the Administration in carrying out a proper
world policy."[23] By early autumn it was increasingly evident
that the war was turning toward its successful conclusion;
1920 would be too late to stop Wilson from shaping the peace
after his own ideas. To Roosevelt's mind a Wilsonian peace
would be a catastrophe.

Throughout the summer and fall of 1918 Roosevelt worked
to unify the Republican party. When ex-Progressives protested against the reactionary tone of Republican state platforms, Roosevelt sought to mollify them. The "prime neces-

[19] Roosevelt to William R. West, January 31, 1917, Roosevelt MSS.
[20] Roosevelt to Taft, March 8, 1918, letters to Roosevelt from Root,
March 5, 1918, and Taft, March 11, 1918, Roosevelt MSS.
[21] Roosevelt to Root, June 29, 1918, Roosevelt MSS.
[22] Taft to Roosevelt, July 19, 1918, Roosevelt MSS.
[23] Taft to Roosevelt, July 4, 1918, Roosevelt MSS.

sity" of any platform, he wrote, is to know that it will be adhered to. That "question of good faith should precede any discussion of theories advanced."[24] The bent of his mind was further revealed in his reply to a demand for a radical program. At the moment Roosevelt was inclined to think that Bolshevism "was a more serious menace to world democracy than any species of capitalism."[25]

A corollary of that viewpoint was that any Republican— progressive, moderate, or reactionary—was better than Wilson and the Democrats. In one week during the campaign of 1918 Roosevelt wrote four political messages. One was to the ex-Progressives of New Hampshire asking them to elect the stalwart George H. Moses to succeed the dead Senator Gallinger.[26] The other three were letters of endorsements for Senators Stirling of South Dakota,[27] Fall of New Mexico, and Weeks of Massachusetts. "To a peculiar degree," Roosevelt wrote, "Fall embodies the best American Spirit."[28] And while Weeks was a "reactionary" and would act like an "Egyptian mummy" on reconstruction problems, he was a mummy "who loved his country" and would "fight the cold-blooded, selfish and tricky creature" in the White House.[29]

The results of the elections of 1918, in which the Republicans won a shaky majority in the Senate, fed Roosevelt's soul. He regretted that two of the senators making the majority were La Follette and Norris. In other years he might have regretted the conservative cast of the Republican victory. But the West, he wrote jubilantly, "had come back with a jump," and with the West once more Republican, Wilson's days were numbered.[30] It was high time. Already the presi-

[24] Roosevelt to Chester H. Rowell, August 4, 1918, Roosevelt MSS.

[25] Roosevelt to William Allen White, May 2, 1918, Roosevelt MSS.

[26] Roosevelt to Irving W. Drew, October 28, 1918, Roosevelt MSS.

[27] Roosevelt to Stitzel X. Way, November 1, 1918 (telegram), Roosevelt MSS.

[28] Roosevelt to A. B. Fall, October 29, 1918 (telegram), Roosevelt MSS.

[29] Roosevelt to Charles S. Bird, November 2, 1918, Roosevelt MSS.

[30] Roosevelt to Lodge, November 12, 1918, Roosevelt MSS.

dent was negotiating an armistice to which Roosevelt was bitterly opposed. Roosevelt agreed with Lodge that the fight ought to end in Berlin and not a minute sooner.[31] Perhaps he believed Lodge's accusation that Wilson was eager to make an armistice to win the German-American votes in 1920.[32] Officially the war ended on November 11, 1918. The suspicion and hate it had created lived on even in America.

Roosevelt was a sick man in the autumn of 1918. In February he had been in the hospital for almost a month. On Armistice Day he went to the hospital again. Two speaking tours within three months and the death of his son Quentin in France had sapped his vitality. The years of strenuous living were collecting their toll. But 1920 was only a step away and Roosevelt had his eye on the presidential election even in the hospital.

Roosevelt would have given his eyeteeth to have been elected president in 1920. Of that there can be little doubt. That would have been the perfect culmination of a historic life. Victory in 1920 would have been ample balm for 1912 and 1916. It would have been a sweeping popular vindication of his struggle with Wilson. As early as February, 1917, plans had been proposed by friends to reunite the Republican party before "any hope or hint of a candidacy for the Colonel in 1920 becomes apparent."[33] To all such suggestions Roosevelt cagily said nothing at the time. But in April, 1918, he wrote that he was going to Washington "by invitation" to sound out the Republican officeholders on their reconstruction views. A few senators, including two old friends, he reported subsequently, were "hopelessly reactionary." But a "great majority" in the House and at least a "large minority" in the Senate were "anxious to have me take some position of leadership." They were equally anxious, he added, to emphasize that their position did not commit them for 1920.[34] A

[31] Lodge to Roosevelt, October 7, 1918, Roosevelt MSS.
[32] Lodge to Roosevelt, September 3, 1918, Roosevelt MSS.
[33] Confidential sources in possession of author.
[34] Roosevelt to William Allen White, April 4, 1918, Roosevelt MSS.

short time later Roosevelt told a friend that if the party wanted him, he would be a candidate. But he would "not lift a finger for the nomination," he added.[35]

Roosevelt was quite aware that there were many men in the party who would oppose him in 1920. He did not fit in with their plans of victory after eight long years of defeat. But apparently he was confident that he could brush them aside as he had done so often in the past. At the opening of 1919 he was telling his friends that the Republican convention would nominate him the following year.[36]

Roosevelt's confidence in the future may have been born of a seeming return of health. A few days before Christmas he had left the hospital to return to Oyster Bay. A short time later he felt strong enough to write for the *Kansas City Star* again. But then the blow fell. Suddenly and without warning he died at four o'clock in the morning on January 6, 1919. The truth was at first hard to grasp. For twenty years Theodore Roosevelt had been an almost elemental force in American politics. Now that he was gone 1920 was left to lesser mortals.

Had Theodore Roosevelt lived and won the election of 1920 the course of American history might have been quite different. He would not have supported Wilson's plans for a league. Years before at Christiania he had proposed a League of Peace between all the world's great nations. Throughout 1914 and 1915 he repeatedly endorsed the league concept. And so in 1918 he obviously could not agree with Leonard Wood's dictum that there was "nothing more dangerous than the world court and the League of Nations idea."[37] Neither could he agree with Wilson. "I am for such a league as I outlined two years ago," he snapped to a slightly bewildered supporter in 1917, "a league which has nothing in common with the policies of Messrs. Wilson and Taft."[38] He elaborated his position

[35] Quoted in Leary, *Talks With T.R.*, 1.
[36] William Allen White, *A Puritan in Babylon* (New York, 1938), 180.
[37] Leonard Wood to Roosevelt, July 4, 1918, Roosevelt MSS.
[38] Roosevelt to William R. West, January 31, 1917, Roosevelt MSS.

in a letter to Taft a year later. Happily Taft had changed his ideas about Wilson's league by that time. They could come "together absolutely," Roosevelt wrote on Taft's program of universal training and self-defense. Then this country could join a league "as an addition to and not a substitute for our defense."[39]

Roosevelt expressed himself again on the league the day before his death. A league was needed, but not Wilson's league. Roosevelt wanted a league of the victorious powers, but only if each power reserved the right to decide which international questions were "non-justiciable."[40] To the end Roosevelt remained a nationalist ready to fight any proposed encroachment on national sovereignty. Henry F. Pringle was right. Had he lived he would have joined Henry Cabot Lodge and the "battalion of death" in killing Wilson's League of Nations.[41]

Had Roosevelt lived and been elected President, however, something might have been salvaged from the peace that was no peace. True, Roosevelt was and would have remained a nationalist. But he had never been opposed to some measure of cooperation in either peace or war. His whole career reflected an understanding of America's growing interest in the world family of nations. Under Roosevelt this country probably would not have joined the League of Nations without drastic reservations. But undoubtedly it would have fulfilled in the years of peace at least some of the obligations it had incurred to world society and to itself by entering the World War in 1917.

The death of Theodore Roosevelt also signified the death of a twenty-year-old political movement. For with him died the last hope of effective progressive action in the Republican party for at least two decades. As the lights went out at Oyster Bay the cold grey shadow of Calvin Coolidge fell across America.

[39] Roosevelt to Taft, August 26, 1918, Roosevelt MSS.
[40] Cited in Bishop, *Roosevelt*, 2: 470.
[41] Pringle, *Roosevelt*, 603.

Roosevelt himself had contributed much to the conservatizing of the Republican party. In 1912 he had skimmed off much progressive talent to support his third party. With Roosevelt and his adherents gone, La Follette, Cummins, Borah, Norris, and the others were no match for the conservative majority of the Republican party. Pitifully outnumbered after 1912, they had little effect on party policy. They were able to remain in political life solely because of their personal hold on their constituencies. Other progressive Republicans were less fortunate. Caught in the crossfire between Progressives and Republicans, Senators Works of California and Clapp of Minnesota and Governor Stubbs of Kansas, to name a few of the more prominent, were defeated and disappeared from political life. The defeat of Senator Joseph L. Bristow of Kansas by Charles Curtis in 1914 was an omen of things to come.[42]

What the split in 1912 had started, the European war and the issues revolving about it helped along. Like Bryan in the Democratic party, many progressive Republicans were peace men to the end. Both they and the principles they represented were hurt by their stand on preparedness and the war. Thus Senators La Follette, Norris, Gronna, Cummins, Clapp, Works, and Kenyon were all thoroughly execrated for their opposition to the armed ship bill in March of 1917. Those of them who persisted in their opposition to intervention down through April 6, 1917, were even more violently attacked. At the head of their belligerent critics was Theodore Roosevelt.

There were certain obvious signs that the progressive spirit was waning even before the declaration of war on Germany. The political pendulum with its almost rhythmic movement in American history was already swinging to the right. But the swing would not have been nearly so sharp nor so extensive had it not been for the impact of international conflict. The mass conformity demanded by war, the necessary industrial leadership, the emphasis upon the tried, and the resultant national weariness and moral exhaustion created a

[42] *New York Times*, August 6, 1914.

social environment inimical to progressive political action.[43] Roosevelt's precipitate turn to the right in 1914 foreshadowed a national movement among the nation's peoples as well as parties.

Even so the almost total absence of progressive Republicanism in the post-war era cannot be wholly explained without reference to the actions of Roosevelt. His destruction of the Progressive party in 1916 and his return to Republicanism left many of his Progressive followers bitter and cynical.[44] Beveridge, for example, changed from an ardent Progressive to a militant reactionary. By 1918 the one-time Indiana Progressive was leading a campaign against income and corporation taxes and against all types of corporate control. With grim satisfaction he invited Roosevelt to speak before a group of his industrialist friends who were "high-minded public spirited, patriotic men." The Indianapolis Associated Employers, Beveridge wrote, stood squarely for an open shop and had been most successful "in the suppression of strikes by force."[45] Other Progressives disheartened by the 1916 proceedings simply retired from politics and were heard of no more.

There were many ex-Progressives, of course, who did not drink the bitter hemlock of despair. They returned to the Republican party with Roosevelt eager to take up the fight where they had left it in 1912. But they did not return to the powerful places in the party they had held in 1912. Their one chance for that was a Roosevelt victory in 1920. And it is probable that their leader, had he been elected, would not have failed them. Roosevelt was temperamentally unable to be a conservative for long. He had returned to the favor of Lodge, Root, and Taft in 1918, but to the end, ideologically, he was not of them. In November, 1918, he wrote Lodge that the people would not stand for the Republican party "unless

[43] George E. Mowry, "Some Effects of the World War on Democracy in America," in *War as a Social Institution: The Historian's Perspective*, ed. by Jesse D. Clarkson and Thomas C. Cochran (New York, 1941).

[44] Bowers, *Beveridge*, 533.

[45] Beveridge to Roosevelt, January 11, 1918, Roosevelt MSS.

we really do go forward."[46] A week later, while in the hospital for the last time, he was planning a conference of progressive followers on reconstruction problems.[47]

But Roosevelt died in January of 1919 and with him died the hopes of progressive Republicanism for post-war control. A few of the men who had followed him out of the party in 1912 managed either to stay in or to make their way back to office. Medill McCormick and Truman Newberry were elected to the Senate before Roosevelt died. In 1922 Smith W. Brookhart was elected to the Senate and Henry J. Allen became governor of Kansas. A decade later Robert D. Carey represented Wyoming in the United States Senate and Gifford Pinchot was governor of Pennsylvania. In 1943 Hiram Johnson still represented California. But these were few against the many. Significantly, the most effective Republican opposition to the party's conservative philosophy throughout the twenties came not from Roosevelt's old followers but from the elder and younger La Follette, from George W. Norris, William E. Borah, Henrik Shipstead, Lynn J. Frazier, and Arthur Capper. Measured by the long-run results, the Roosevelt revolt of 1912 had hurt progressive Republicanism instead of helping it.

Still Theodore Roosevelt had done much for the evolution of progressive politics in the United States. In the days of its infancy he had lent the progressive movement the prestige of his great name. Without his support of varying intensity many progressive proposals would not have been written into statutes between 1901 and 1909. His rebellion of 1912 had assured the election of Woodrow Wilson, who by 1916 had achieved more than Bryan had proposed in 1896. Roosevelt's New Nationalism and the Progressive platform of 1912 were in themselves major steps in the development of progressive principles. By their insistence upon paternalistic federal regulation they looked forward to another great progressive movement in the 1930's. In fact, in some ways the New Nationalism and not the New Freedom was the ideological predecessor of the New Deal. It was Woodrow Wilson who remarked in the campaign of 1912 that the history of human liberty had been the history of the curtailment of governmental powers.

The administrations of Franklin D. Roosevelt had other lines of kinship with Theodore Roosevelt and the Progressive party. In the early days of the New Deal few men were more ardent in their defense of its cardinal measures than Harold Ickes, Edward P. Costigan, and Bronson Cutting. Later when stormy international questions intruded upon domestic reform Frank Knox joined the Democratic Cabinet. All of these men were Bull Moosers. None of them was inconsistent in his transfer of political support. For the post-war Republican party had totally rejected the principles of Progressivism. By officially accepting Warren G. Harding's Boston program it had in particular buried Roosevelt's domestic and foreign policies in the dust of party history. The restless spirit of Theodore Roosevelt was and ever would be at war with Harding's "healing," "normalcy," "restoration," and "serenity."

Bibliography and Index

Manuscripts and Works Cited

MANUSCRIPTS

ALLISON, WILLIAM B. Allison MSS. Historical Memorial and Art Department of Iowa, Des Moines, Iowa.

BONAPARTE, CHARLES J. Bonaparte MSS. Library of Congress.

CARNEGIE, ANDREW. Carnegie MSS. Library of Congress.

CARTER, THOMAS H. Carter MSS. Library of Congress.

CUMMINS, ALBERT B. Cummins MSS. Historical Memorial and Art Department of Iowa, Des Moines, Iowa.

DODGE, GRENVILLE M. Dodge MSS. Historical Memorial and Art Department of Iowa, Des Moines, Iowa.

DOLLIVER, JONATHAN P. Dolliver MSS. State Historical Society of Iowa, Iowa City, Iowa.

FORAKER, JOSEPH B. Foraker MSS. Library of Congress and Historical and Philosophical Society of Ohio, Cincinnati, Ohio.

FOULKE, WILLIAM DUDLEY. Foulke MSS. Library of Congress.

HULL, COLONEL JOHN A. T. Hull MSS. Historical Memorial and Art Department of Iowa, Des Moines, Iowa.

KEYES, E. M. Keyes MSS. State Historical Society of Wisconsin, Madison, Wisconsin.

KNOX, PHILANDER C. Knox MSS. Library of Congress.

LACEY, JOHN C. Lacey MSS. Historical Memorial and Art Department of Iowa, Des Moines, Iowa.

ROOSEVELT, THEODORE. Roosevelt MSS. Library of Congress.

PUBLIC DOCUMENTS

Canadian Reciprocity. United States Senate, 61 Congress, 3 Session, Document 787. Washington, 1911.

Cases Brought in the Commerce Court of the United States. United States Senate, 62 Congress, 2 Session, Document 789. Washington, 1912.

Conditions of Employment in the Iron and Steel Industry in the United States. United States Senate, 62 Congress, 1 Session, Document 110. 4 vols. Washington, 1912.

Congressional Record, 1909–1913.

Decisions of the Interstate Commerce Commission of the United States, vol. 31, no. 6569: In re Financial Transactions of the New York, New Haven and Hartford Railroad Company. Washington, 1915.

Department of the Interior. United States Senate, 61 Congress, 2 Session, Document 248. Washington, 1911.

Election of William Lorimer. United States Senate, 62 Congress, 2 Session, Document 484. 9 vols. Washington, 1912.

Federal Anti-Trust Decisions. United States Senate, 62 Congress, 1 Session, Document 111. 4 vols. Washington, 1912.

Hearings on the Commerce Court. House of Representatives, 61 Congress, 2 Session, Document 967. Washington, 1911.

Investigation of the Department of the Interior and of the Bureau of Forestry. United States Senate, 61 Congress, 3 Session, Document 719. 13 vols. Washington, 1911.

Iowa Documents, vol. 1. Des Moines, Iowa, 1902.

Iowa Official Register. Des Moines, Iowa, 1910.

Official Proceedings of the Thirteenth Republican National Convention. New York, 1904.

Preliminary Report on Trusts and Industrial Combinations. Congressional Industrial Commission. Washington, 1900.

Report of the Commissioner of Corporations. House of Representatives, 58 Congress, 3 Session, Document 165. Washington, 1905.

Report of the Select Committee on Wages and Prices of Commodities. United States Senate, 61 Congress, 2 Session, Document 912. Washington, 1910.

Report of the Tariff Board on Schedule K. House of Representatives, 62 Congress, 2 Session, Document 342. 4 vols. Washington, 1912.

Thirteenth Census of the United States, vol. 8: *Manufactures.* Washington, 1910.

Yearbook of the Department of Agriculture. Washington, 1911, 1925.

NEWSPAPERS AND PERIODICALS

American Federationist, 1909–1916.

Bankers' Magazine, 1909–1916.

Boston Transcript. Scattered references.

Brooklyn Eagle. Scattered references.
Chicago Inter-Ocean. Scattered references.
Chicago Tribune. Scattered references.
Cincinnati Times Star. Scattered references.
Cleveland Leader. Scattered references.
Cleveland Plain Dealer. Scattered references.
Denver Post. Scattered references.
Des Moines Register and Leader, 1909–1913.
Harper's Weekly, 1912–1916.
Kansas City Star, 1909–1919.
La Follette's Weekly (Madison, Wisconsin), 1909–1913.
Literary Digest. Scattered references.
Metropolitan, 1914–1916.
Milwaukee Sentinel. Scattered references.
The Nation, 1909–1918.
New Orleans Times Picayune. Scattered references.
New Republic 1914–1920.
New York Sun, 1909–1916.
New York Times, 1909–1918.
New York World, 1909–1913.
North American Review. Scattered references.
Outlook, 1909–1916.
Philadelphia North American, 1909–1916.
Railway Age Gazette. Scattered references.
St. Louis Daily Globe Democrat. Scattered references.
Sioux City Journal, 1910.
Springfield Republican. Scattered references.
Wall Street Journal. Scattered references.
Washington Times. Scattered references.

AUTOBIOGRAPHIES, MEMOIRS, AND PUBLISHED COLLECTIONS OF LETTERS

ABBOTT, LYMAN. *Reminiscences.* New York, 1915.
ADAMS, HENRY. *The Education of Henry Adams.* New York, 1918.
——— *Letters of Henry Adams.* Boston and New York, 1938.
BRYAN, WILLIAM JENNINGS AND MARY BAIRD. *The Memoirs of William Jennings Bryan.* Philadelphia, 1925.
BUTLER, NICHOLAS MURRAY. *Across the Busy Years.* New York, 1939.

BUTT, ARCHIE. *Taft and Roosevelt.* 2 vols. New York, 1930.

CLARK, CHAMP. *My Quarter Century of American Politics.* 2 vols. New York, 1920.

COLE, CYRENUS. *I Remember, I Remember: A Book of Recollections.* Iowa City, Iowa, 1936.

CULLOM, SHELBY M. *Fifty Years of Public Service.* Chicago, 1911.

DAVIS, OSCAR KING. *Released for Publication.* New York, 1925.

DEPEW, CHAUNCEY M. *My Memoirs of Eighty Years.* New York, 1922.

DYER, DAVID P. *Autobiography and Reminiscences.* St. Louis, 1922.

FLINT, CHARLES R. *Memoirs of an Active Life.* New York, 1923.

FORAKER, JOSEPH BENSON. *Notes of a Busy Life.* Cincinnati, 1916.

FORAKER, JULIA B. *I Would Live It Again.* New York, 1932.

FOULKE, WILLIAM DUDLEY. *A Hoosier Autobiography.* New York, 1922.

GARDNER, AUGUSTUS P. *Some Letters of Augustus Peabody Gardner,* edited by Constance Gardner. New York, 1920.

GOMPERS, SAMUEL. *Seventy Years of Life and Labor.* 2 vols. New York, 1925.

HARRISON, CARTER HENRY. *Stormy Years.* New York, 1935.

HOUSE, E. M. *The Intimate Papers of Colonel House,* edited by Charles Seymour. 4 vols. New York, 1926–28.

JOHNSON, TOM LOFTEN. *My Story,* edited by Elizabeth J. Hauser. New York, 1911.

KOHLSAAT, H. H. *From McKinley to Harding.* New York, 1923.

LA FOLLETTE, ROBERT M. *Autobiography.* Madison, Wisconsin, 1911.

LANE, FRANKLIN K. *The Letters of Franklin K. Lane,* edited by Anne Wintermute Lane and Louise Herrick Wall. New York, 1922.

LEARY, JOHN J., JR. *Talks With T.R.* New York, 1920.

LONGWORTH, ALICE ROOSEVELT. *Crowded Hours.* New York, 1933.

McADOO, WILLIAM G. *Crowded Years.* New York, 1931.

McCLURE, S. S. *My Autobiography.* New York, 1914.

MORGENTHAU, HENRY. *All in a Life-Time.* New York, 1922.

ROOSEVELT, THEODORE. *An Autobiography.* New York, 1921.

——— *Letters from Theodore Roosevelt to Anna Roosevelt Cowles, 1870–1918.* New York, 1924.

——— *Selections from the Correspondence of Theodore Roosevelt and Henry Cabot Lodge, 1884–1918,* edited by Henry Cabot Lodge. 2 vols. New York, 1925.

——— *Works.* 20 vols. New York, 1925.

ROSEWATER, VICTOR. *Backstage in 1912.* Philadelphia, 1932.

RUSSELL, CHARLES EDWARD. *Bare Hands and Stone Walls: Some Recollections of a Side-Line Reformer.* New York, 1933.

STEFFENS, LINCOLN. *The Autobiography of Lincoln Steffens.* New York, 1931.

——— *The Letters of Lincoln Steffens, 1899–1919.* New York, 1938.

STEPHENSON, ISAAC. *Recollections of a Long Life, 1829–1915.* Chicago, 1915.

STODDARD, HENRY L. *As I Knew Them.* New York, 1927.

STRAUS, OSCAR S. *Under Four Administrations: From Cleveland to Taft.* New York, 1922.

TAFT, HELEN H. *Recollections of Full Years.* New York, 1914.

UNDERWOOD, OSCAR W. *Drifting Sands of Party Politics.* New York, 1928.

VARE, WILLIAM S. *My Forty Years in Politics.* Philadelphia, 1933.

WATSON, JAMES E. *As I Knew Them.* Indianapolis, 1936.

WHITLOCK, BRAND. *Forty Years of It.* New York, 1914.

SECONDARY WORKS

ABBOTT, LAWRENCE F. *Impressions of Theodore Roosevelt.* New York, 1919.

ACHESON, SAM HANNA. *Joe Bailey, the Last Democrat.* New York, 1932.

BAKER, RAY S. *Woodrow Wilson, Life and Letters.* 7 vols. New York, 1927–39.

BEARD, CHARLES A. *An Economic Interpretation of the Constitution of the United States.* New York, 1912.

BEARD, CHARLES A. AND MARY. *The Rise of American Civilization.* 2 vols. New York, 1930.

BEASLEY, NORMAN. *Frank Knox.* New York, 1936.

BISHOP, JOSEPH BUCKLIN. *Charles Joseph Bonaparte: His Life and Public Services.* New York, 1922.

———— *Presidential Nominations and Elections.* New York, 1916.

———— *Theodore Roosevelt and His Time.* New York, 1920.

BOWDEN, R. D. *The Evolution of the Politician.* Boston, 1924.

BOWERS, CLAUDE G. *Beveridge and the Progressive Era.* Boston, 1932.

BRIGGS, JOHN ELY. *William Peters Hepburn.* Iowa City, 1919.

BROWN, WILLIAM GARROTT. *The New Politics and Other Papers.* New York, 1914.

BRYAN, WILLIAM JENNINGS. *A Tale of Two Conventions.* New York, 1912.

BURR, ANNA ROBESON. *The Portrait of a Banker: James Stillman, 1850–1918.* New York, 1927.

BUSBEY, L. WHITE. *Uncle Joe Cannon: The Story of a Pioneer American.* New York, 1927.

CARNEGIE, ANDREW. *Problems of Today: Wealth—Labor—Socialism.* New York, 1908.

CARROLL, MOLLIE RAY. *Labor and Politics.* Boston, 1923.

CHAMBERLAIN, JOHN. *Farewell to Reform.* New York, 1932.

CHARNWOOD, LORD. *Theodore Roosevelt.* Boston, 1923.

Chicago Conference on Trusts . . . Civic Federation of Chicago, 1900.

CLARK, JOHN D. *The Federal Trust Policy.* Baltimore, 1931.

COLEMAN, McALISTER. *Eugene V. Debs: A Man Unafraid.* New York, 1930.

COOK, SHERWIN LAWRENCE. *Torchlight Parade.* New York, 1929.

CROLY, HERBERT D. *The Promise of American Life.* New York, 1909.

DE CHAMBRUN, CLARA. *The Making of Nicholas Longworth.* New York, 1933.

DE WITT, BENJAMIN PARKE. *The Progressive Movement.* New York, 1915.

DOUGLAS, PAUL H. *Real Wages in the United States.* New York, 1930.

DREIER, THOMAS. *Heroes of Insurgency.* New York, 1910.

DUFFY, HERBERT S. *William Howard Taft.* New York, 1930.

DUMOND, DWIGHT L. *Roosevelt to Roosevelt.* New York, 1937.

DUNN, ARTHUR WALLACE. *From Harrison to Harding.* New York, 1922.

FLINT, WINSLOW ALLEN. *Progressive Movement in Vermont.* Washington, 1942.

GIBBONS, HERBERT ADAMS. *John Wanamaker.* 2 vols. New York, 1926.

GRIFFIN, SOLOMON BULKLEY. *People and Politics.* Boston, 1923.

———— *W. Murray Crane.* Boston, 1926.

HARRIMAN, MRS. J. BORDEN. *From Pinafores to Politics.* New York, 1923.

HARVEY, GEORGE. *Henry Clay Frick, the Man.* New York, 1928.

HARVEY, ROWLAND HILL. *Samuel Gompers, Champion of the Toiling Masses.* Stanford University Press, 1935.

HAYNES, GEORGE H. *The Life of Charles G. Washburn.* Boston, 1931.

HIBBEN, PAXTON. *The Peerless Leader William Jennings Bryan.* New York, 1929.

HICKS, JOHN D. *The Populist Revolt.* Minneapolis, 1931.

HOBSON, JOHN H. *The Evolution of Modern Capitalism: A Study of Machine Production.* London, 1907.

HOWE, FREDERIC C. *Confessions of a Reformer.* New York, 1925.

HOWE, M. A. DEWOLFE. *George von Lengerke Meyer: His Life and Public Service.* New York, 1920.

———— *Portrait of an Independent: Moorfield Storey.* New York, 1932.

HOWLAND, HAROLD. *Theodore Roosevelt and His Times.* New Haven, 1921.

JESSUP, PHILIP C. *Elihu Root.* 2 vols. New York, 1938.

JOHNSON, CLAUDIUS O. *Borah of Idaho.* New York, 1936.

JOHNSON, WILLIS FLETCHER. *George Harvey: A Passionate Patriot.* Cambridge, 1929.

LIPPMAN, WALTER. *A Preface to Politics.* New York, 1913.

LONG, JOHN CUTHBERT. *Bryan, the Great Commoner.* New York, 1928.

McCALEB, WALTER F. *Theodore Roosevelt.* New York, 1931.

MADDEN, JAMES WILLIAM. *Charles Allen Culberson: His Life, Character, and Public Service.* Austin, Texas, 1929.

MASON, ALPHEUS T. *Bureaucracy Convicts Itself.* Princeton, 1941

MILLER, WILLIAM T. *The Progressive Movement in Missouri.* Columbia, Missouri, 1928.

MOODY, JOHN. *The Truth about the Trusts.* New York, 1904.

MOORE, J. HAMPTON. *Roosevelt and the Old Guard.* Philadelphia, 1925.

MOTT, COLONEL T. BENTLEY. *Myron T. Herrick, Friend of France.* New York, 1929.

MYERS, GUSTAVUS. *History of the Great American Fortunes.* Chicago, 1910.

NEVINS, ALLEN. *Henry White: Thirty Years of American Diplomacy.* New York, 1930.

ODLAND, MARTIN W. *The Life of Knute Nelson.* Minneapolis, 1926.

OGG, FREDERIC AUSTIN. *National Progress 1907–1917.* New York, 1918.

ORCUTT, WILLIAM DANA. *Burrows of Michigan and the Republican Party.* 2 vols. New York, 1917.

PAXSON, FREDERIC LOGAN. *Recent History of the United States.* Boston, 1929.

PERLMAN, SELIG. *History of Trade Unionism in the United States.* New York, 1923.

PERLMAN, SELIG, AND PHILIP TAFT. *History of Labor in the United States,* vol. 4: *Labor Movements.* New York, 1935.

PERRY, BLISS. *Life and Letters of Henry Lee Higginson.* Boston, 1921.

PRINGLE, HENRY F. *The Life and Times of William Howard Taft.* 2 vols. New York, 1939.

——— *Theodore Roosevelt.* New York, 1931.

REGIER, C. C. *The Era of the Muckrakers.* Chapel Hill, 1932.

RING, ELIZABETH. *The Progressive Movement of 1912 and Third Party Movement of 1924 in Maine.* Orono, Maine, 1933.

ROSEWATER, VICTOR. *Backstage in 1912.* Philadelphia, 1932.

ROSS, EDWARD A. *Sin and Society.* Boston, 1907.

RUSSELL, JOHN ANDREW. *Joseph Warren Fordney, an American Legislator.* Boston, 1928.

SELIGMAN, EDWIN R. A. *The Economic Interpretation of History.* New York, 1903.

SMITH, JAMES ALLEN. *The Spirit of American Government: A Study of the Constitution, Its Origin, Influence, and Relation to Democracy.* New York, 1907.

STAHL, ROSE MILDRED. *The Ballinger-Pinchot Controversy.* Northampton, Massachusetts, 1926.

STEPHENSON, NATHANIEL W. *Nelson W. Aldrich.* New York, 1930.

SULLIVAN, MARK. *Our Times,* vol. 4: *The War Begins* (1904–14). New York, 1932.

TARBELL, IDA M. *The Life of Elbert H. Gary.* New York, 1925.

TAUSSIG, F. W. *Free Trade, the Tariff, and Reciprocity.* New York, 1920.

——— *The Tariff History of the United States.* New York, 1914.

THAYER, WILLIAM ROSCOE. *Theodore Roosevelt.* New York, 1919.

THOMPSON, CHARLES WILLIS. *Party Leaders of the Time.* New York, 1906.

VEBLEN, THORSTEIN. *The Theory of the Leisure Class: An Economic Study of Institutions.* New York, 1899.

WARREN, CHARLES. *The Supreme Court in United States History,* vol. 2. Boston, 1926.

WERNER, MORRIS ROBERT. *Bryan.* New York, 1929.

WEYL, WALTER E. *The New Democracy.* New York, 1912.

WHITE, WILLIAM ALLEN. *Masks in a Pageant.* New York, 1928.

——— *A Puritan in Babylon.* New York, 1938.

WILCOX, BENTON H. "A Reconsideration of the Character and Economic Basis of Northwestern Radicalism." Unpublished thesis, 1933, Library of the University of Wisconsin.

WILLIAMSON, HAROLD FRANCIS. *Edward Atkinson: The Biography of an American Liberal, 1827–1905.* Boston, 1934.

WISTER, OWEN. *Roosevelt: The Story of a Friendship.* New York, 1930.

WOOD, FREDERICK S. *Roosevelt As We Knew Him.* Chicago, 1927.

Index